AGENTS OF ATLAS

VERSUS

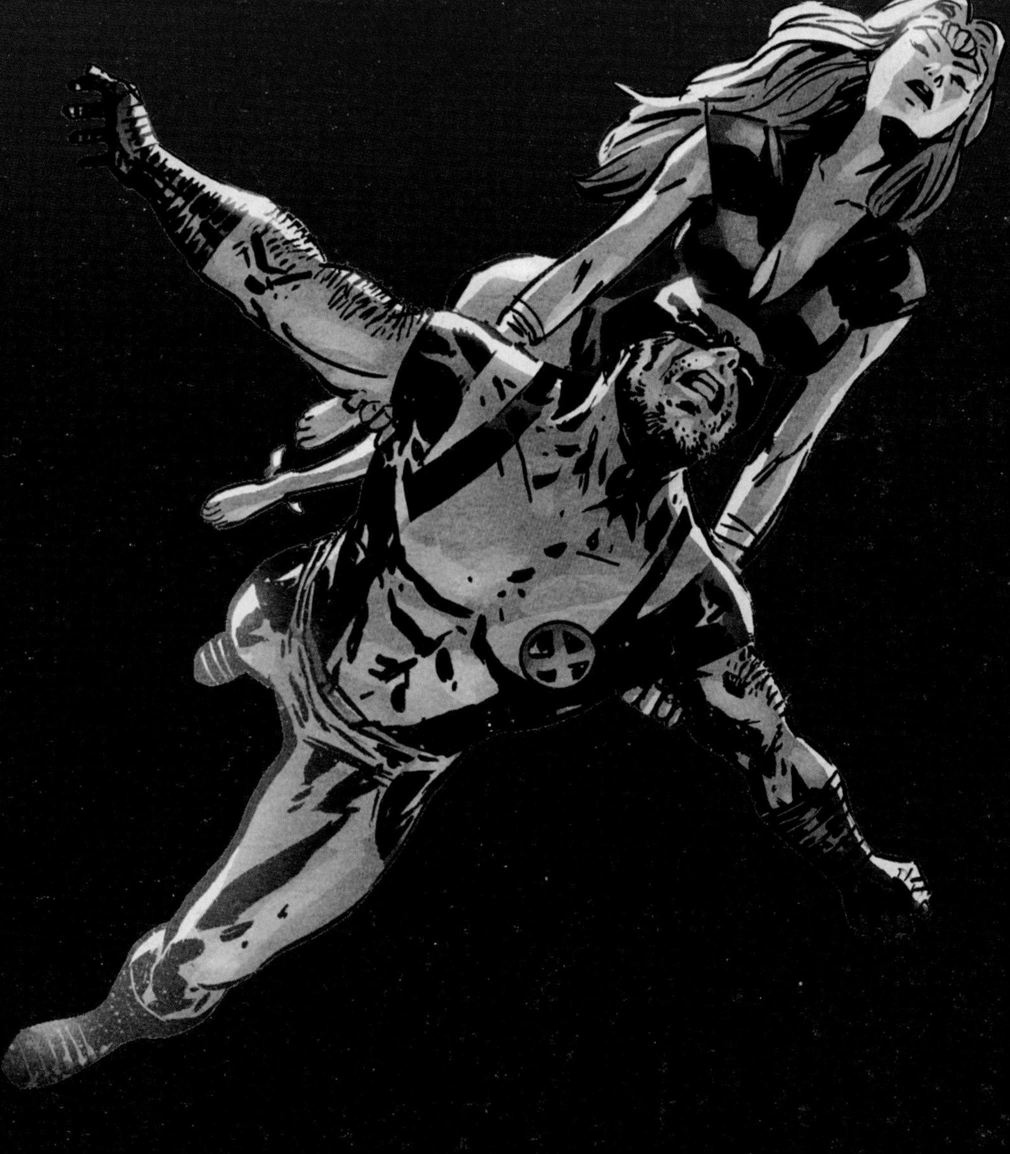

VERSUS

X-MEN

WRITER
Jeff Parker

PENCILERS
Carlo Pagulayan, Chris Samnee,
Gabriel Hardman & Carlos Rodriguez

INKERS
Jason Paz, Chris Samnee,
Gabriel Hardman & Terry Pallot

COLORISTS
Wilfredo Quintana & Veronica Gandini

LETTERER
Virtual Calligraphy's Joe Caramagna

COVER ARTISTS
Ed McGuinness, Dexter Vines, Justin Ponsor
& Adi Granov

ASSISTANT EDITOR
Michael Horwitz

ASSOCIATE EDITOR
Nathan Cosby

EDITOR
Mark Paniccia

Special Thanks to Lauren Sankovitch

AVENGERS

WRITER
Jeff Parker

ARTIST
Gabriel Hardman

COLORISTS
Elizabeth Breitweiser

LETTERER
Tom Orzechowski

COVER ARTISTS
Humberto Ramos & Edgar Delgado

ASSOCIATE EDITOR
Nathan Cosby

EDITOR
Mark Paniccia

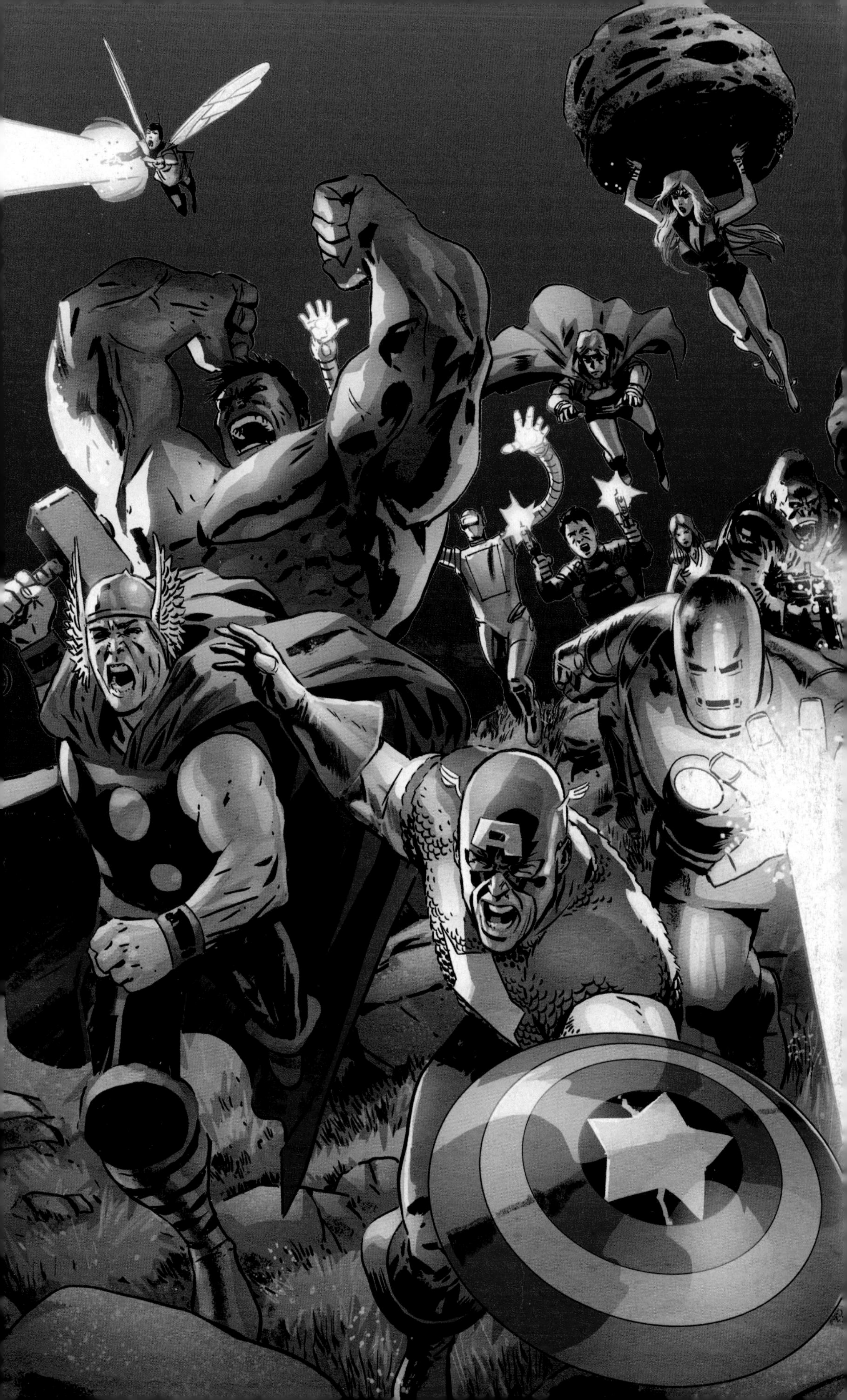

COLLECTION EDITOR: Cory Levine
ASSISTANT EDITOR: Alex Starbuck
ASSOCIATE EDITOR: John Denning
EDITORS, SPECIAL PROJECTS: Jennifer Grünwald & Mark D. Beazley
SENIOR EDITOR, SPECIAL PROJECTS: Jeff Youngquist
SENIOR VICE PRESIDENT OF SALES: David Gabriel

EDITOR IN CHIEF: Joe Quesada
PUBLISHER: Dan Buckley
EXECUTIVE PRODUCER: Alan Fine

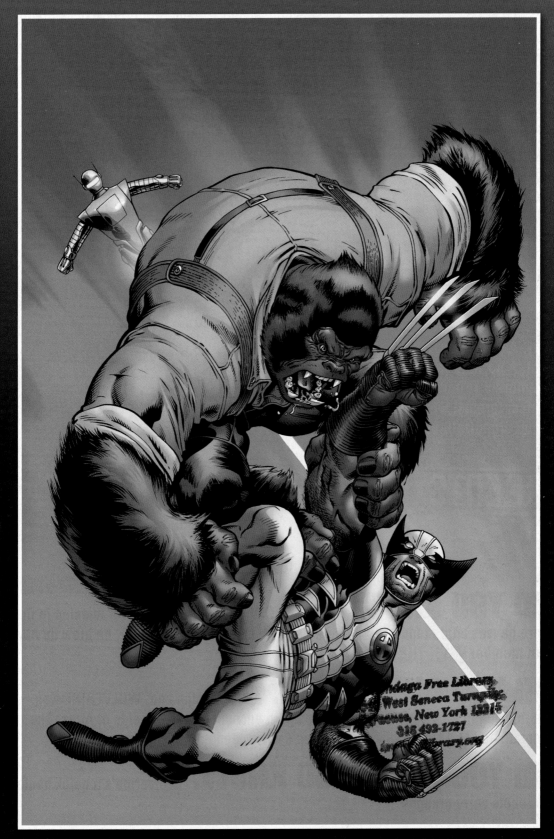

X-MEN VS. AGENTS OF ATLAS

#1

Some people are born different. They are gifted with powers and abilities surpassing normal humans. They are mutants. And in a world that hates and fears them, some of these mutants have banded together to defend themselves against those that would wipe them from the earth. These are the

A spy. A spaceman. A siren. A mermaid. A robot. A gorilla. They are a team of 1950s adventurers re-formed to battle Earth's greatest threats, while under the guise of an evil organization. They are the

DID YOU KNOW:
In 1958, WOLVERINE was on a secret mission in Cuba, where he was apprehended by the Agents of Atlas. In order to escape, he blew up Atlas team member M-11, THE HUMAN ROBOT.

DID YOU ALSO KNOW:
A few months ago, WOLVERINE was on a mission in New York City, where he again encountered the Agents of Atlas. The reconstructed M-11 recognized Wolverine's voice, and melted his arm off.

DID YOU ALSO ALSO KNOW:
Wolverine's a quick healer, and robots carry grudges.

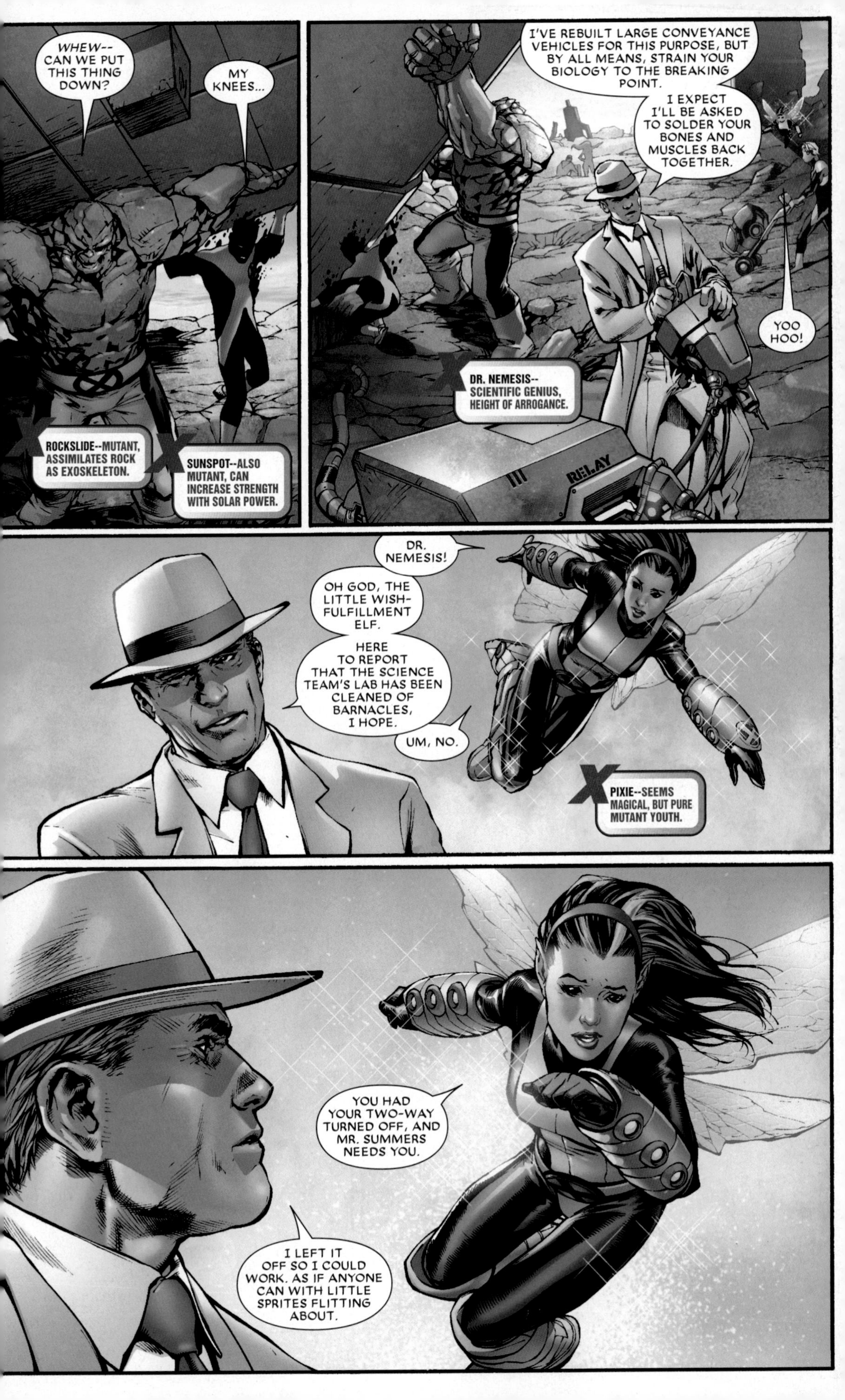
WHEW--
CAN WE PUT THIS THING DOWN?
MY KNEES...
ROCKSLIDE--MUTANT, ASSIMILATES ROCK AS EXOSKELETON.
SUNSPOT--ALSO MUTANT, CAN INCREASE STRENGTH WITH SOLAR POWER.
I'VE REBUILT LARGE CONVEYANCE VEHICLES FOR THIS PURPOSE, BUT BY ALL MEANS, STRAIN YOUR BIOLOGY TO THE BREAKING POINT.
I EXPECT I'LL BE ASKED TO SOLDER YOUR BONES AND MUSCLES BACK TOGETHER.
YOO HOO!
DR. NEMESIS--SCIENTIFIC GENIUS, HEIGHT OF ARROGANCE.
RELAY
DR. NEMESIS!
OH GOD, THE LITTLE WISH-FULFILLMENT ELF.
HERE TO REPORT THAT THE SCIENCE TEAM'S LAB HAS BEEN CLEANED OF BARNACLES, I HOPE.
UM, NO.
PIXIE--SEEMS MAGICAL, BUT PURE MUTANT YOUTH.
YOU HAD YOUR TWO-WAY TURNED OFF, AND MR. SUMMERS NEEDS YOU.
I LEFT IT OFF SO I COULD WORK. AS IF ANYONE CAN WITH LITTLE SPRITES FLITTING ABOUT.

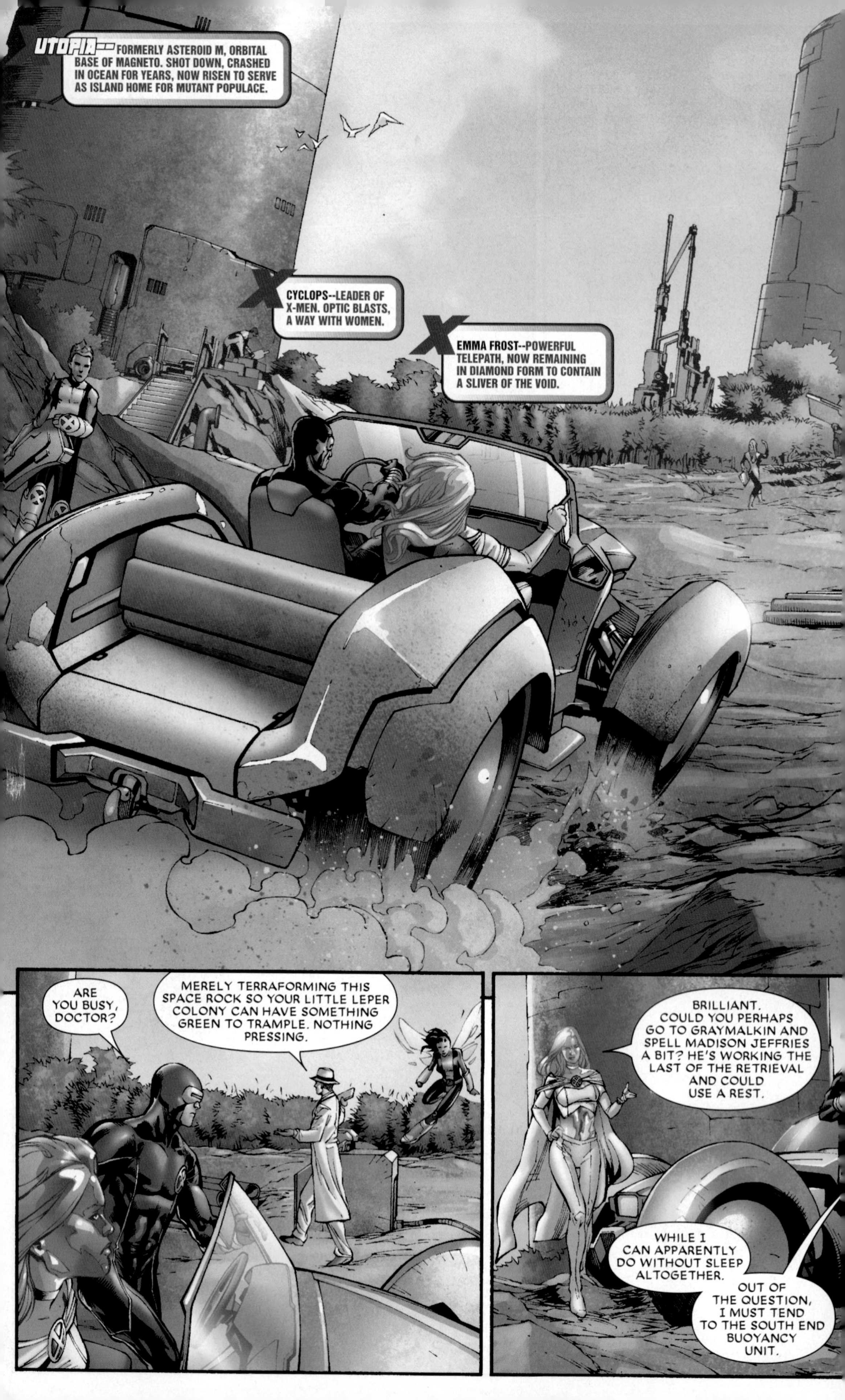
UTOPIA--FORMERLY ASTEROID M, ORBITAL BASE OF MAGNETO. SHOT DOWN, CRASHED IN OCEAN FOR YEARS, NOW RISEN TO SERVE AS ISLAND HOME FOR MUTANT POPULACE.
CYCLOPS--LEADER OF X-MEN. OPTIC BLASTS, A WAY WITH WOMEN.
EMMA FROST--POWERFUL TELEPATH, NOW REMAINING IN DIAMOND FORM TO CONTAIN A SLIVER OF THE VOID.
ARE YOU BUSY, DOCTOR?
MERELY TERRAFORMING THIS SPACE ROCK SO YOUR LITTLE LEPER COLONY CAN HAVE SOMETHING GREEN TO TRAMPLE. NOTHING PRESSING.
BRILLIANT. COULD YOU PERHAPS GO TO GRAYMALKIN AND SPELL MADISON JEFFRIES A BIT? HE'S WORKING THE LAST OF THE RETRIEVAL AND COULD USE A REST.
WHILE I CAN APPARENTLY DO WITHOUT SLEEP ALTOGETHER.
OUT OF THE QUESTION, I MUST TEND TO THE SOUTH END BUOYANCY UNIT.

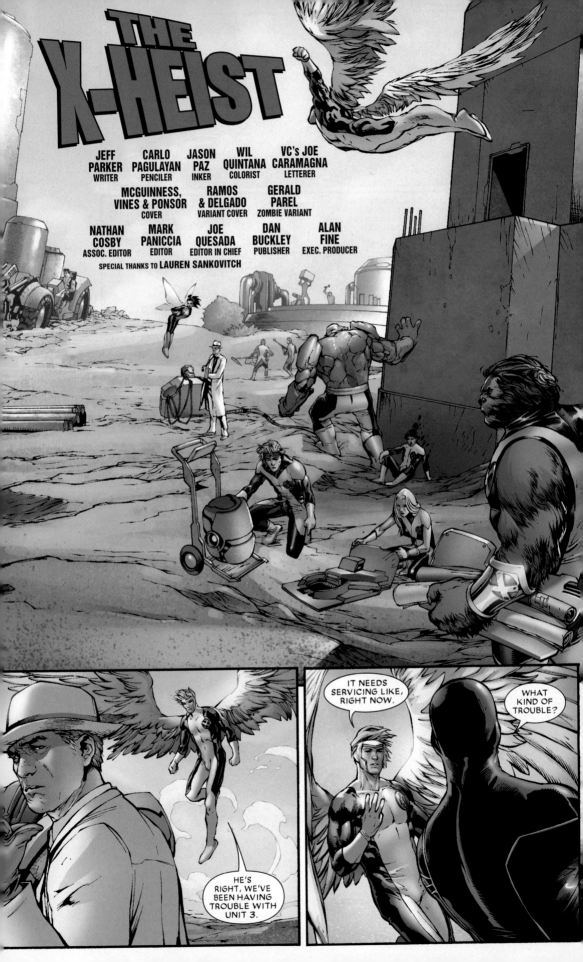

THE X-HEIST

JEFF
PARKER
WRITER

CARLO
PAGULAYAN
PENCILER

JASON
PAZ
INKER

WIL
QUINTANA
COLORIST

VC's JOE
CARAMAGNA
LETTERER

McGUINNESS,
VINES & PONSOR
COVER

RAMOS
& DELGADO
VARIANT COVER

GERALD
PAREL
ZOMBIE VARIANT

NATHAN
COSBY
ASSOC. EDITOR

MARK
PANICCIA
EDITOR

JOE
QUESADA
EDITOR IN CHIEF

DAN
BUCKLEY
PUBLISHER

ALAN
FINE
EXEC. PRODUCER

SPECIAL THANKS TO LAUREN SANKOVITCH

HE'S RIGHT, WE'VE BEEN HAVING TROUBLE WITH UNIT 3.

IT NEEDS SERVICING LIKE, RIGHT NOW.

WHAT KIND OF TROUBLE?

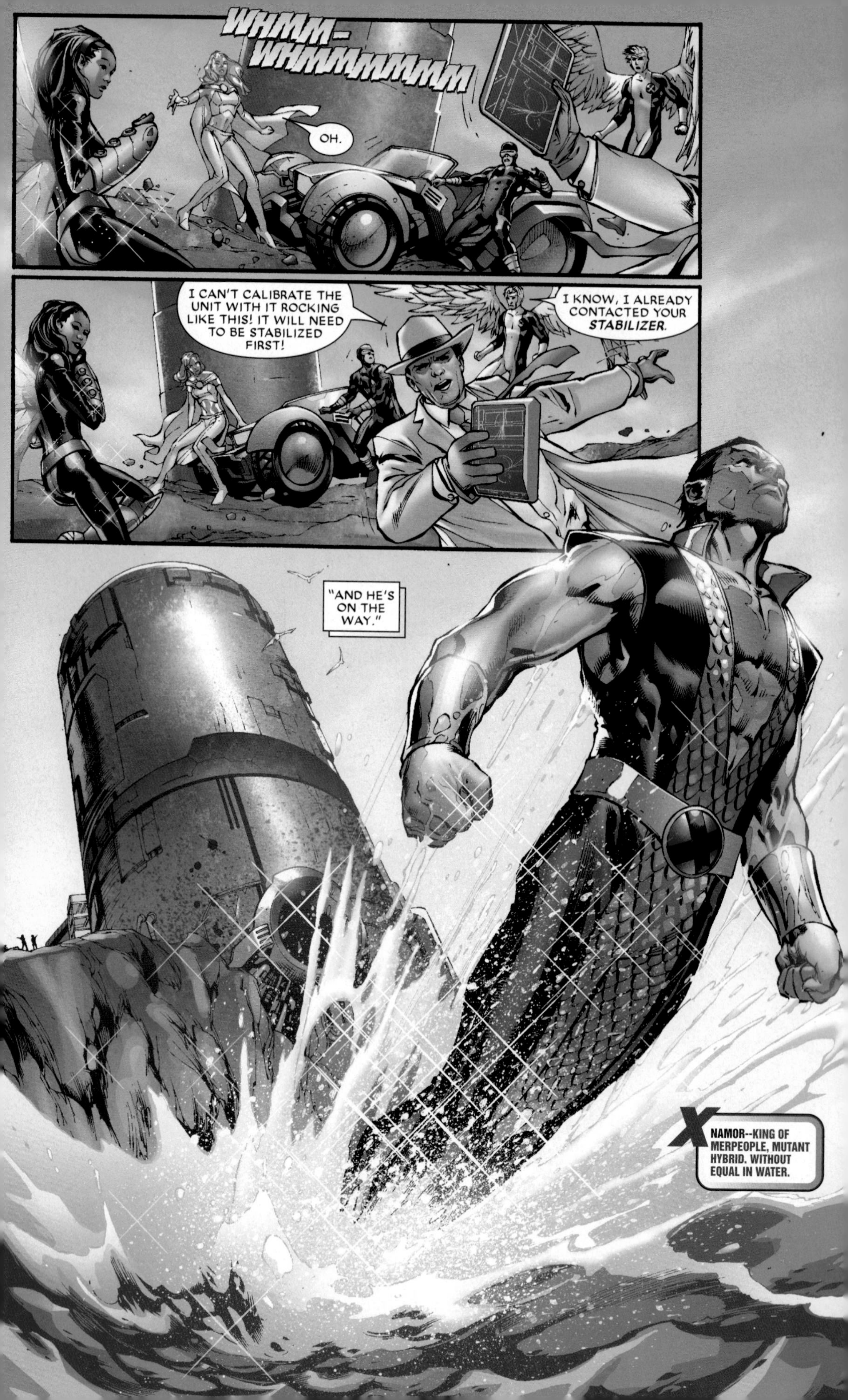
WHMM-WHMMMMMMM
OH.
I CAN'T CALIBRATE THE UNIT WITH IT ROCKING LIKE THIS! IT WILL NEED TO BE STABILIZED FIRST!
I KNOW, I ALREADY CONTACTED YOUR STABILIZER.
"AND HE'S ON THE WAY."
NAMOR--KING OF MERPEOPLE, MUTANT HYBRID. WITHOUT EQUAL IN WATER.

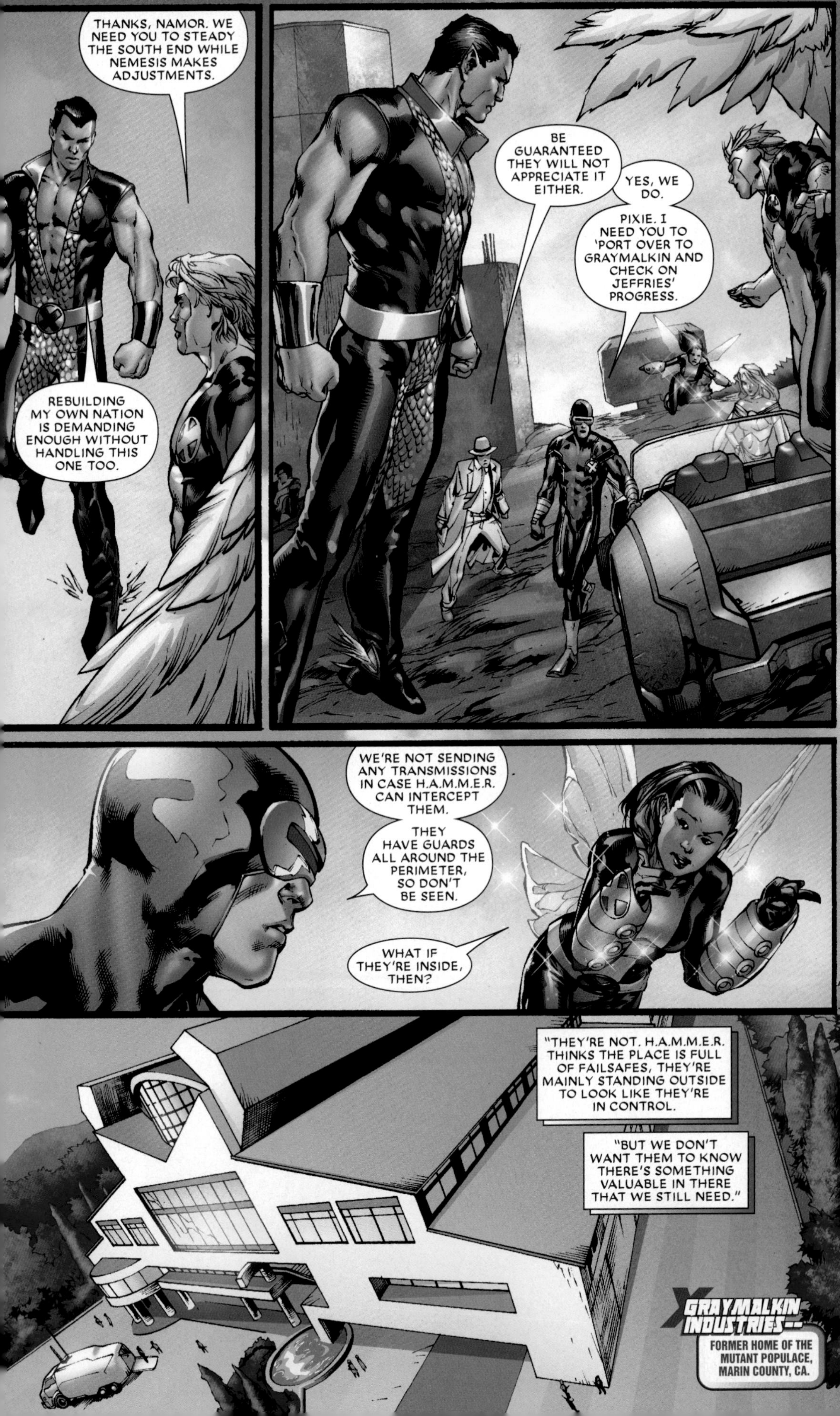
THANKS, NAMOR. WE NEED YOU TO STEADY THE SOUTH END WHILE NEMESIS MAKES ADJUSTMENTS.
REBUILDING MY OWN NATION IS DEMANDING ENOUGH WITHOUT HANDLING THIS ONE TOO.
BE GUARANTEED THEY WILL NOT APPRECIATE IT EITHER.
YES, WE DO.
PIXIE. I NEED YOU TO 'PORT OVER TO GRAYMALKIN AND CHECK ON JEFFRIES' PROGRESS.
WE'RE NOT SENDING ANY TRANSMISSIONS IN CASE H.A.M.M.E.R. CAN INTERCEPT THEM.
THEY HAVE GUARDS ALL AROUND THE PERIMETER, SO DON'T BE SEEN.
WHAT IF THEY'RE INSIDE, THEN?
"THEY'RE NOT. H.A.M.M.E.R. THINKS THE PLACE IS FULL OF FAILSAFES, THEY'RE MAINLY STANDING OUTSIDE TO LOOK LIKE THEY'RE IN CONTROL.
"BUT WE DON'T WANT THEM TO KNOW THERE'S SOMETHING VALUABLE IN THERE THAT WE STILL NEED."
GRAYMALKIN INDUSTRIES--
FORMER HOME OF THE MUTANT POPULACE, MARIN COUNTY, CA.

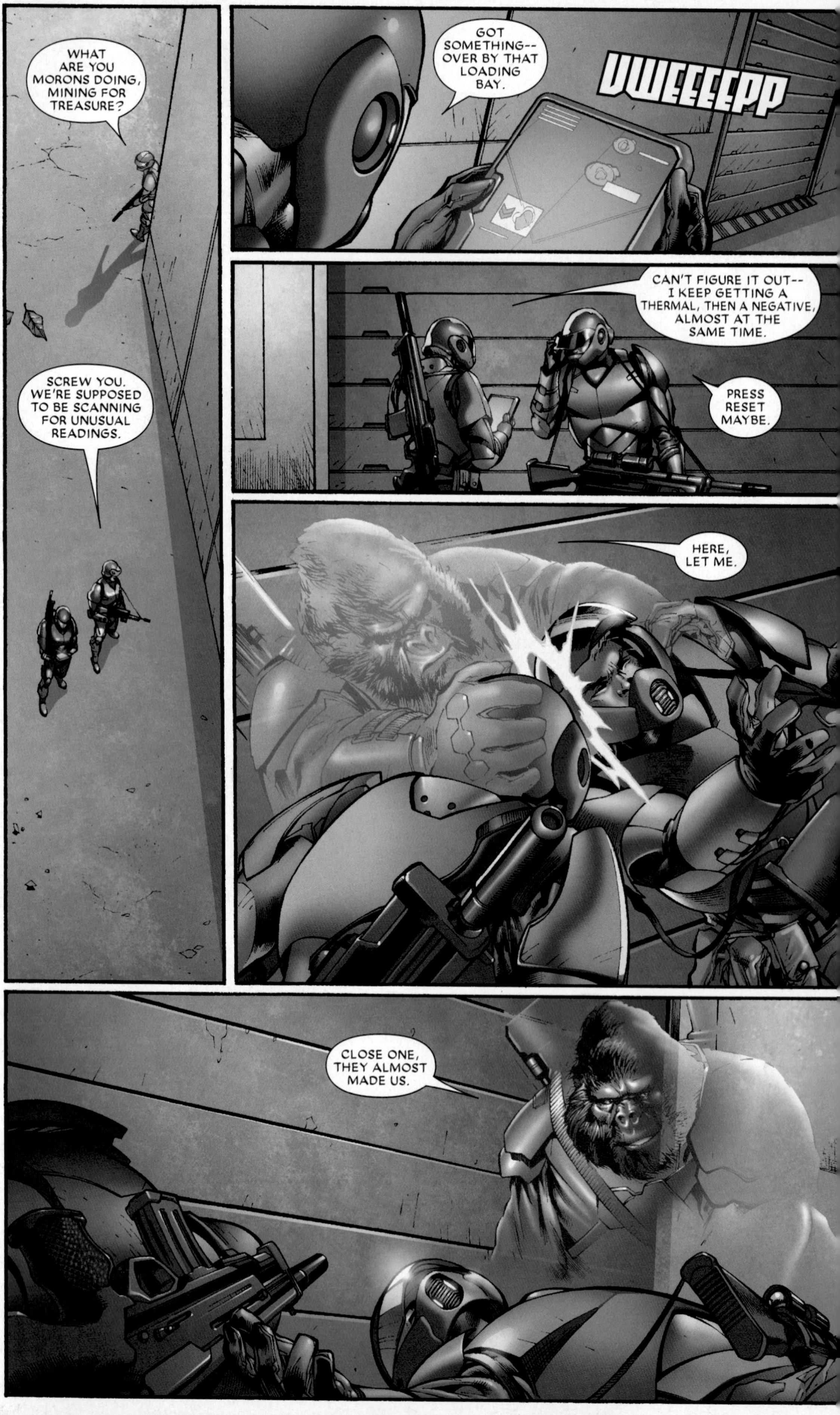
WHAT ARE YOU MORONS DOING, MINING FOR TREASURE?
SCREW YOU. WE'RE SUPPOSED TO BE SCANNING FOR UNUSUAL READINGS.
GOT SOMETHING-- OVER BY THAT LOADING BAY.
VWEEEEPP
CAN'T FIGURE IT OUT-- I KEEP GETTING A THERMAL, THEN A NEGATIVE, ALMOST AT THE SAME TIME.
PRESS RESET MAYBE.
HERE, LET ME.
CLOSE ONE, THEY ALMOST MADE US.

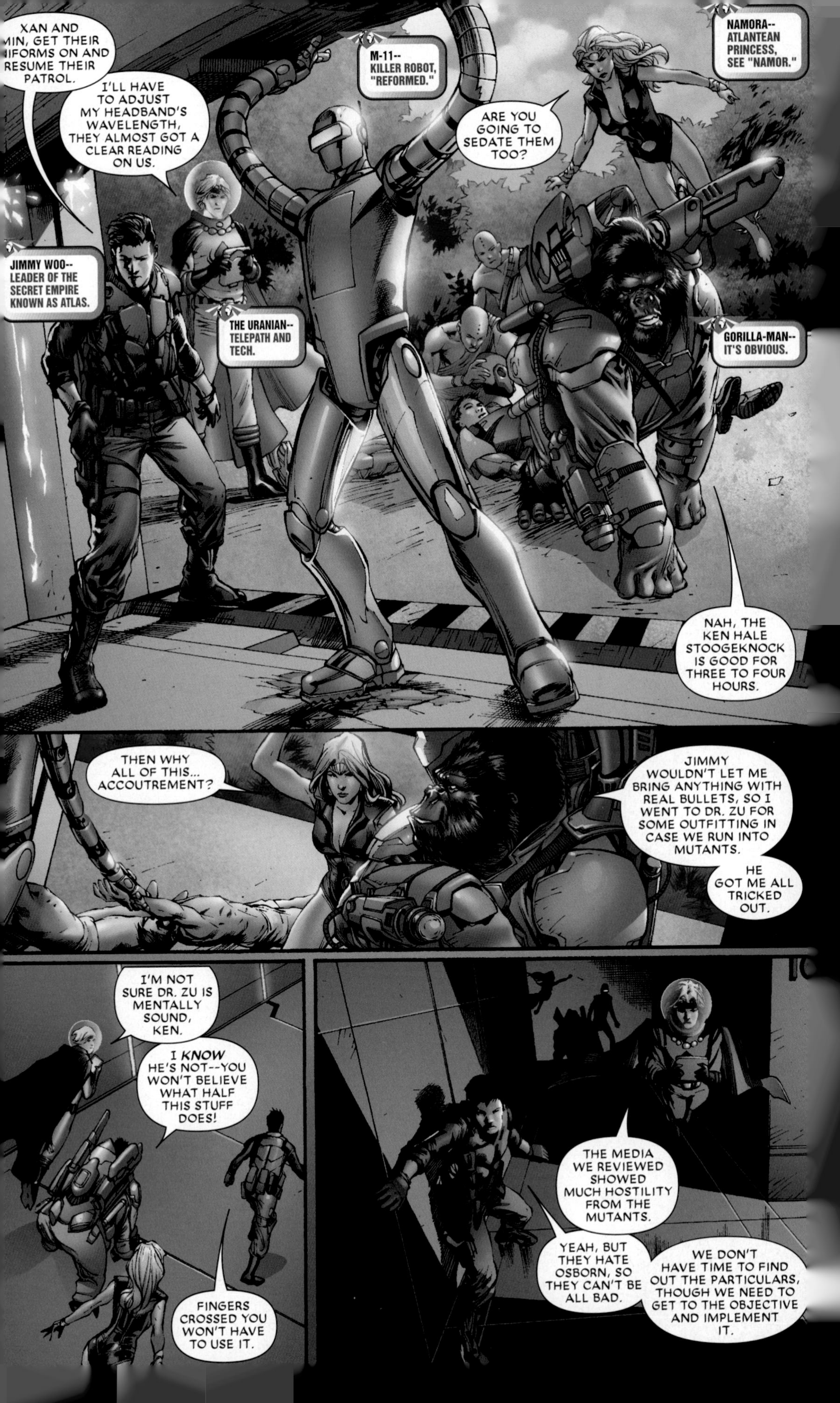
XAN AND MIN, GET THEIR UNIFORMS ON AND RESUME THEIR PATROL.
I'LL HAVE TO ADJUST MY HEADBAND'S WAVELENGTH, THEY ALMOST GOT A CLEAR READING ON US.
M-11-- KILLER ROBOT, "REFORMED."
ARE YOU GOING TO SEDATE THEM TOO?
NAMORA-- ATLANTEAN PRINCESS, SEE "NAMOR."
JIMMY WOO-- LEADER OF THE SECRET EMPIRE KNOWN AS ATLAS.
THE URANIAN-- TELEPATH AND TECH.
GORILLA-MAN-- IT'S OBVIOUS.
NAH, THE KEN HALE STOOGEKNOCK IS GOOD FOR THREE TO FOUR HOURS.
THEN WHY ALL OF THIS... ACCOUTREMENT?
JIMMY WOULDN'T LET ME BRING ANYTHING WITH REAL BULLETS, SO I WENT TO DR. ZU FOR SOME OUTFITTING IN CASE WE RUN INTO MUTANTS.
HE GOT ME ALL TRICKED OUT.
I'M NOT SURE DR. ZU IS MENTALLY SOUND, KEN.
I *KNOW* HE'S NOT--YOU WON'T BELIEVE WHAT HALF THIS STUFF DOES!
FINGERS CROSSED YOU WON'T HAVE TO USE IT.
THE MEDIA WE REVIEWED SHOWED MUCH HOSTILITY FROM THE MUTANTS.
YEAH, BUT THEY HATE OSBORN, SO THEY CAN'T BE ALL BAD.
WE DON'T HAVE TIME TO FIND OUT THE PARTICULARS, THOUGH WE NEED TO GET TO THE OBJECTIVE AND IMPLEMENT IT.

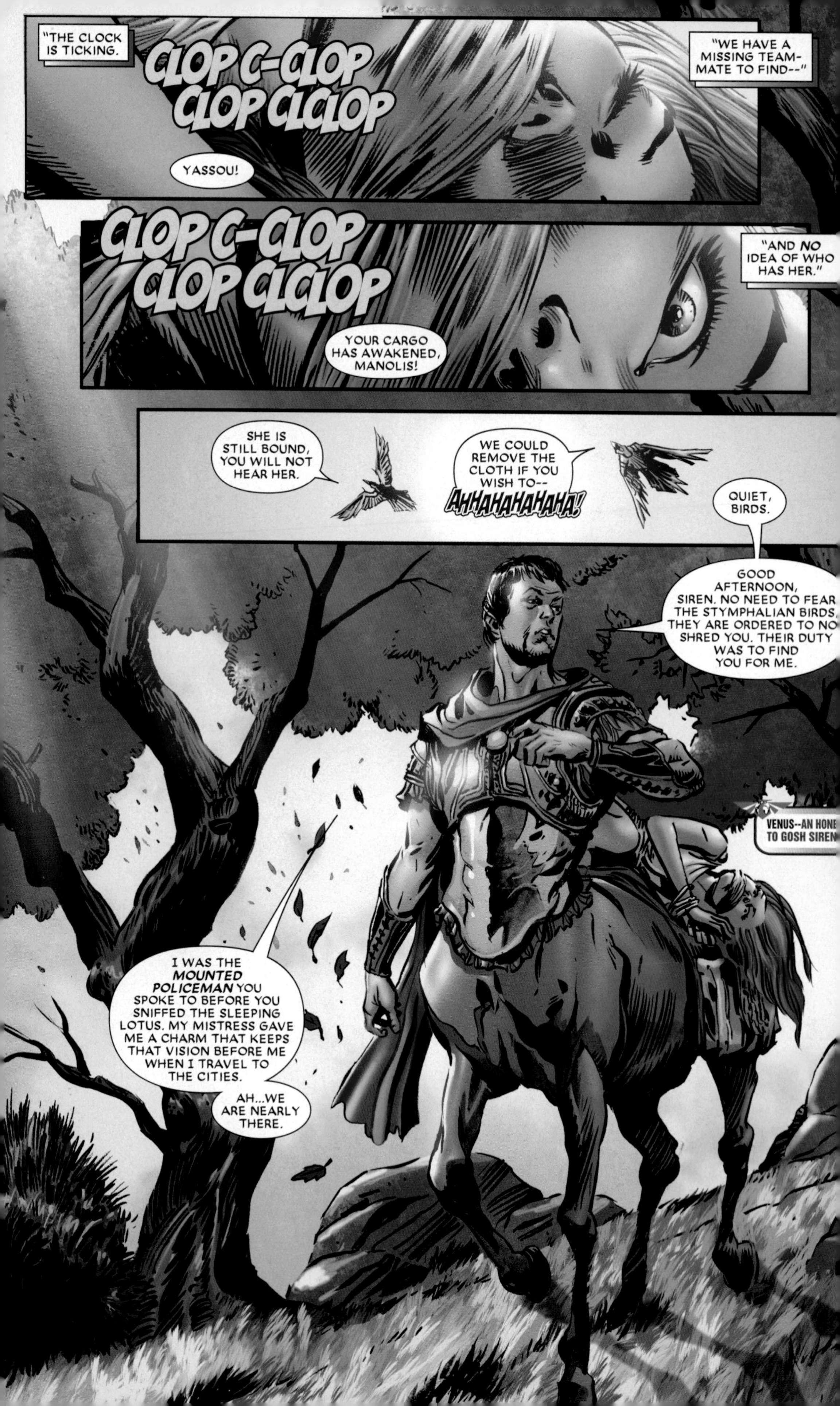
"THE CLOCK IS TICKING.
CLOP C-CLOP CLOP CLCLOP
"WE HAVE A MISSING TEAM-MATE TO FIND--"
YASSOU!
CLOP C-CLOP CLOP CLCLOP
"AND NO IDEA OF WHO HAS HER."
YOUR CARGO HAS AWAKENED, MANOLIS!
SHE IS STILL BOUND, YOU WILL NOT HEAR HER.
WE COULD REMOVE THE CLOTH IF YOU WISH TO--
AHHAHAHAHAHA!
QUIET, BIRDS.
GOOD AFTERNOON, SIREN. NO NEED TO FEAR THE STYMPHALIAN BIRDS. THEY ARE ORDERED TO NO SHRED YOU. THEIR DUTY WAS TO FIND YOU FOR ME.
VENUS--AN HONE TO GOSH SIREN
I WAS THE MOUNTED POLICEMAN YOU SPOKE TO BEFORE YOU SNIFFED THE SLEEPING LOTUS. MY MISTRESS GAVE ME A CHARM THAT KEEPS THAT VISION BEFORE ME WHEN I TRAVEL TO THE CITIES.
AH...WE ARE NEARLY THERE.

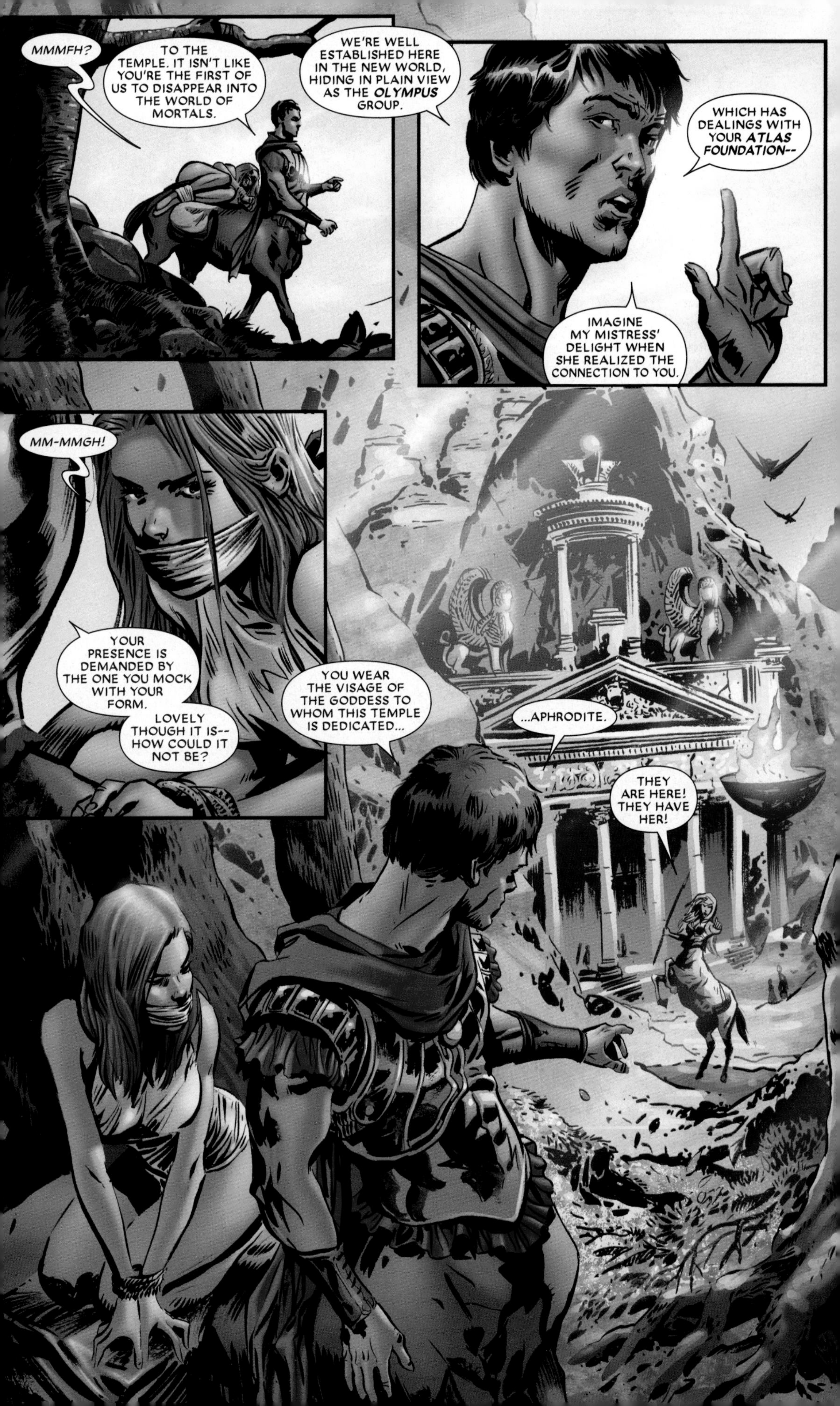
MMMFH?
TO THE TEMPLE. IT ISN'T LIKE YOU'RE THE FIRST OF US TO DISAPPEAR INTO THE WORLD OF MORTALS.
WE'RE WELL ESTABLISHED HERE IN THE NEW WORLD, HIDING IN PLAIN VIEW AS THE OLYMPUS GROUP.
WHICH HAS DEALINGS WITH YOUR ATLAS FOUNDATION--
IMAGINE MY MISTRESS' DELIGHT WHEN SHE REALIZED THE CONNECTION TO YOU.
MM-MMGH!
YOUR PRESENCE IS DEMANDED BY THE ONE YOU MOCK WITH YOUR FORM.
LOVELY THOUGH IT IS-- HOW COULD IT NOT BE?
YOU WEAR THE VISAGE OF THE GODDESS TO WHOM THIS TEMPLE IS DEDICATED...
...APHRODITE.
THEY ARE HERE! THEY HAVE HER!

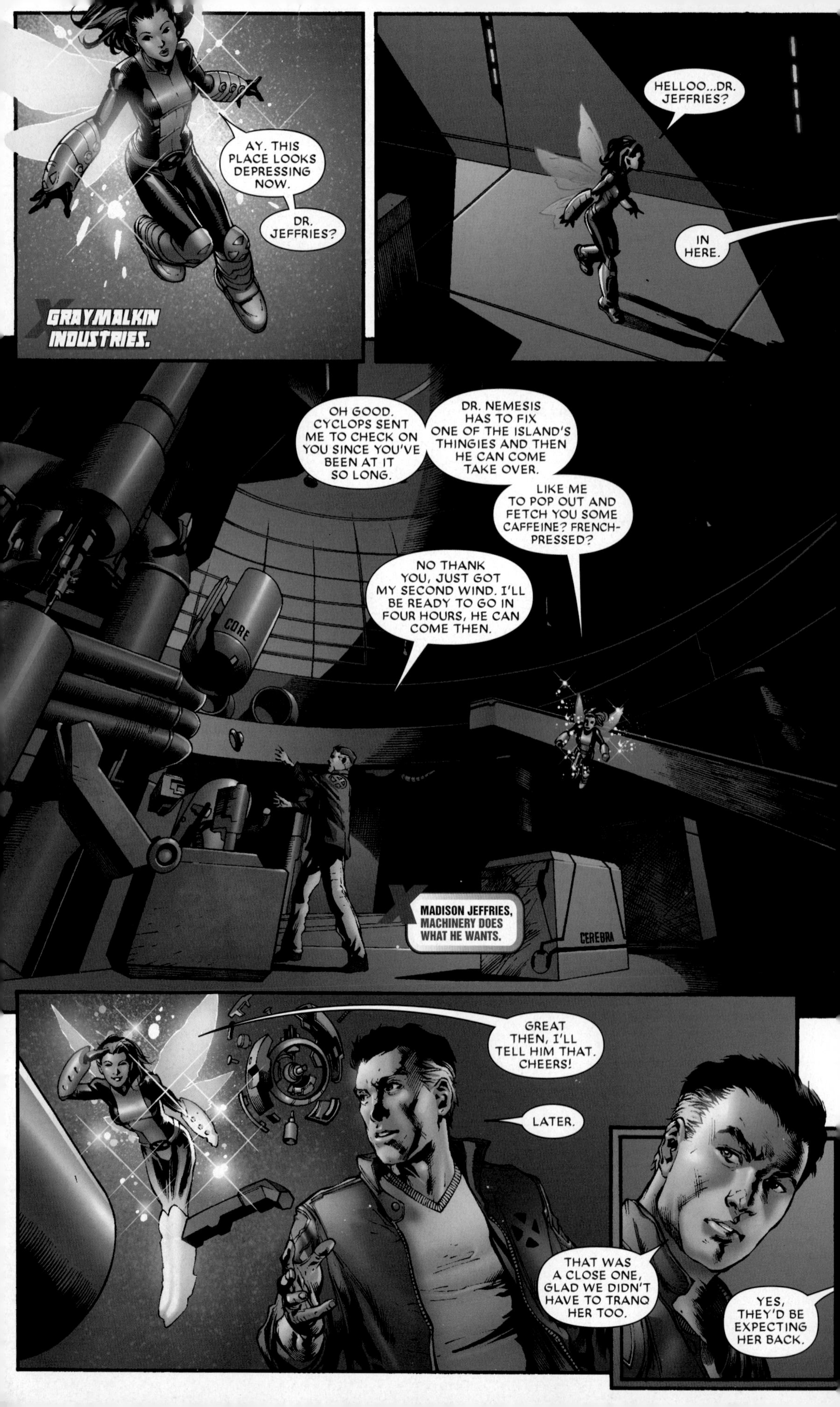
GRAYMALKIN INDUSTRIES.
AY. THIS PLACE LOOKS DEPRESSING NOW.
DR. JEFFRIES?
HELLOO...DR. JEFFRIES?
IN HERE.
OH GOOD. CYCLOPS SENT ME TO CHECK ON YOU SINCE YOU'VE BEEN AT IT SO LONG.
DR. NEMESIS HAS TO FIX ONE OF THE ISLAND'S THINGIES AND THEN HE CAN COME TAKE OVER.
LIKE ME TO POP OUT AND FETCH YOU SOME CAFFEINE? FRENCH-PRESSED?
NO THANK YOU, JUST GOT MY SECOND WIND. I'LL BE READY TO GO IN FOUR HOURS, HE CAN COME THEN.
CORE
MADISON JEFFRIES, MACHINERY DOES WHAT HE WANTS.
CEREBRA
GREAT THEN, I'LL TELL HIM THAT. CHEERS!
LATER.
THAT WAS A CLOSE ONE, GLAD WE DIDN'T HAVE TO TRANQ HER TOO.
YES, THEY'D BE EXPECTING HER BACK.

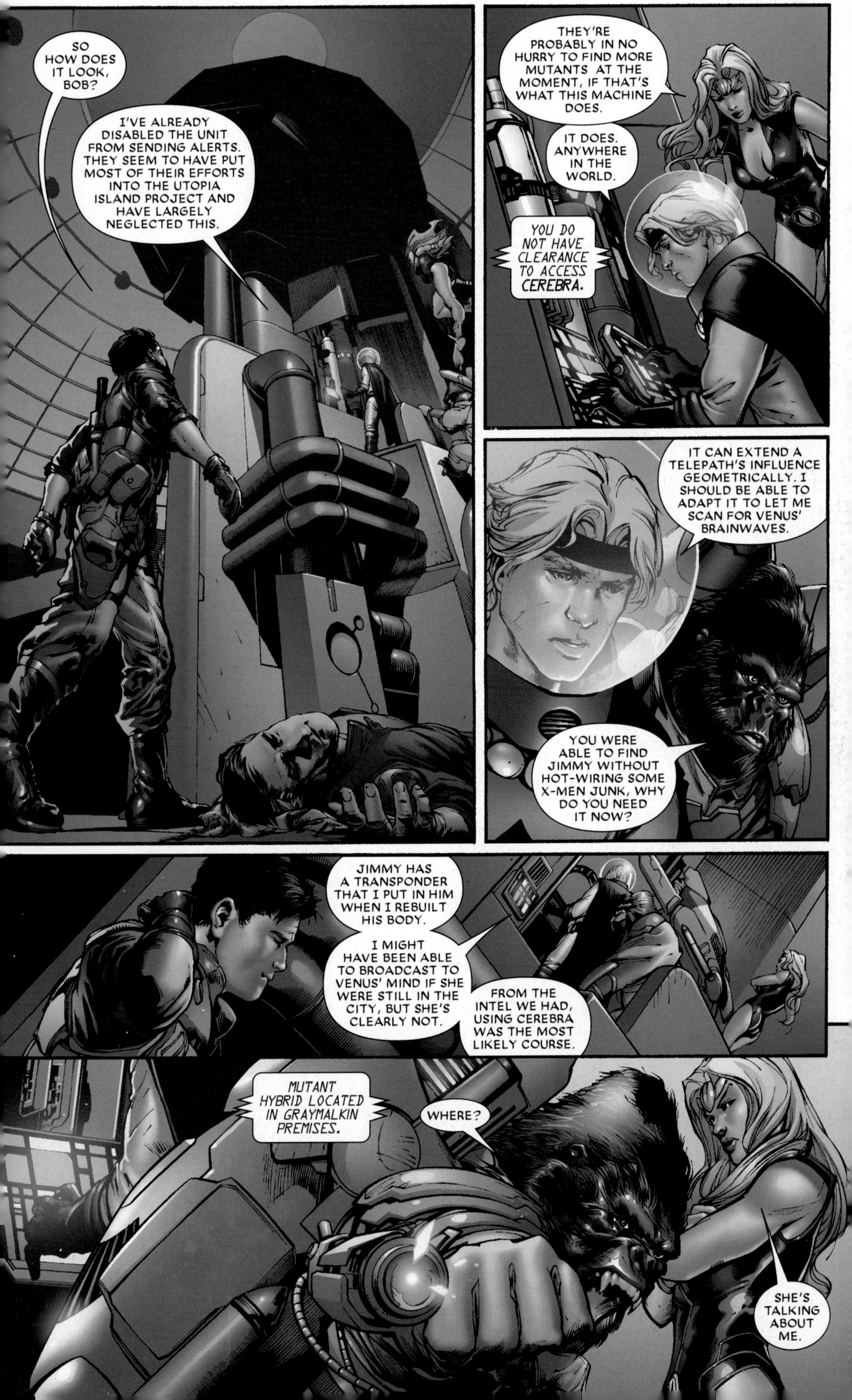
SO HOW DOES IT LOOK, BOB?
I'VE ALREADY DISABLED THE UNIT FROM SENDING ALERTS. THEY SEEM TO HAVE PUT MOST OF THEIR EFFORTS INTO THE UTOPIA ISLAND PROJECT AND HAVE LARGELY NEGLECTED THIS.
THEY'RE PROBABLY IN NO HURRY TO FIND MORE MUTANTS AT THE MOMENT, IF THAT'S WHAT THIS MACHINE DOES.
IT DOES. ANYWHERE IN THE WORLD.
YOU DO NOT HAVE CLEARANCE TO ACCESS CEREBRA.
IT CAN EXTEND A TELEPATH'S INFLUENCE GEOMETRICALLY. I SHOULD BE ABLE TO ADAPT IT TO LET ME SCAN FOR VENUS' BRAINWAVES.
YOU WERE ABLE TO FIND JIMMY WITHOUT HOT-WIRING SOME X-MEN JUNK, WHY DO YOU NEED IT NOW?
JIMMY HAS A TRANSPONDER THAT I PUT IN HIM WHEN I REBUILT HIS BODY.
I MIGHT HAVE BEEN ABLE TO BROADCAST TO VENUS' MIND IF SHE WERE STILL IN THE CITY, BUT SHE'S CLEARLY NOT.
FROM THE INTEL WE HAD, USING CEREBRA WAS THE MOST LIKELY COURSE.
MUTANT HYBRID LOCATED IN GRAYMALKIN PREMISES.
WHERE?
SHE'S TALKING ABOUT ME.

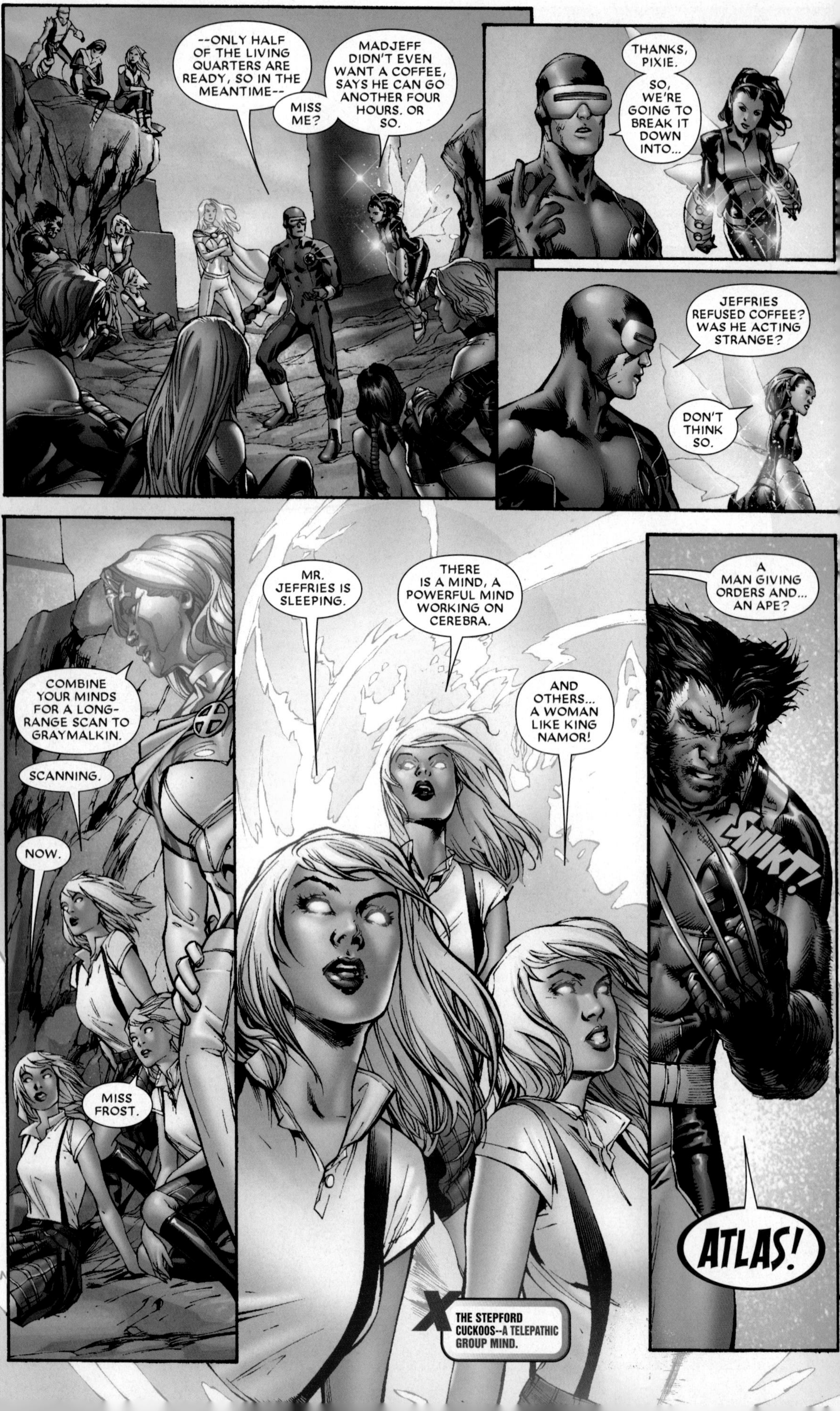
--ONLY HALF OF THE LIVING QUARTERS ARE READY, SO IN THE MEANTIME--
MISS ME?
MADJEFF DIDN'T EVEN WANT A COFFEE, SAYS HE CAN GO ANOTHER FOUR HOURS. OR SO.
THANKS, PIXIE.
SO, WE'RE GOING TO BREAK IT DOWN INTO...
JEFFRIES REFUSED COFFEE? WAS HE ACTING STRANGE?
DON'T THINK SO.
COMBINE YOUR MINDS FOR A LONG-RANGE SCAN TO GRAYMALKIN.
SCANNING.
NOW.
MISS FROST.
MR. JEFFRIES IS SLEEPING.
THERE IS A MIND, A POWERFUL MIND WORKING ON CEREBRA.
AND OTHERS... A WOMAN LIKE KING NAMOR!
THE STEPFORD CUCKOOS--A TELEPATHIC GROUP MIND.
A MAN GIVING ORDERS AND... AN APE?
SNIKT!
ATLAS!

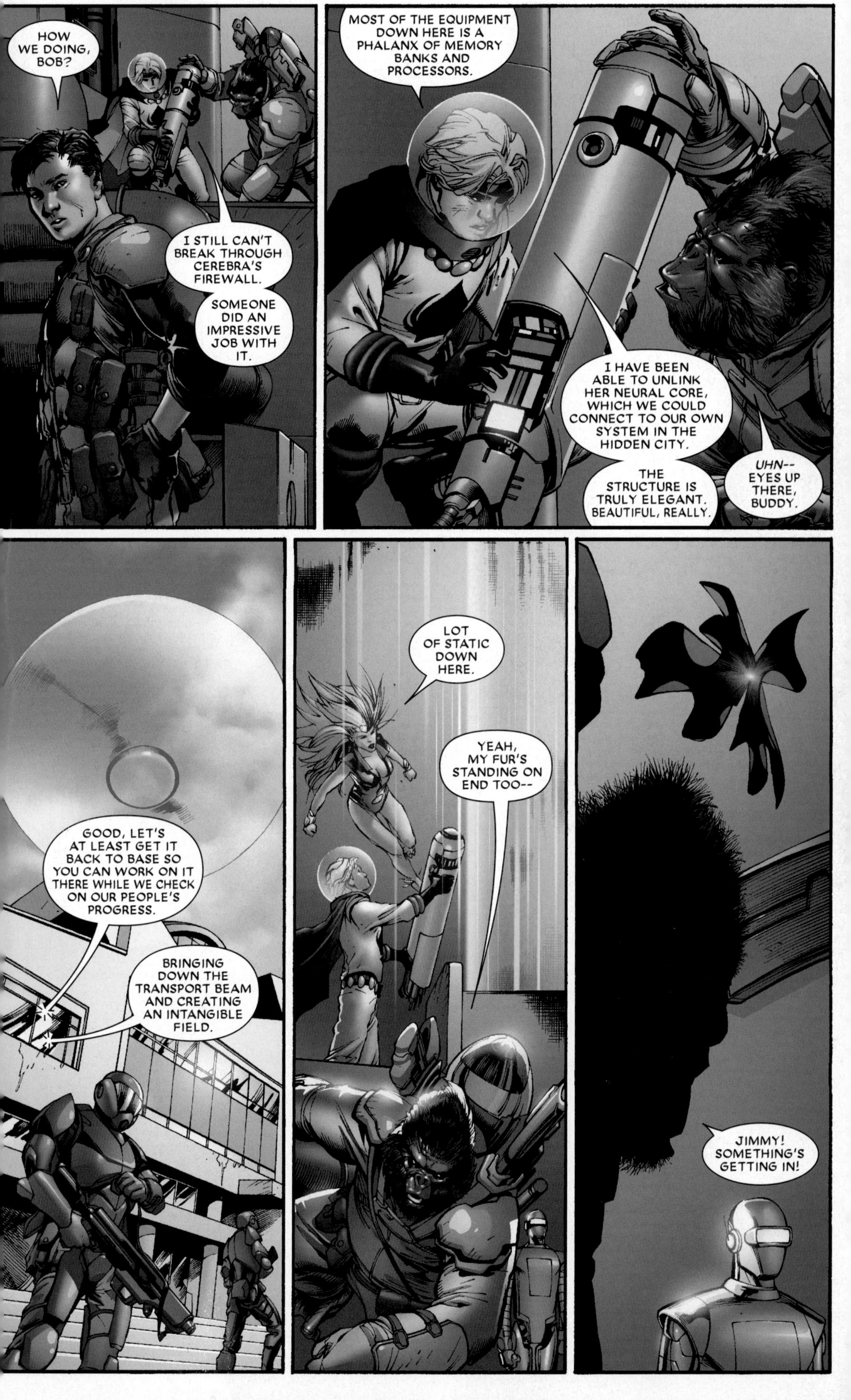
HOW WE DOING, BOB?
I STILL CAN'T BREAK THROUGH CEREBRA'S FIREWALL.
SOMEONE DID AN IMPRESSIVE JOB WITH IT.
MOST OF THE EQUIPMENT DOWN HERE IS A PHALANX OF MEMORY BANKS AND PROCESSORS.
I HAVE BEEN ABLE TO UNLINK HER NEURAL CORE, WHICH WE COULD CONNECT TO OUR OWN SYSTEM IN THE HIDDEN CITY.
THE STRUCTURE IS TRULY ELEGANT. BEAUTIFUL, REALLY.
UHN-- EYES UP THERE, BUDDY.
GOOD, LET'S AT LEAST GET IT BACK TO BASE SO YOU CAN WORK ON IT THERE WHILE WE CHECK ON OUR PEOPLE'S PROGRESS.
BRINGING DOWN THE TRANSPORT BEAM AND CREATING AN INTANGIBLE FIELD.
LOT OF STATIC DOWN HERE.
YEAH, MY FUR'S STANDING ON END TOO--
JIMMY! SOMETHING'S GETTING IN!

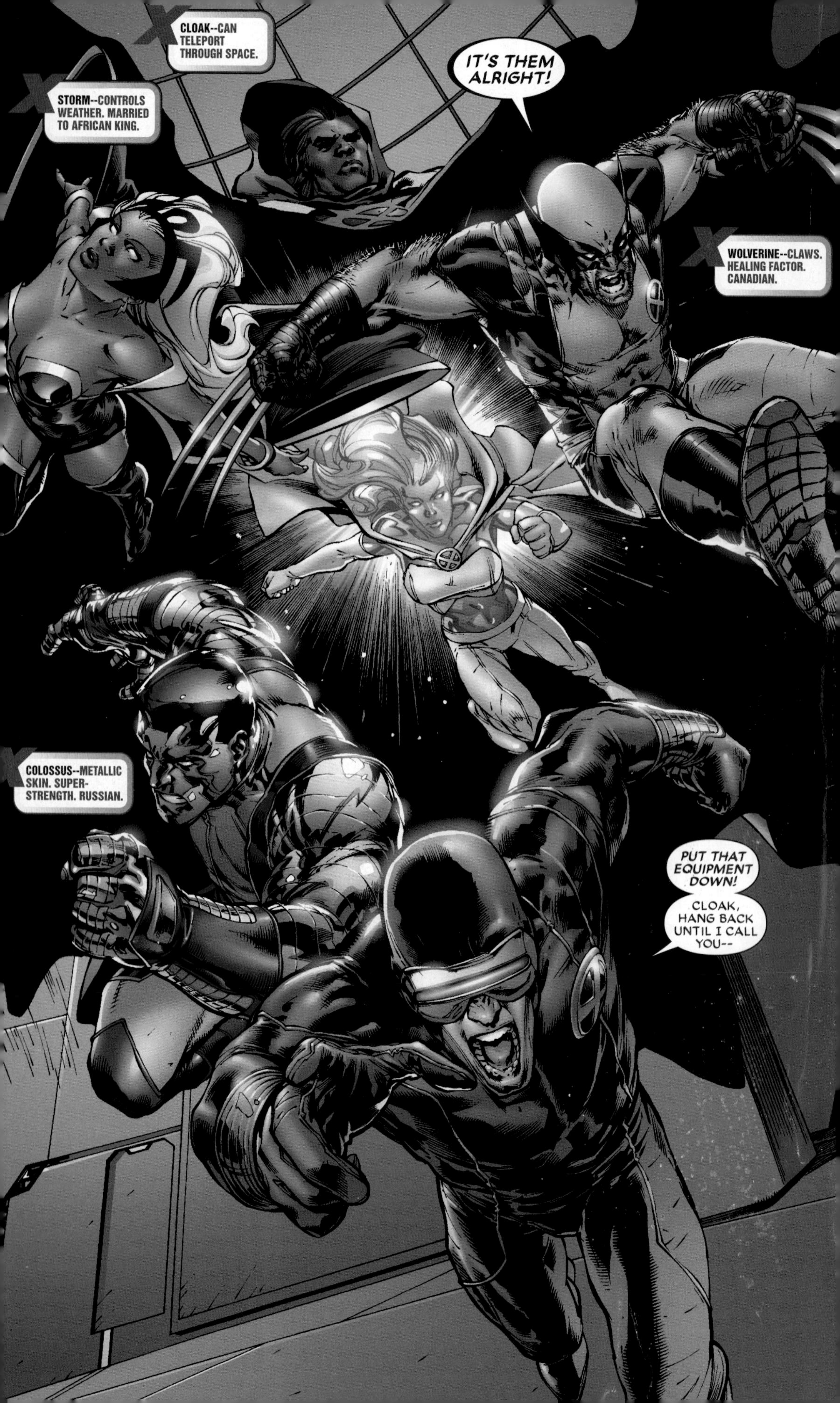

CLOAK--CAN TELEPORT THROUGH SPACE.
STORM--CONTROLS WEATHER. MARRIED TO AFRICAN KING.
IT'S THEM ALRIGHT!
WOLVERINE--CLAWS. HEALING FACTOR. CANADIAN.
COLOSSUS--METALLIC SKIN. SUPER-STRENGTH. RUSSIAN.
PUT THAT EQUIPMENT DOWN!
CLOAK, HANG BACK UNTIL I CALL YOU--

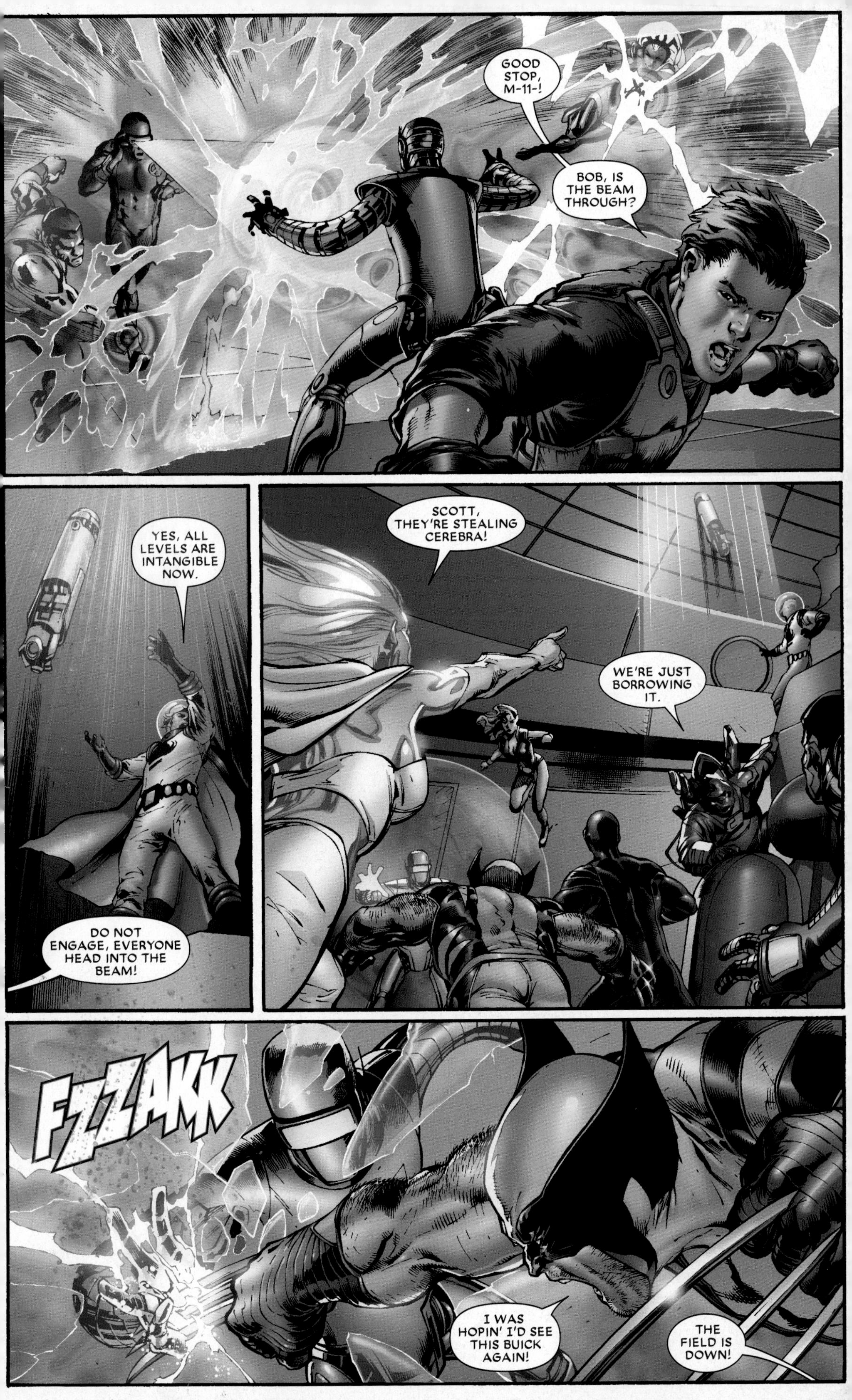
GOOD STOP, M-11-!
BOB, IS THE BEAM THROUGH?
YES, ALL LEVELS ARE INTANGIBLE NOW.
DO NOT ENGAGE, EVERYONE HEAD INTO THE BEAM!
SCOTT, THEY'RE STEALING CEREBRA!
WE'RE JUST BORROWING IT.
FZZAKK
I WAS HOPIN' I'D SEE THIS BUICK AGAIN!
THE FIELD IS DOWN!

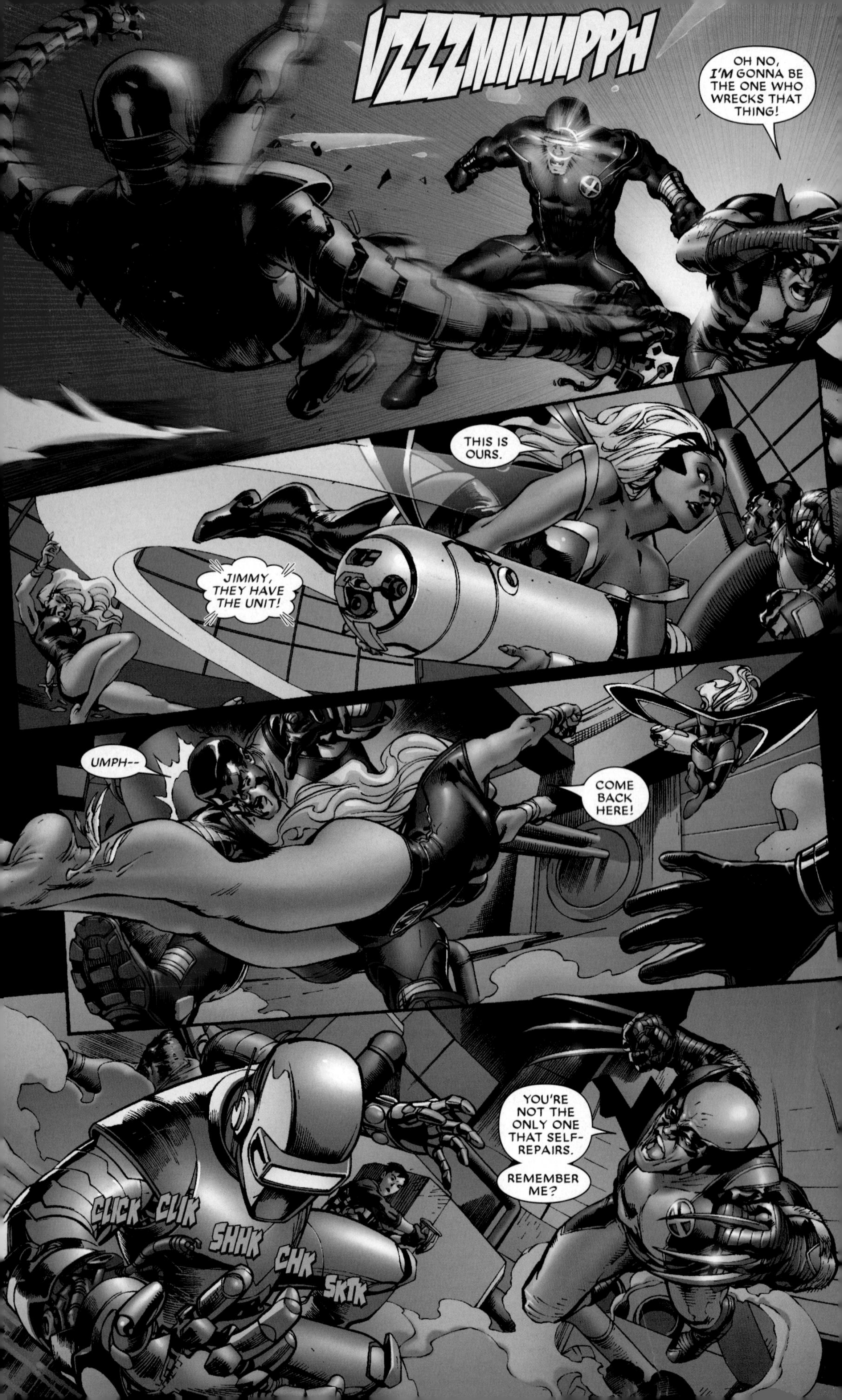
VZZZMMMMPPH
OH NO, I'M GONNA BE THE ONE WHO WRECKS THAT THING!
THIS IS OURS.
JIMMY, THEY HAVE THE UNIT!
UMPH--
COME BACK HERE!
YOU'RE NOT THE ONLY ONE THAT SELF-REPAIRS.
REMEMBER ME?
CLICK CLIK
SHHK
CHK
SKTK

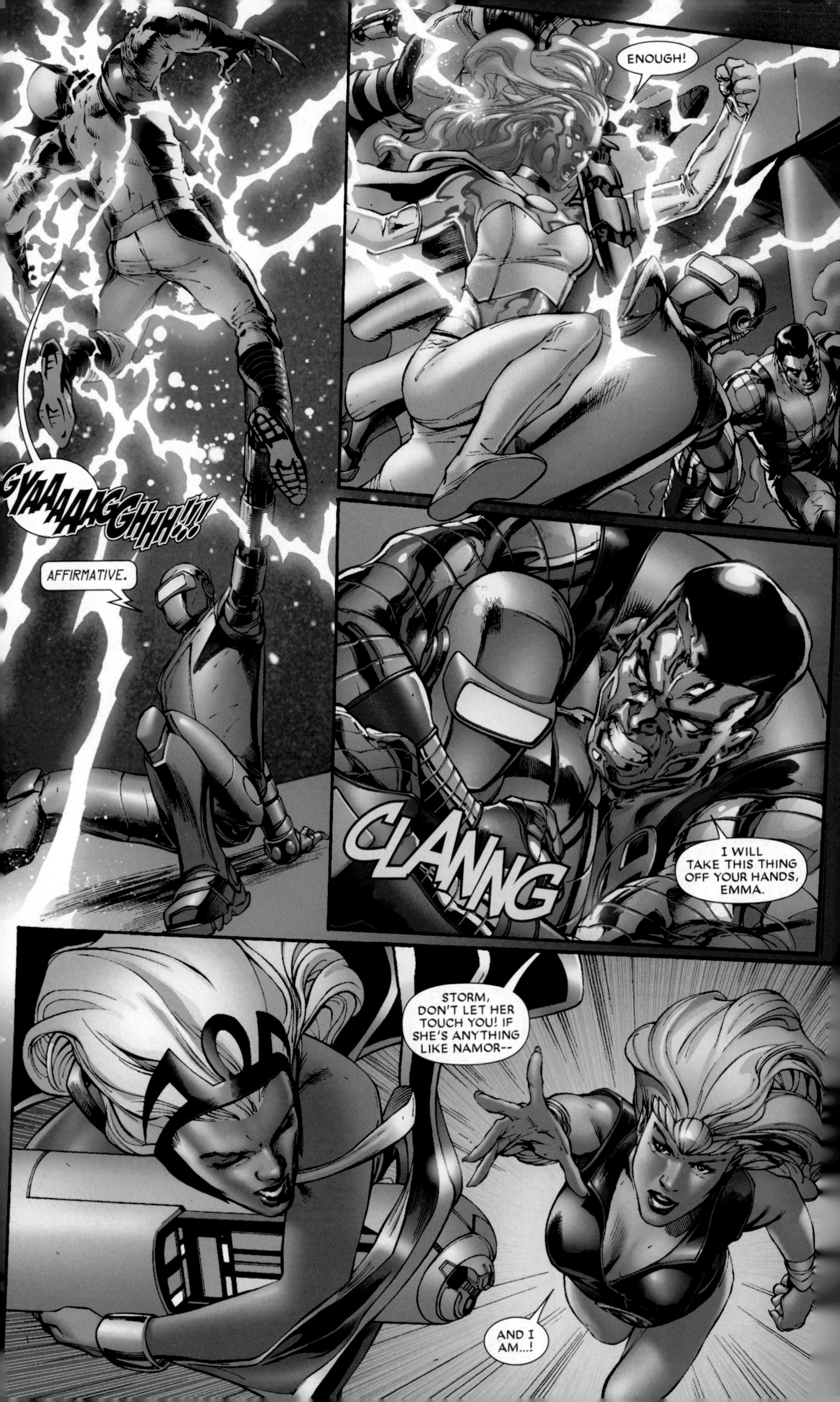
GYAAAAAGGHHH!!!
AFFIRMATIVE.
ENOUGH!
CLANNG
I WILL TAKE THIS THING OFF YOUR HANDS, EMMA.
STORM, DON'T LET HER TOUCH YOU! IF SHE'S ANYTHING LIKE NAMOR--
AND I AM...!

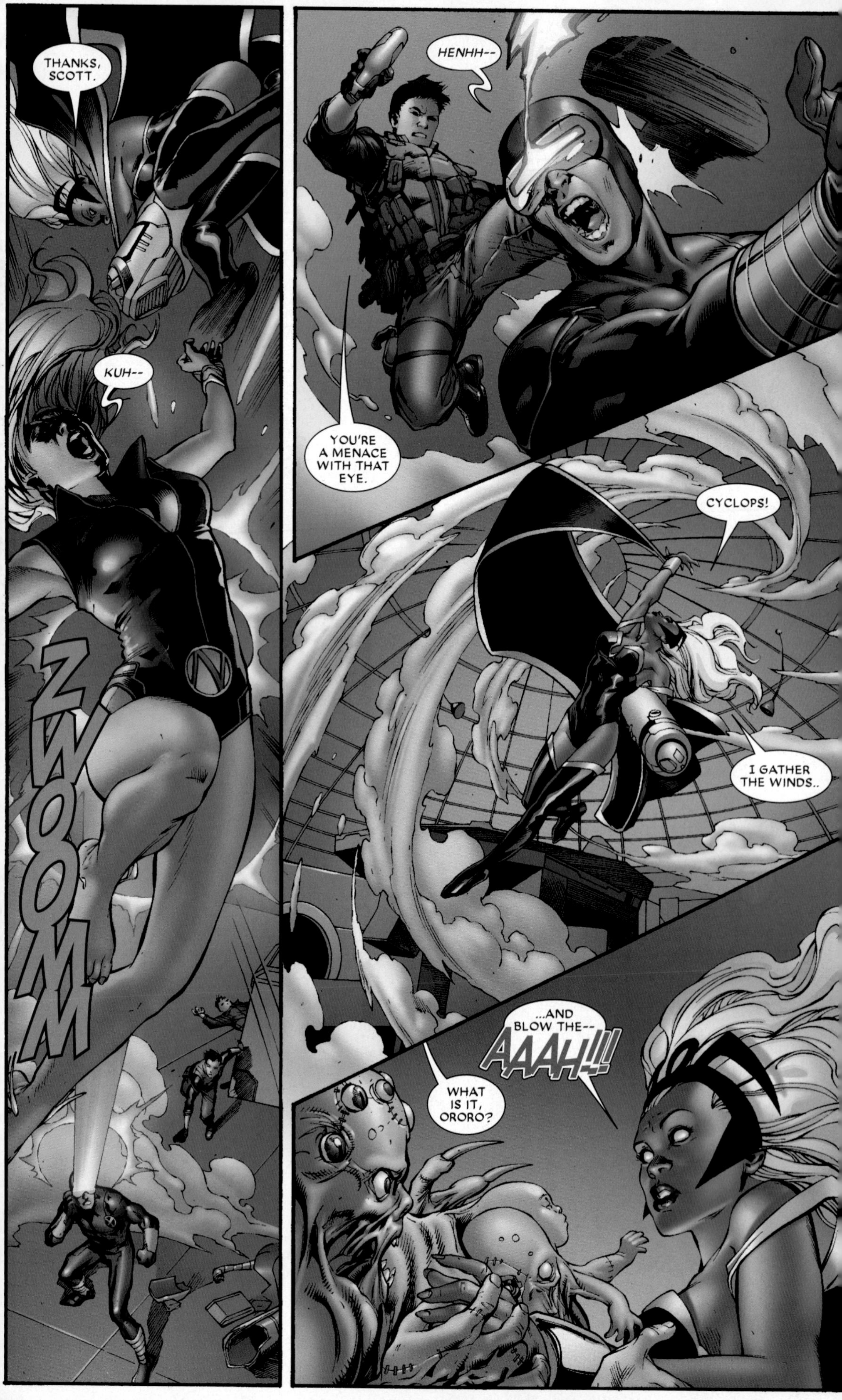
THANKS, SCOTT.
KUH--
ZWOOOM
HENHH--
YOU'RE A MENACE WITH THAT EYE.
CYCLOPS!
I GATHER THE WINDS..
...AND BLOW THE--
AAAH!!!
WHAT IS IT, ORORO?

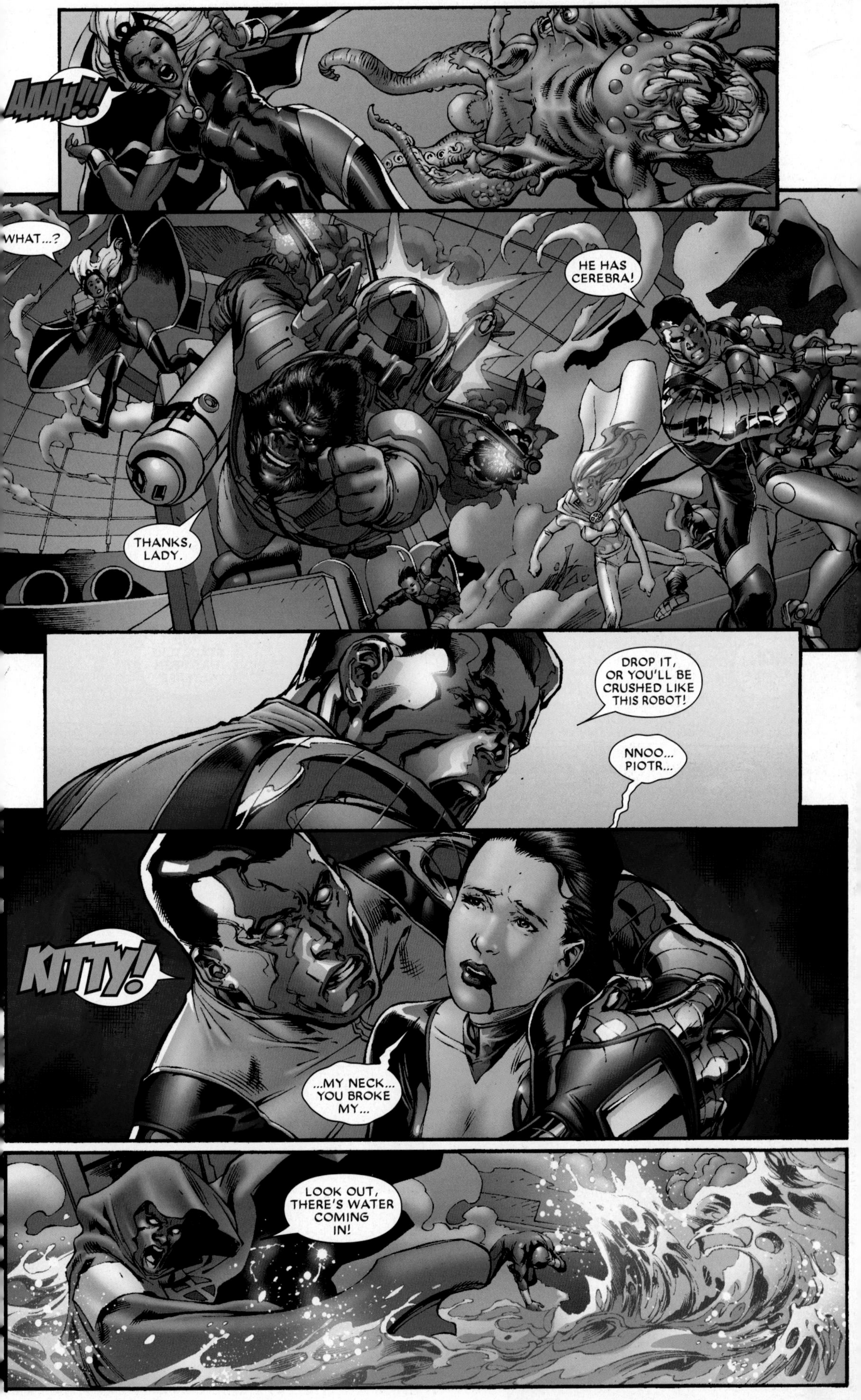

AAAH!!!
WHAT...?
HE HAS CEREBRA!
THANKS, LADY.
DROP IT, OR YOU'LL BE CRUSHED LIKE THIS ROBOT!
NNOO... PIOTR...
KITTY!
...MY NECK... YOU BROKE MY...
LOOK OUT, THERE'S WATER COMING IN!

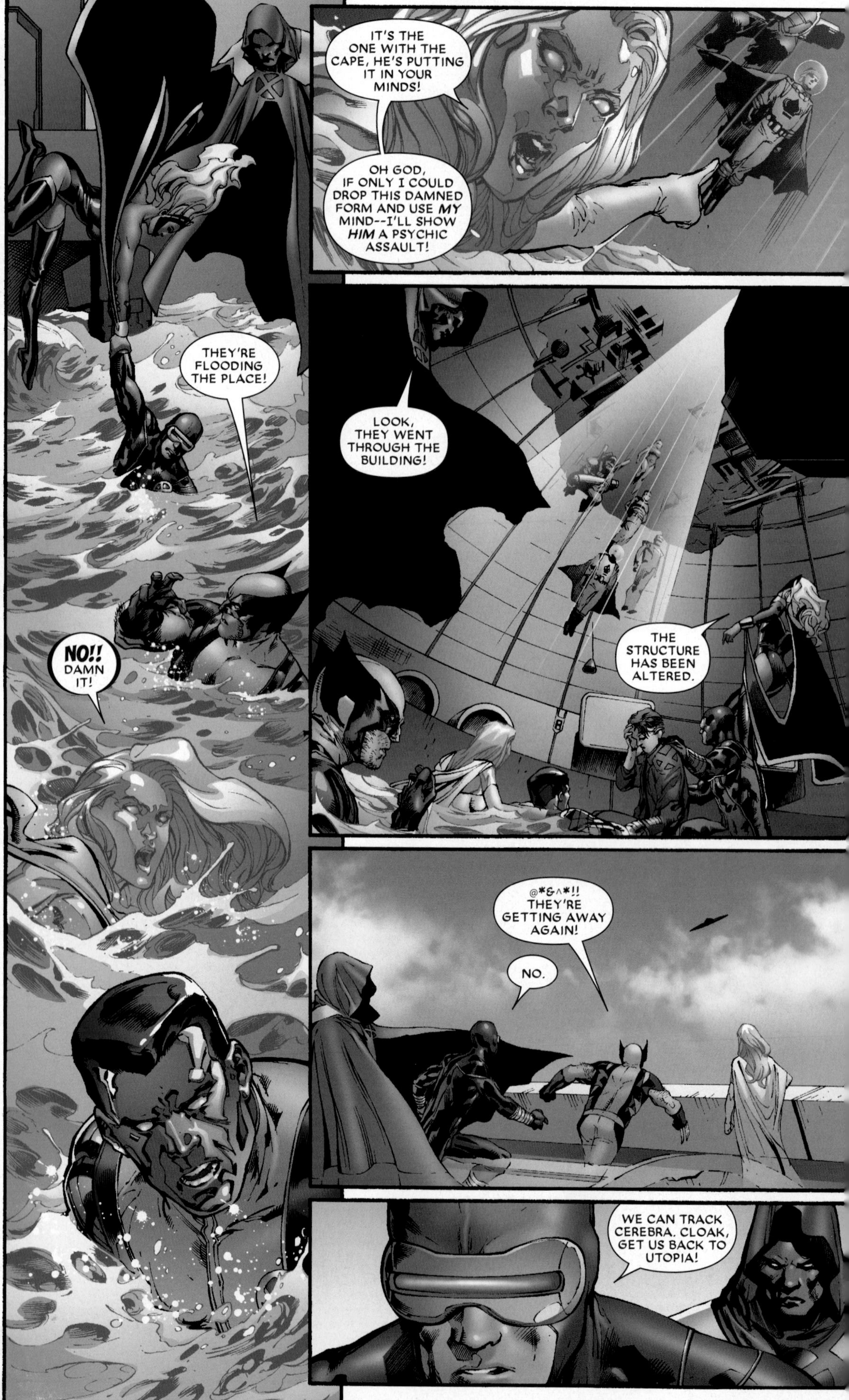
IT'S THE ONE WITH THE CAPE, HE'S PUTTING IT IN YOUR MINDS!
OH GOD, IF ONLY I COULD DROP THIS DAMNED FORM AND USE MY MIND--I'LL SHOW HIM A PSYCHIC ASSAULT!
THEY'RE FLOODING THE PLACE!
NO!! DAMN IT!
LOOK, THEY WENT THROUGH THE BUILDING!
THE STRUCTURE HAS BEEN ALTERED.
@*&^*!! THEY'RE GETTING AWAY AGAIN!
NO.
WE CAN TRACK CEREBRA. CLOAK, GET US BACK TO UTOPIA!

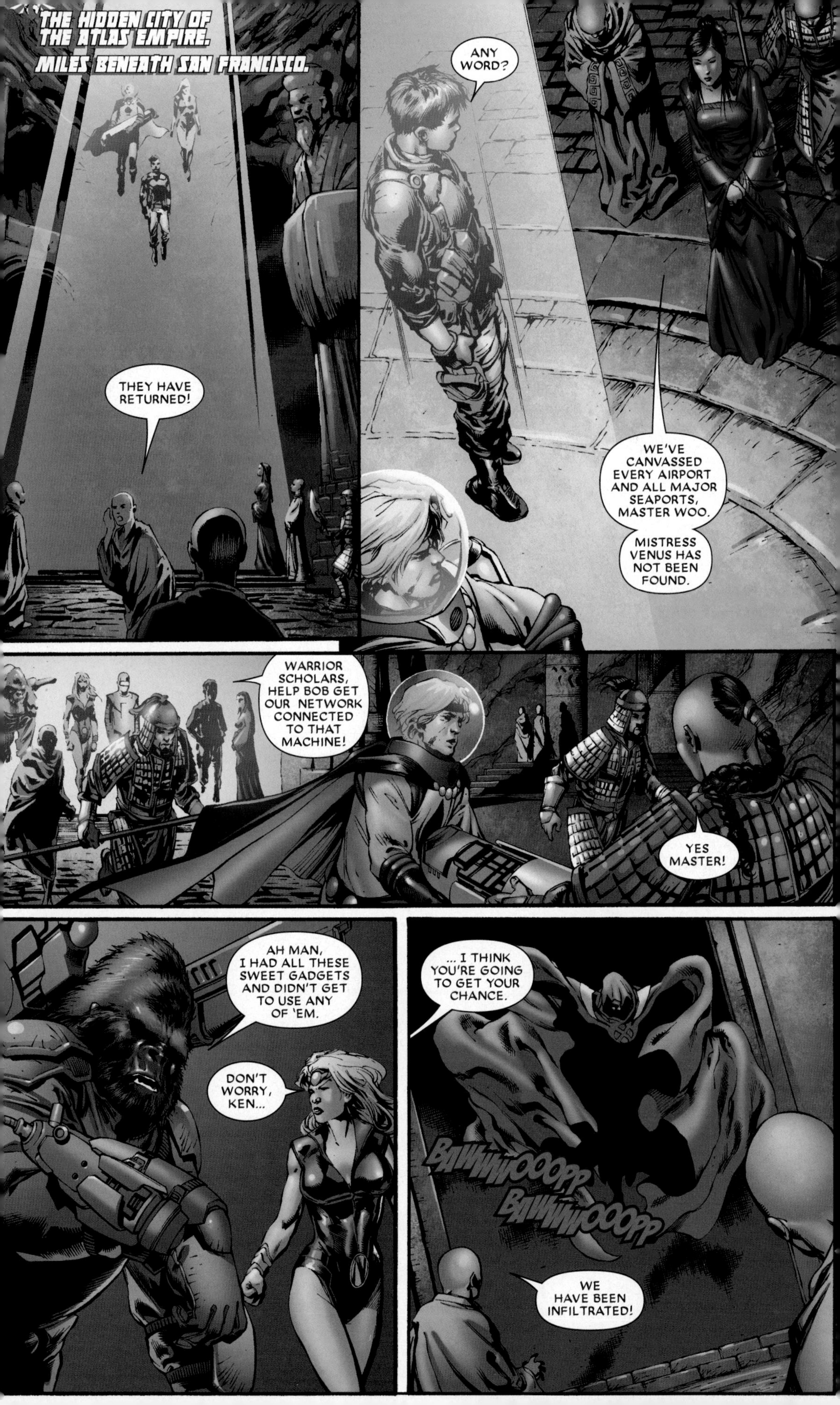
THE HIDDEN CITY OF THE ATLAS EMPIRE.
MILES BENEATH SAN FRANCISCO.
THEY HAVE RETURNED!
ANY WORD?
WE'VE CANVASSED EVERY AIRPORT AND ALL MAJOR SEAPORTS, MASTER WOO.
MISTRESS VENUS HAS NOT BEEN FOUND.
WARRIOR SCHOLARS, HELP BOB GET OUR NETWORK CONNECTED TO THAT MACHINE!
YES MASTER!
AH MAN, I HAD ALL THESE SWEET GADGETS AND DIDN'T GET TO USE ANY OF 'EM.
DON'T WORRY, KEN...
... I THINK YOU'RE GOING TO GET YOUR CHANCE.
BAWWWOOOPP
BAWWWOOOPP
WE HAVE BEEN INFILTRATED!

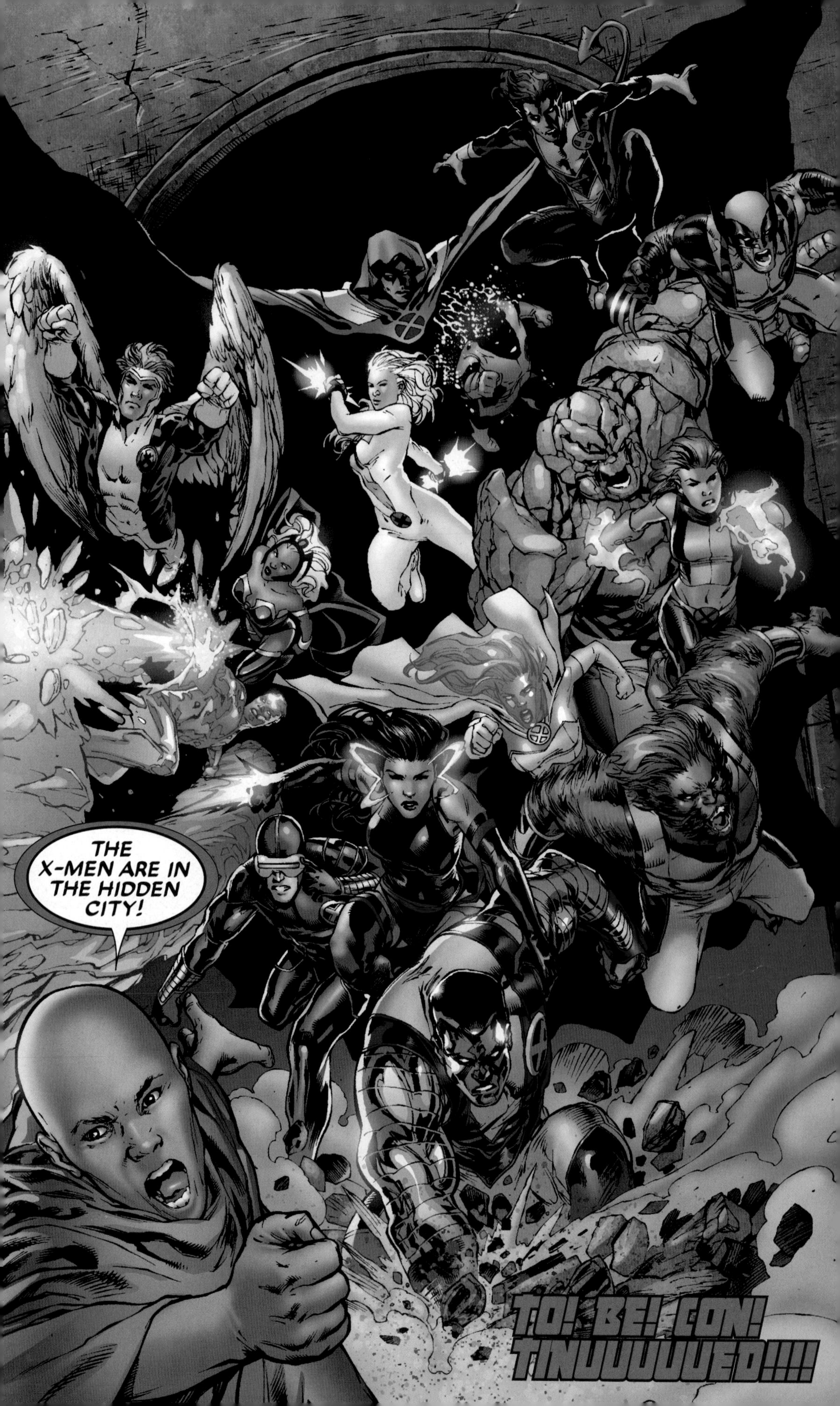
THE X-MEN ARE IN THE HIDDEN CITY!
T.O! BE! CON! TINUUUUUED!!!!

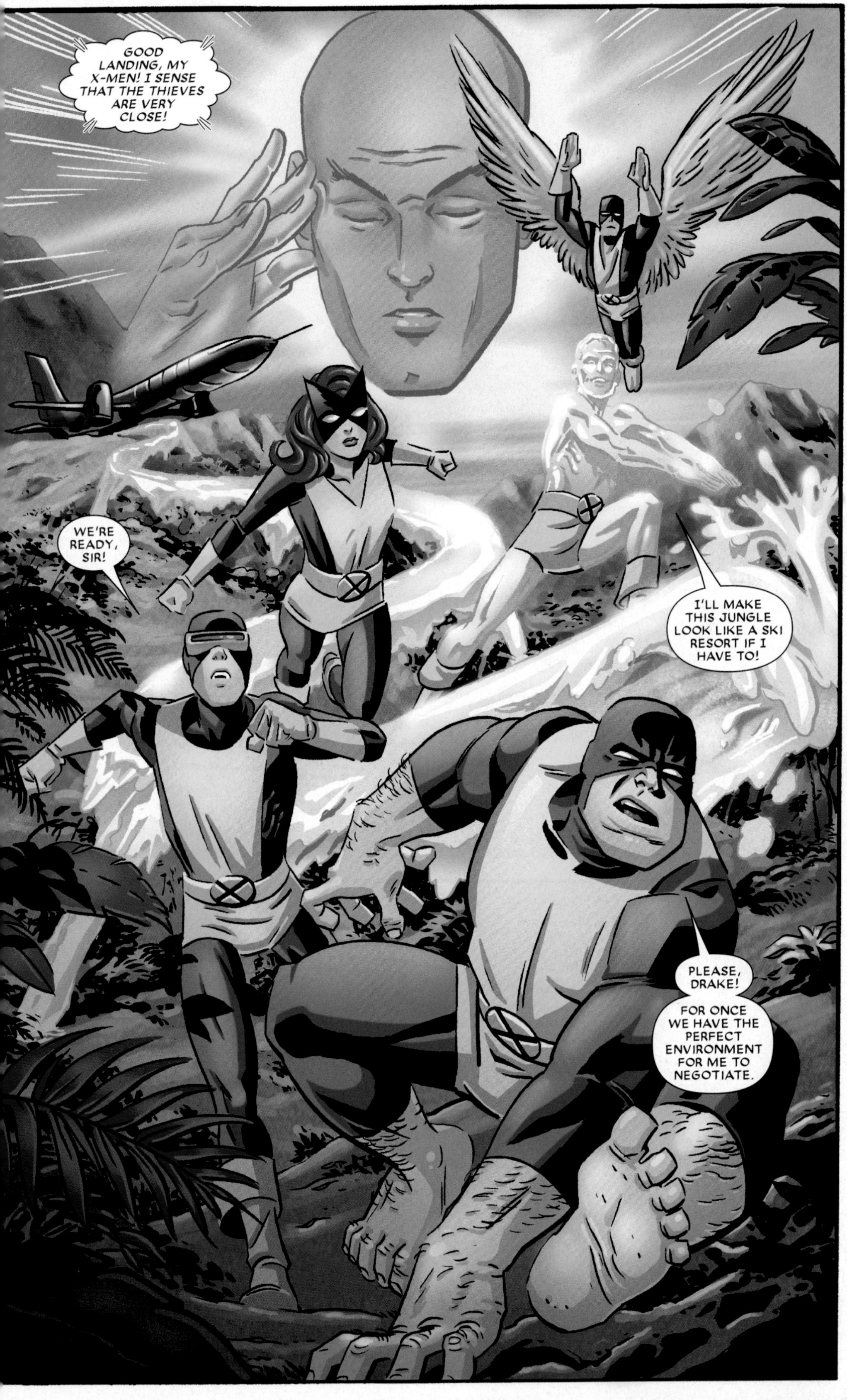
GOOD LANDING, MY X-MEN! I SENSE THAT THE THIEVES ARE VERY CLOSE!
WE'RE READY, SIR!
I'LL MAKE THIS JUNGLE LOOK LIKE A SKI RESORT IF I HAVE TO!
PLEASE, DRAKE!
FOR ONCE WE HAVE THE PERFECT ENVIRONMENT FOR ME TO NEGOTIATE.

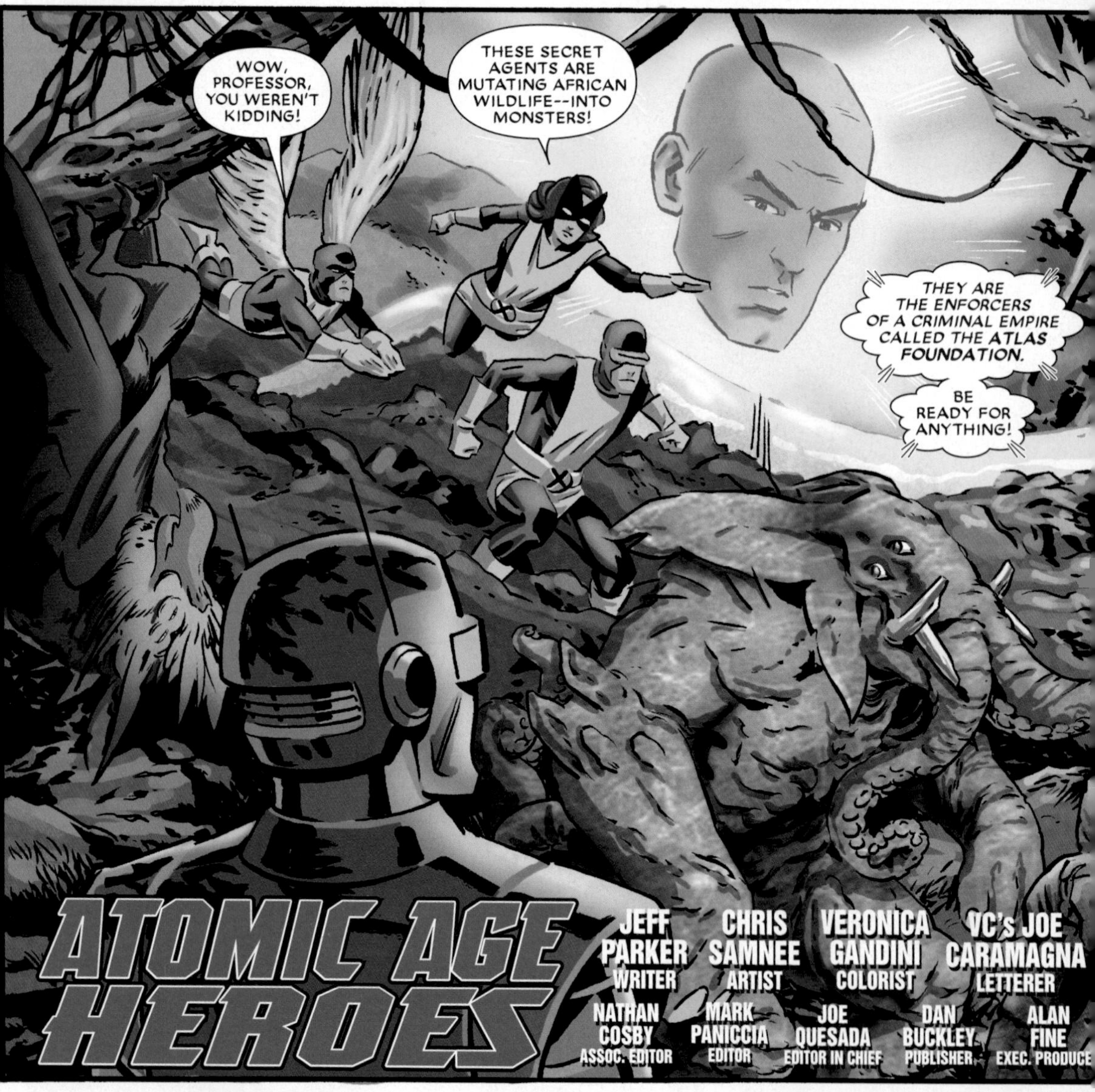
WOW, PROFESSOR, YOU WEREN'T KIDDING!
THESE SECRET AGENTS ARE MUTATING AFRICAN WILDLIFE--INTO MONSTERS!
THEY ARE THE ENFORCERS OF A CRIMINAL EMPIRE CALLED THE ATLAS FOUNDATION.
BE READY FOR ANYTHING!
ATOMIC AGE HEROES
JEFF PARKER WRITER
CHRIS SAMNEE ARTIST
VERONICA GANDINI COLORIST
VC's JOE CARAMAGNA LETTERER
NATHAN COSBY ASSOC. EDITOR
MARK PANICCIA EDITOR
JOE QUESADA EDITOR IN CHIEF
DAN BUCKLEY PUBLISHER
ALAN FINE EXEC. PRODUCE

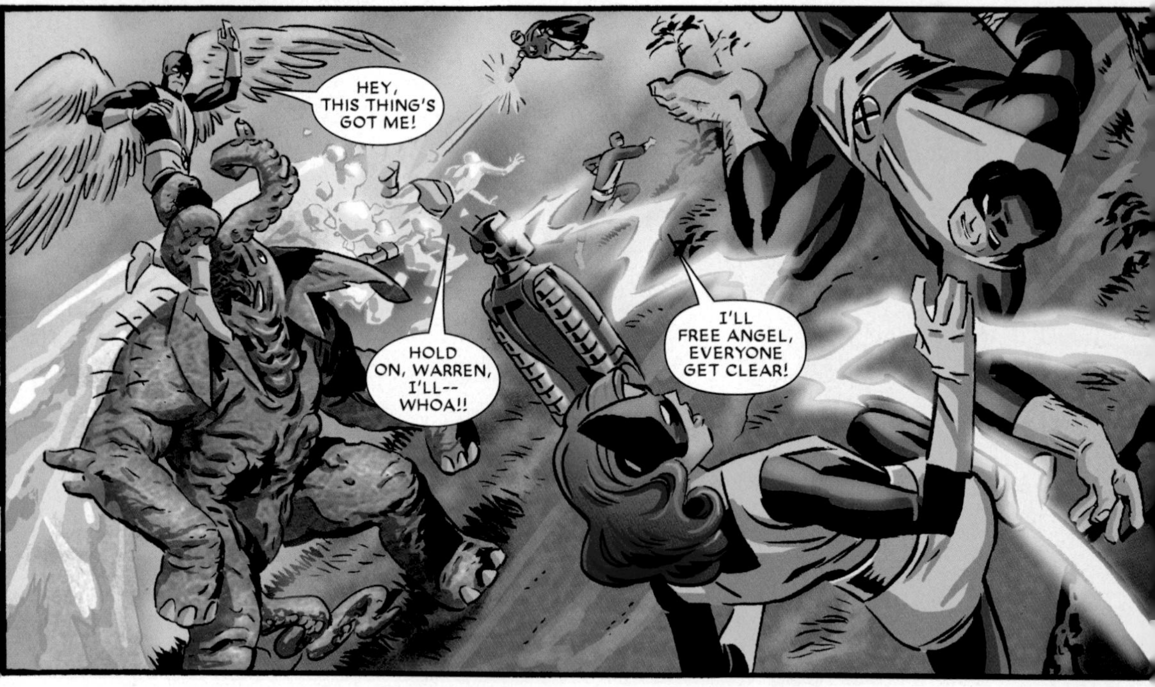
HEY, THIS THING'S GOT ME!
HOLD ON, WARREN, I'LL-- WHOA!!
I'LL FREE ANGEL, EVERYONE GET CLEAR!

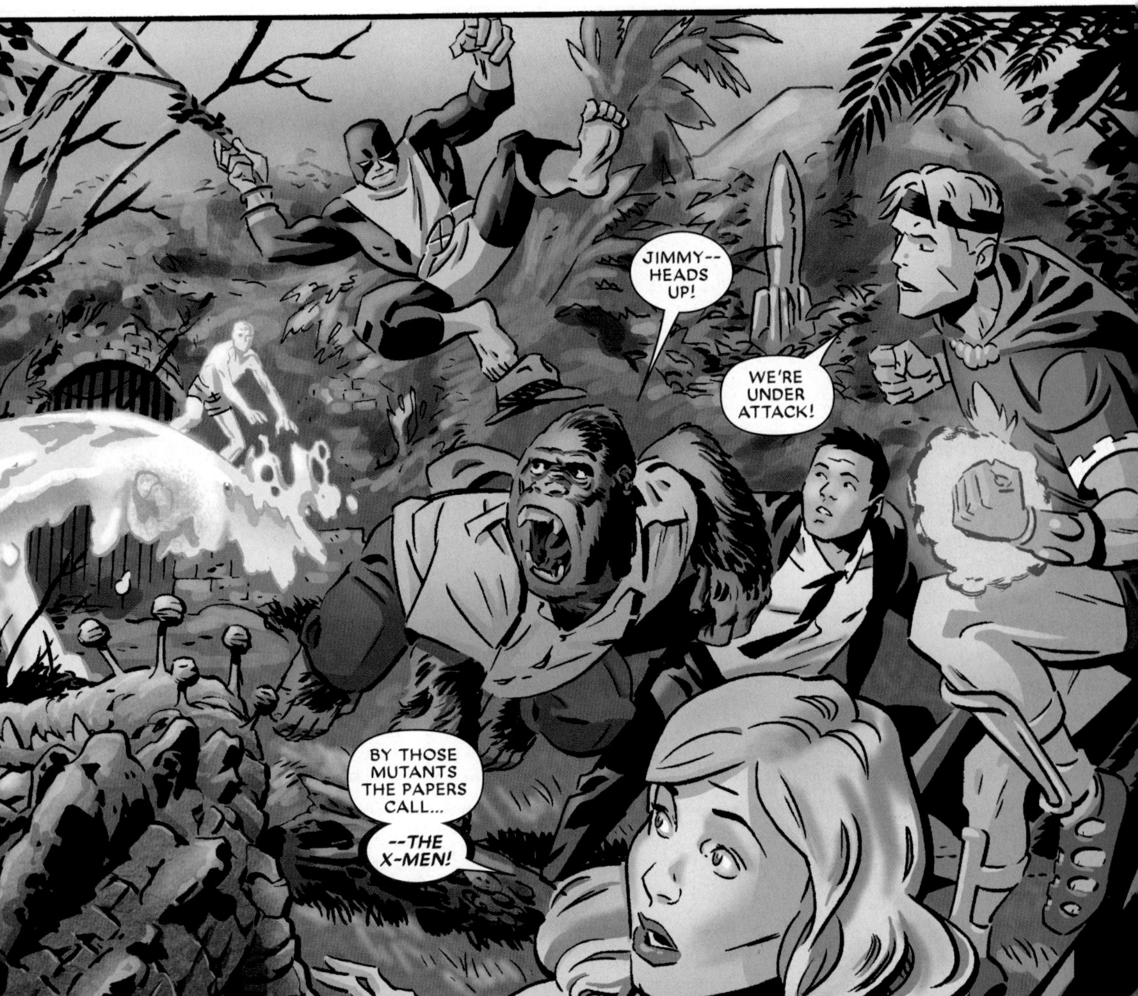
JIMMY--
HEADS
UP!
WE'RE
UNDER
ATTACK!
BY THOSE
MUTANTS
THE PAPERS
CALL...
--THE
X-MEN!

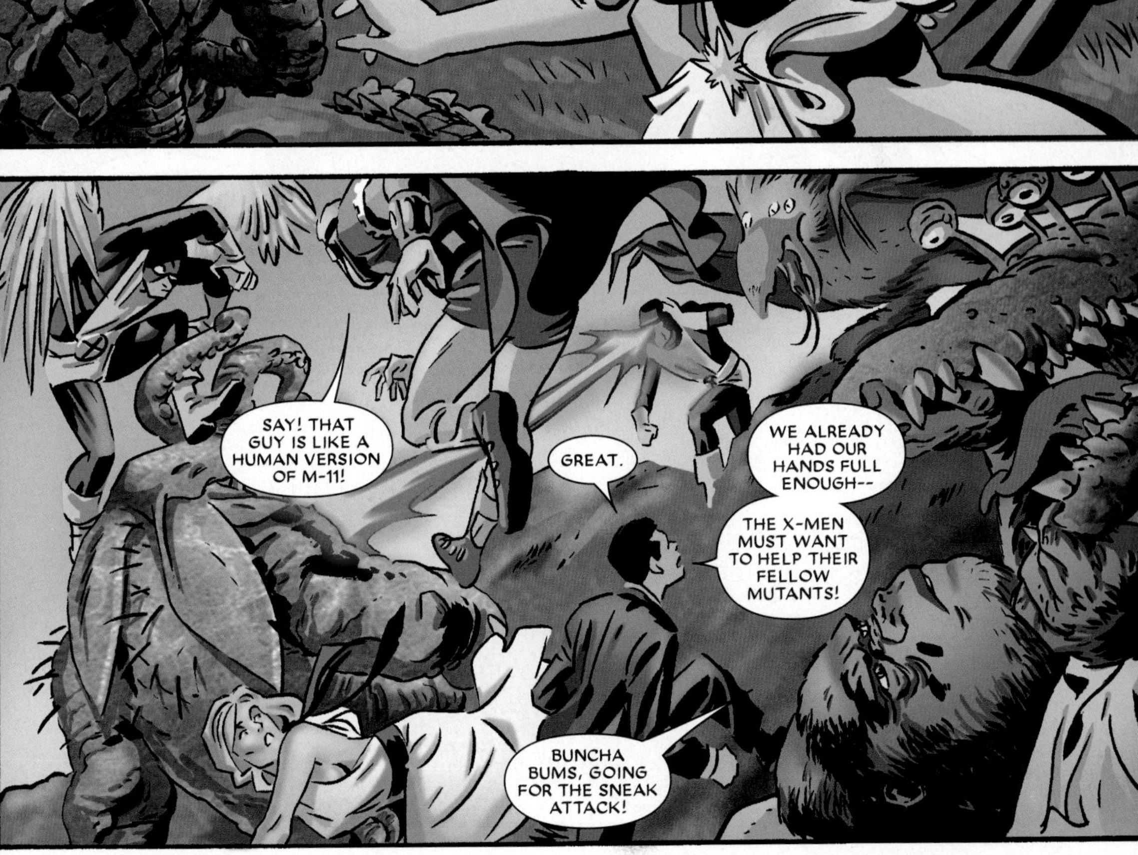
SAY! THAT
GUY IS LIKE A
HUMAN VERSION
OF M-11!
GREAT.
WE ALREADY
HAD OUR
HANDS FULL
ENOUGH--
THE X-MEN
MUST WANT
TO HELP THEIR
FELLOW
MUTANTS!
BUNCHA
BUMS, GOING
FOR THE SNEAK
ATTACK!

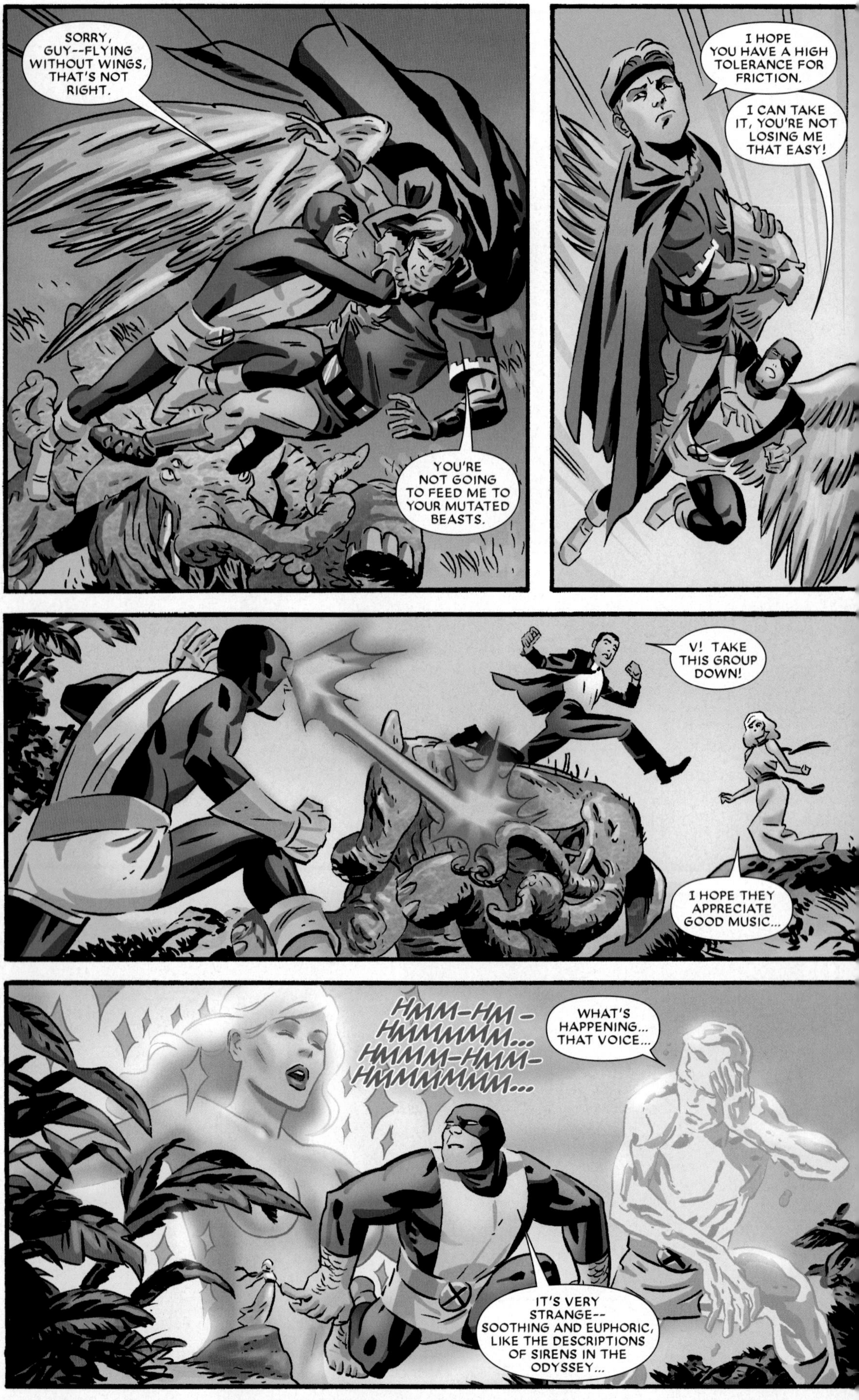

SORRY, GUY--FLYING WITHOUT WINGS, THAT'S NOT RIGHT.
YOU'RE NOT GOING TO FEED ME TO YOUR MUTATED BEASTS.
I HOPE YOU HAVE A HIGH TOLERANCE FOR FRICTION.
I CAN TAKE IT, YOU'RE NOT LOSING ME THAT EASY!
V! TAKE THIS GROUP DOWN!
I HOPE THEY APPRECIATE GOOD MUSIC...
HMM-HM-HMMMMM... HMMM-HMM-HMMMMMM...
WHAT'S HAPPENING... THAT VOICE...
IT'S VERY STRANGE--SOOTHING AND EUPHORIC, LIKE THE DESCRIPTIONS OF SIRENS IN THE ODYSSEY...

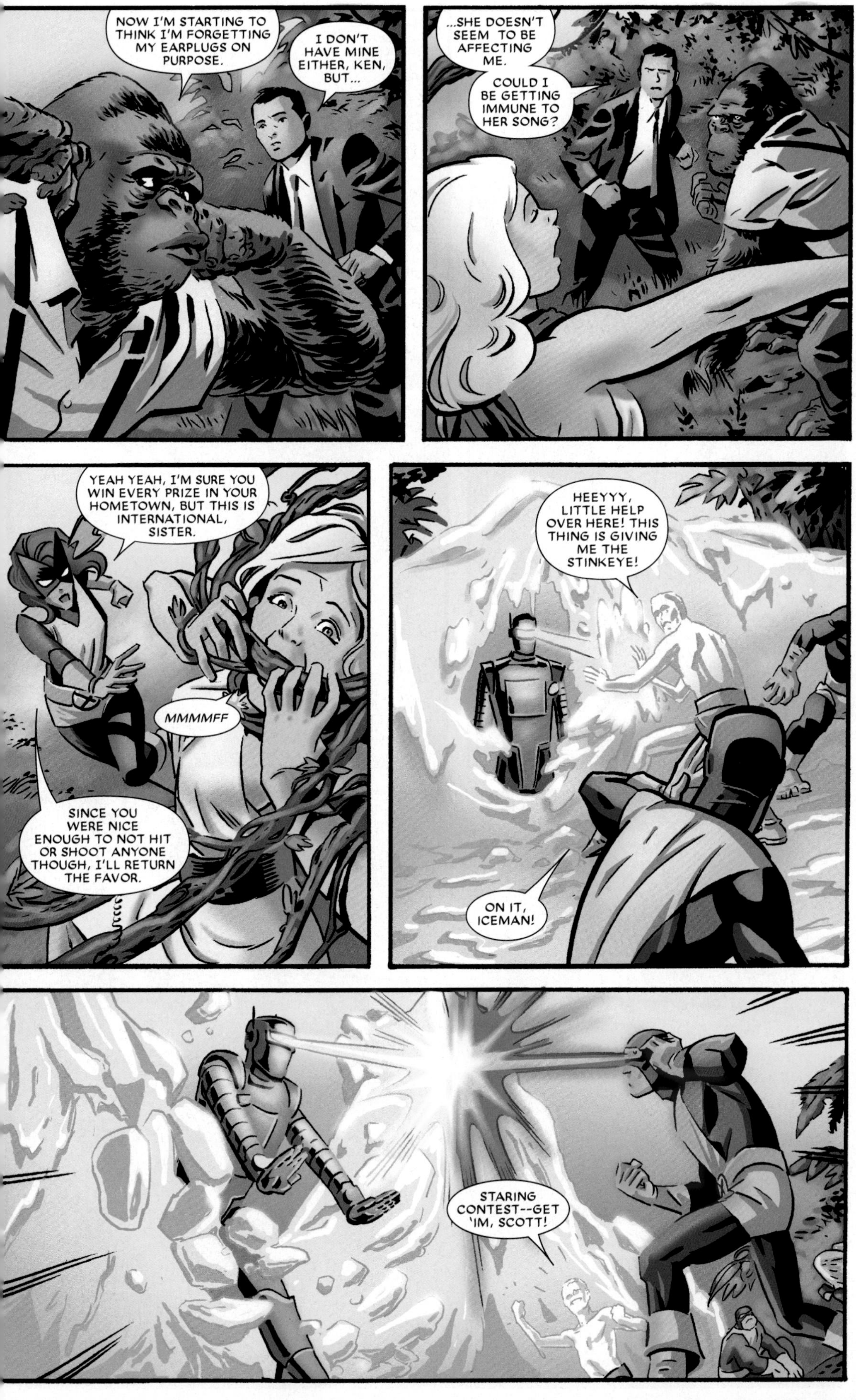
NOW I'M STARTING TO THINK I'M FORGETTING MY EARPLUGS ON PURPOSE.
I DON'T HAVE MINE EITHER, KEN, BUT...
...SHE DOESN'T SEEM TO BE AFFECTING ME.
COULD I BE GETTING IMMUNE TO HER SONG?
YEAH YEAH, I'M SURE YOU WIN EVERY PRIZE IN YOUR HOMETOWN, BUT THIS IS INTERNATIONAL, SISTER.
MMMMFF
SINCE YOU WERE NICE ENOUGH TO NOT HIT OR SHOOT ANYONE THOUGH, I'LL RETURN THE FAVOR.
HEEYYY, LITTLE HELP OVER HERE! THIS THING IS GIVING ME THE STINKEYE!
ON IT, ICEMAN!
STARING CONTEST--GET 'IM, SCOTT!

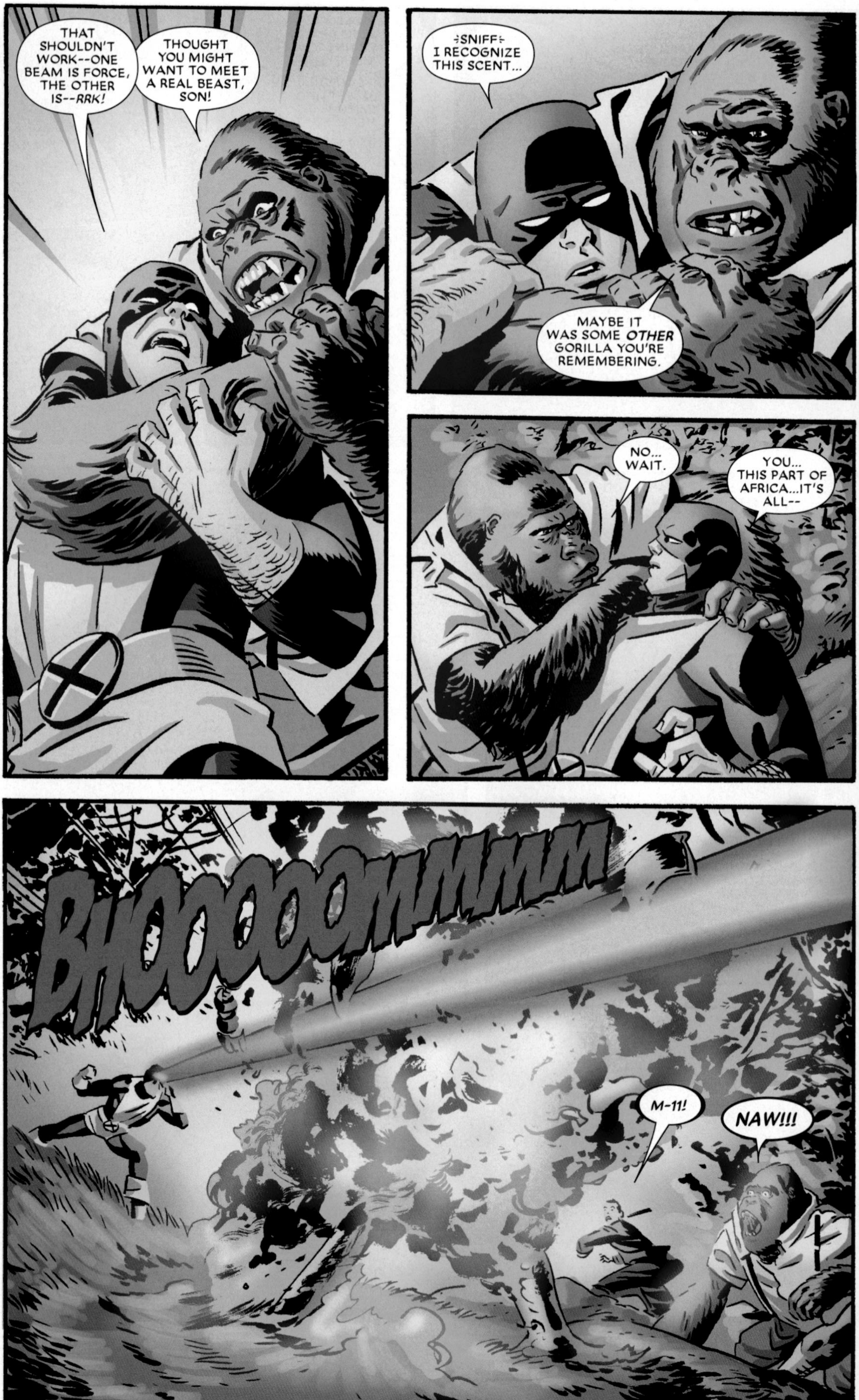
THAT SHOULDN'T WORK--ONE BEAM IS FORCE, THE OTHER IS--*RRK!*
THOUGHT YOU MIGHT WANT TO MEET A REAL BEAST, SON!
SNIFF I RECOGNIZE THIS SCENT...
MAYBE IT WAS SOME *OTHER* GORILLA YOU'RE REMEMBERING.
NO... WAIT.
YOU... THIS PART OF AFRICA...IT'S ALL--
BHOOOOOMMMMMM
M-11!
NAW!!!

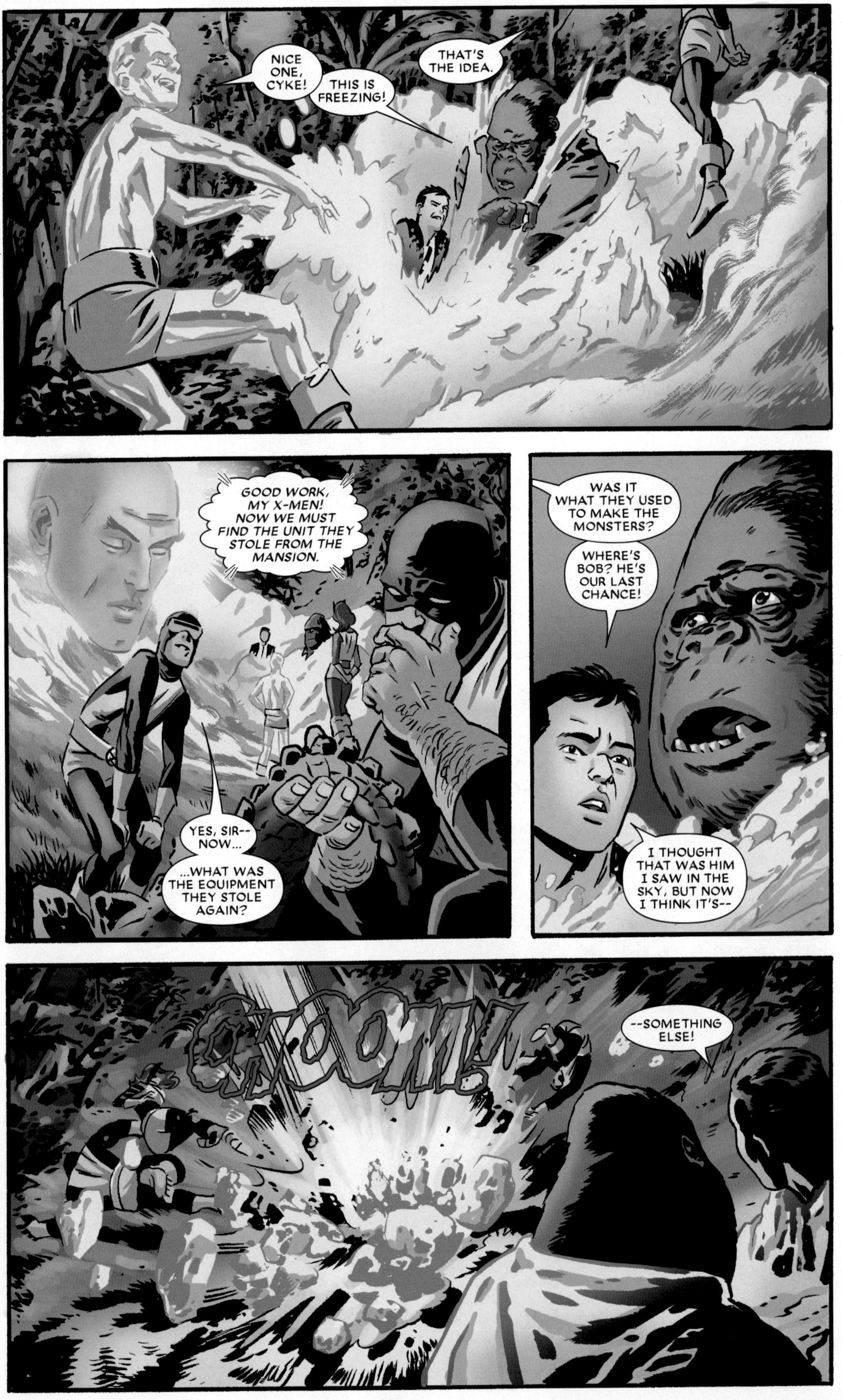
NICE ONE, CYKE!
THIS IS FREEZING!
THAT'S THE IDEA.
GOOD WORK, MY X-MEN! NOW WE MUST FIND THE UNIT THEY STOLE FROM THE MANSION.
YES, SIR-- NOW...
...WHAT WAS THE EQUIPMENT THEY STOLE AGAIN?
WAS IT WHAT THEY USED TO MAKE THE MONSTERS?
WHERE'S BOB? HE'S OUR LAST CHANCE!
I THOUGHT THAT WAS HIM I SAW IN THE SKY, BUT NOW I THINK IT'S--
--SOMETHING ELSE!

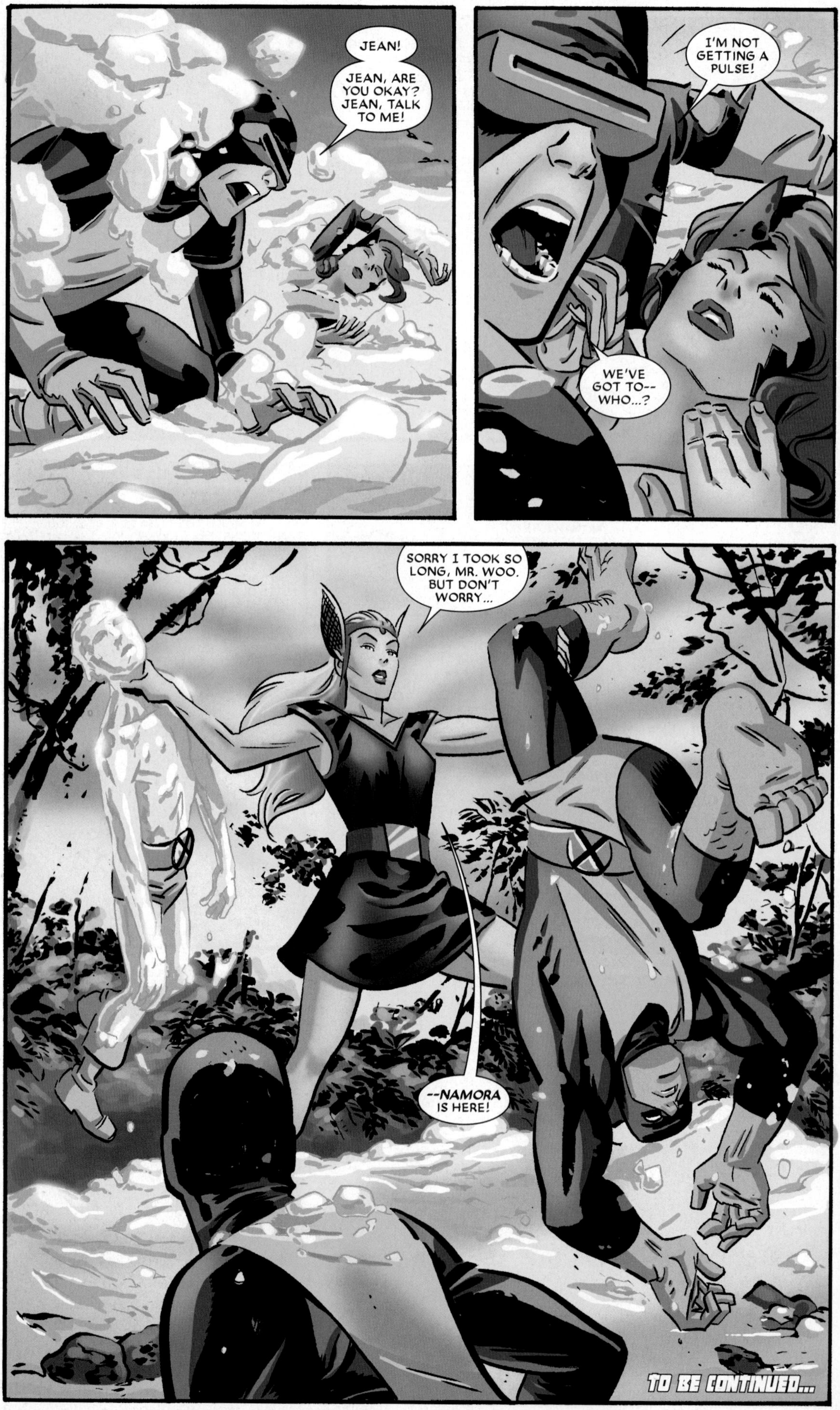

JEAN!
JEAN, ARE YOU OKAY? JEAN, TALK TO ME!
I'M NOT GETTING A PULSE!
WE'VE GOT TO-- WHO...?
SORRY I TOOK SO LONG, MR. WOO. BUT DON'T WORRY...
--NAMORA IS HERE!
TO BE CONTINUED...

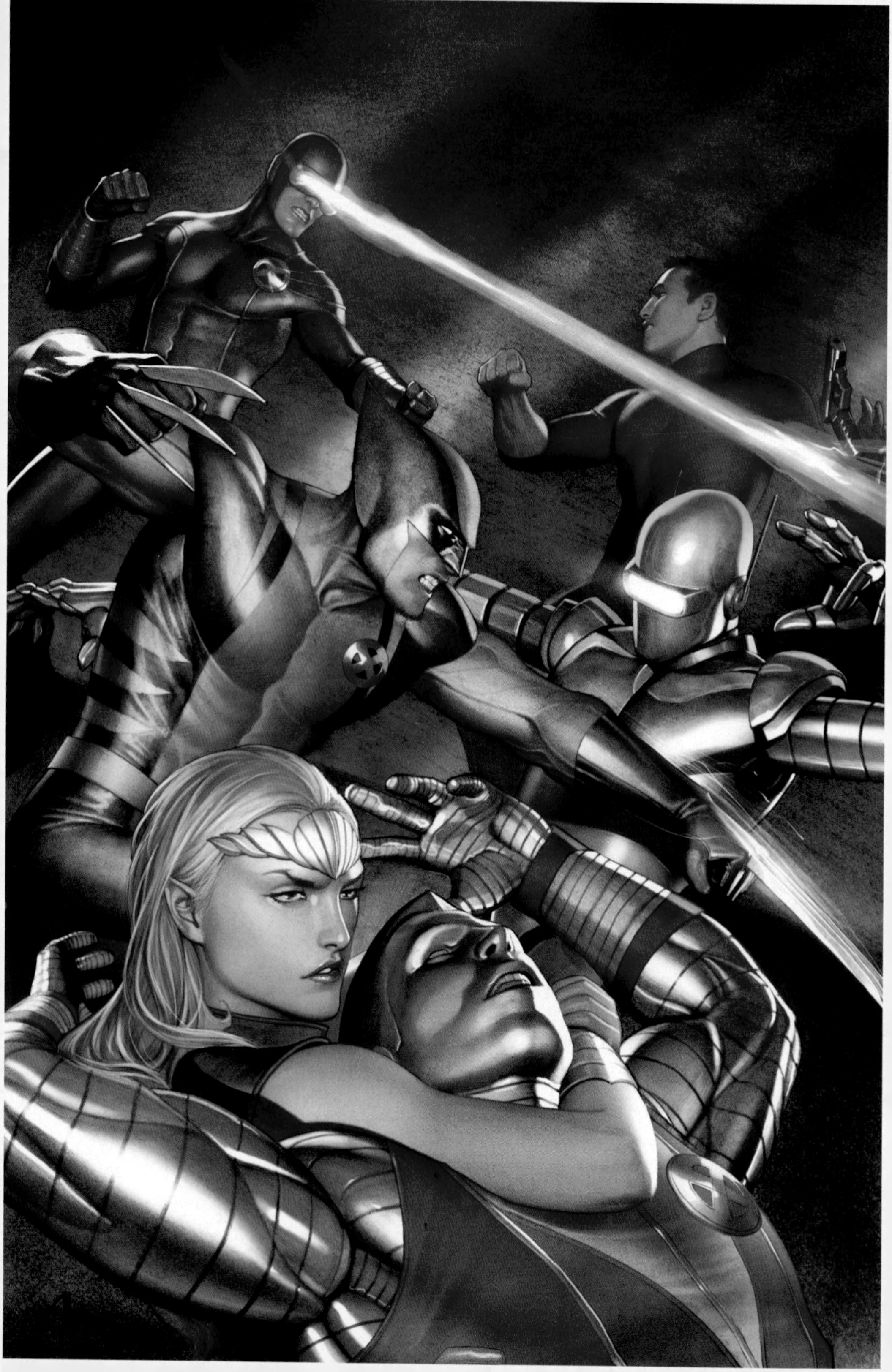

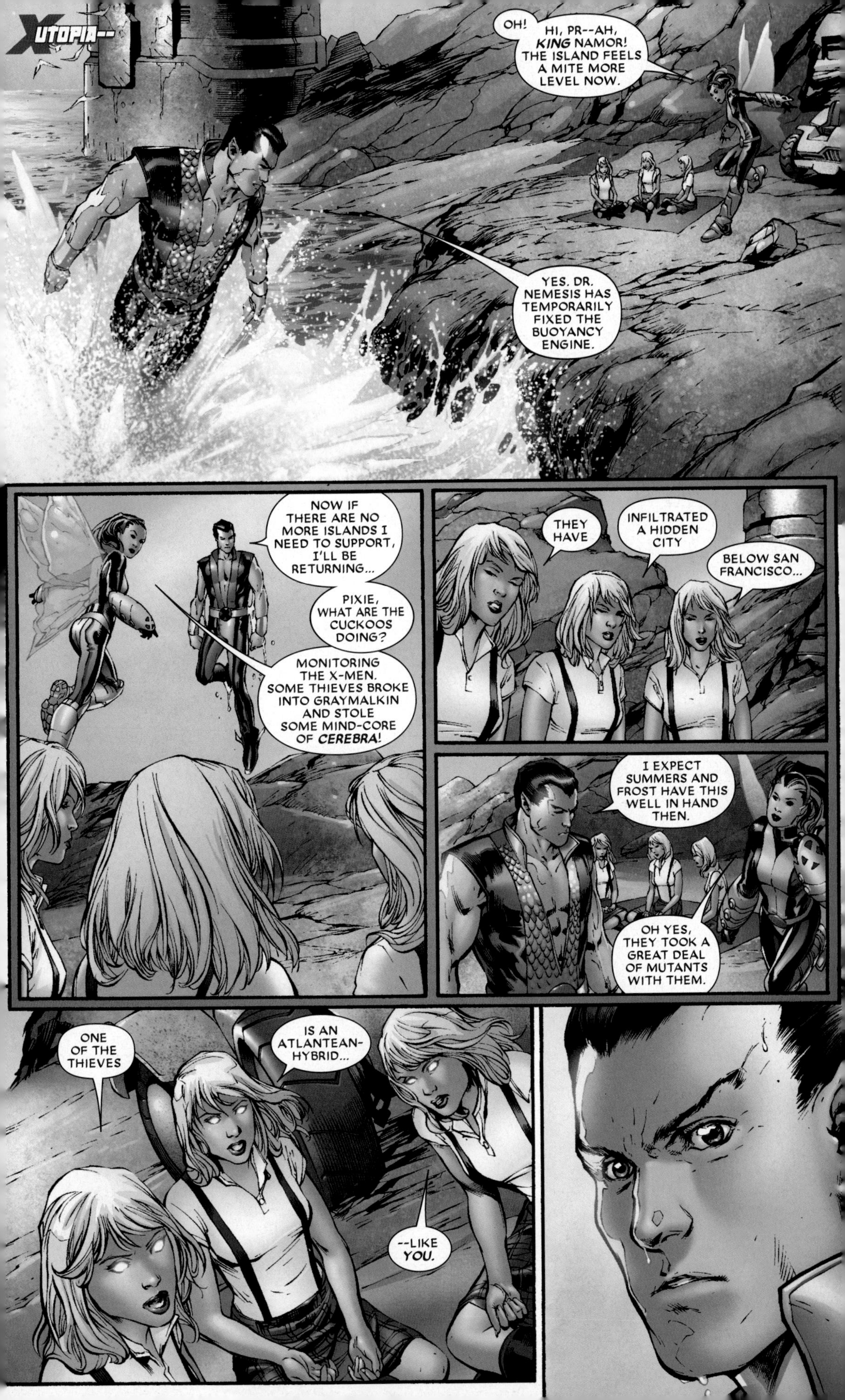
UTOPIA--
OH!
HI, PR--AH, KING NAMOR! THE ISLAND FEELS A MITE MORE LEVEL NOW.
YES. DR. NEMESIS HAS TEMPORARILY FIXED THE BUOYANCY ENGINE.
NOW IF THERE ARE NO MORE ISLANDS I NEED TO SUPPORT, I'LL BE RETURNING...
PIXIE, WHAT ARE THE CUCKOOS DOING?
MONITORING THE X-MEN. SOME THIEVES BROKE INTO GRAYMALKIN AND STOLE SOME MIND-CORE OF CEREBRA!
THEY HAVE
INFILTRATED A HIDDEN CITY
BELOW SAN FRANCISCO...
I EXPECT SUMMERS AND FROST HAVE THIS WELL IN HAND THEN.
OH YES, THEY TOOK A GREAT DEAL OF MUTANTS WITH THEM.
ONE OF THE THIEVES
IS AN ATLANTEAN-HYBRID...
--LIKE YOU.

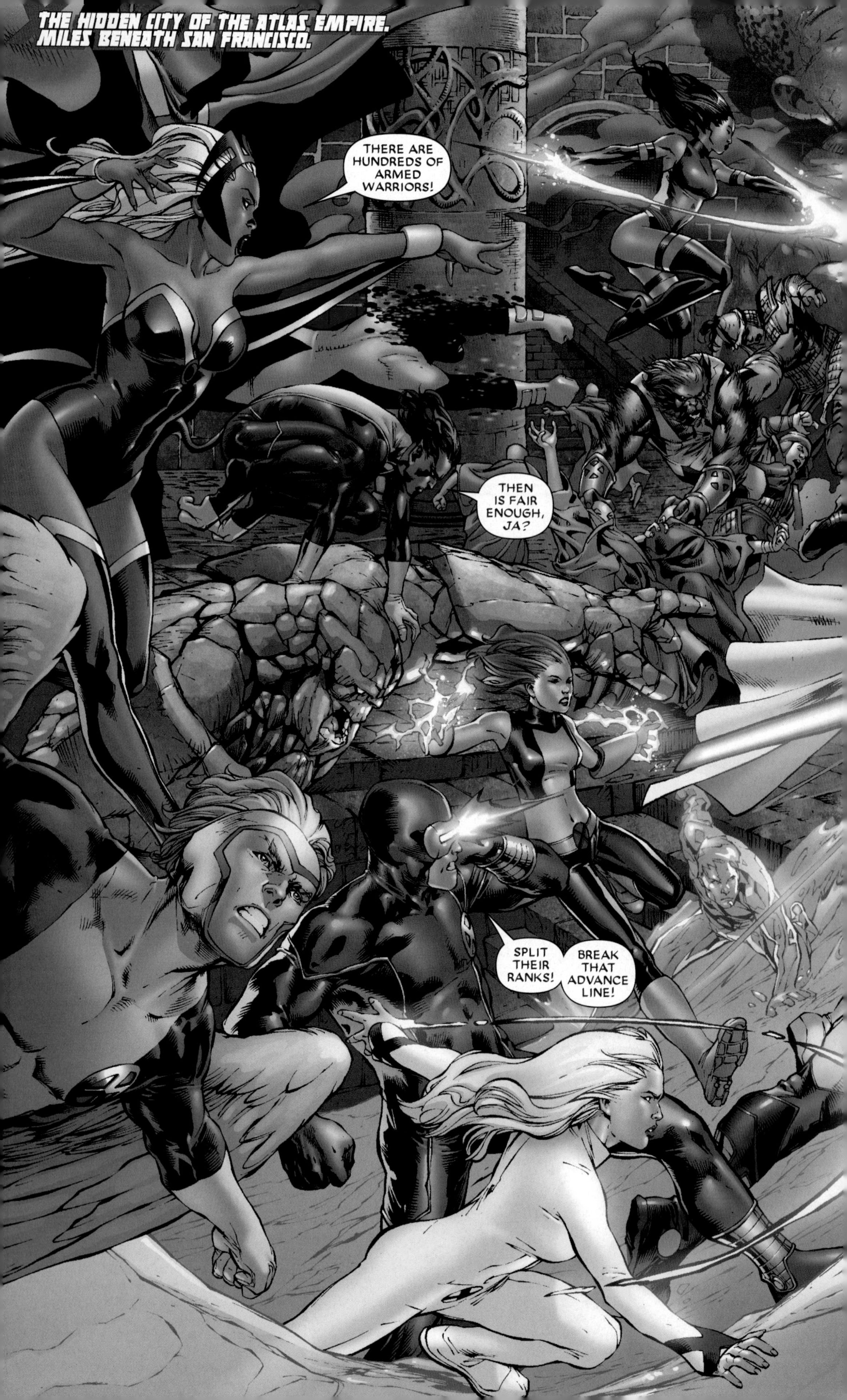
THE HIDDEN CITY OF THE ATLAS EMPIRE. MILES BENEATH SAN FRANCISCO.
THERE ARE HUNDREDS OF ARMED WARRIORS!
THEN IS FAIR ENOUGH, JA?
SPLIT THEIR RANKS!
BREAK THAT ADVANCE LINE!

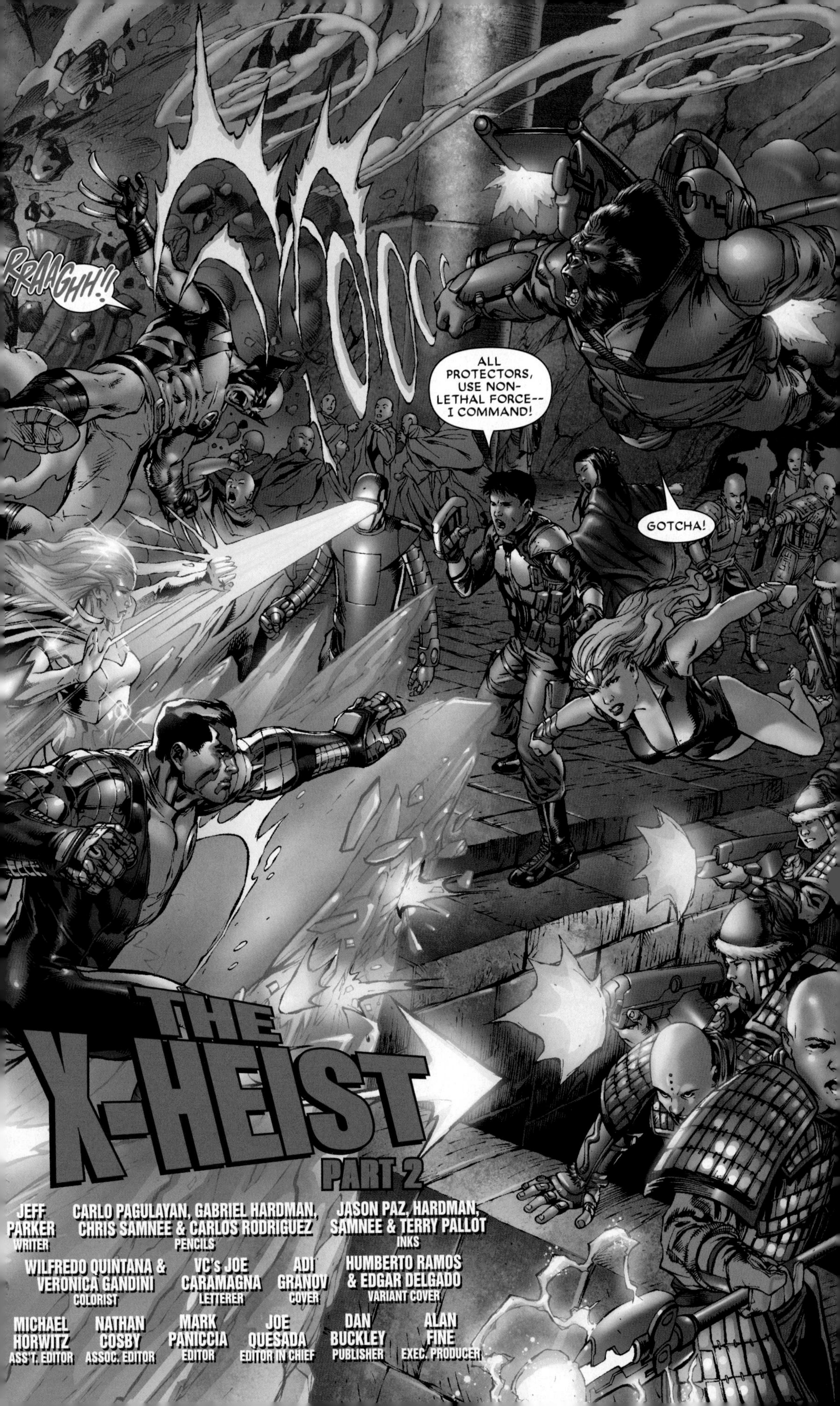
RRAAGHH!!
ALL PROTECTORS, USE NON-LETHAL FORCE-- I COMMAND!
GOTCHA!
THE X-HEIST
PART 2
JEFF PARKER WRITER
CARLO PAGULAYAN, GABRIEL HARDMAN, CHRIS SAMNEE & CARLOS RODRIGUEZ PENCILS
JASON PAZ, HARDMAN, SAMNEE & TERRY PALLOT INKS
WILFREDO QUINTANA & VERONICA GANDINI COLORIST
VC's JOE CARAMAGNA LETTERER
ADI GRANOV COVER
HUMBERTO RAMOS & EDGAR DELGADO VARIANT COVER
MICHAEL HORWITZ ASS'T. EDITOR
NATHAN COSBY ASSOC. EDITOR
MARK PANICCIA EDITOR
JOE QUESADA EDITOR IN CHIEF
DAN BUCKLEY PUBLISHER
ALAN FINE EXEC. PRODUCER

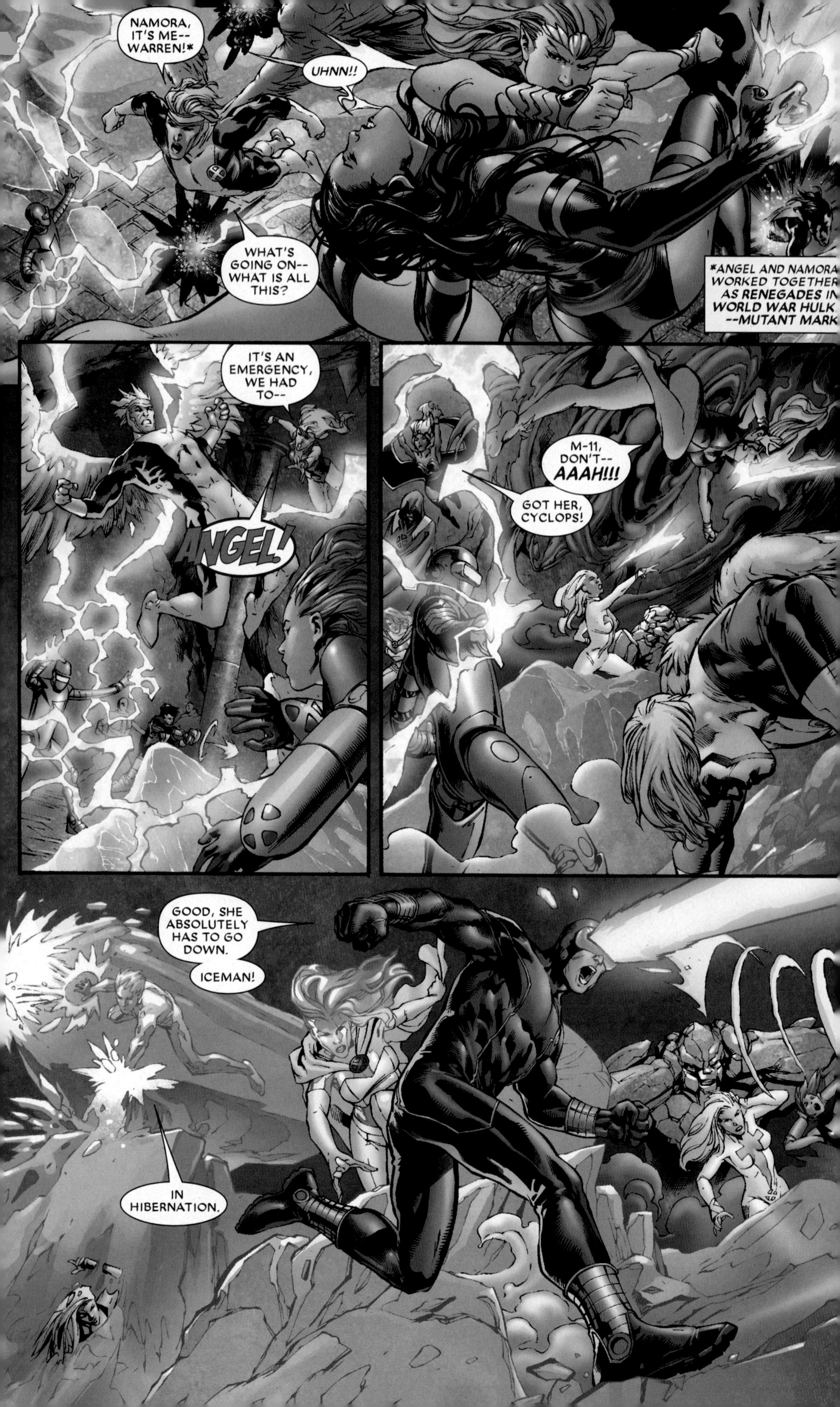
NAMORA, IT'S ME-- WARREN!*
UHNN!!
WHAT'S GOING ON-- WHAT IS ALL THIS?
*ANGEL AND NAMORA WORKED TOGETHER AS RENEGADES IN WORLD WAR HULK. --MUTANT MARK
IT'S AN EMERGENCY, WE HAD TO--
ANGEL!
M-11, DON'T-- AAAH!!!
GOT HER, CYCLOPS!
GOOD, SHE ABSOLUTELY HAS TO GO DOWN.
ICEMAN!
IN HIBERNATION.

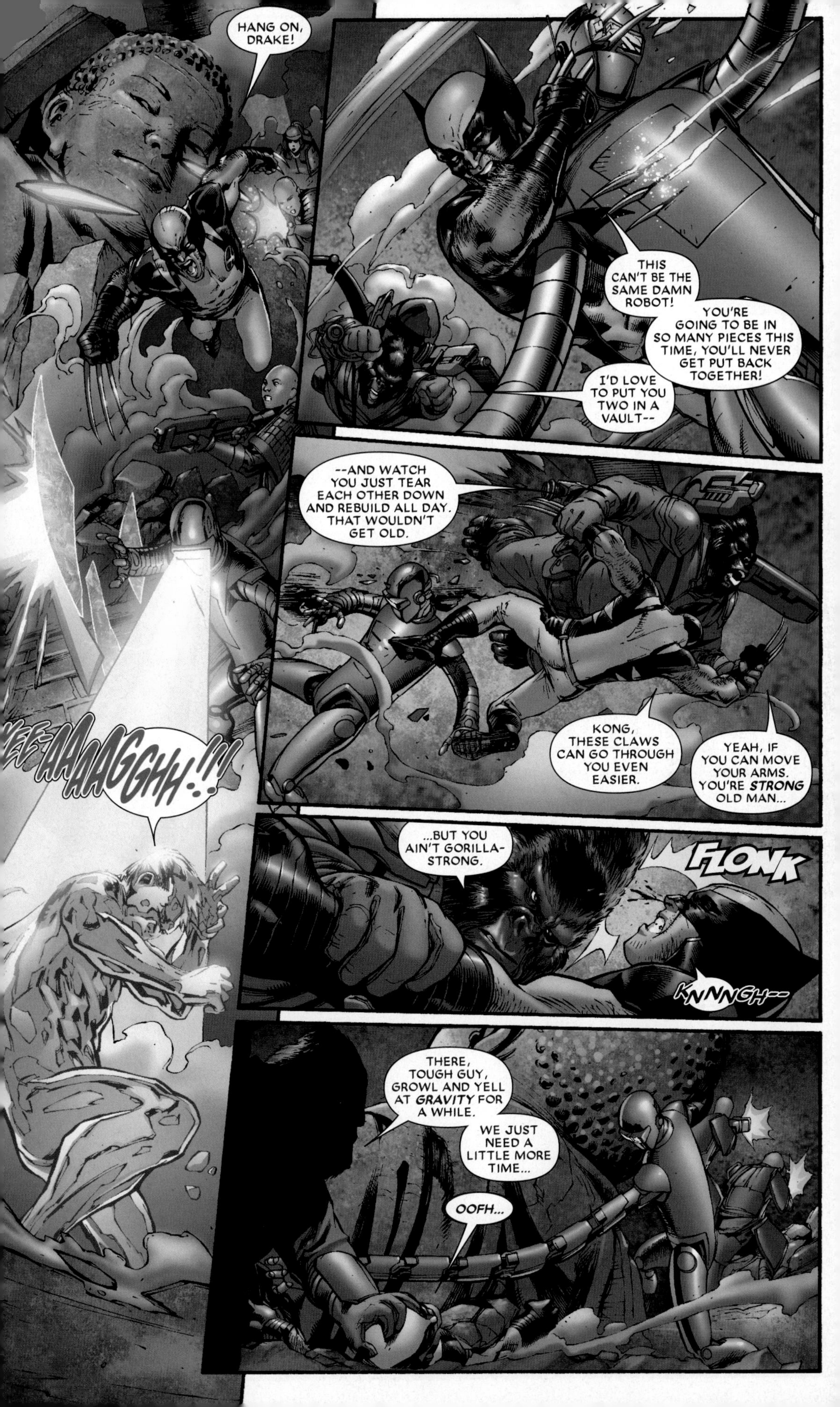
HANG ON, DRAKE!
THIS CAN'T BE THE SAME DAMN ROBOT!
YOU'RE GOING TO BE IN SO MANY PIECES THIS TIME, YOU'LL NEVER GET PUT BACK TOGETHER!
I'D LOVE TO PUT YOU TWO IN A VAULT--
--AND WATCH YOU JUST TEAR EACH OTHER DOWN AND REBUILD ALL DAY. THAT WOULDN'T GET OLD.
KONG, THESE CLAWS CAN GO THROUGH YOU EVEN EASIER.
YEAH, IF YOU CAN MOVE YOUR ARMS. YOU'RE STRONG OLD MAN...
EEE-AAAAAGGHH!!!
...BUT YOU AIN'T GORILLA-STRONG.
FLONK
KNNNGH--
THERE, TOUGH GUY, GROWL AND YELL AT GRAVITY FOR A WHILE.
WE JUST NEED A LITTLE MORE TIME...
OOFH...

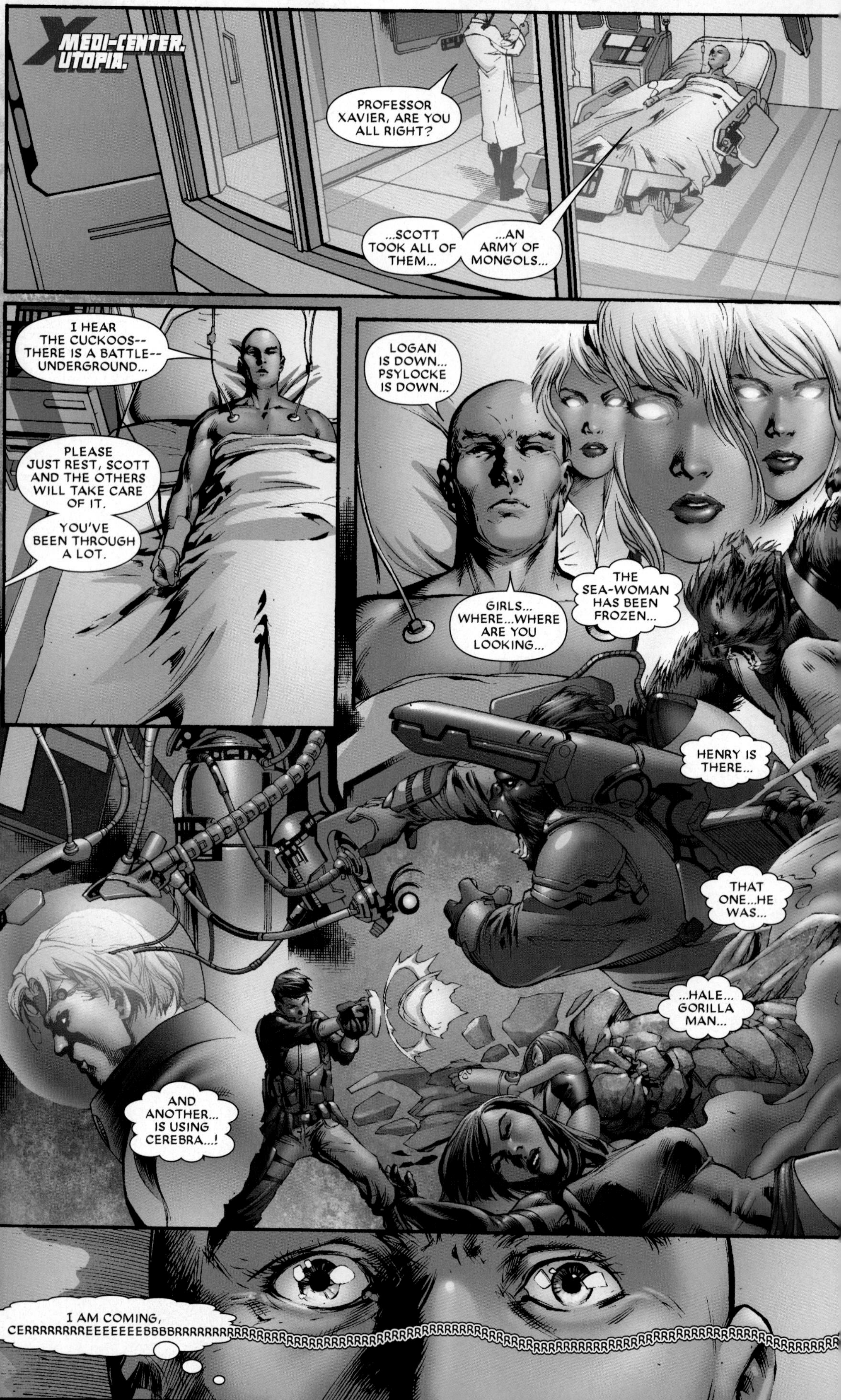
MEDI-CENTER, UTOPIA.
PROFESSOR XAVIER, ARE YOU ALL RIGHT?
...SCOTT TOOK ALL OF THEM...
...AN ARMY OF MONGOLS...
I HEAR THE CUCKOOS-- THERE IS A BATTLE-- UNDERGROUND...
PLEASE JUST REST, SCOTT AND THE OTHERS WILL TAKE CARE OF IT.
YOU'VE BEEN THROUGH A LOT.
LOGAN IS DOWN... PSYLOCKE IS DOWN...
GIRLS... WHERE...WHERE ARE YOU LOOKING...
THE SEA-WOMAN HAS BEEN FROZEN...
HENRY IS THERE...
THAT ONE...HE WAS...
...HALE... GORILLA MAN...
AND ANOTHER... IS USING CEREBRA...!
I AM COMING, CERRRRRRRREEEEEEEBBBBRRRRRRRRRRRRRRRRRRRRRRRRRRRRRRRRRRRRRRRRRRRRRRRRRRRRRRRRRRRRRRRRRRRRRRRRRRRRRRRRRRRRR

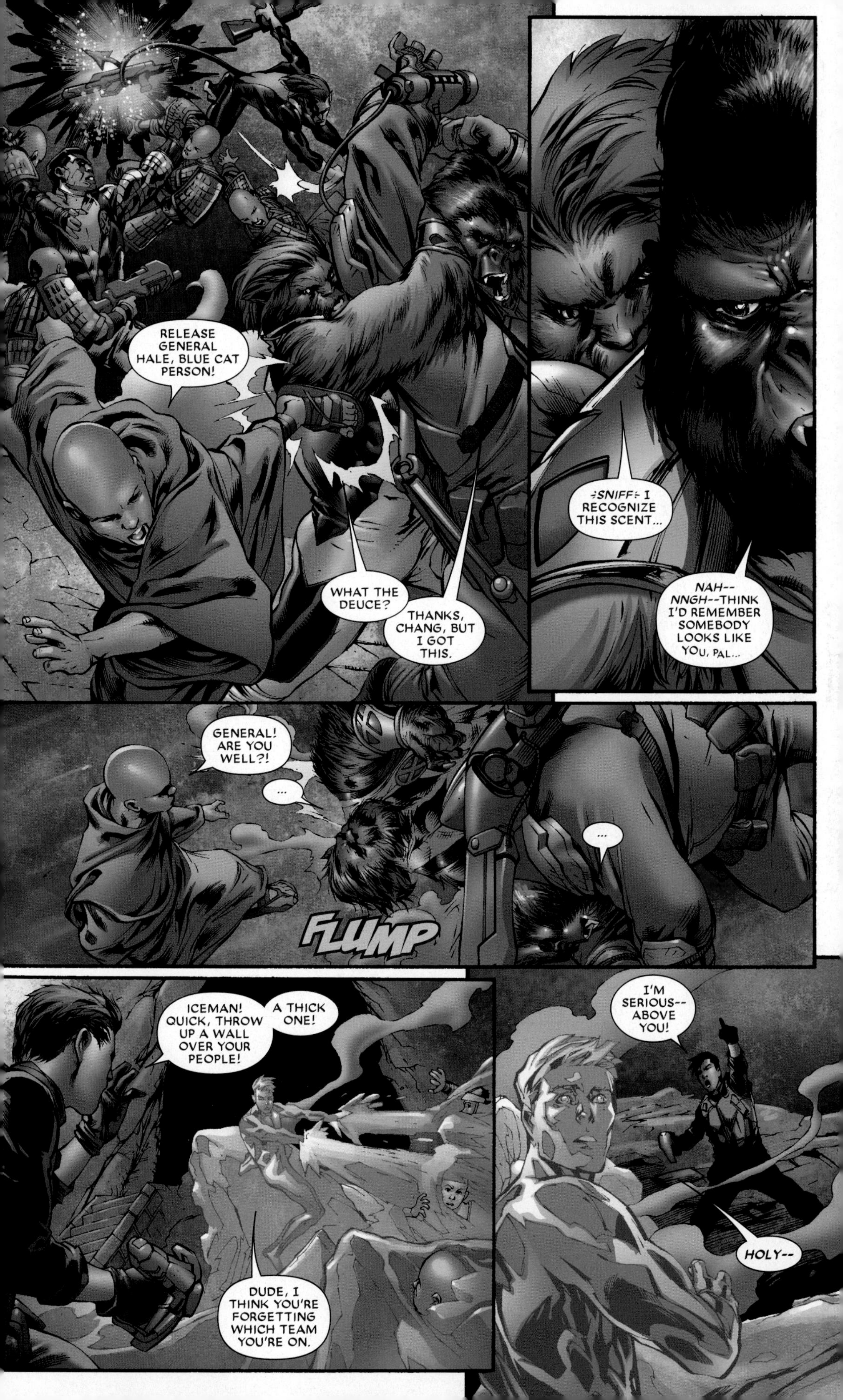
RELEASE GENERAL HALE, BLUE CAT PERSON!
WHAT THE DEUCE?
THANKS, CHANG, BUT I GOT THIS.
=SNIFF= I RECOGNIZE THIS SCENT...
NAH--NNGH--THINK I'D REMEMBER SOMEBODY LOOKS LIKE YOU, PAL...
GENERAL! ARE YOU WELL?!
...
...
FLUMP
ICEMAN! QUICK, THROW UP A WALL OVER YOUR PEOPLE!
A THICK ONE!
DUDE, I THINK YOU'RE FORGETTING WHICH TEAM YOU'RE ON.
I'M SERIOUS--ABOVE YOU!
HOLY--

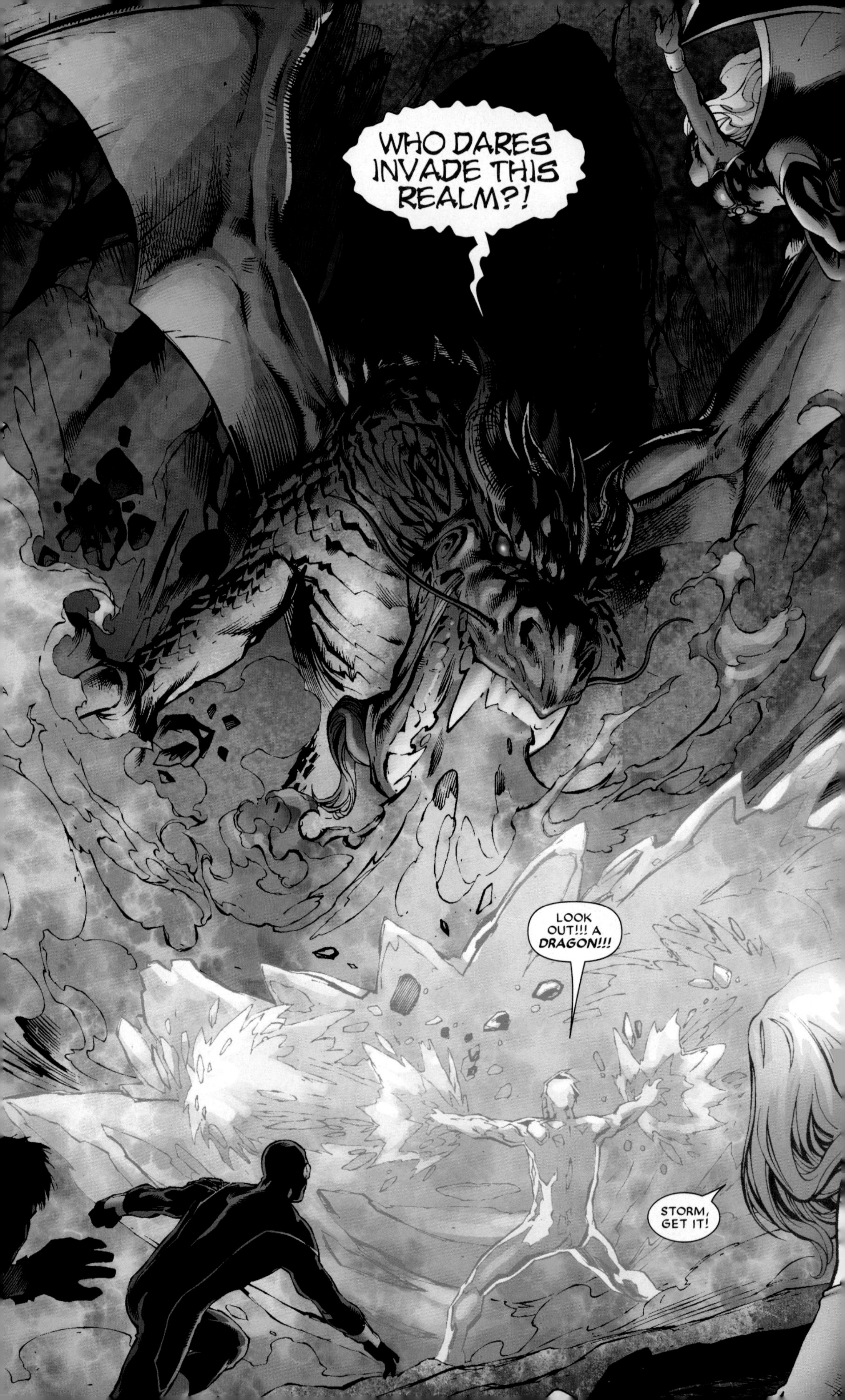
WHO DARES INVADE THIS REALM?!
LOOK OUT!!! A DRAGON!!!
STORM, GET IT!

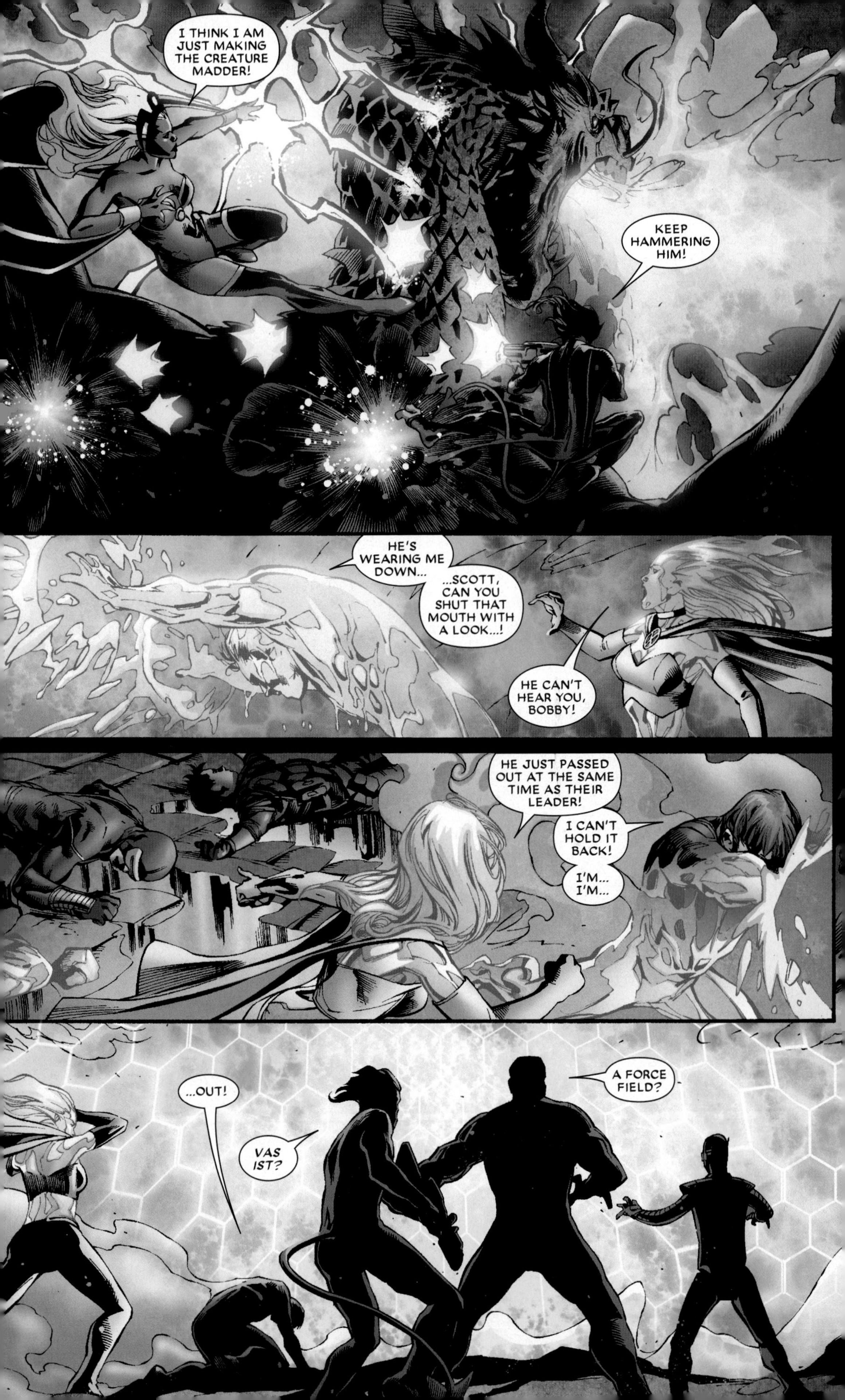
I THINK I AM JUST MAKING THE CREATURE MADDER!
KEEP HAMMERING HIM!
HE'S WEARING ME DOWN...
...SCOTT, CAN YOU SHUT THAT MOUTH WITH A LOOK...!
HE CAN'T HEAR YOU, BOBBY!
HE JUST PASSED OUT AT THE SAME TIME AS THEIR LEADER!
I CAN'T HOLD IT BACK!
I'M... I'M...
...OUT!
VAS IST?
A FORCE FIELD?

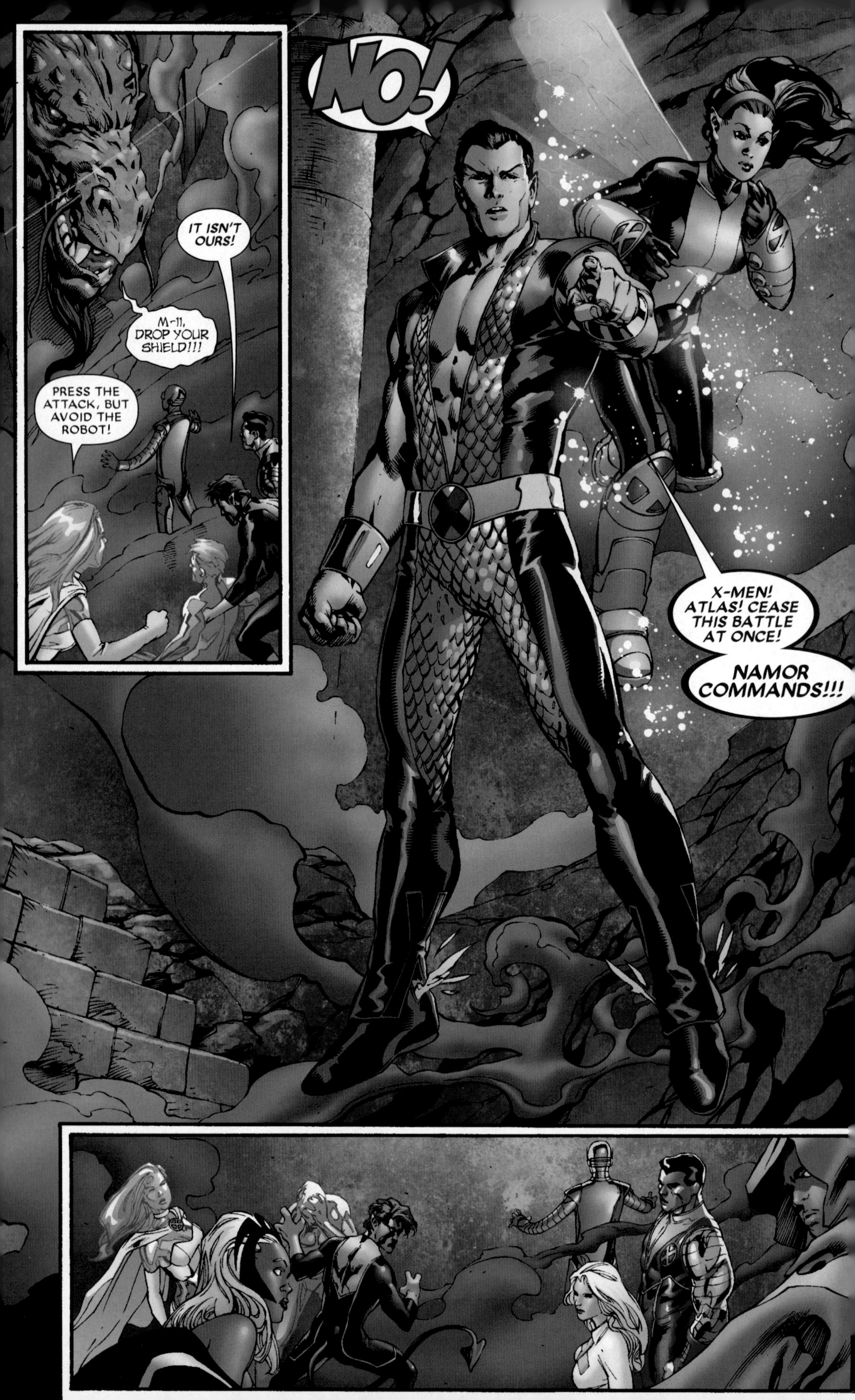
IT ISN'T OURS!
M-11, DROP YOUR SHIELD!!!
PRESS THE ATTACK, BUT AVOID THE ROBOT!
NO!
X-MEN! ATLAS! CEASE THIS BATTLE AT ONCE!
NAMOR COMMANDS!!!

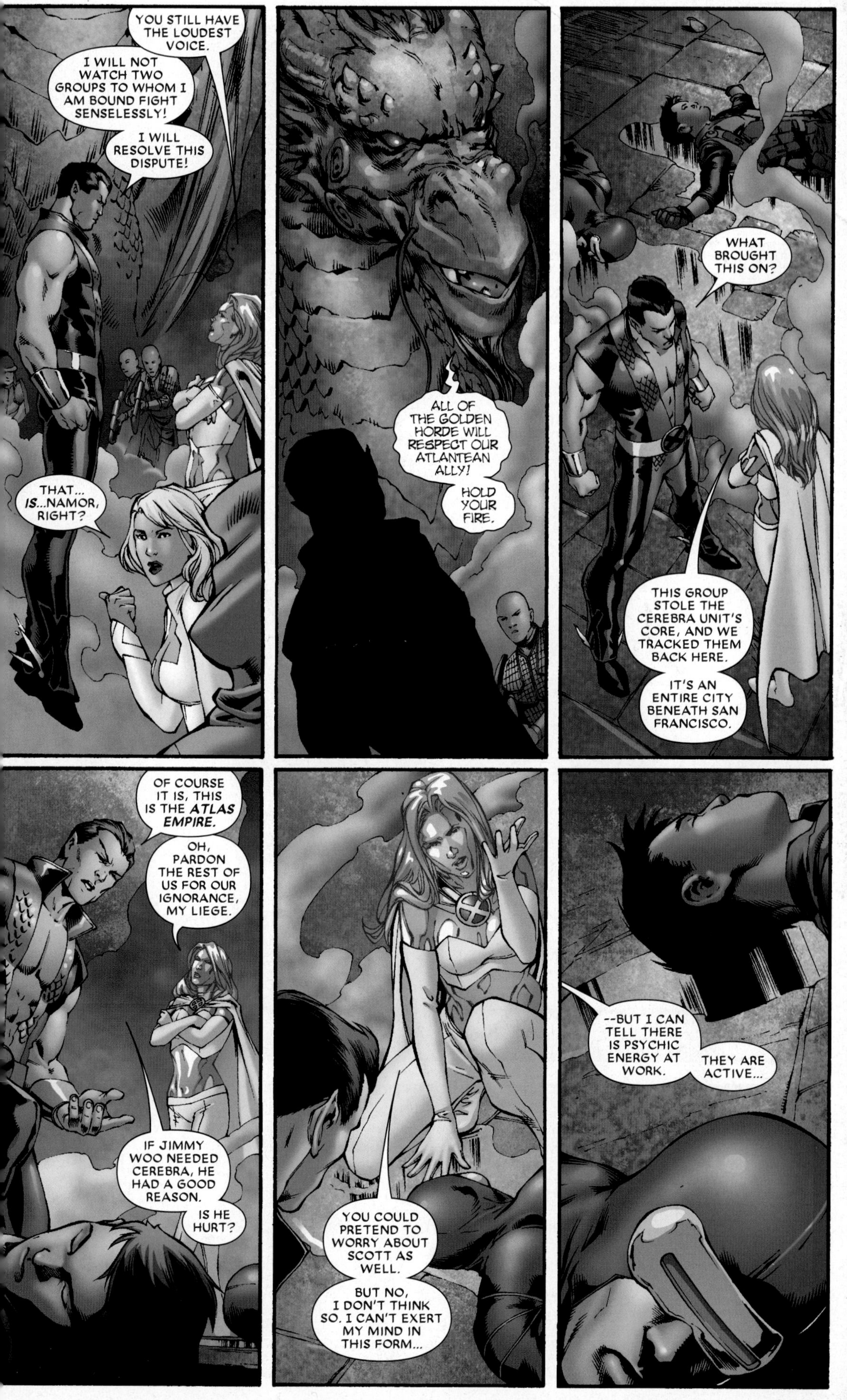

YOU STILL HAVE THE LOUDEST VOICE.
I WILL NOT WATCH TWO GROUPS TO WHOM I AM BOUND FIGHT SENSELESSLY!
I WILL RESOLVE THIS DISPUTE!
THAT... *IS*...NAMOR, RIGHT?
ALL OF THE GOLDEN HORDE WILL RESPECT OUR ATLANTEAN ALLY!
HOLD YOUR FIRE.
WHAT BROUGHT THIS ON?
THIS GROUP STOLE THE CEREBRA UNIT'S CORE, AND WE TRACKED THEM BACK HERE.
IT'S AN ENTIRE CITY BENEATH SAN FRANCISCO.
OF COURSE IT IS, THIS IS THE *ATLAS EMPIRE.*
OH, PARDON THE REST OF US FOR OUR IGNORANCE, MY LIEGE.
IF JIMMY WOO NEEDED CEREBRA, HE HAD A GOOD REASON.
IS HE HURT?
YOU COULD PRETEND TO WORRY ABOUT SCOTT AS WELL.
BUT NO, I DON'T THINK SO. I CAN'T EXERT MY MIND IN THIS FORM...
--BUT I CAN TELL THERE IS PSYCHIC ENERGY AT WORK.
THEY ARE ACTIVE...

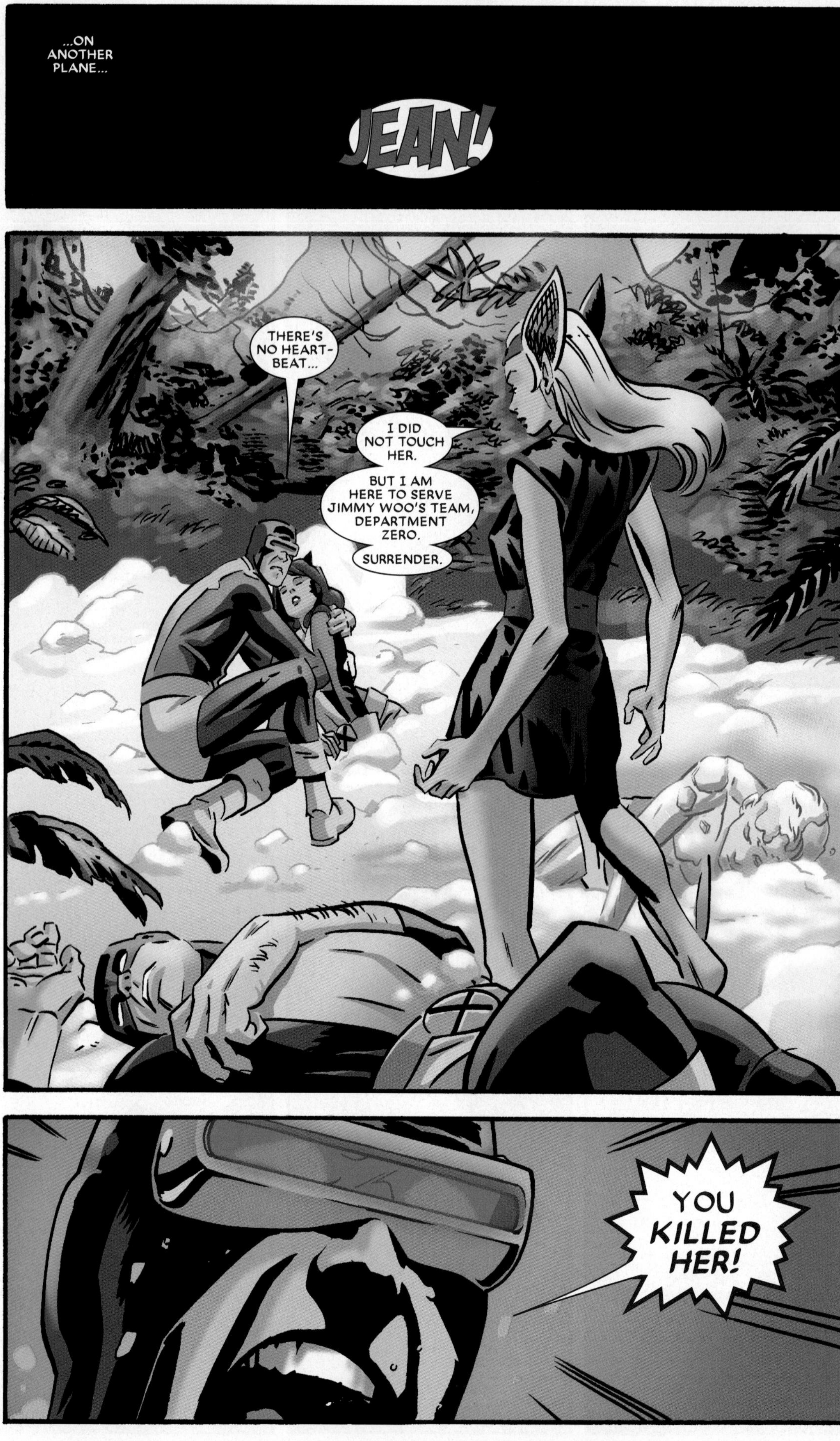
...ON ANOTHER PLANE...
JEAN!
THERE'S NO HEART-BEAT...
I DID NOT TOUCH HER.
BUT I AM HERE TO SERVE JIMMY WOO'S TEAM, DEPARTMENT ZERO.
SURRENDER.
YOU KILLED HER!

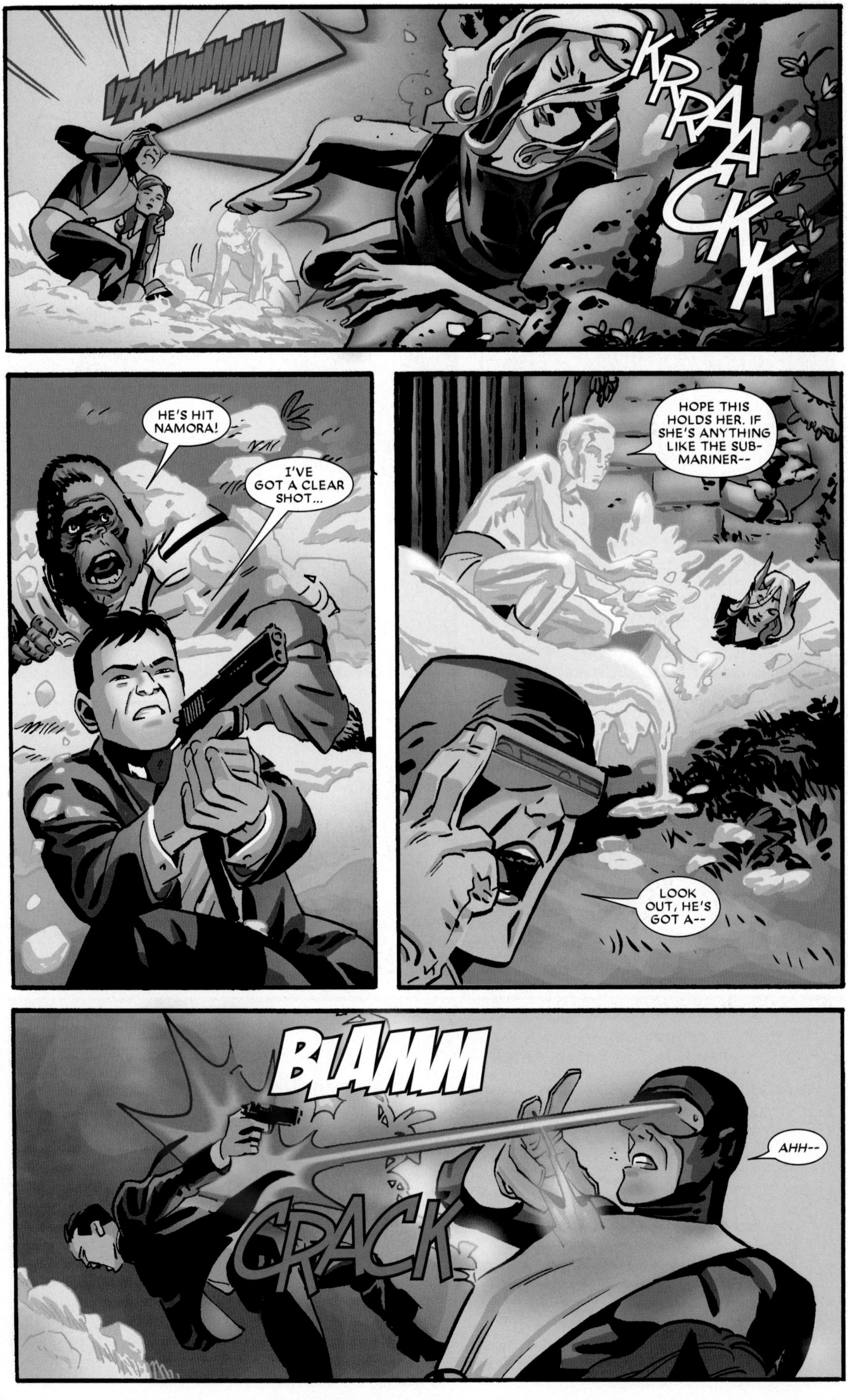
VZAAMMMMMMM
KRRAACKKK
HE'S HIT NAMORA!
I'VE GOT A CLEAR SHOT...
HOPE THIS HOLDS HER. IF SHE'S ANYTHING LIKE THE SUB-MARINER--
LOOK OUT, HE'S GOT A--
BLAMM
CRACK
AHH--

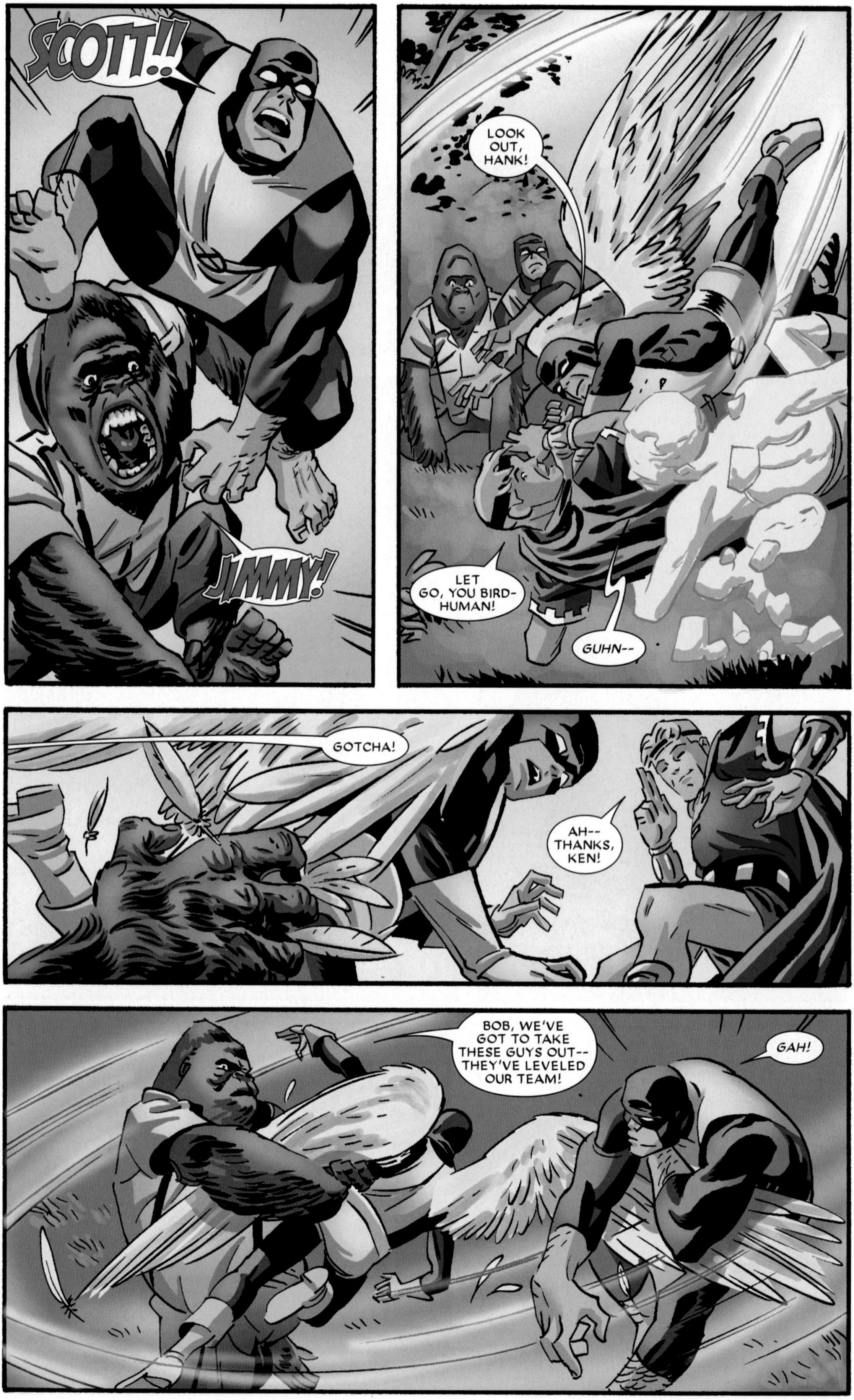
SCOTT!!
JIMMY!
LOOK OUT, HANK!
LET GO, YOU BIRD-HUMAN!
GUHN--
GOTCHA!
AH-- THANKS, KEN!
BOB, WE'VE GOT TO TAKE THESE GUYS OUT-- THEY'VE LEVELED OUR TEAM!
GAH!

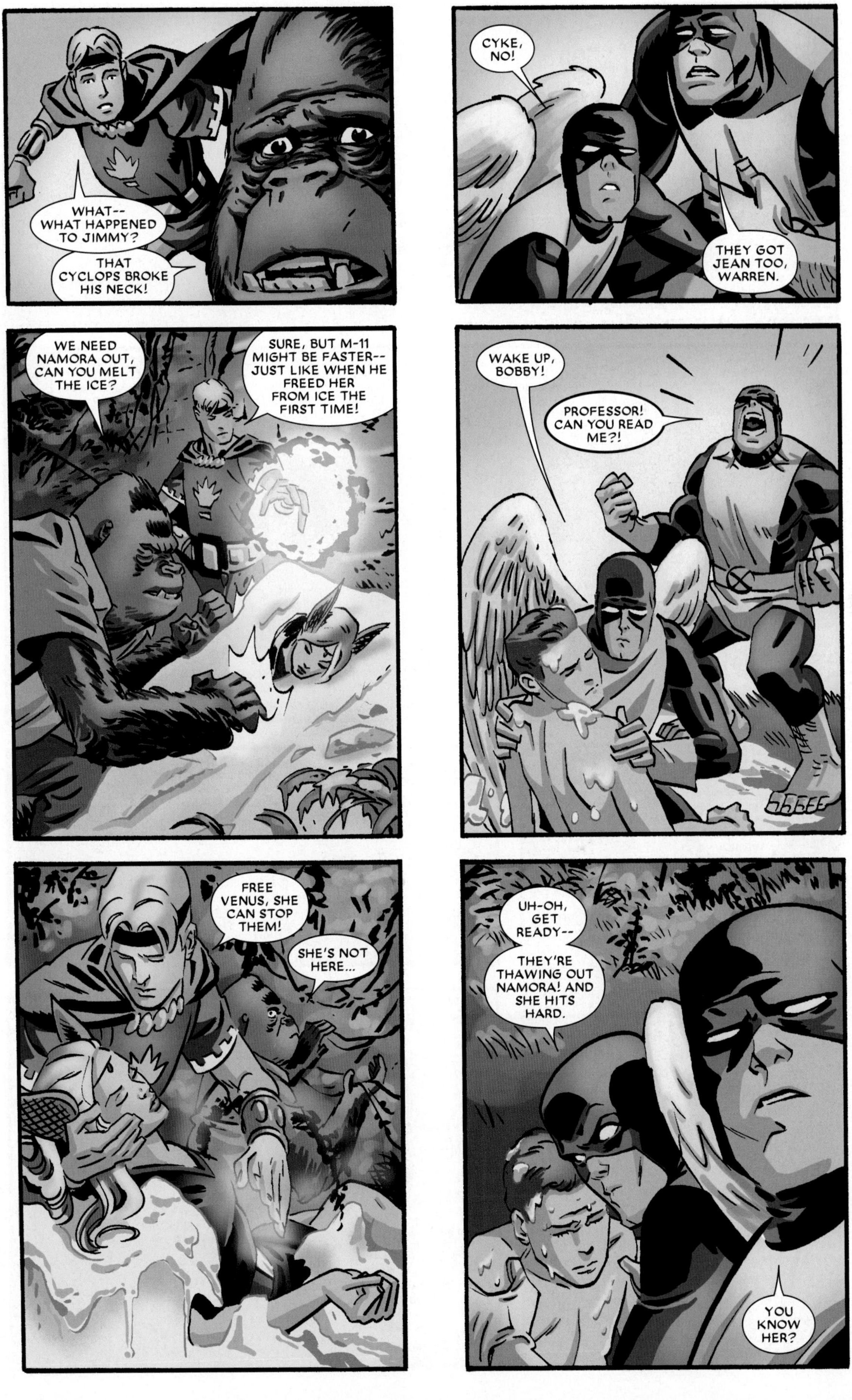
WHAT-- WHAT HAPPENED TO JIMMY?
THAT CYCLOPS BROKE HIS NECK!
CYKE, NO!
THEY GOT JEAN TOO, WARREN.
WE NEED NAMORA OUT, CAN YOU MELT THE ICE?
SURE, BUT M-11 MIGHT BE FASTER-- JUST LIKE WHEN HE FREED HER FROM ICE THE FIRST TIME!
WAKE UP, BOBBY!
PROFESSOR! CAN YOU READ ME?!
FREE VENUS, SHE CAN STOP THEM!
SHE'S NOT HERE...
UH-OH, GET READY--
THEY'RE THAWING OUT NAMORA! AND SHE HITS HARD.
YOU KNOW HER?

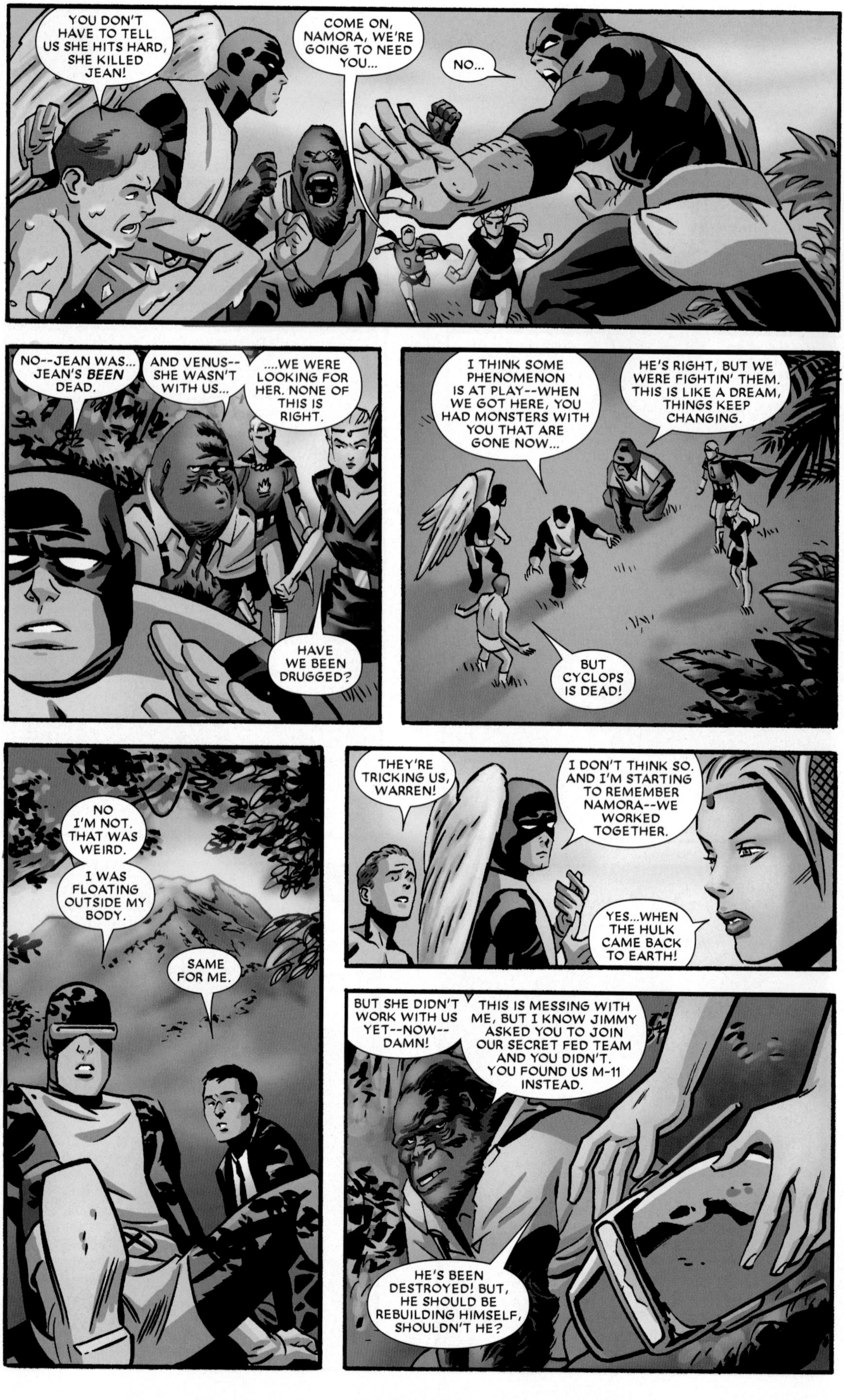
YOU DON'T HAVE TO TELL US SHE HITS HARD, SHE KILLED JEAN!
COME ON, NAMORA, WE'RE GOING TO NEED YOU...
NO...
NO--JEAN WAS... JEAN'S BEEN DEAD.
AND VENUS-- SHE WASN'T WITH US...
....WE WERE LOOKING FOR HER. NONE OF THIS IS RIGHT.
HAVE WE BEEN DRUGGED?
I THINK SOME PHENOMENON IS AT PLAY--WHEN WE GOT HERE, YOU HAD MONSTERS WITH YOU THAT ARE GONE NOW...
HE'S RIGHT, BUT WE WERE FIGHTIN' THEM. THIS IS LIKE A DREAM, THINGS KEEP CHANGING.
BUT CYCLOPS IS DEAD!
NO I'M NOT. THAT WAS WEIRD.
I WAS FLOATING OUTSIDE MY BODY.
SAME FOR ME.
THEY'RE TRICKING US, WARREN!
I DON'T THINK SO. AND I'M STARTING TO REMEMBER NAMORA--WE WORKED TOGETHER.
YES...WHEN THE HULK CAME BACK TO EARTH!
BUT SHE DIDN'T WORK WITH US YET--NOW-- DAMN!
THIS IS MESSING WITH ME, BUT I KNOW JIMMY ASKED YOU TO JOIN OUR SECRET FED TEAM AND YOU DIDN'T. YOU FOUND US M-11 INSTEAD.
HE'S BEEN DESTROYED! BUT, HE SHOULD BE REBUILDING HIMSELF, SHOULDN'T HE?

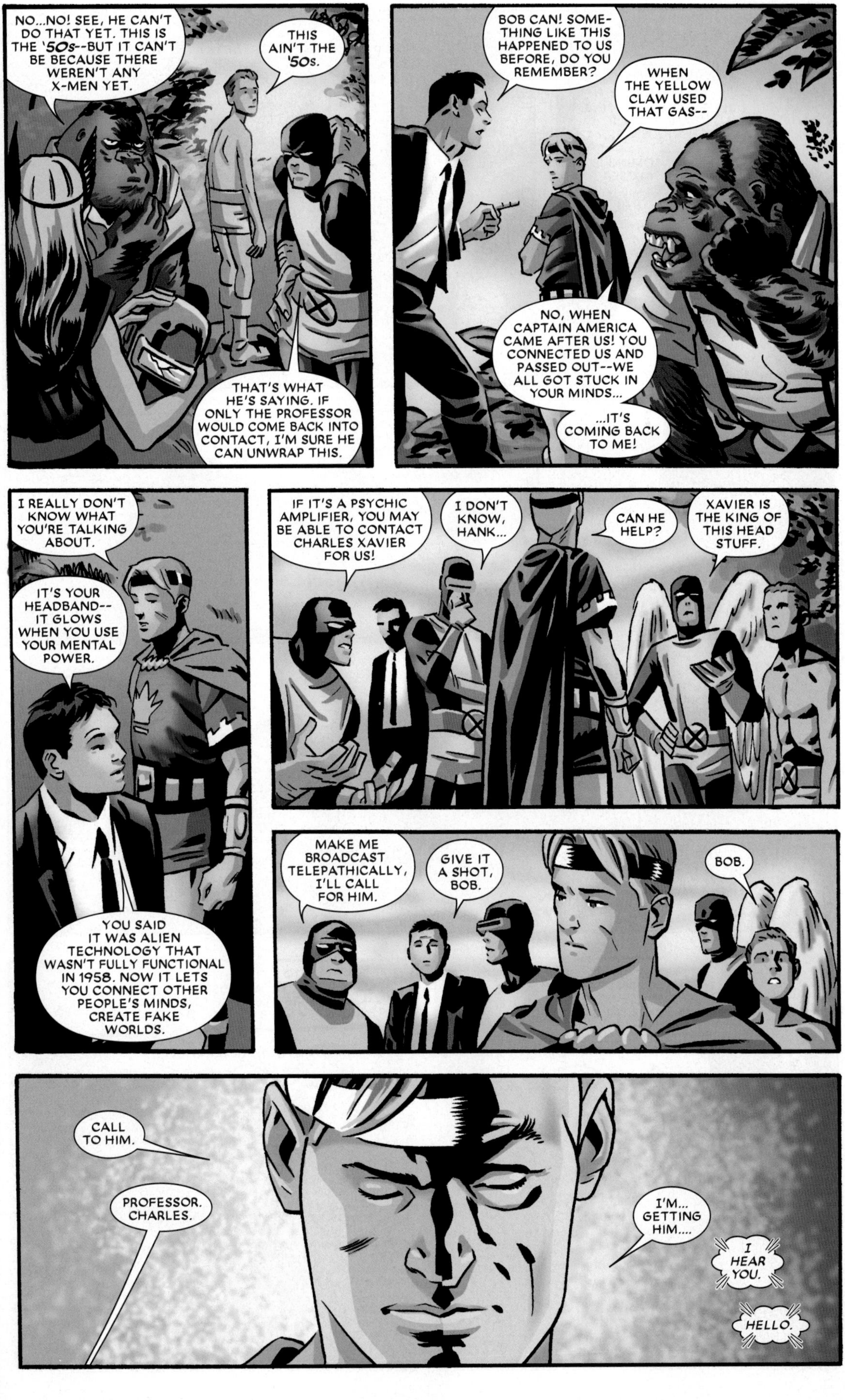
NO...NO! SEE, HE CAN'T DO THAT YET. THIS IS THE '50s--BUT IT CAN'T BE BECAUSE THERE WEREN'T ANY X-MEN YET.
THIS AIN'T THE '50s.
THAT'S WHAT HE'S SAYING. IF ONLY THE PROFESSOR WOULD COME BACK INTO CONTACT, I'M SURE HE CAN UNWRAP THIS.
BOB CAN! SOMETHING LIKE THIS HAPPENED TO US BEFORE, DO YOU REMEMBER?
WHEN THE YELLOW CLAW USED THAT GAS--
NO, WHEN CAPTAIN AMERICA CAME AFTER US! YOU CONNECTED US AND PASSED OUT--WE ALL GOT STUCK IN YOUR MINDS...
...IT'S COMING BACK TO ME!
I REALLY DON'T KNOW WHAT YOU'RE TALKING ABOUT.
IT'S YOUR HEADBAND-- IT GLOWS WHEN YOU USE YOUR MENTAL POWER.
YOU SAID IT WAS ALIEN TECHNOLOGY THAT WASN'T FULLY FUNCTIONAL IN 1958. NOW IT LETS YOU CONNECT OTHER PEOPLE'S MINDS, CREATE FAKE WORLDS.
IF IT'S A PSYCHIC AMPLIFIER, YOU MAY BE ABLE TO CONTACT CHARLES XAVIER FOR US!
I DON'T KNOW, HANK...
CAN HE HELP?
XAVIER IS THE KING OF THIS HEAD STUFF.
MAKE ME BROADCAST TELEPATHICALLY, I'LL CALL FOR HIM.
GIVE IT A SHOT, BOB.
BOB.
CALL TO HIM.
PROFESSOR. CHARLES.
I'M... GETTING HIM....
I HEAR YOU.
HELLO.

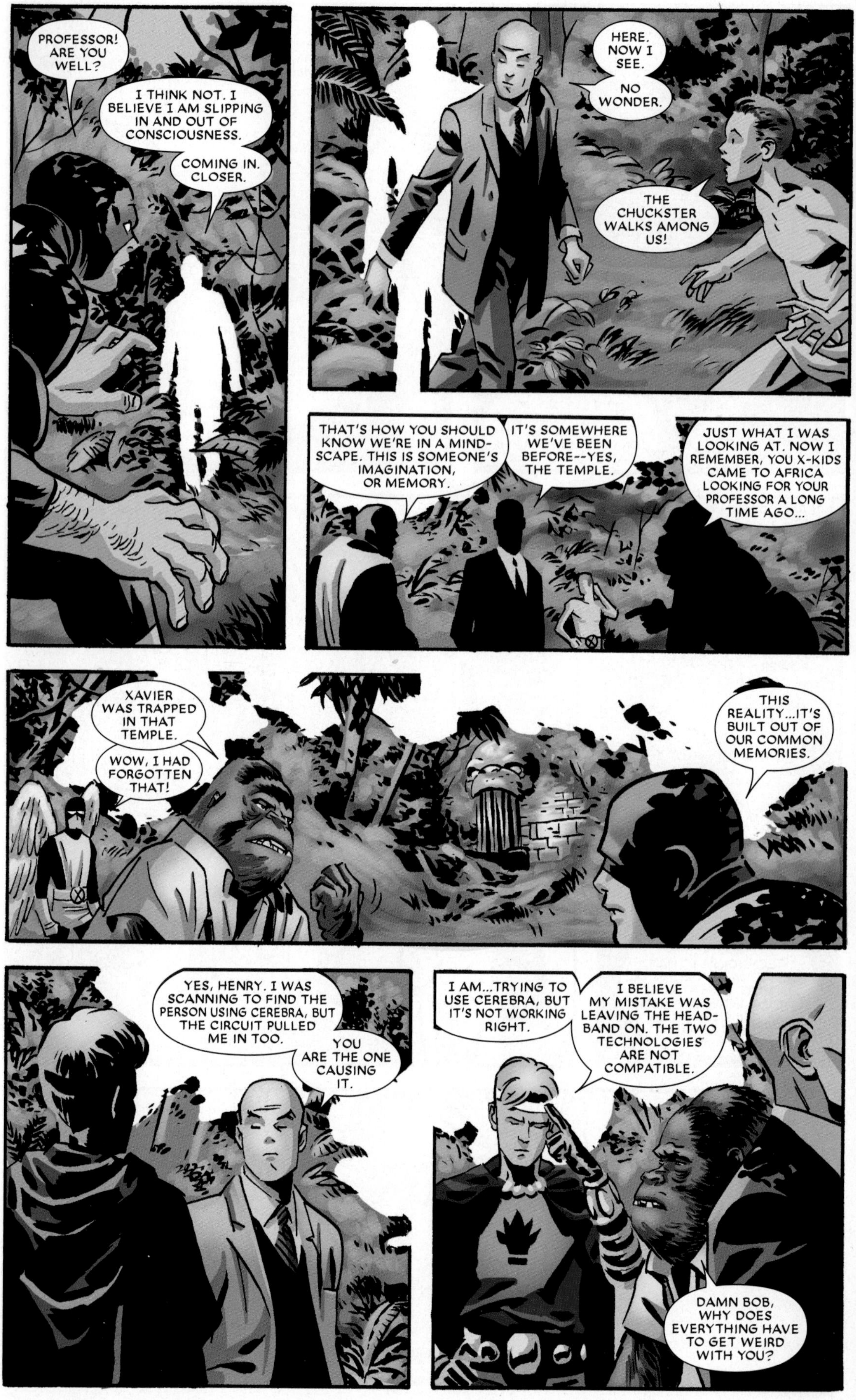
PROFESSOR! ARE YOU WELL?
I THINK NOT. I BELIEVE I AM SLIPPING IN AND OUT OF CONSCIOUSNESS.
COMING IN. CLOSER.
HERE. NOW I SEE.
NO WONDER.
THE CHUCKSTER WALKS AMONG US!
THAT'S HOW YOU SHOULD KNOW WE'RE IN A MIND-SCAPE. THIS IS SOMEONE'S IMAGINATION, OR MEMORY.
IT'S SOMEWHERE WE'VE BEEN BEFORE--YES, THE TEMPLE.
JUST WHAT I WAS LOOKING AT. NOW I REMEMBER, YOU X-KIDS CAME TO AFRICA LOOKING FOR YOUR PROFESSOR A LONG TIME AGO...
XAVIER WAS TRAPPED IN THAT TEMPLE.
WOW, I HAD FORGOTTEN THAT!
THIS REALITY...IT'S BUILT OUT OF OUR COMMON MEMORIES.
YES, HENRY. I WAS SCANNING TO FIND THE PERSON USING CEREBRA, BUT THE CIRCUIT PULLED ME IN TOO.
YOU ARE THE ONE CAUSING IT.
I AM...TRYING TO USE CEREBRA, BUT IT'S NOT WORKING RIGHT.
I BELIEVE MY MISTAKE WAS LEAVING THE HEAD-BAND ON. THE TWO TECHNOLOGIES ARE NOT COMPATIBLE.
DAMN BOB, WHY DOES EVERYTHING HAVE TO GET WEIRD WITH YOU?

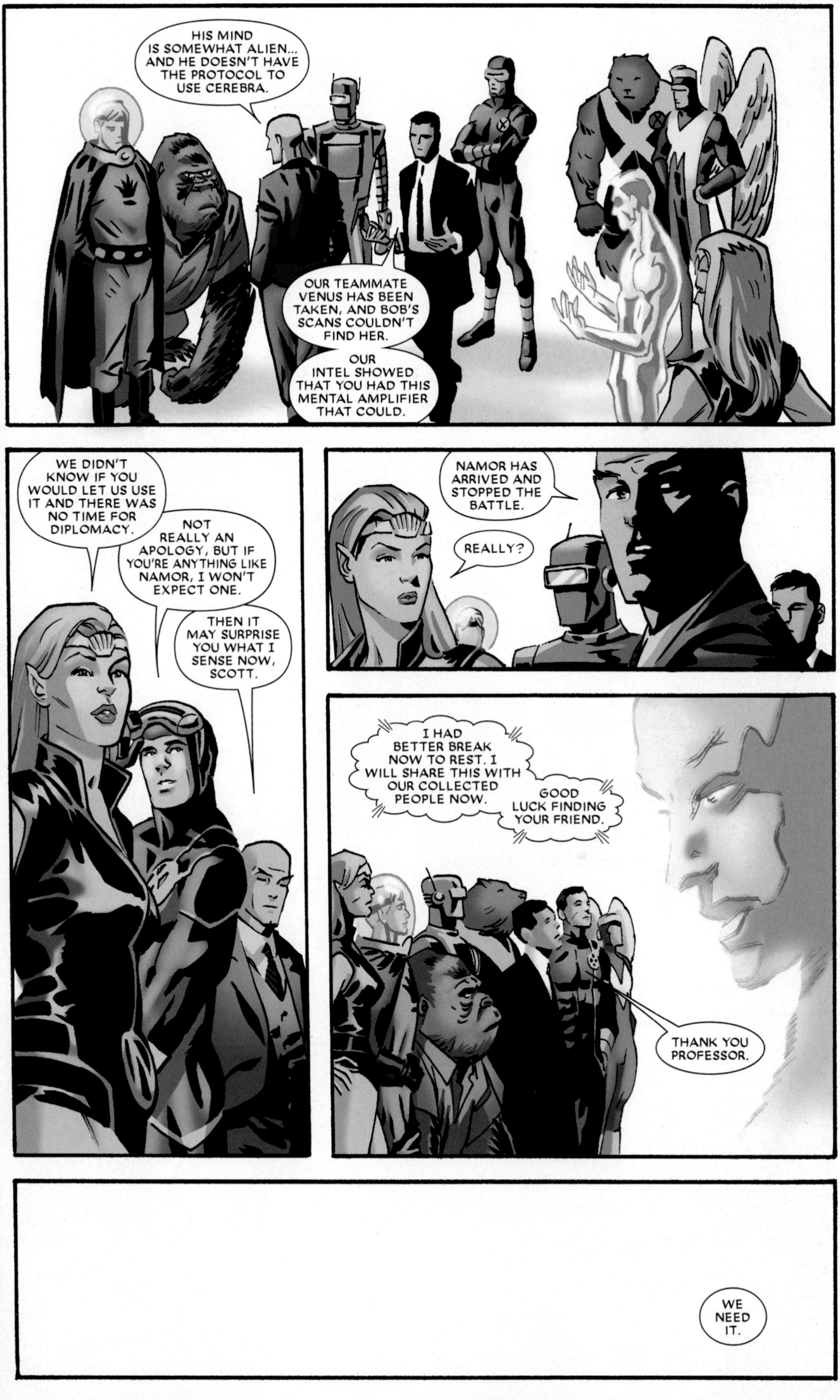
HIS MIND IS SOMEWHAT ALIEN... AND HE DOESN'T HAVE THE PROTOCOL TO USE CEREBRA.
OUR TEAMMATE VENUS HAS BEEN TAKEN, AND BOB'S SCANS COULDN'T FIND HER.
OUR INTEL SHOWED THAT YOU HAD THIS MENTAL AMPLIFIER THAT COULD.
WE DIDN'T KNOW IF YOU WOULD LET US USE IT AND THERE WAS NO TIME FOR DIPLOMACY.
NOT REALLY AN APOLOGY, BUT IF YOU'RE ANYTHING LIKE NAMOR, I WON'T EXPECT ONE.
THEN IT MAY SURPRISE YOU WHAT I SENSE NOW, SCOTT.
NAMOR HAS ARRIVED AND STOPPED THE BATTLE.
REALLY?
I HAD BETTER BREAK NOW TO REST. I WILL SHARE THIS WITH OUR COLLECTED PEOPLE NOW.
GOOD LUCK FINDING YOUR FRIEND.
THANK YOU PROFESSOR.
WE NEED IT.

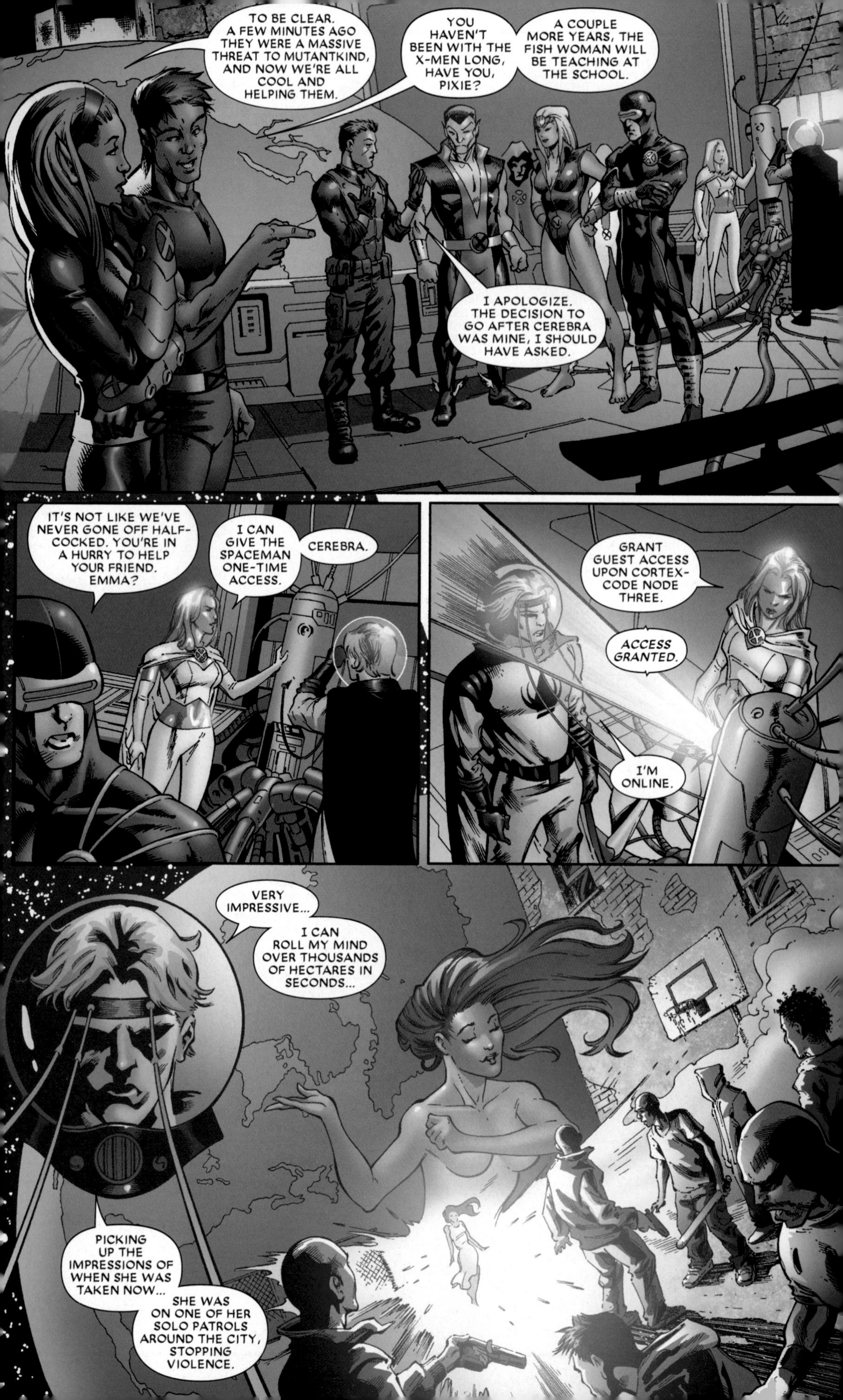
TO BE CLEAR. A FEW MINUTES AGO THEY WERE A MASSIVE THREAT TO MUTANTKIND, AND NOW WE'RE ALL COOL AND HELPING THEM.
YOU HAVEN'T BEEN WITH THE X-MEN LONG, HAVE YOU, PIXIE?
A COUPLE MORE YEARS, THE FISH WOMAN WILL BE TEACHING AT THE SCHOOL.
I APOLOGIZE. THE DECISION TO GO AFTER CEREBRA WAS MINE, I SHOULD HAVE ASKED.
IT'S NOT LIKE WE'VE NEVER GONE OFF HALF-COCKED. YOU'RE IN A HURRY TO HELP YOUR FRIEND. EMMA?
I CAN GIVE THE SPACEMAN ONE-TIME ACCESS.
CEREBRA.
GRANT GUEST ACCESS UPON CORTEX-CODE NODE THREE.
ACCESS GRANTED.
I'M ONLINE.
VERY IMPRESSIVE...
I CAN ROLL MY MIND OVER THOUSANDS OF HECTARES IN SECONDS...
PICKING UP THE IMPRESSIONS OF WHEN SHE WAS TAKEN NOW...
SHE WAS ON ONE OF HER SOLO PATROLS AROUND THE CITY, STOPPING VIOLENCE.

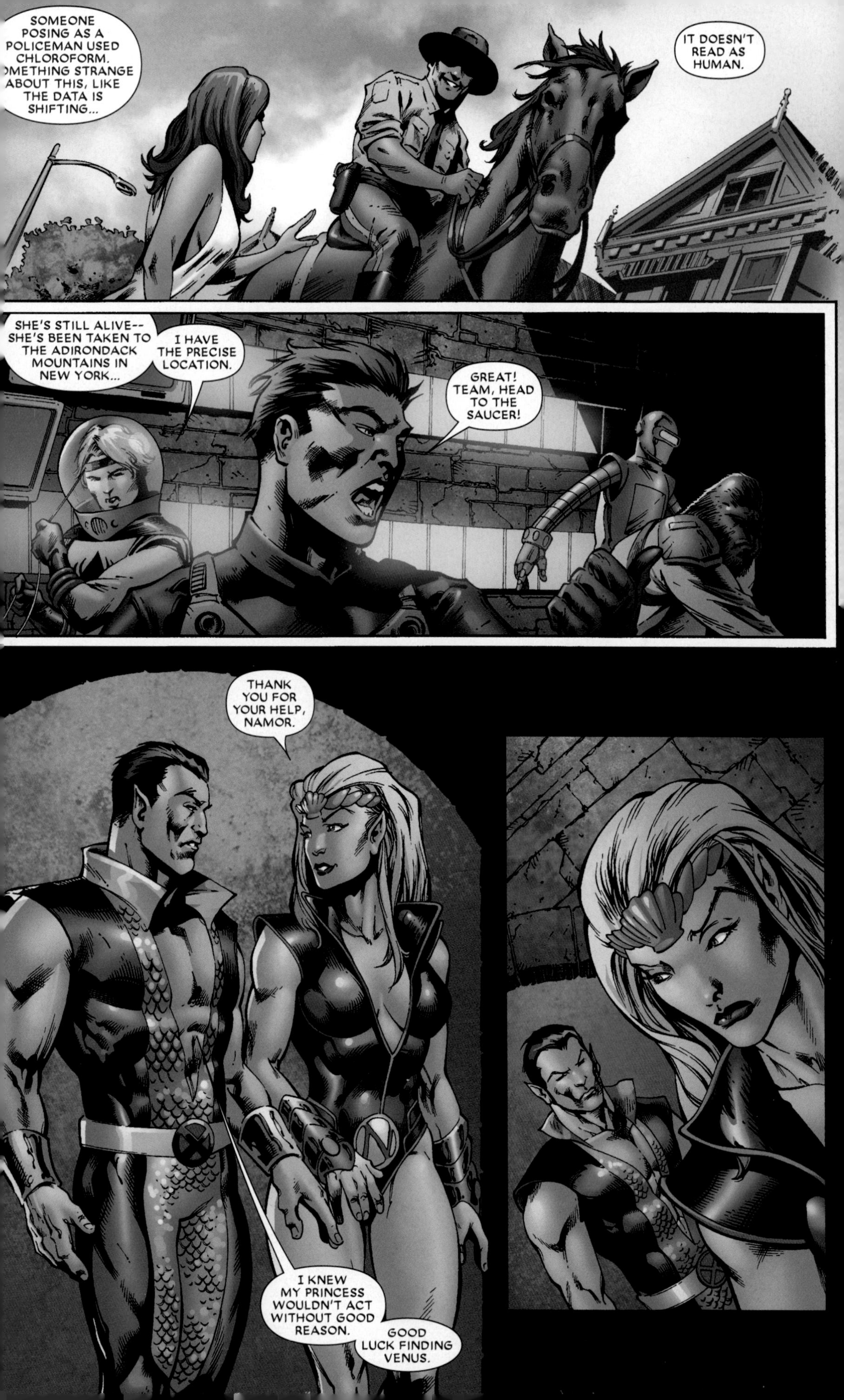
SOMEONE POSING AS A POLICEMAN USED CHLOROFORM. OMETHING STRANGE ABOUT THIS, LIKE THE DATA IS SHIFTING...
IT DOESN'T READ AS HUMAN.
SHE'S STILL ALIVE-- SHE'S BEEN TAKEN TO THE ADIRONDACK MOUNTAINS IN NEW YORK...
I HAVE THE PRECISE LOCATION.
GREAT! TEAM, HEAD TO THE SAUCER!
THANK YOU FOR YOUR HELP, NAMOR.
I KNEW MY PRINCESS WOULDN'T ACT WITHOUT GOOD REASON.
GOOD LUCK FINDING VENUS.

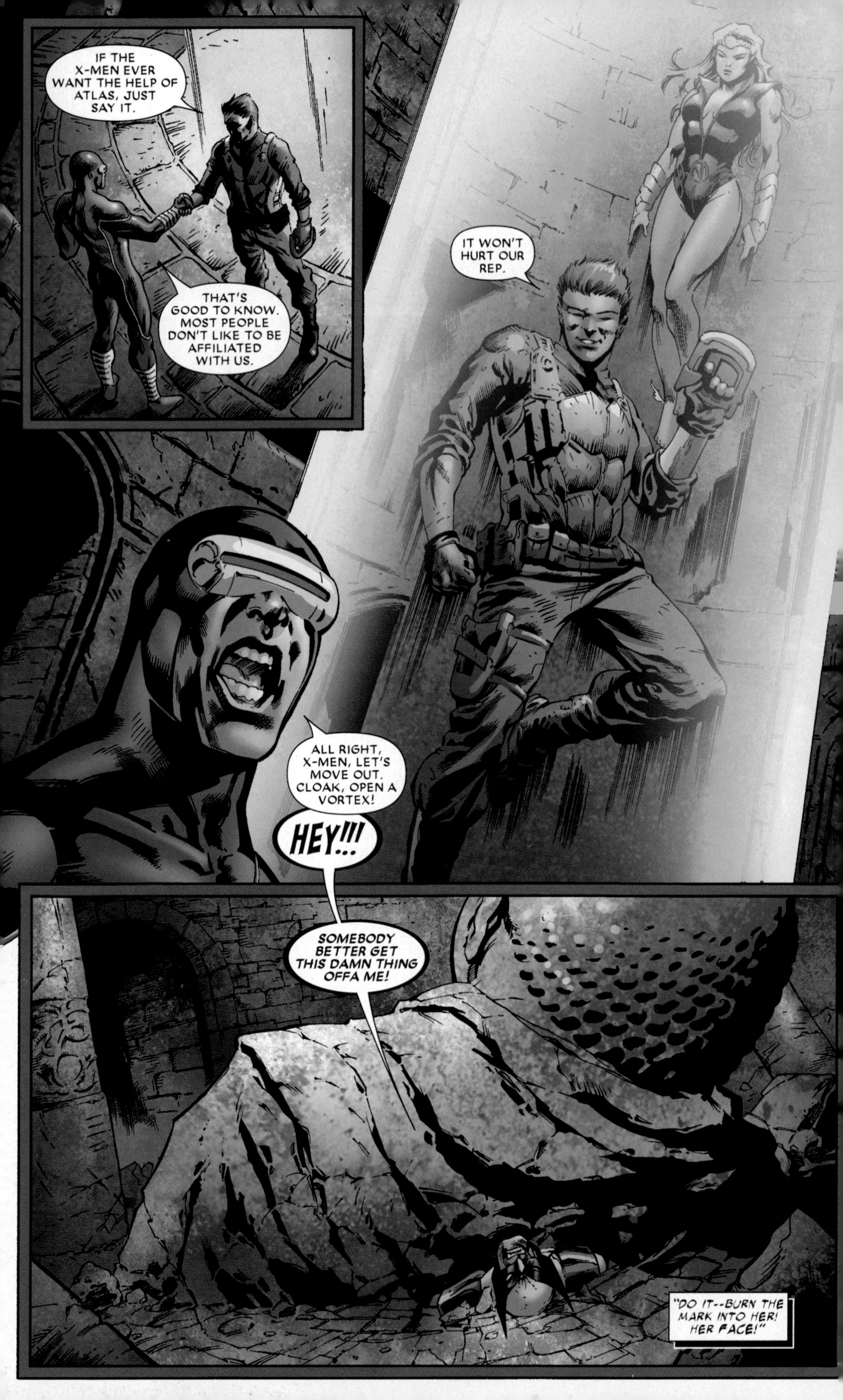
IF THE X-MEN EVER WANT THE HELP OF ATLAS, JUST SAY IT.
THAT'S GOOD TO KNOW. MOST PEOPLE DON'T LIKE TO BE AFFILIATED WITH US.
IT WON'T HURT OUR REP.
ALL RIGHT, X-MEN, LET'S MOVE OUT. CLOAK, OPEN A VORTEX!
HEY!!!
SOMEBODY BETTER GET THIS DAMN THING OFFA ME!
"DO IT--BURN THE MARK INTO HER! HER FACE!"

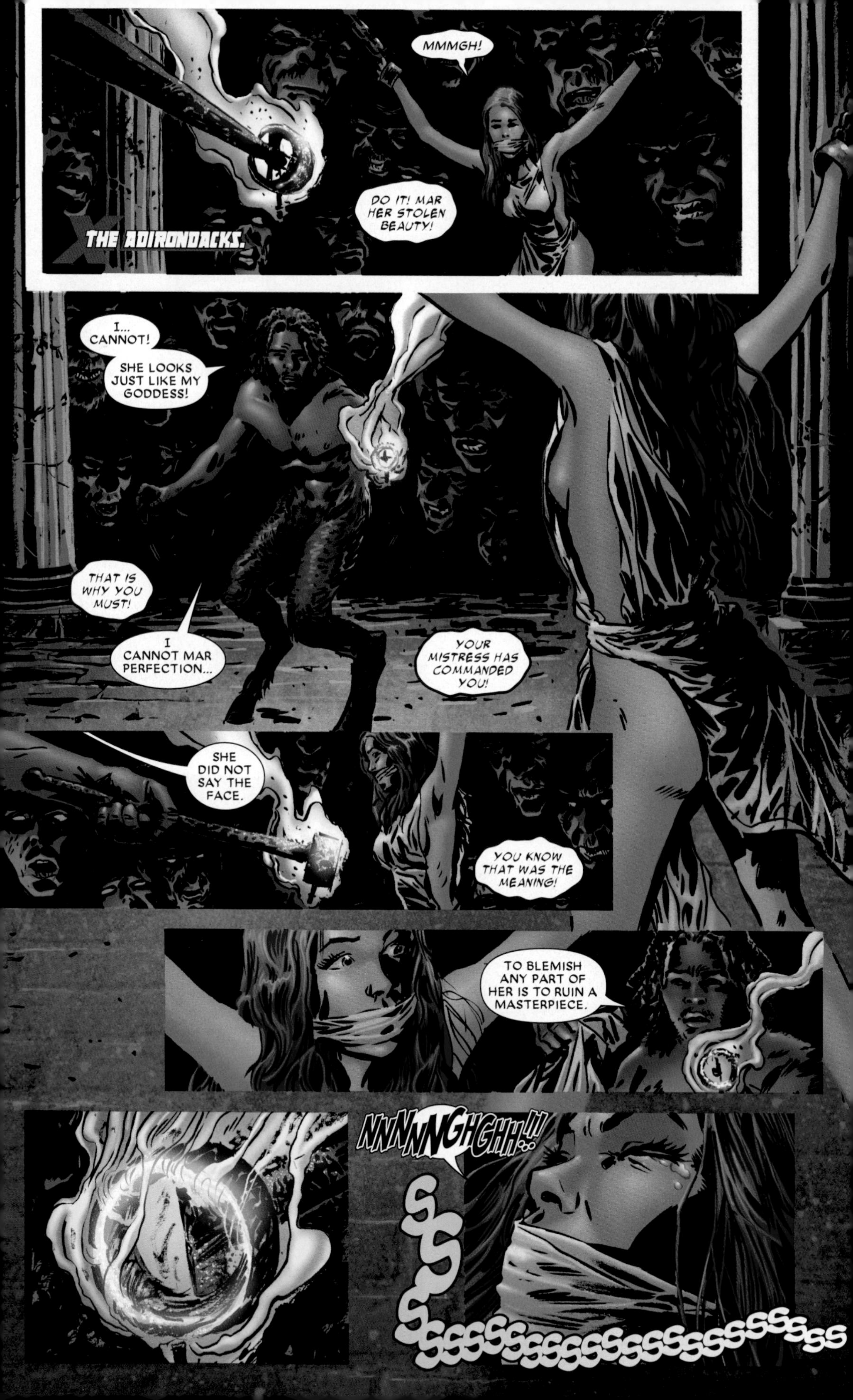
THE ADIRONDACKS.
MMMGH!
DO IT! MAR HER STOLEN BEAUTY!
I... CANNOT!
SHE LOOKS JUST LIKE MY GODDESS!
THAT IS WHY YOU MUST!
I CANNOT MAR PERFECTION...
YOUR MISTRESS HAS COMMANDED YOU!
SHE DID NOT SAY THE FACE.
YOU KNOW THAT WAS THE MEANING!
TO BLEMISH ANY PART OF HER IS TO RUIN A MASTERPIECE.
NNNNNGHGHH!!
SSSSSSSSSSSSSSSSSSSSSSSSSSSSSSS

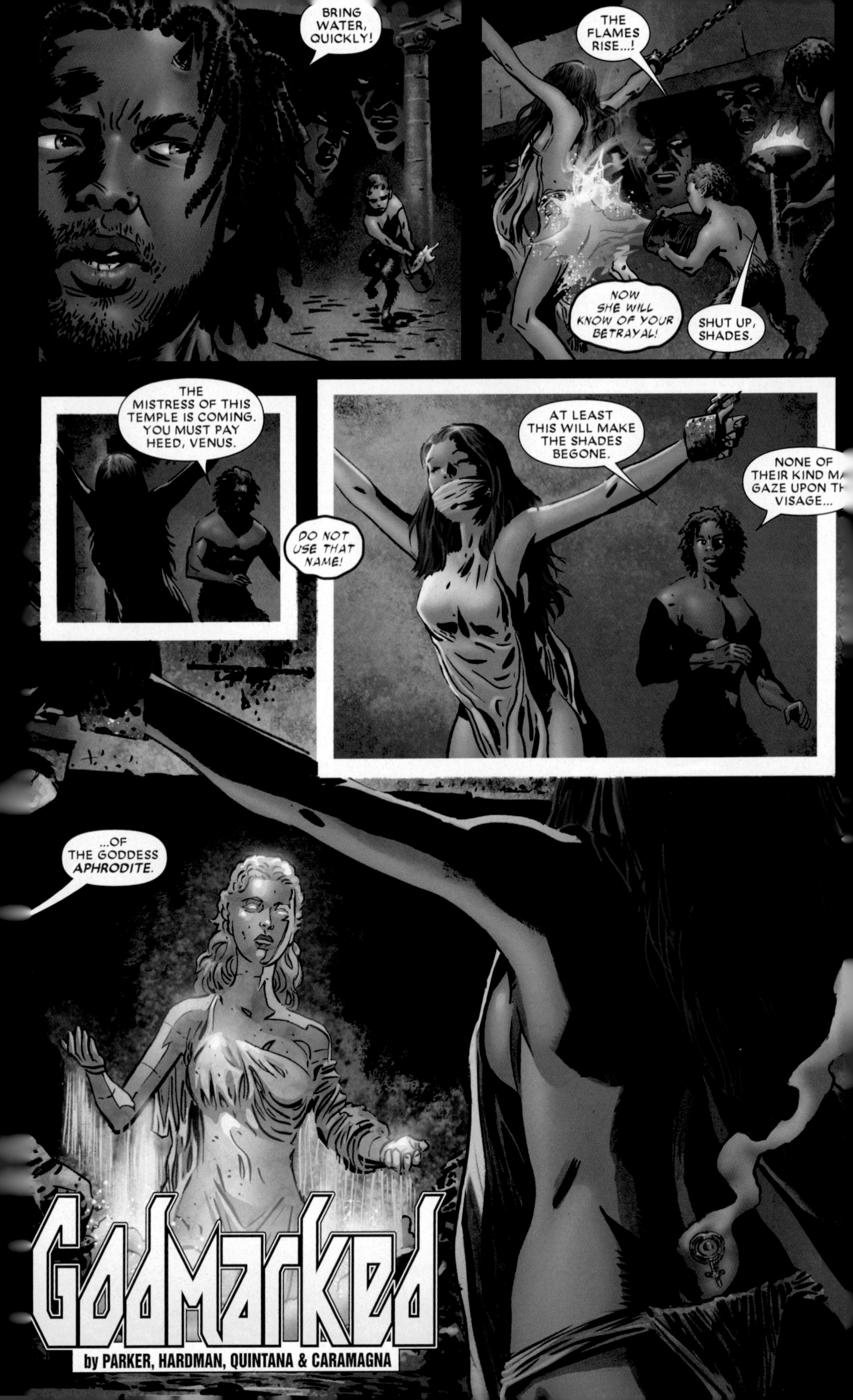

BRING WATER, QUICKLY!
THE FLAMES RISE...!
NOW SHE WILL KNOW OF YOUR BETRAYAL!
SHUT UP, SHADES.
THE MISTRESS OF THIS TEMPLE IS COMING. YOU MUST PAY HEED, VENUS.
DO NOT USE THAT NAME!
AT LEAST THIS WILL MAKE THE SHADES BEGONE.
NONE OF THEIR KIND MA GAZE UPON TH VISAGE...
...OF THE GODDESS APHRODITE.
GodMarked
by PARKER, HARDMAN, QUINTANA & CARAMAGNA

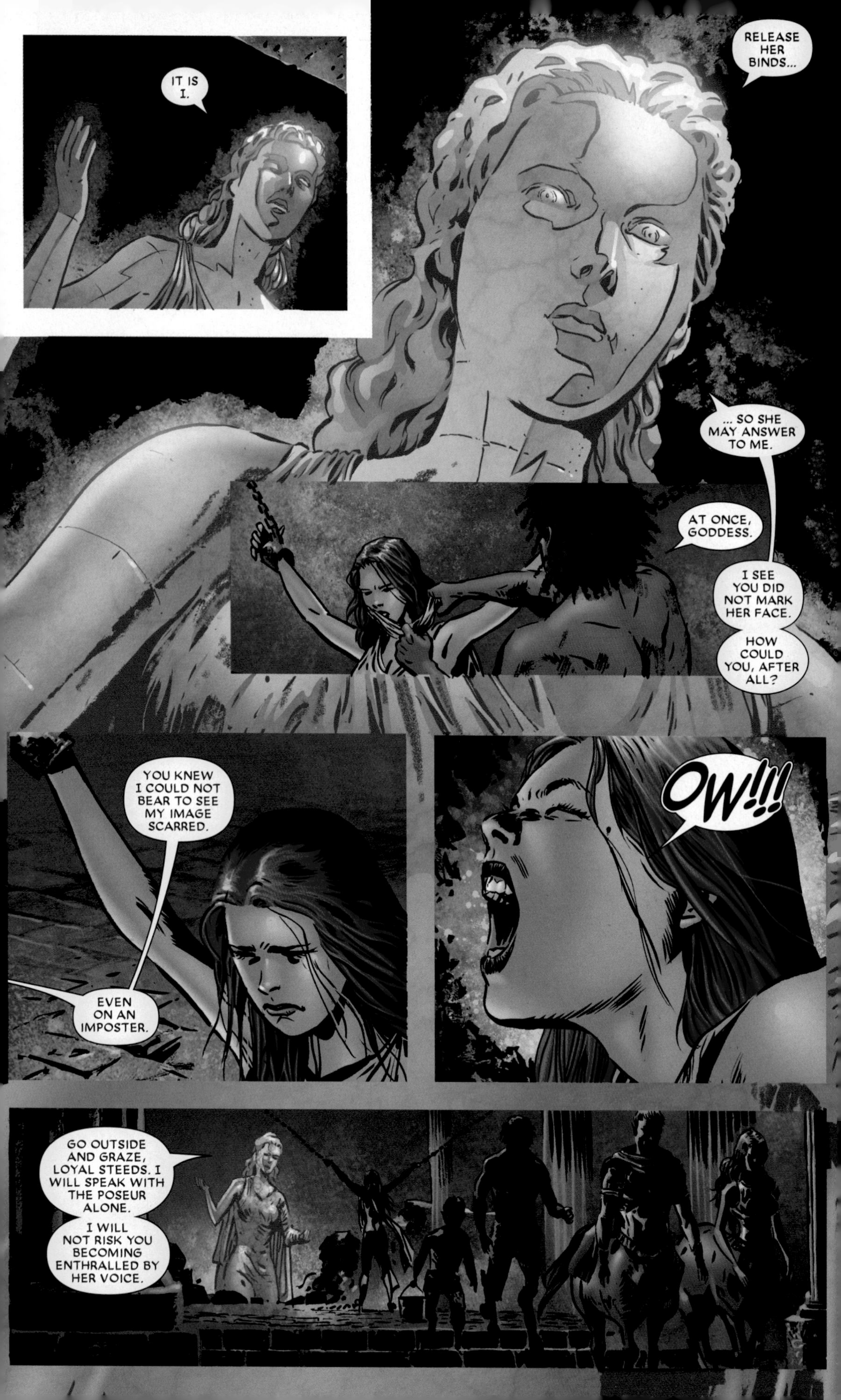

IT IS I.
RELEASE HER BINDS...
... SO SHE MAY ANSWER TO ME.
AT ONCE, GODDESS.
I SEE YOU DID NOT MARK HER FACE.
HOW COULD YOU, AFTER ALL?
YOU KNEW I COULD NOT BEAR TO SEE MY IMAGE SCARRED.
EVEN ON AN IMPOSTER.
OW!!!
GO OUTSIDE AND GRAZE, LOYAL STEEDS. I WILL SPEAK WITH THE POSEUR ALONE.
I WILL NOT RISK YOU BECOMING ENTHRALLED BY HER VOICE.

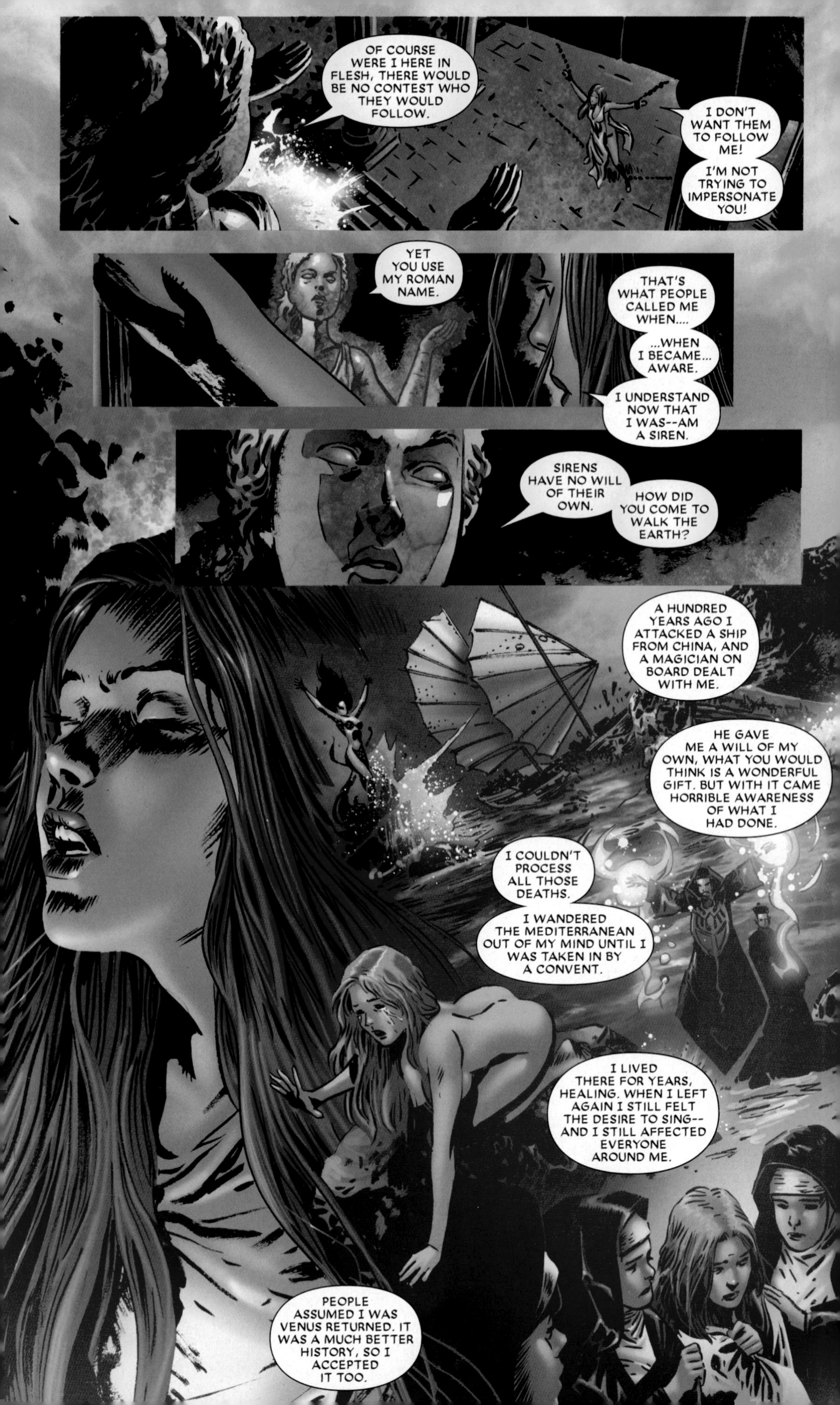

OF COURSE WERE I HERE IN FLESH, THERE WOULD BE NO CONTEST WHO THEY WOULD FOLLOW.
I DON'T WANT THEM TO FOLLOW ME!
I'M NOT TRYING TO IMPERSONATE YOU!
YET YOU USE MY ROMAN NAME.
THAT'S WHAT PEOPLE CALLED ME WHEN....
...WHEN I BECAME... AWARE.
I UNDERSTAND NOW THAT I WAS--AM A SIREN.
SIRENS HAVE NO WILL OF THEIR OWN.
HOW DID YOU COME TO WALK THE EARTH?
A HUNDRED YEARS AGO I ATTACKED A SHIP FROM CHINA, AND A MAGICIAN ON BOARD DEALT WITH ME.
HE GAVE ME A WILL OF MY OWN, WHAT YOU WOULD THINK IS A WONDERFUL GIFT. BUT WITH IT CAME HORRIBLE AWARENESS OF WHAT I HAD DONE.
I COULDN'T PROCESS ALL THOSE DEATHS.
I WANDERED THE MEDITERRANEAN OUT OF MY MIND UNTIL I WAS TAKEN IN BY A CONVENT.
I LIVED THERE FOR YEARS, HEALING. WHEN I LEFT AGAIN I STILL FELT THE DESIRE TO SING-- AND I STILL AFFECTED EVERYONE AROUND ME.
PEOPLE ASSUMED I WAS VENUS RETURNED. IT WAS A MUCH BETTER HISTORY, SO I ACCEPTED IT TOO.

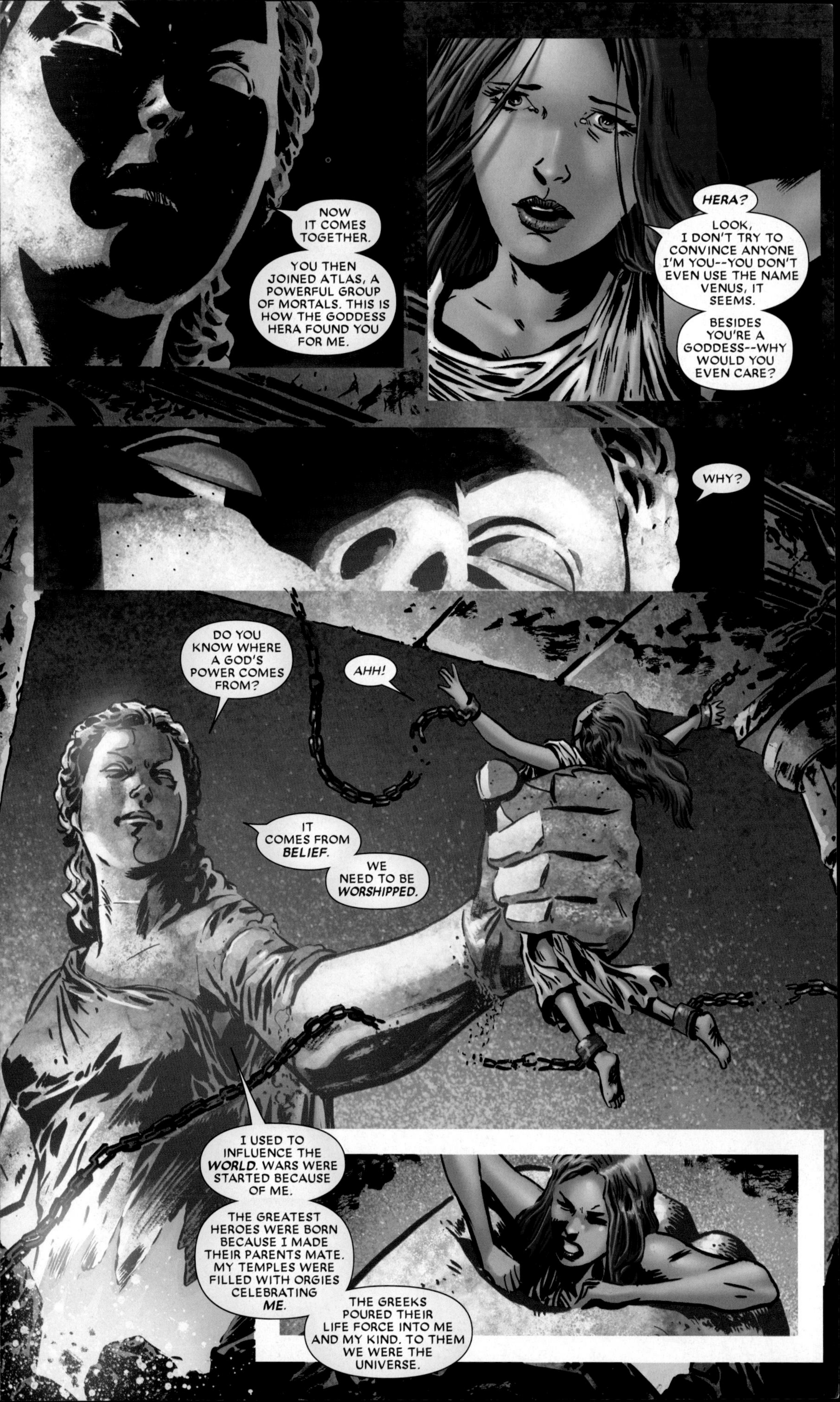

NOW IT COMES TOGETHER.
YOU THEN JOINED ATLAS, A POWERFUL GROUP OF MORTALS. THIS IS HOW THE GODDESS HERA FOUND YOU FOR ME.
HERA?
LOOK, I DON'T TRY TO CONVINCE ANYONE I'M YOU--YOU DON'T EVEN USE THE NAME VENUS, IT SEEMS.
BESIDES YOU'RE A GODDESS--WHY WOULD YOU EVEN CARE?
WHY?
DO YOU KNOW WHERE A GOD'S POWER COMES FROM?
AHH!
IT COMES FROM BELIEF.
WE NEED TO BE WORSHIPPED.
I USED TO INFLUENCE THE WORLD. WARS WERE STARTED BECAUSE OF ME.
THE GREATEST HEROES WERE BORN BECAUSE I MADE THEIR PARENTS MATE. MY TEMPLES WERE FILLED WITH ORGIES CELEBRATING ME.
THE GREEKS POURED THEIR LIFE FORCE INTO ME AND MY KIND. TO THEM WE WERE THE UNIVERSE.

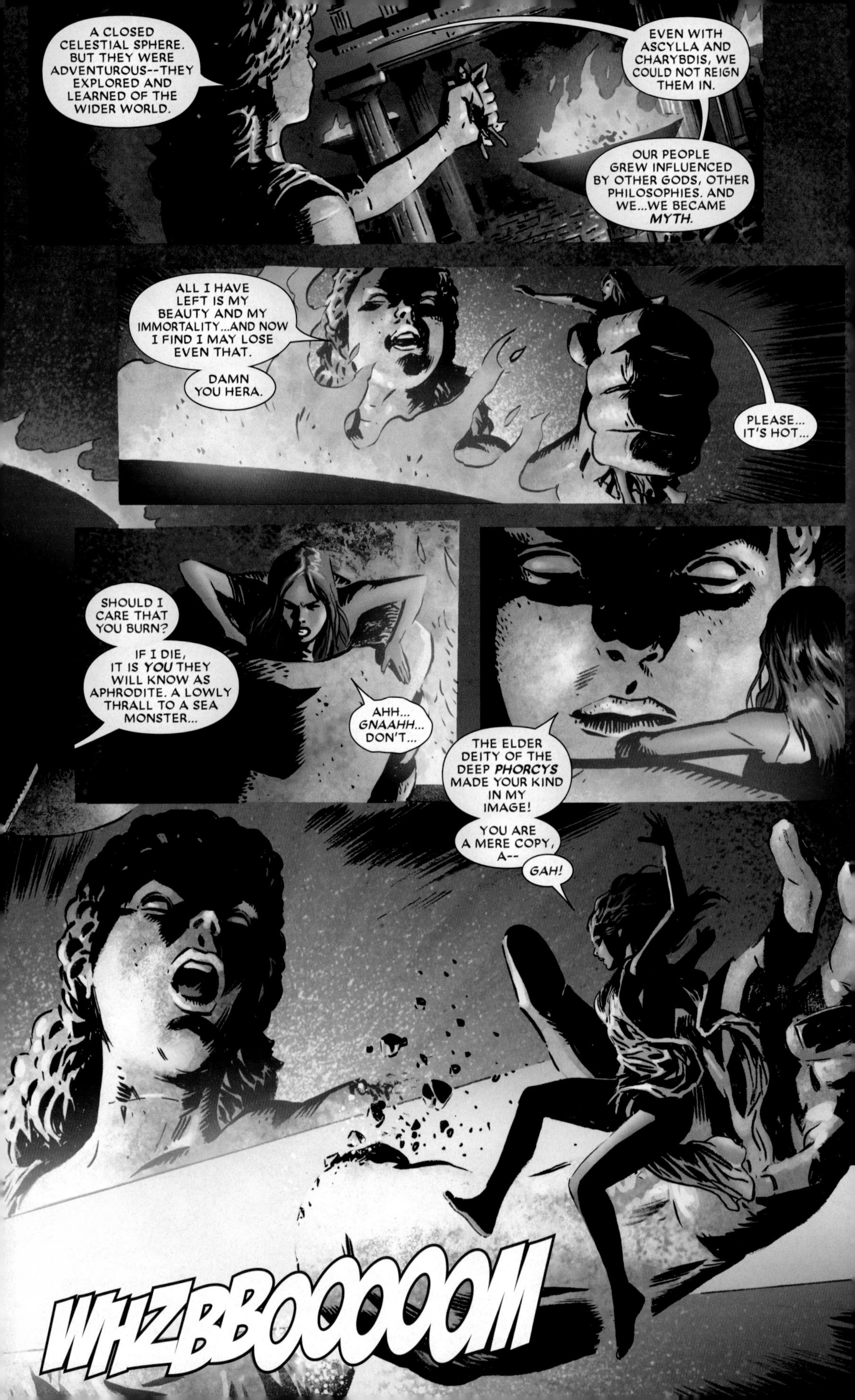

A CLOSED CELESTIAL SPHERE. BUT THEY WERE ADVENTUROUS--THEY EXPLORED AND LEARNED OF THE WIDER WORLD.
EVEN WITH ASCYLLA AND CHARYBDIS, WE COULD NOT REIGN THEM IN.
OUR PEOPLE GREW INFLUENCED BY OTHER GODS, OTHER PHILOSOPHIES. AND WE...WE BECAME *MYTH.*
ALL I HAVE LEFT IS MY BEAUTY AND MY IMMORTALITY...AND NOW I FIND I MAY LOSE EVEN THAT.
DAMN YOU HERA.
PLEASE... IT'S HOT...
SHOULD I CARE THAT YOU BURN?
IF I DIE, IT IS *YOU* THEY WILL KNOW AS APHRODITE. A LOWLY THRALL TO A SEA MONSTER...
AHH... *GNAAHH...* DON'T...
THE ELDER DEITY OF THE DEEP *PHORCYS* MADE YOUR KIND IN MY IMAGE!
YOU ARE A MERE COPY, A--
GAH!
WHZBBOOOOOM

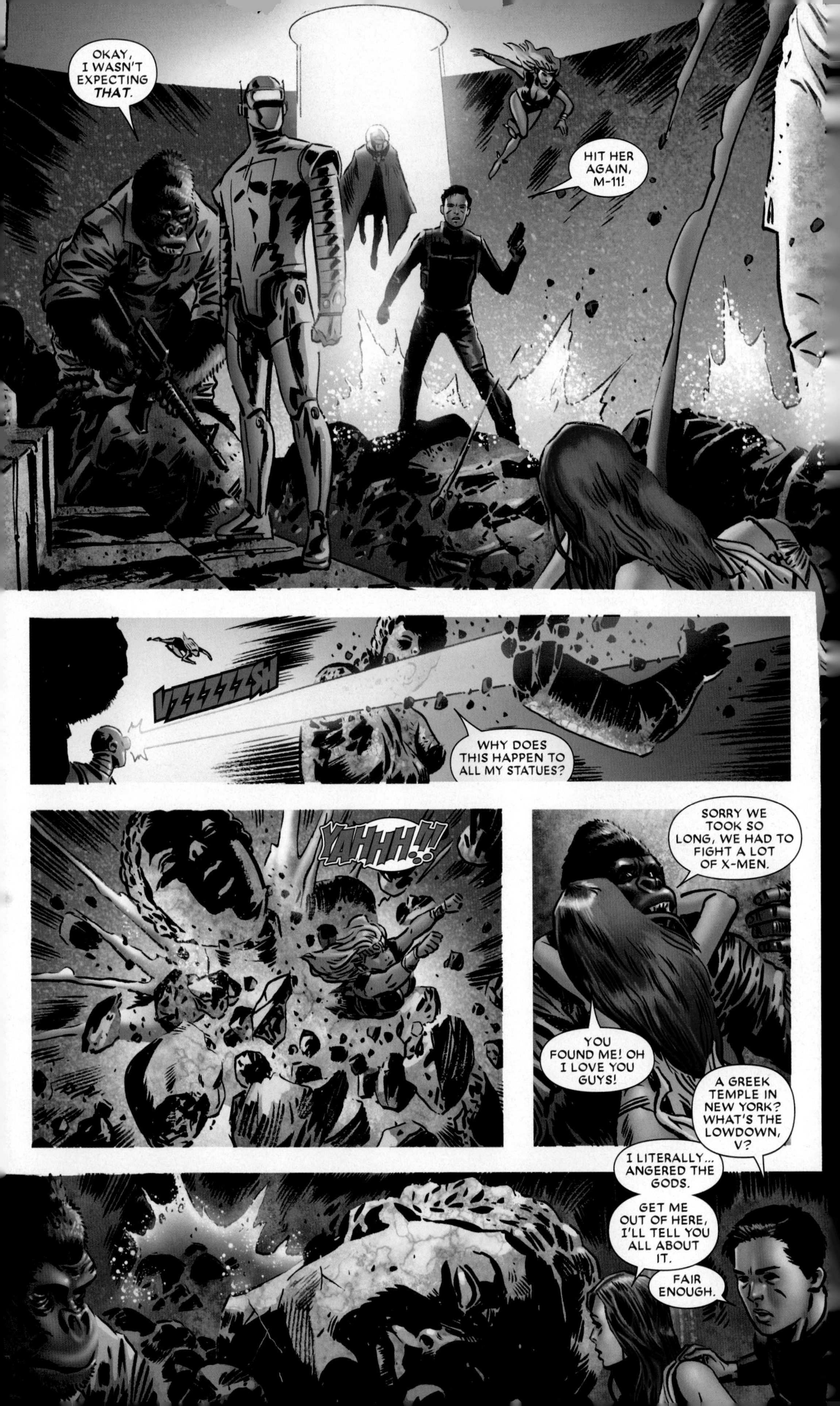
OKAY, I WASN'T EXPECTING THAT.
HIT HER AGAIN, M-11!
VZZZZZZSH
WHY DOES THIS HAPPEN TO ALL MY STATUES?
YAHHH!!
SORRY WE TOOK SO LONG, WE HAD TO FIGHT A LOT OF X-MEN.
YOU FOUND ME! OH I LOVE YOU GUYS!
A GREEK TEMPLE IN NEW YORK? WHAT'S THE LOWDOWN, V?
I LITERALLY... ANGERED THE GODS.
GET ME OUT OF HERE, I'LL TELL YOU ALL ABOUT IT.
FAIR ENOUGH.

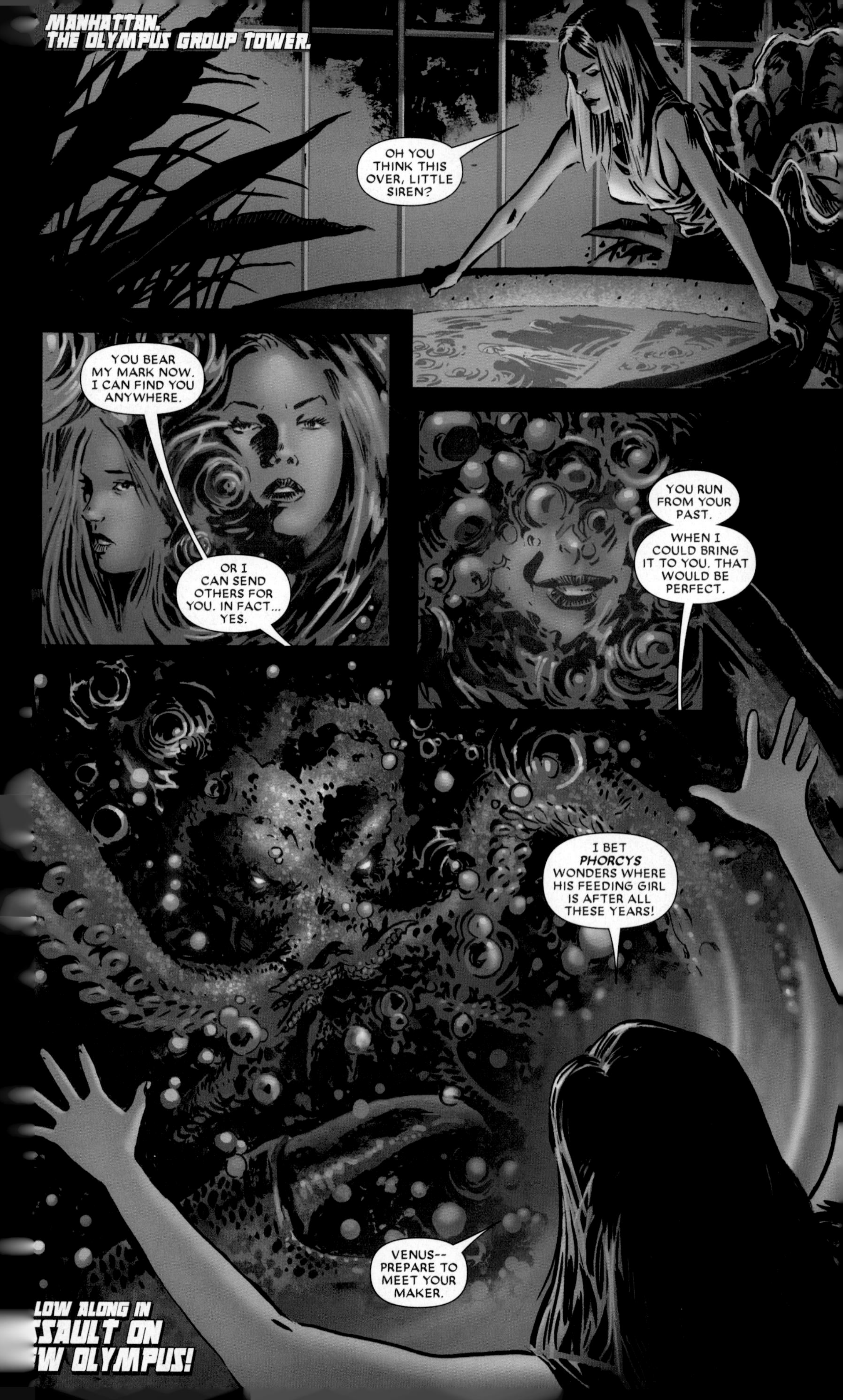
MANHATTAN.
THE OLYMPUS GROUP TOWER.
OH YOU THINK THIS OVER, LITTLE SIREN?
YOU BEAR MY MARK NOW. I CAN FIND YOU ANYWHERE.
OR I CAN SEND OTHERS FOR YOU. IN FACT... YES.
YOU RUN FROM YOUR PAST.
WHEN I COULD BRING IT TO YOU. THAT WOULD BE PERFECT.
I BET PHORCYS WONDERS WHERE HIS FEEDING GIRL IS AFTER ALL THESE YEARS!
VENUS-- PREPARE TO MEET YOUR MAKER.
LOW ALONG IN
SSAULT ON
W OLYMPUS!

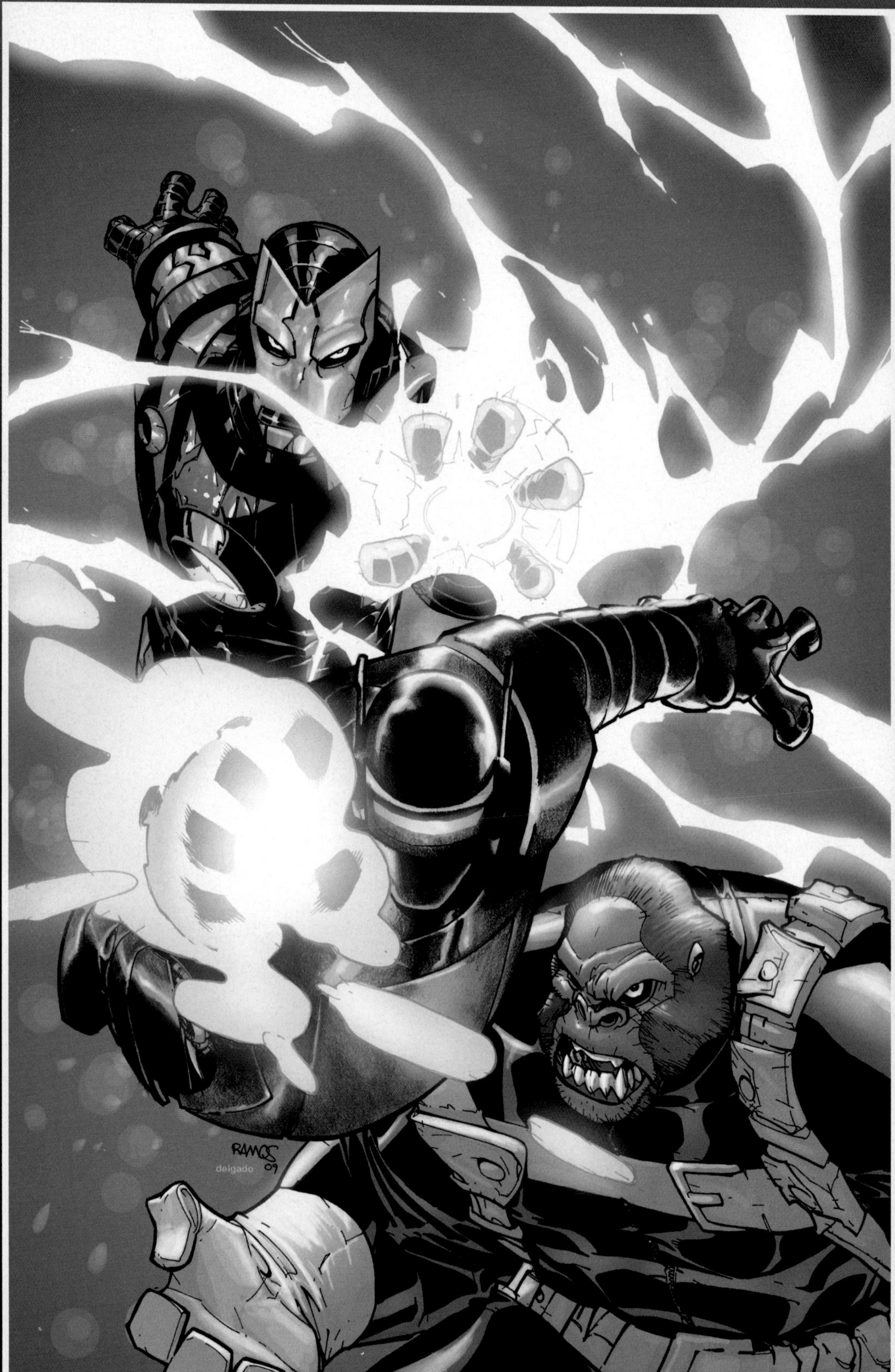
RAMOS
'09
delgado

AVENGERS VS. ATLAS

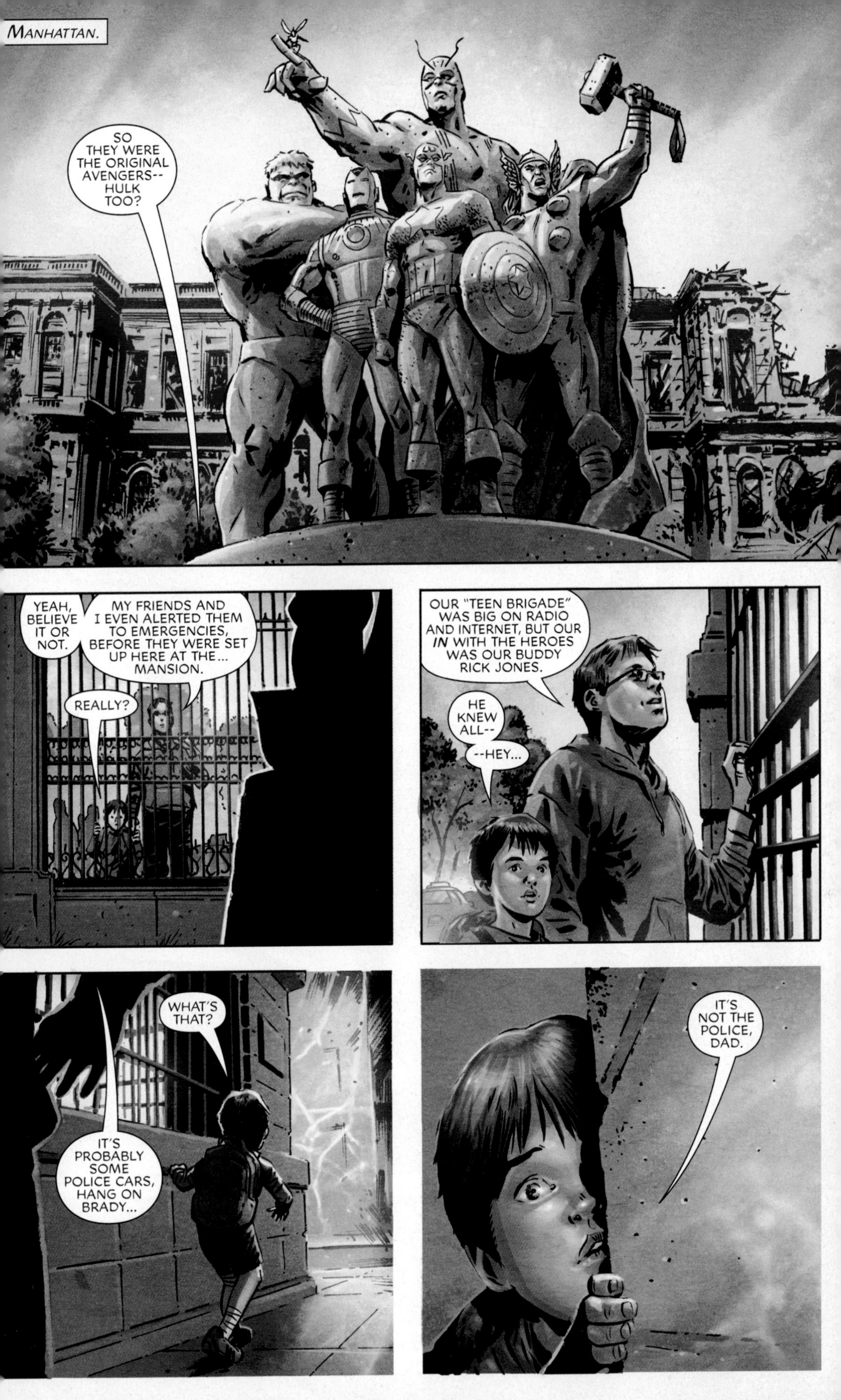
MANHATTAN.
SO THEY WERE THE ORIGINAL AVENGERS-- HULK TOO?
YEAH, BELIEVE IT OR NOT.
MY FRIENDS AND I EVEN ALERTED THEM TO EMERGENCIES, BEFORE THEY WERE SET UP HERE AT THE... MANSION.
REALLY?
OUR "TEEN BRIGADE" WAS BIG ON RADIO AND INTERNET, BUT OUR *IN* WITH THE HEROES WAS OUR BUDDY RICK JONES.
HE KNEW ALL--
--HEY...
WHAT'S THAT?
IT'S PROBABLY SOME POLICE CARS, HANG ON BRADY...
IT'S NOT THE POLICE, DAD.

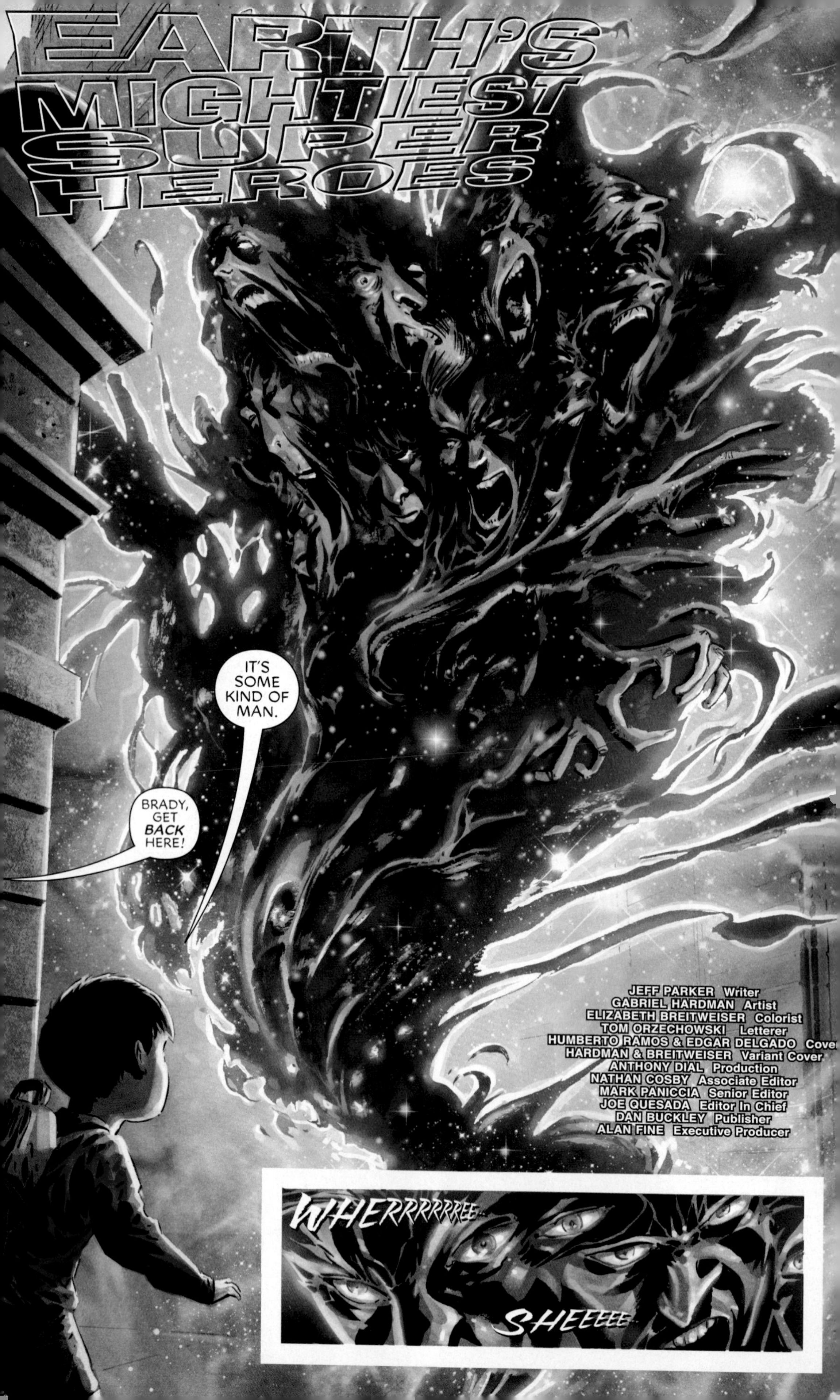
EARTH'S MIGHTIEST SUPER HEROES
IT'S SOME KIND OF MAN.
BRADY, GET BACK HERE!
JEFF PARKER Writer
GABRIEL HARDMAN Artist
ELIZABETH BREITWEISER Colorist
TOM ORZECHOWSKI Letterer
HUMBERTO RAMOS & EDGAR DELGADO Cover
HARDMAN & BREITWEISER Variant Cover
ANTHONY DIAL Production
NATHAN COSBY Associate Editor
MARK PANICCIA Senior Editor
JOE QUESADA Editor In Chief
DAN BUCKLEY Publisher
ALAN FINE Executive Producer
WHERRRRRRREE
SHEEEEE

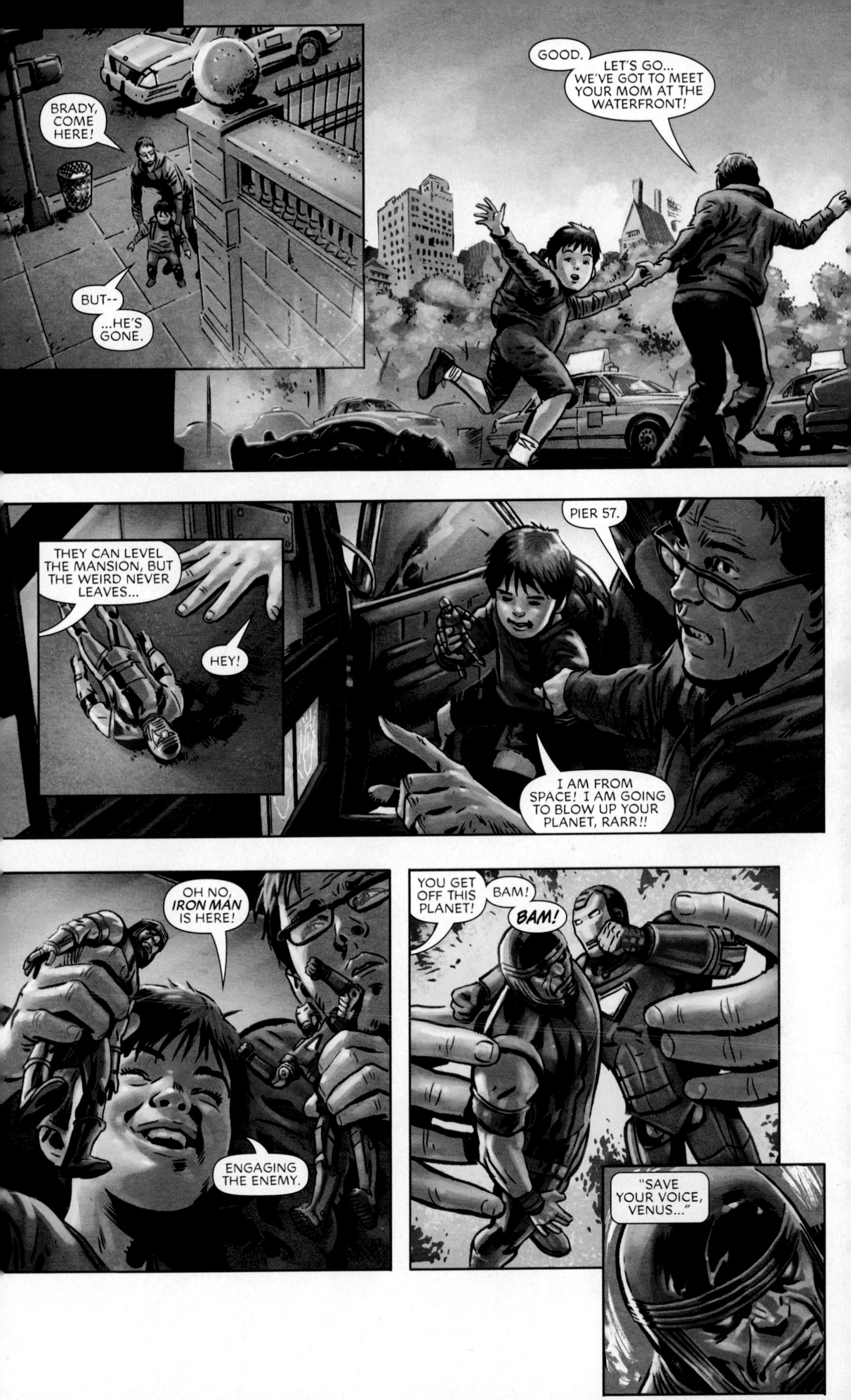
BRADY, COME HERE!
BUT--
...HE'S GONE.
GOOD.
LET'S GO... WE'VE GOT TO MEET YOUR MOM AT THE WATERFRONT!
THEY CAN LEVEL THE MANSION, BUT THE WEIRD NEVER LEAVES...
HEY!
PIER 57.
I AM FROM SPACE! I AM GOING TO BLOW UP YOUR PLANET, RARR!!
OH NO, IRON MAN IS HERE!
ENGAGING THE ENEMY.
YOU GET OFF THIS PLANET!
BAM!
BAM!
"SAVE YOUR VOICE, VENUS..."

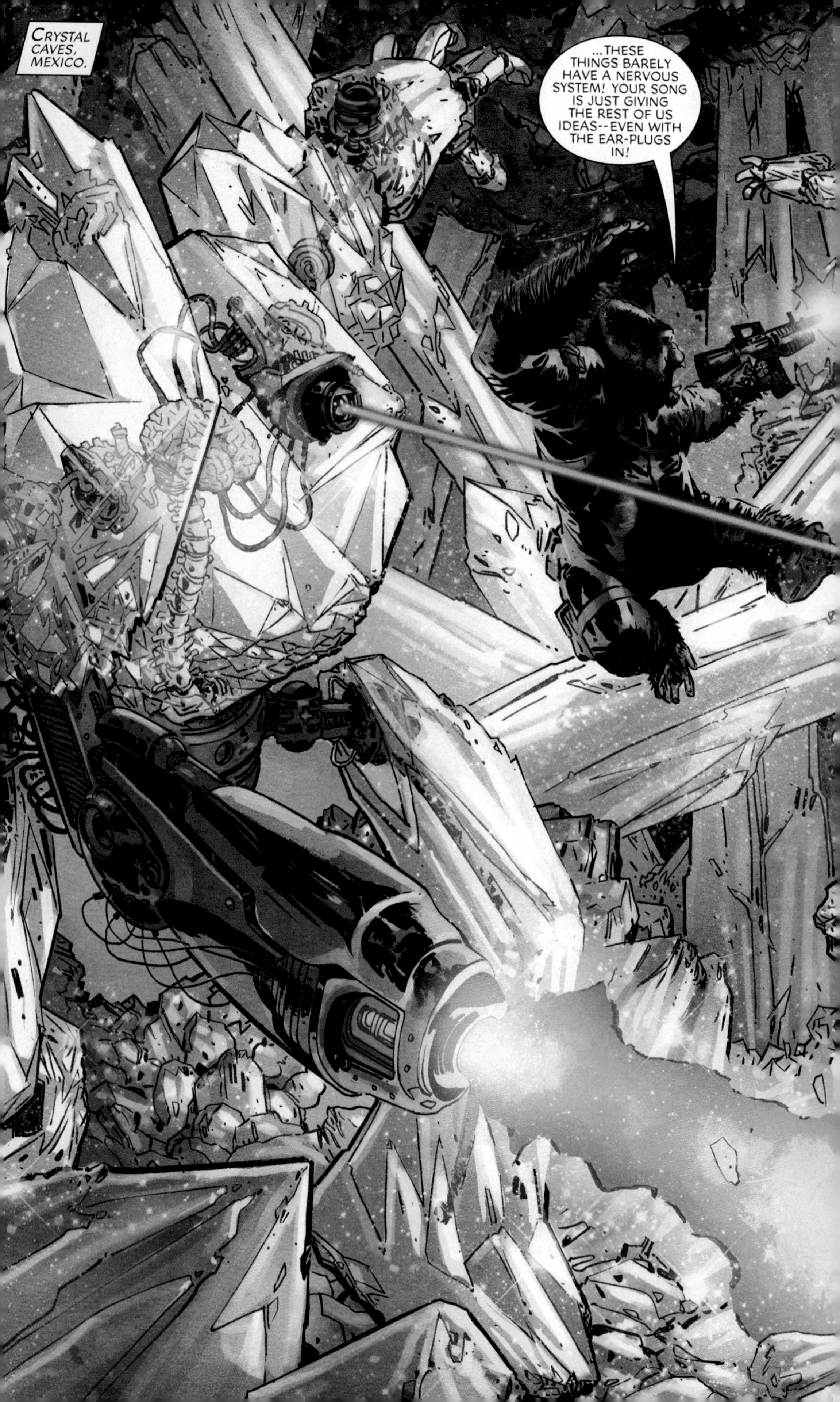
CRYSTAL CAVES, MEXICO.
...THESE THINGS BARELY HAVE A NERVOUS SYSTEM! YOUR SONG IS JUST GIVING THE REST OF US IDEAS--EVEN WITH THE EAR-PLUGS IN!

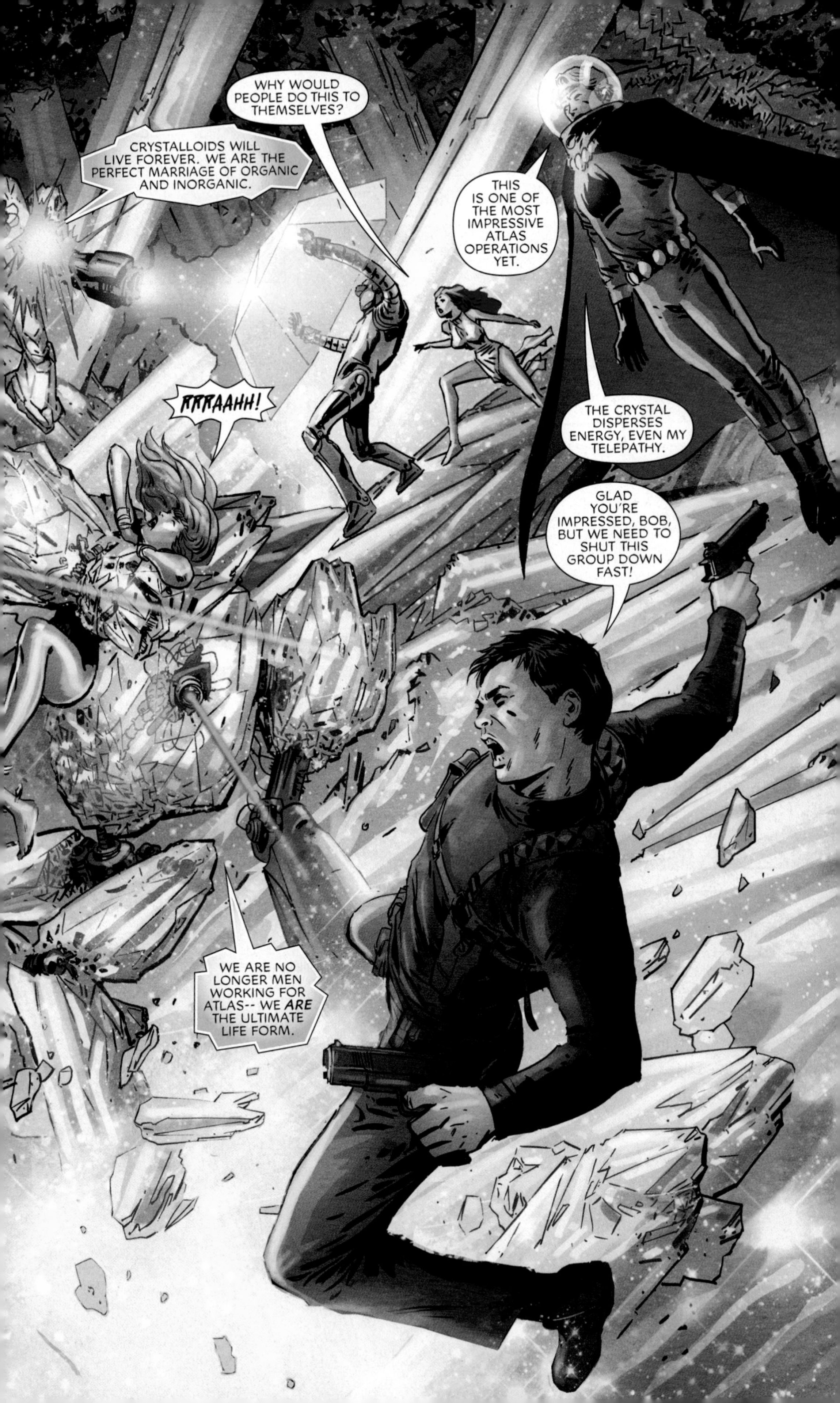

CRYSTALLOIDS WILL LIVE FOREVER. WE ARE THE PERFECT MARRIAGE OF ORGANIC AND INORGANIC.
WHY WOULD PEOPLE DO THIS TO THEMSELVES?
THIS IS ONE OF THE MOST IMPRESSIVE ATLAS OPERATIONS YET.
RRRAAHH!
THE CRYSTAL DISPERSES ENERGY, EVEN MY TELEPATHY.
GLAD YOU'RE IMPRESSED, BOB, BUT WE NEED TO SHUT THIS GROUP DOWN FAST!
WE ARE NO LONGER MEN WORKING FOR ATLAS-- WE *ARE* THE ULTIMATE LIFE FORM.

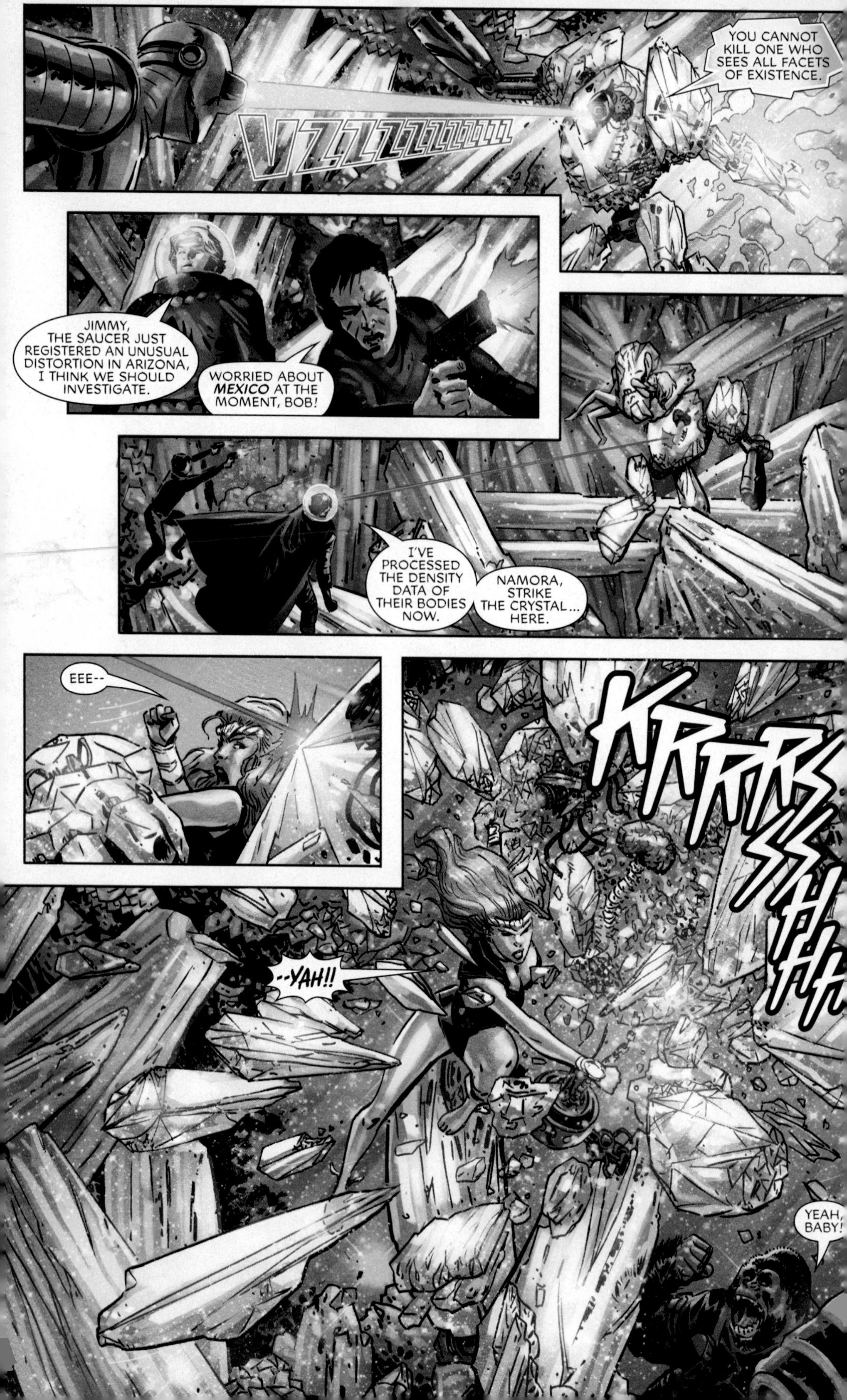

YOU CANNOT KILL ONE WHO SEES ALL FACETS OF EXISTENCE.
VZZZZZZZZZ
JIMMY, THE SAUCER JUST REGISTERED AN UNUSUAL DISTORTION IN ARIZONA, I THINK WE SHOULD INVESTIGATE.
WORRIED ABOUT MEXICO AT THE MOMENT, BOB!
I'VE PROCESSED THE DENSITY DATA OF THEIR BODIES NOW.
NAMORA, STRIKE THE CRYSTAL... HERE.
EEE--
KRRRSSHHH
--YAH!!
YEAH, BABY!

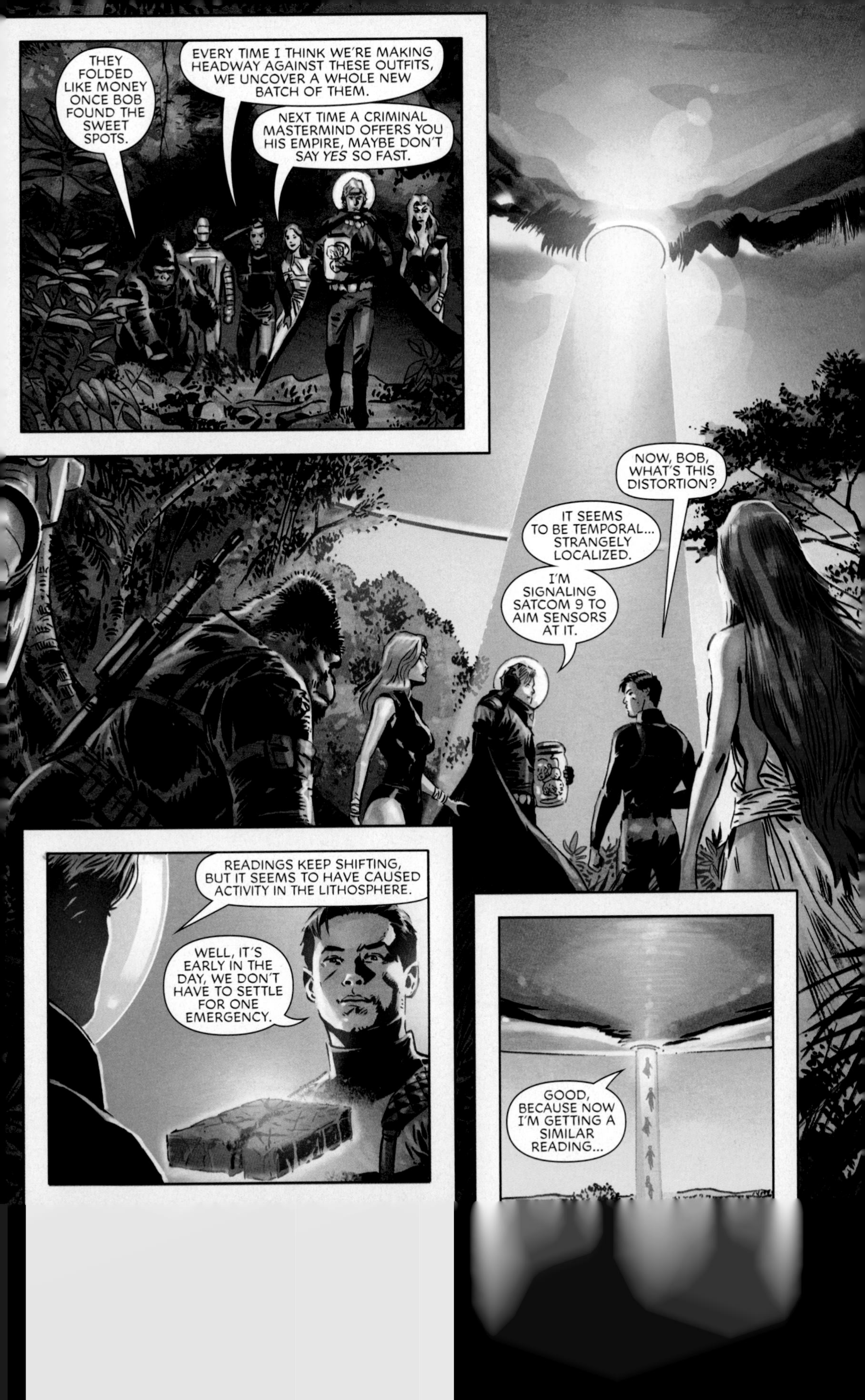
THEY FOLDED LIKE MONEY ONCE BOB FOUND THE SWEET SPOTS.
EVERY TIME I THINK WE'RE MAKING HEADWAY AGAINST THESE OUTFITS, WE UNCOVER A WHOLE NEW BATCH OF THEM.
NEXT TIME A CRIMINAL MASTERMIND OFFERS YOU HIS EMPIRE, MAYBE DON'T SAY *YES* SO FAST.
NOW, BOB, WHAT'S THIS DISTORTION?
IT SEEMS TO BE TEMPORAL... STRANGELY LOCALIZED.
I'M SIGNALING SATCOM 9 TO AIM SENSORS AT IT.
READINGS KEEP SHIFTING, BUT IT SEEMS TO HAVE CAUSED ACTIVITY IN THE LITHOSPHERE.
WELL, IT'S EARLY IN THE DAY, WE DON'T HAVE TO SETTLE FOR ONE EMERGENCY.
GOOD, BECAUSE NOW I'M GETTING A SIMILAR READING...

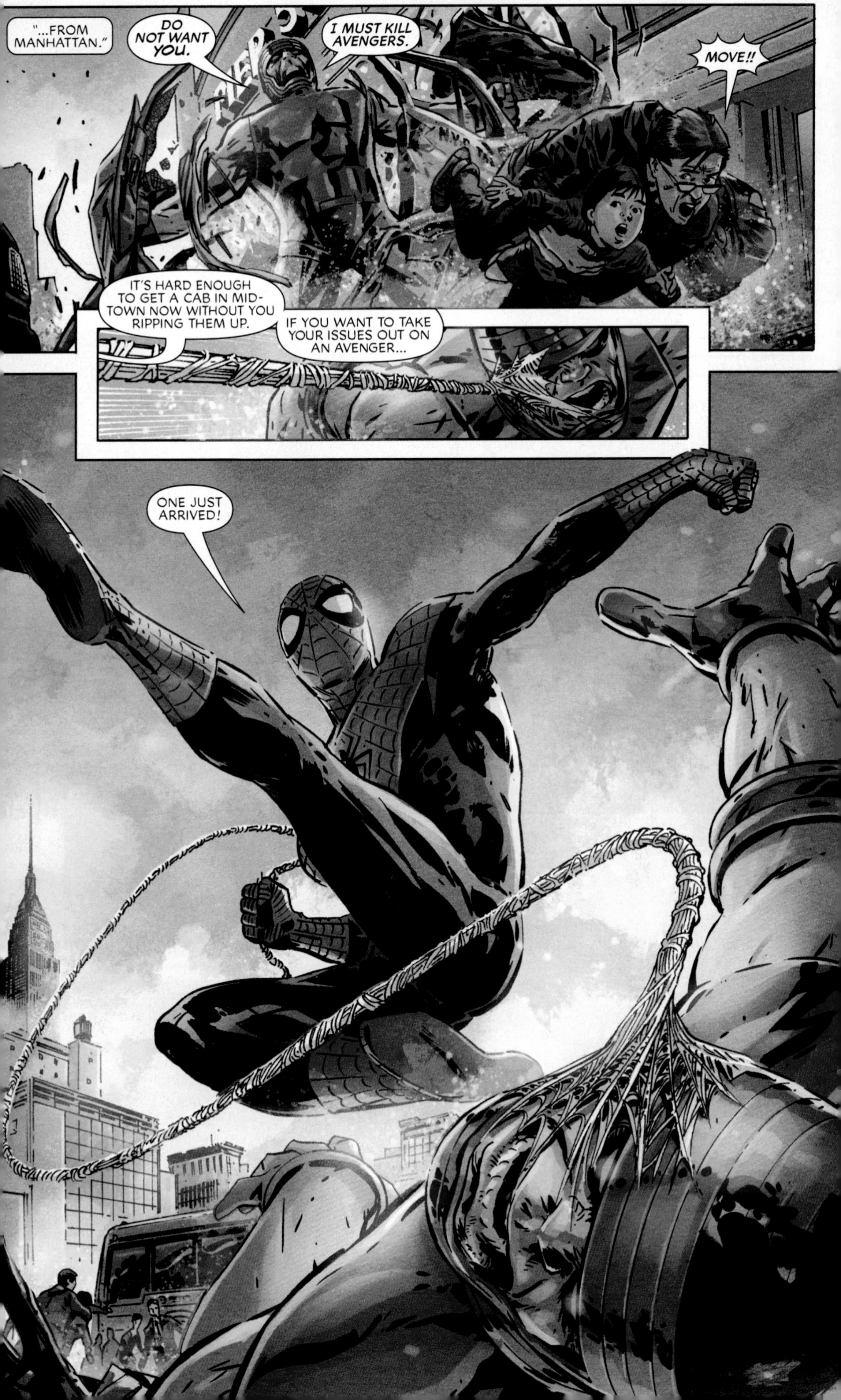
"...FROM MANHATTAN."
DO NOT WANT YOU.
I MUST KILL AVENGERS.
MOVE!!
IT'S HARD ENOUGH TO GET A CAB IN MID-TOWN NOW WITHOUT YOU RIPPING THEM UP.
IF YOU WANT TO TAKE YOUR ISSUES OUT ON AN AVENGER...
ONE JUST ARRIVED!

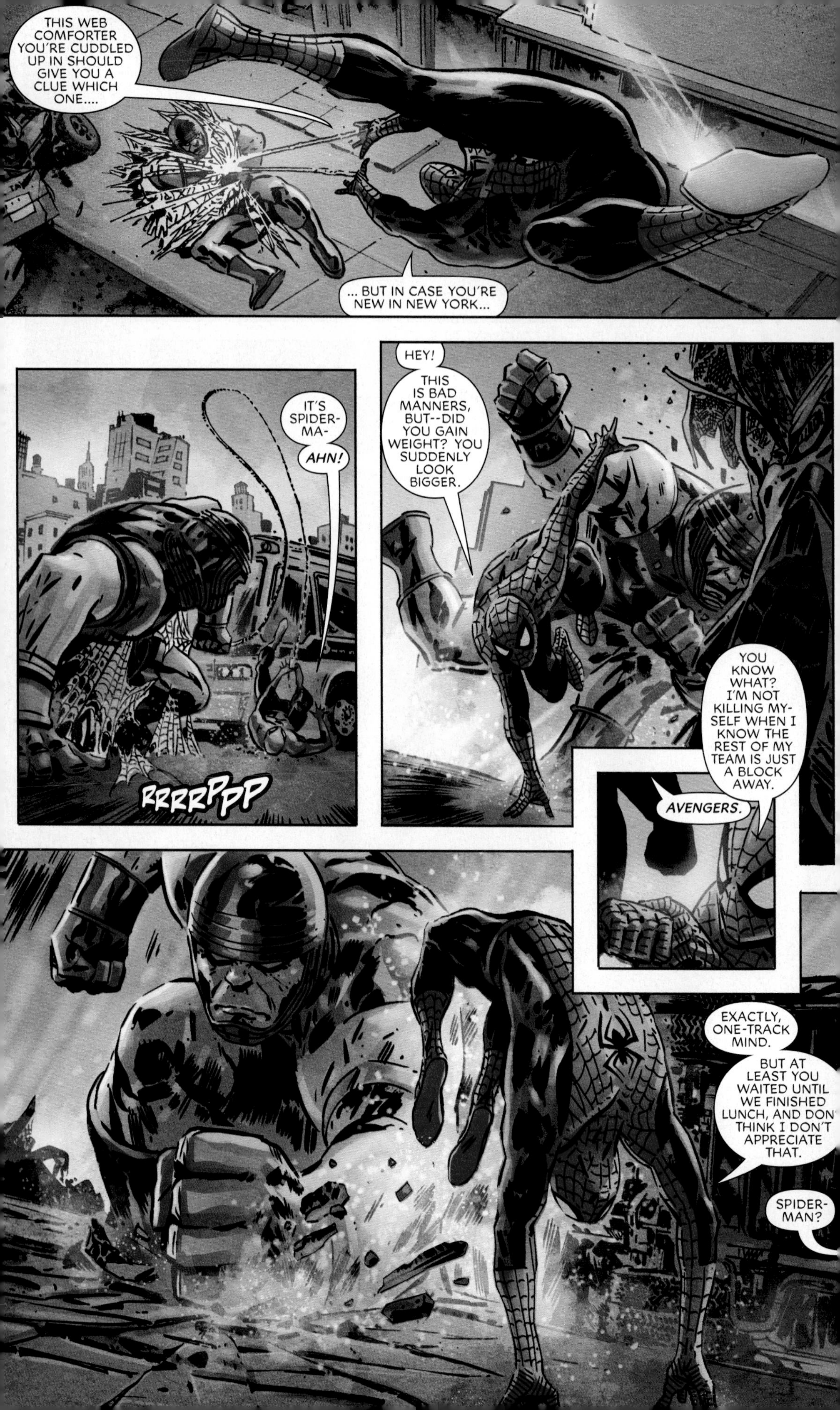

THIS WEB COMFORTER YOU'RE CUDDLED UP IN SHOULD GIVE YOU A CLUE WHICH ONE....
... BUT IN CASE YOU'RE NEW IN NEW YORK...
IT'S SPIDER-MA-
AHN!
RRRRPPP
HEY!
THIS IS BAD MANNERS, BUT--DID YOU GAIN WEIGHT? YOU SUDDENLY LOOK BIGGER.
YOU KNOW WHAT? I'M NOT KILLING MY-SELF WHEN I KNOW THE REST OF MY TEAM IS JUST A BLOCK AWAY.
AVENGERS.
EXACTLY, ONE-TRACK MIND.
BUT AT LEAST YOU WAITED UNTIL WE FINISHED LUNCH, AND DON THINK I DON'T APPRECIATE THAT.
SPIDER-MAN?

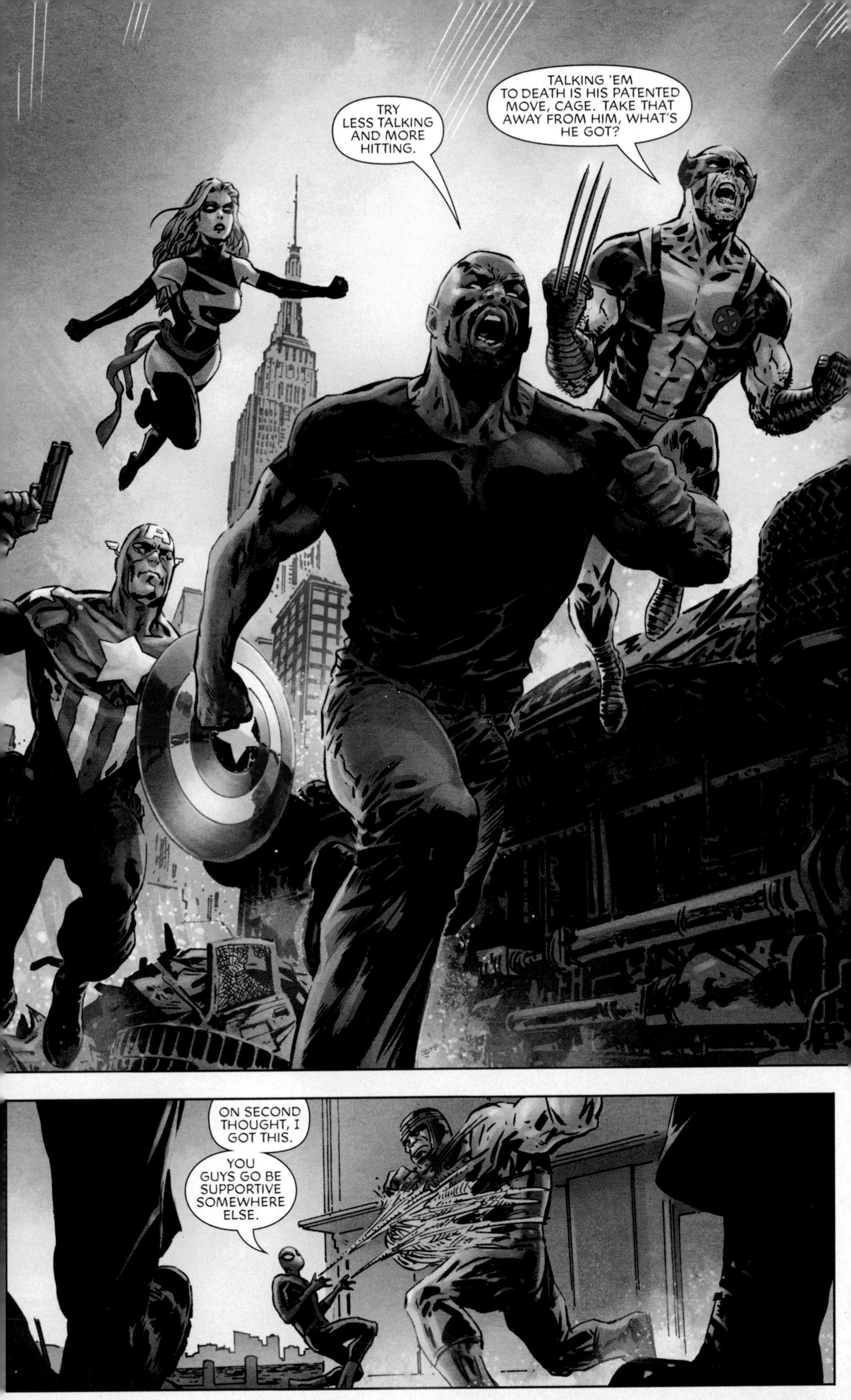
TRY LESS TALKING AND MORE HITTING.
TALKING 'EM TO DEATH IS HIS PATENTED MOVE, CAGE. TAKE THAT AWAY FROM HIM, WHAT'S HE GOT?
ON SECOND THOUGHT, I GOT THIS.
YOU GUYS GO BE SUPPORTIVE SOMEWHERE ELSE.

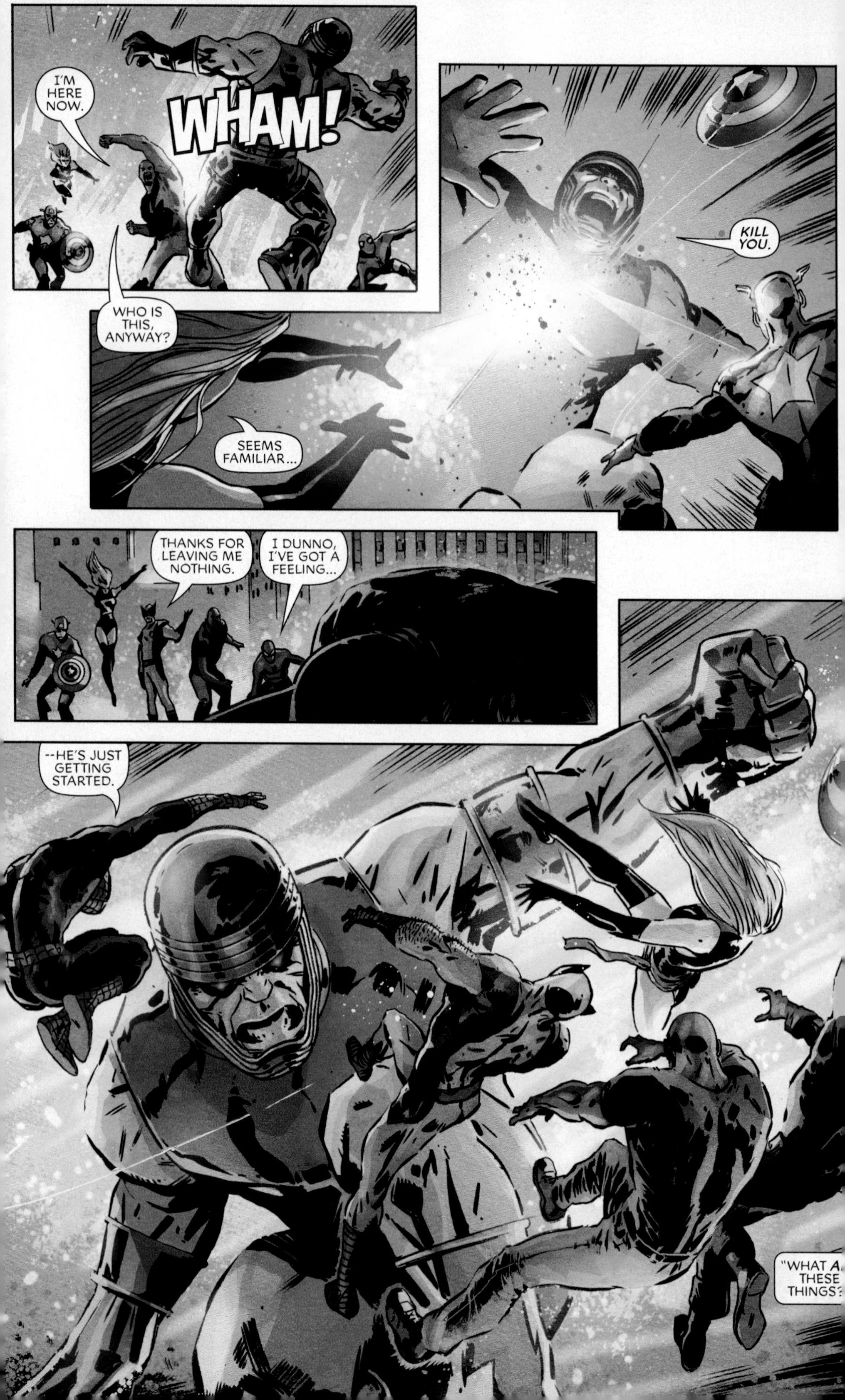
I'M HERE NOW.
WHAM!
WHO IS THIS, ANYWAY?
KILL YOU.
SEEMS FAMILIAR...
THANKS FOR LEAVING ME NOTHING.
I DUNNO, I'VE GOT A FEELING...
--HE'S JUST GETTING STARTED.
"WHAT A THESE THINGS?

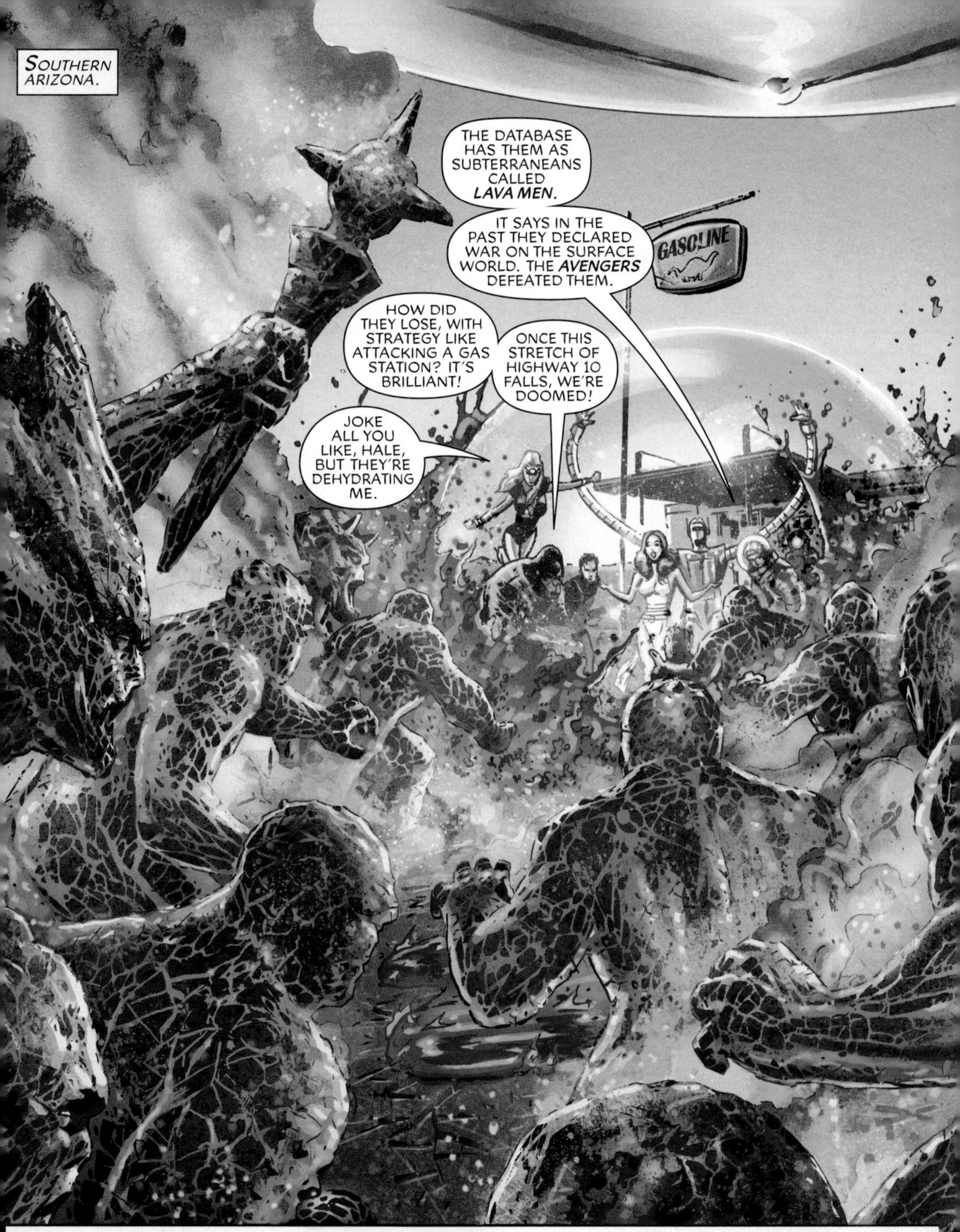
SOUTHERN ARIZONA.
THE DATABASE HAS THEM AS SUBTERRANEANS CALLED LAVA MEN.
IT SAYS IN THE PAST THEY DECLARED WAR ON THE SURFACE WORLD. THE AVENGERS DEFEATED THEM.
GASOLINE
HOW DID THEY LOSE, WITH STRATEGY LIKE ATTACKING A GAS STATION? IT'S BRILLIANT!
ONCE THIS STRETCH OF HIGHWAY 10 FALLS, WE'RE DOOMED!
JOKE ALL YOU LIKE, HALE, BUT THEY'RE DEHYDRATING ME.

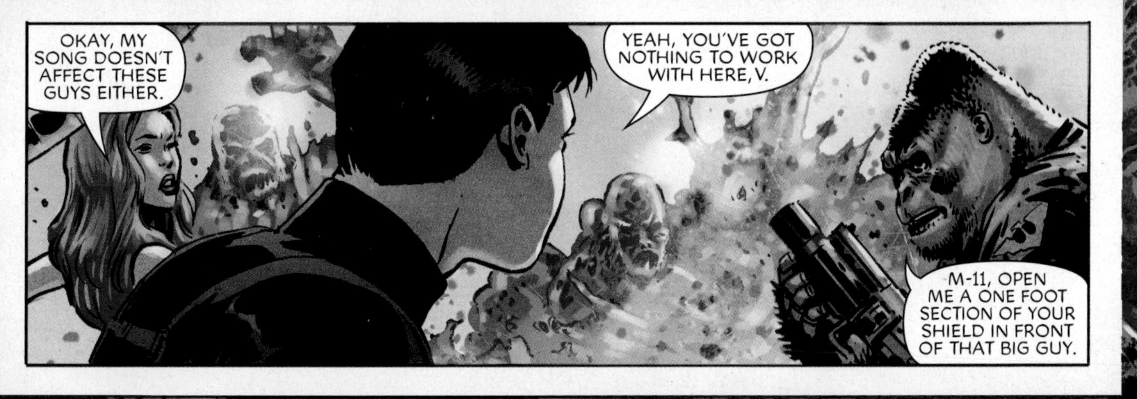
OKAY, MY SONG DOESN'T AFFECT THESE GUYS EITHER.
YEAH, YOU'VE GOT NOTHING TO WORK WITH HERE, V.
M-11, OPEN ME A ONE FOOT SECTION OF YOUR SHIELD IN FRONT OF THAT BIG GUY.

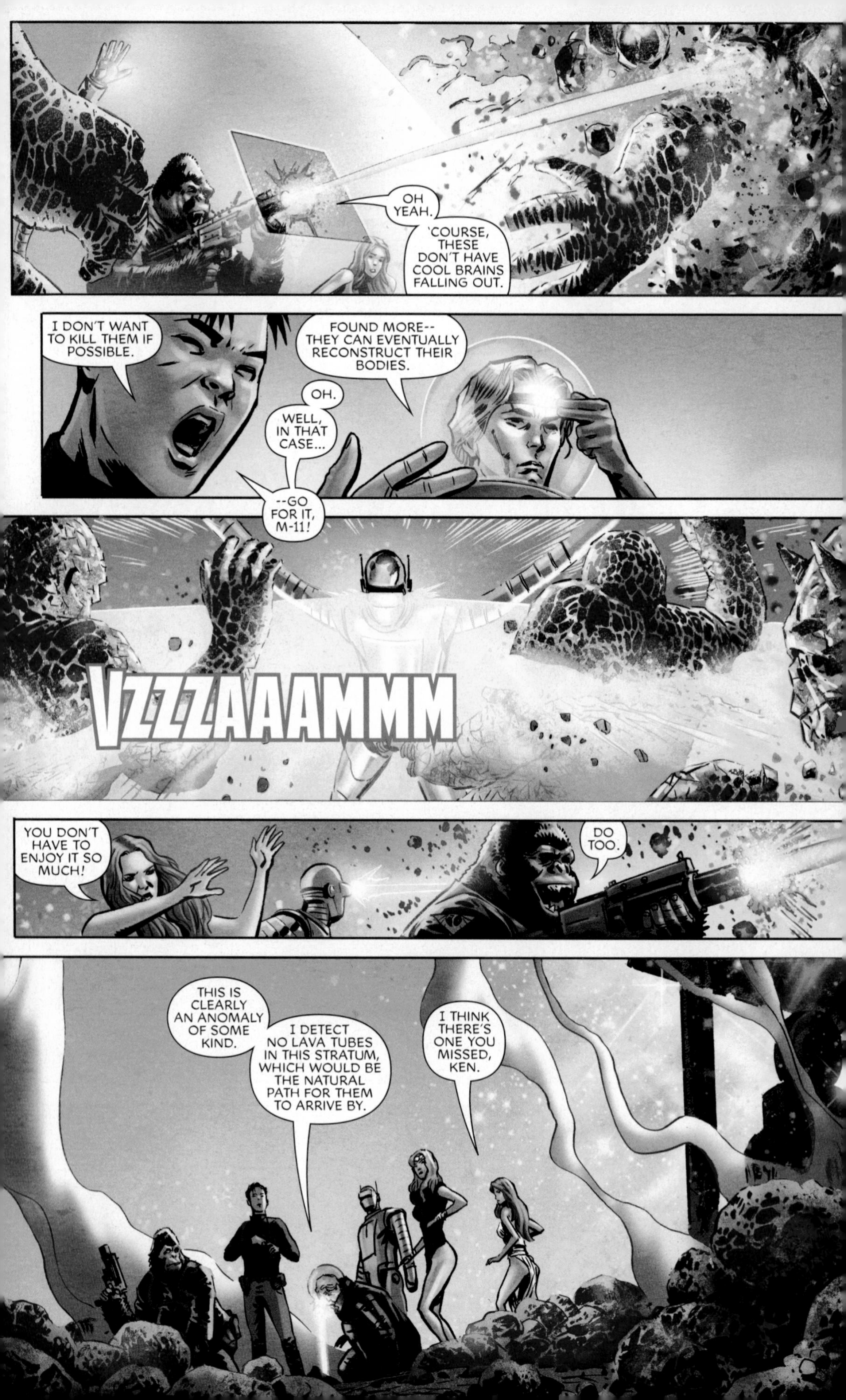
OH YEAH.
'COURSE, THESE DON'T HAVE COOL BRAINS FALLING OUT.
I DON'T WANT TO KILL THEM IF POSSIBLE.
FOUND MORE-- THEY CAN EVENTUALLY RECONSTRUCT THEIR BODIES.
OH.
WELL, IN THAT CASE...
--GO FOR IT, M-11!
VZZZAAAMMMM
YOU DON'T HAVE TO ENJOY IT SO MUCH!
DO TOO.
THIS IS CLEARLY AN ANOMALY OF SOME KIND.
I DETECT NO LAVA TUBES IN THIS STRATUM, WHICH WOULD BE THE NATURAL PATH FOR THEM TO ARRIVE BY.
I THINK THERE'S ONE YOU MISSED, KEN.

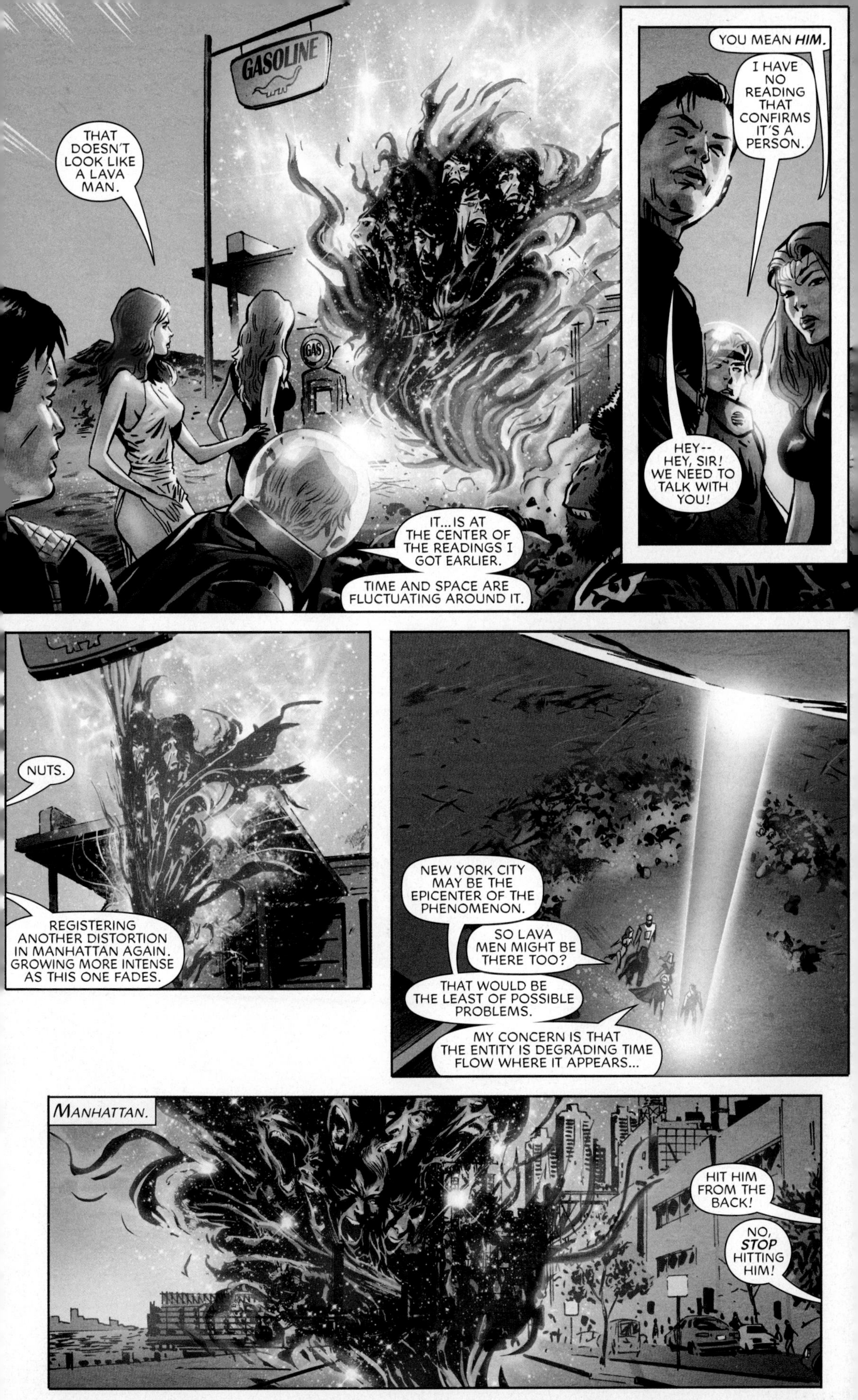
GASOLINE
THAT DOESN'T LOOK LIKE A LAVA MAN.
GAS
YOU MEAN *HIM*.
I HAVE NO READING THAT CONFIRMS IT'S A PERSON.
HEY-- HEY, SIR! WE NEED TO TALK WITH YOU!
IT...IS AT THE CENTER OF THE READINGS I GOT EARLIER.
TIME AND SPACE ARE FLUCTUATING AROUND IT.
NUTS.
REGISTERING ANOTHER DISTORTION IN MANHATTAN AGAIN. GROWING MORE INTENSE AS THIS ONE FADES.
NEW YORK CITY MAY BE THE EPICENTER OF THE PHENOMENON.
SO LAVA MEN MIGHT BE THERE TOO?
THAT WOULD BE THE LEAST OF POSSIBLE PROBLEMS.
MY CONCERN IS THAT THE ENTITY IS DEGRADING TIME FLOW WHERE IT APPEARS...
MANHATTAN.
HIT HIM FROM THE BACK!
NO, *STOP* HITTING HIM!

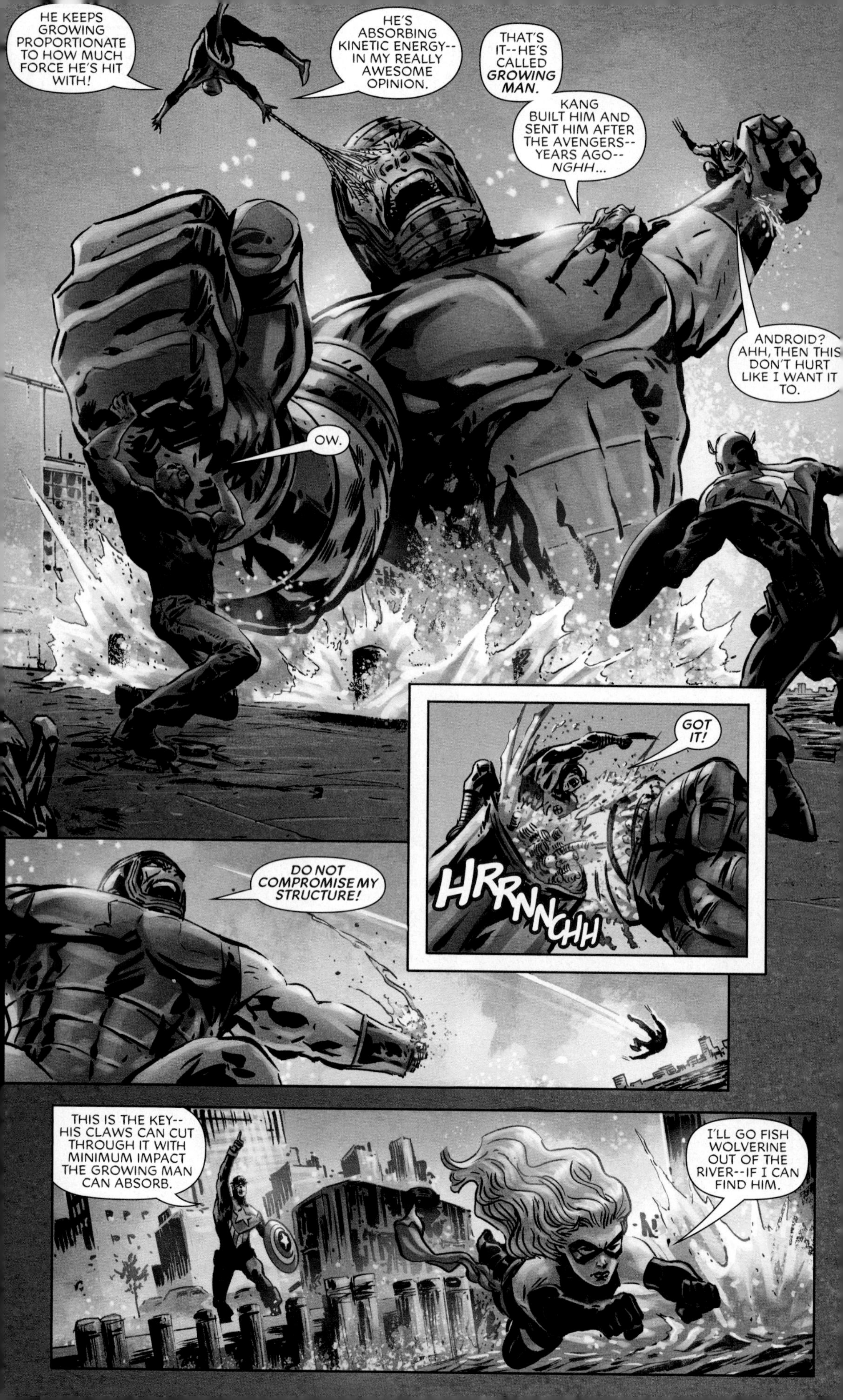
HE KEEPS GROWING PROPORTIONATE TO HOW MUCH FORCE HE'S HIT WITH!
HE'S ABSORBING KINETIC ENERGY-- IN MY REALLY AWESOME OPINION.
THAT'S IT--HE'S CALLED *GROWING MAN.*
KANG BUILT HIM AND SENT HIM AFTER THE AVENGERS-- YEARS AGO-- *NGHH...*
ANDROID? AHH, THEN THIS DON'T HURT LIKE I WANT IT TO.
OW.
GOT IT!
HRRNNNGHH
DO NOT COMPROMISE MY STRUCTURE!
THIS IS THE KEY-- HIS CLAWS CAN CUT THROUGH IT WITH MINIMUM IMPACT THE GROWING MAN CAN ABSORB.
I'LL GO FISH WOLVERINE OUT OF THE RIVER--IF I CAN FIND HIM.

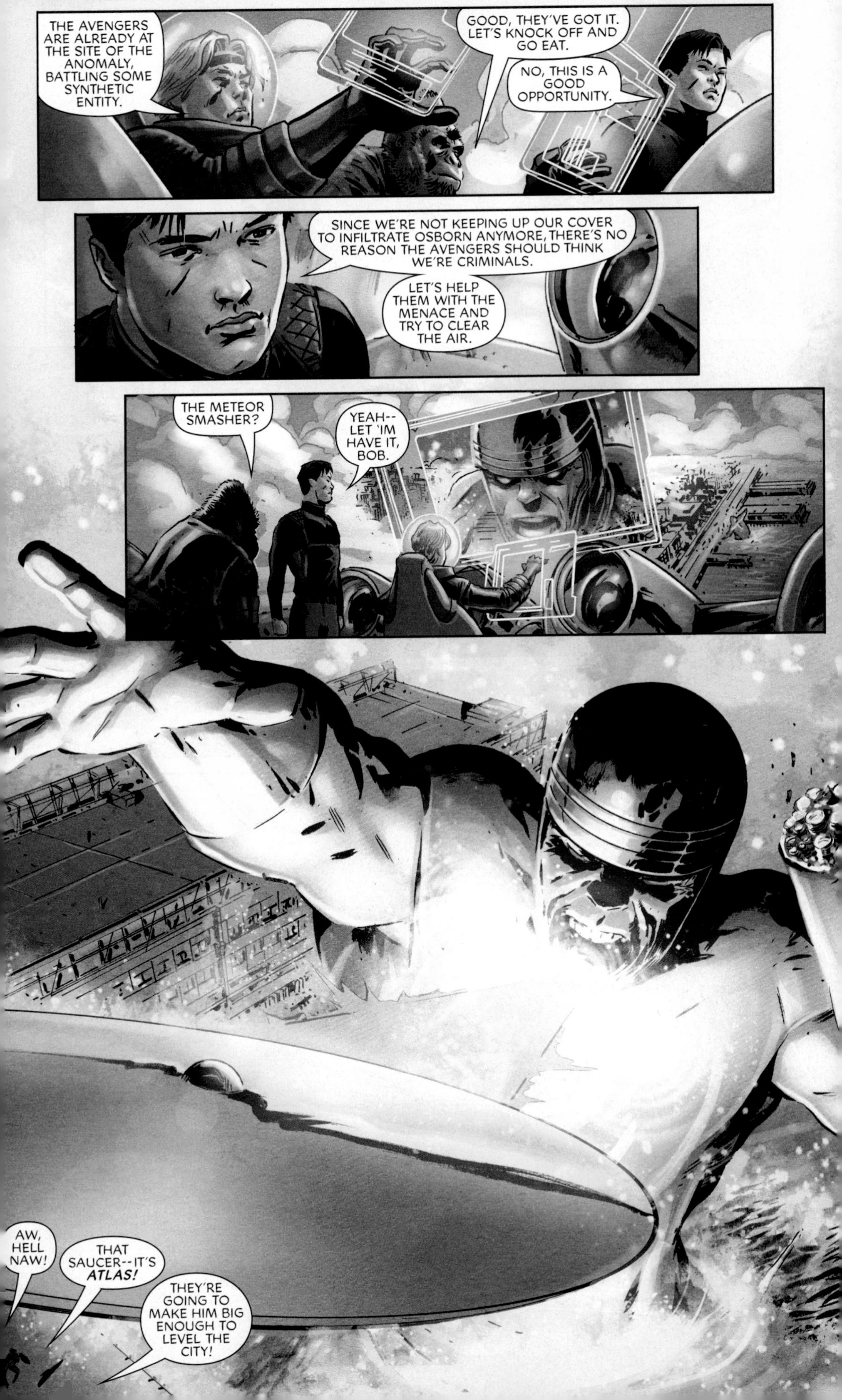

THE AVENGERS ARE ALREADY AT THE SITE OF THE ANOMALY, BATTLING SOME SYNTHETIC ENTITY.
GOOD, THEY'VE GOT IT. LET'S KNOCK OFF AND GO EAT.
NO, THIS IS A GOOD OPPORTUNITY.
SINCE WE'RE NOT KEEPING UP OUR COVER TO INFILTRATE OSBORN ANYMORE, THERE'S NO REASON THE AVENGERS SHOULD THINK WE'RE CRIMINALS.
LET'S HELP THEM WITH THE MENACE AND TRY TO CLEAR THE AIR.
THE METEOR SMASHER?
YEAH-- LET 'IM HAVE IT, BOB.
AW, HELL NAW!
THAT SAUCER--IT'S *ATLAS!*
THEY'RE GOING TO MAKE HIM BIG ENOUGH TO LEVEL THE CITY!

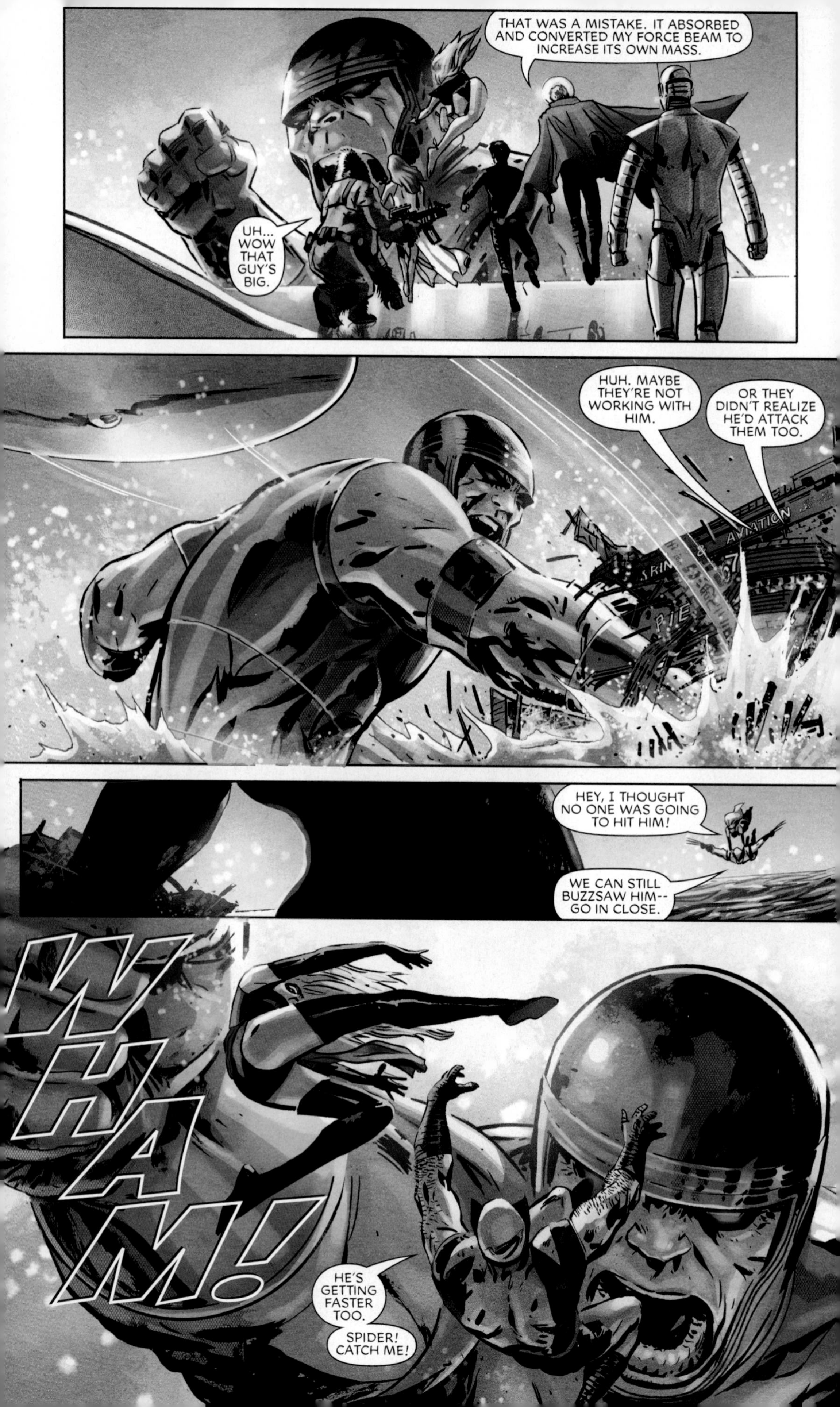
THAT WAS A MISTAKE. IT ABSORBED AND CONVERTED MY FORCE BEAM TO INCREASE ITS OWN MASS.
UH... WOW THAT GUY'S BIG.
HUH. MAYBE THEY'RE NOT WORKING WITH HIM.
OR THEY DIDN'T REALIZE HE'D ATTACK THEM TOO.
AVIATION
HEY, I THOUGHT NO ONE WAS GOING TO HIT HIM!
WE CAN STILL BUZZSAW HIM-- GO IN CLOSE.
WHAM!
HE'S GETTING FASTER TOO.
SPIDER! CATCH ME!

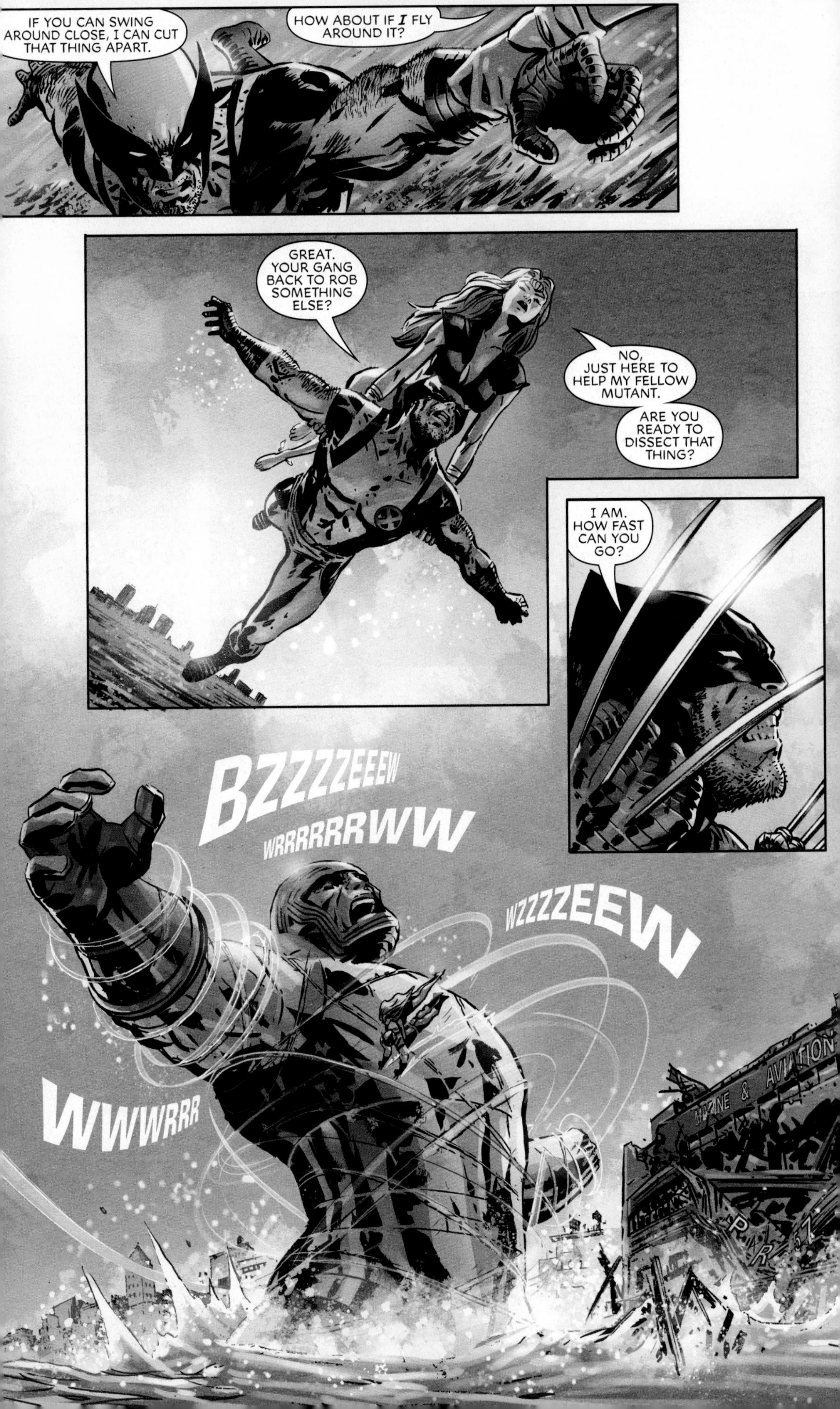

IF YOU CAN SWING AROUND CLOSE, I CAN CUT THAT THING APART.
HOW ABOUT IF I FLY AROUND IT?
GREAT. YOUR GANG BACK TO ROB SOMETHING ELSE?
NO, JUST HERE TO HELP MY FELLOW MUTANT.
ARE YOU READY TO DISSECT THAT THING?
I AM. HOW FAST CAN YOU GO?
BZZZZEEEW
WRRRRRRWW
WZZZZEEW
WWWRRR
MARINE & AVIATION

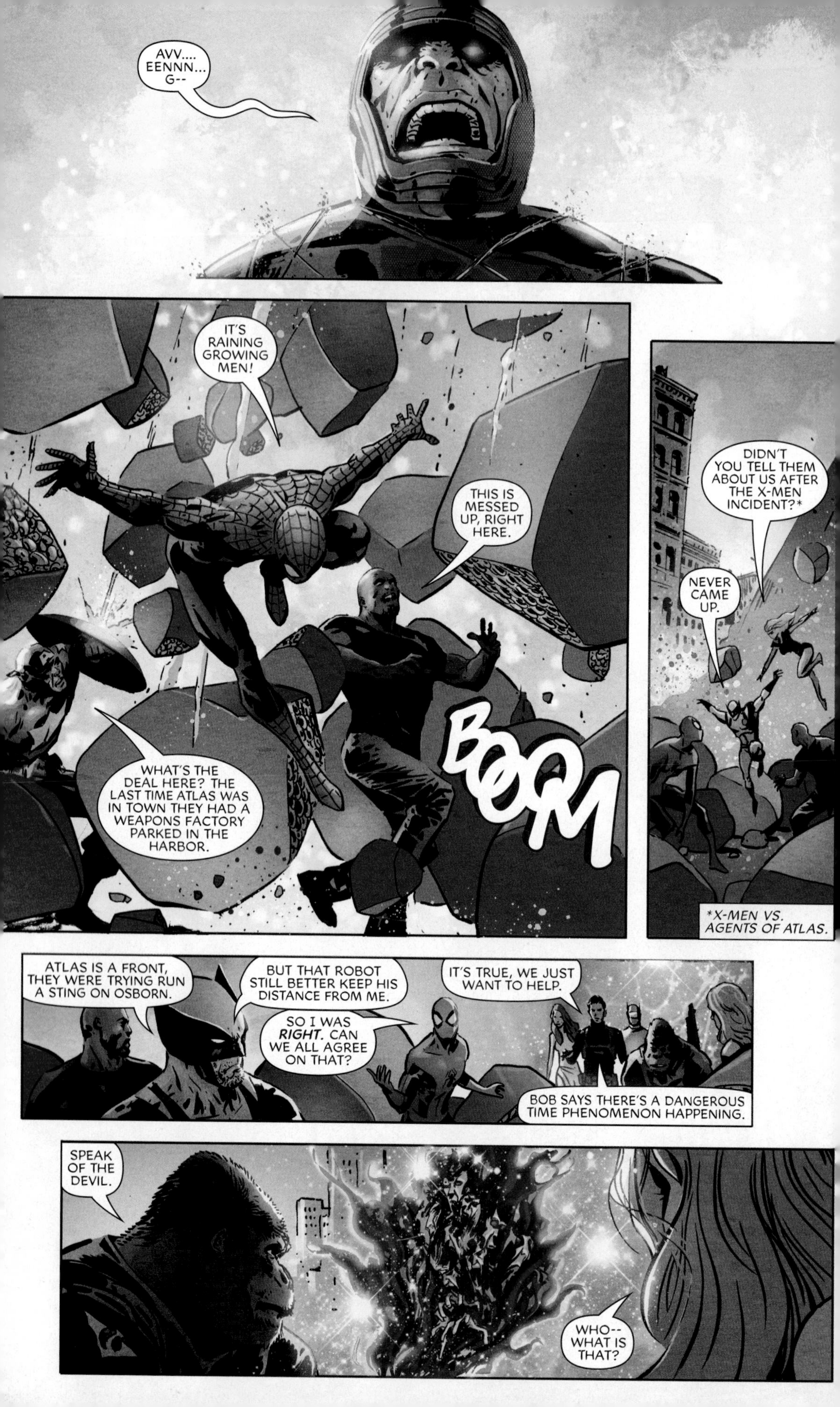
AVV.... EENNN... G--
IT'S RAINING GROWING MEN!
THIS IS MESSED UP, RIGHT HERE.
WHAT'S THE DEAL HERE? THE LAST TIME ATLAS WAS IN TOWN THEY HAD A WEAPONS FACTORY PARKED IN THE HARBOR.
BOOM
DIDN'T YOU TELL THEM ABOUT US AFTER THE X-MEN INCIDENT?*
NEVER CAME UP.
*X-MEN VS. AGENTS OF ATLAS.
ATLAS IS A FRONT, THEY WERE TRYING RUN A STING ON OSBORN.
BUT THAT ROBOT STILL BETTER KEEP HIS DISTANCE FROM ME.
SO I WAS RIGHT. CAN WE ALL AGREE ON THAT?
IT'S TRUE, WE JUST WANT TO HELP.
BOB SAYS THERE'S A DANGEROUS TIME PHENOMENON HAPPENING.
SPEAK OF THE DEVIL.
WHO-- WHAT IS THAT?

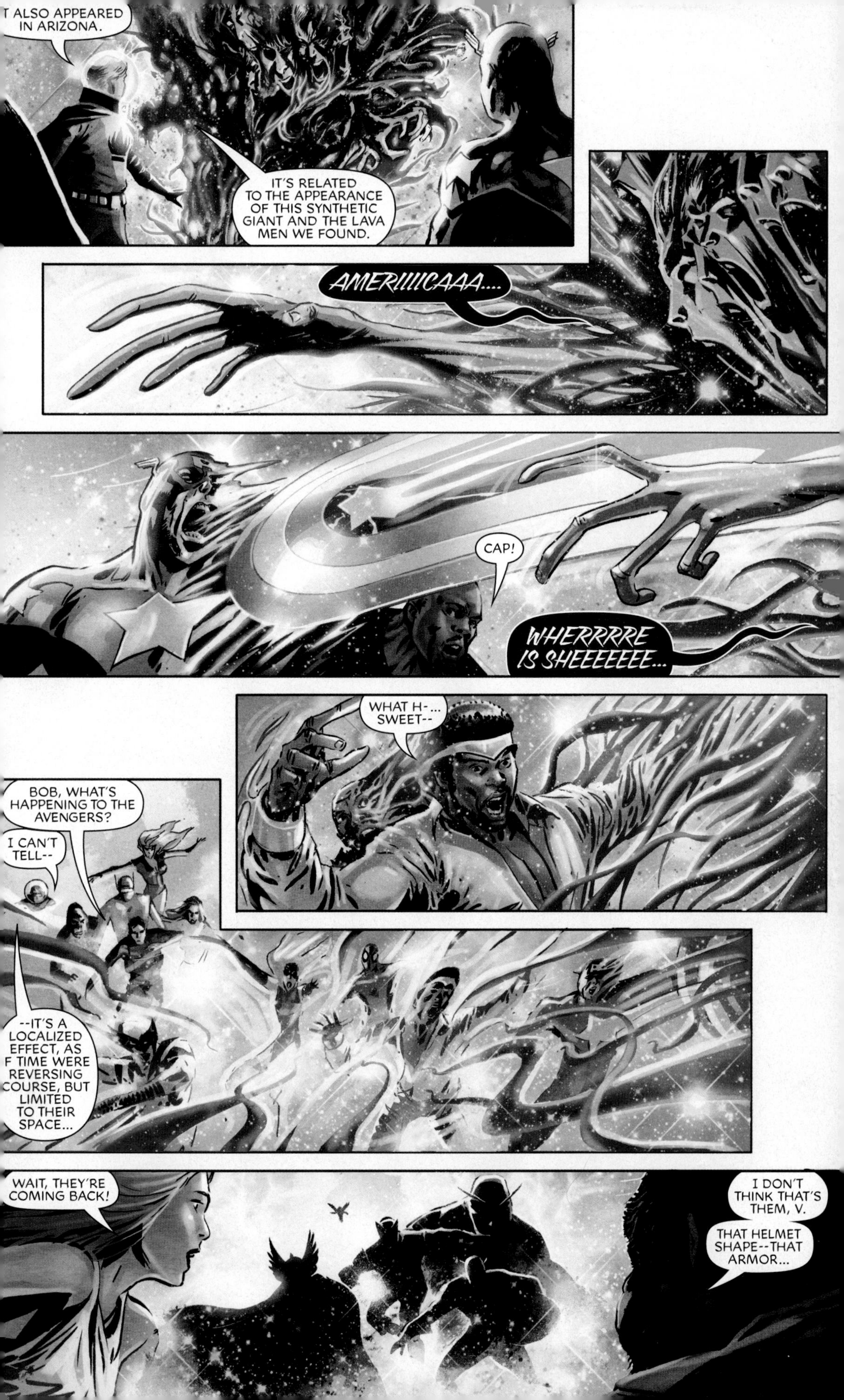
T ALSO APPEARED IN ARIZONA.
IT'S RELATED TO THE APPEARANCE OF THIS SYNTHETIC GIANT AND THE LAVA MEN WE FOUND.
AMERIIIICAAA....
CAP!
WHERRRRE IS SHEEEEEEE...
WHAT H-... SWEET--
BOB, WHAT'S HAPPENING TO THE AVENGERS?
I CAN'T TELL--
--IT'S A LOCALIZED EFFECT, AS F TIME WERE REVERSING COURSE, BUT LIMITED TO THEIR SPACE...
WAIT, THEY'RE COMING BACK!
I DON'T THINK THAT'S THEM, V.
THAT HELMET SHAPE--THAT ARMOR...

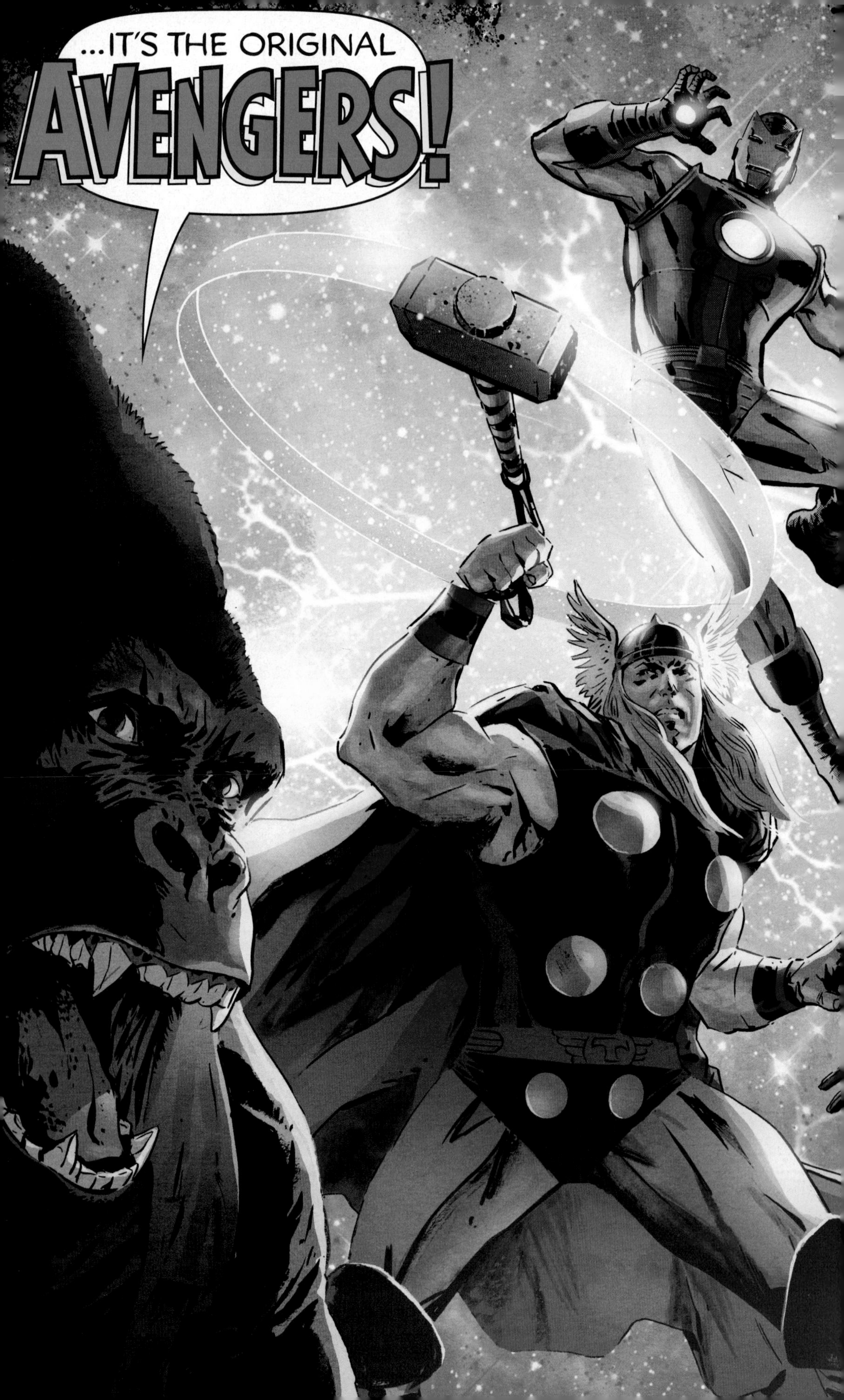
...IT'S THE ORIGINAL AVENGERS!

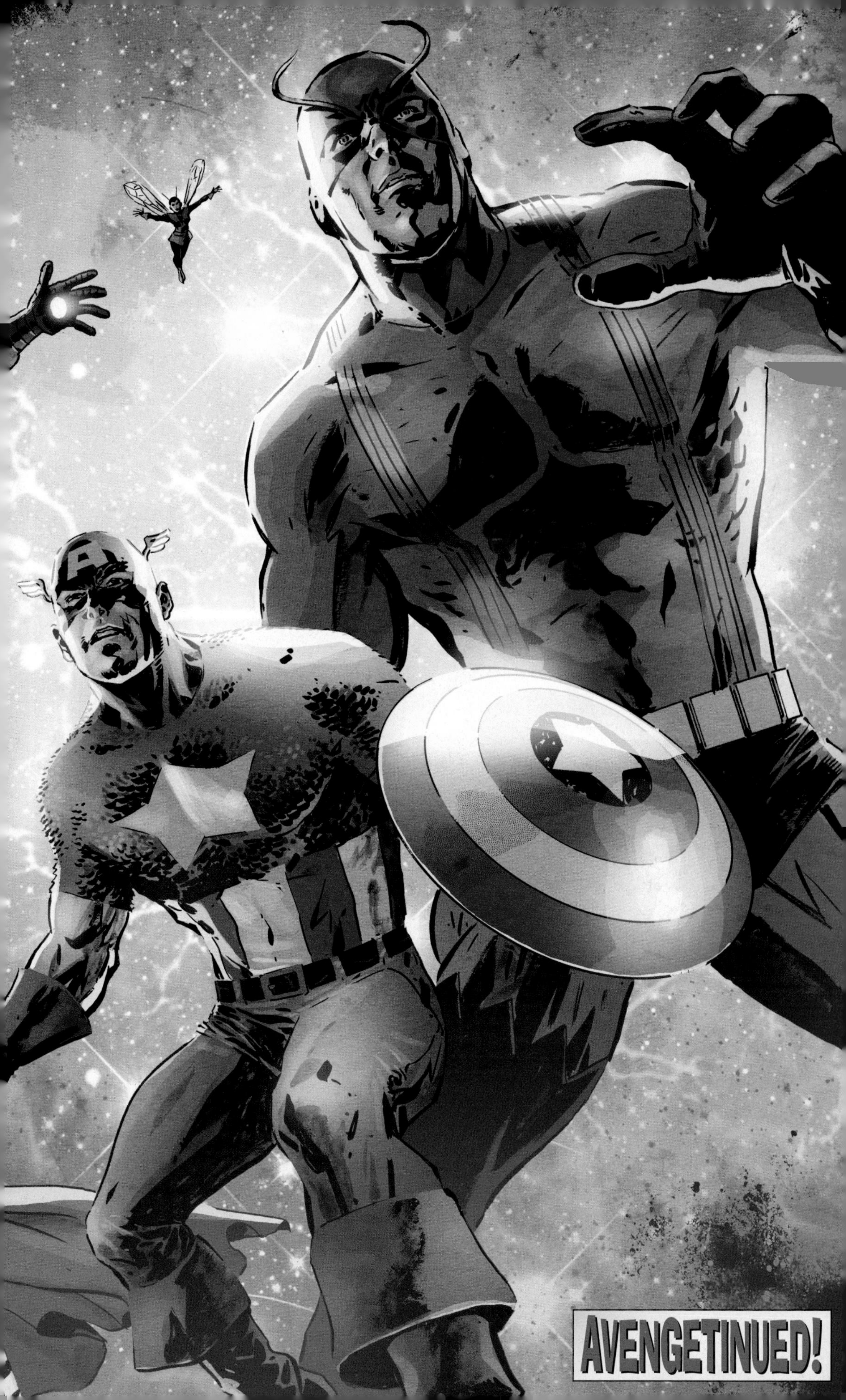
AVENGETINUED!

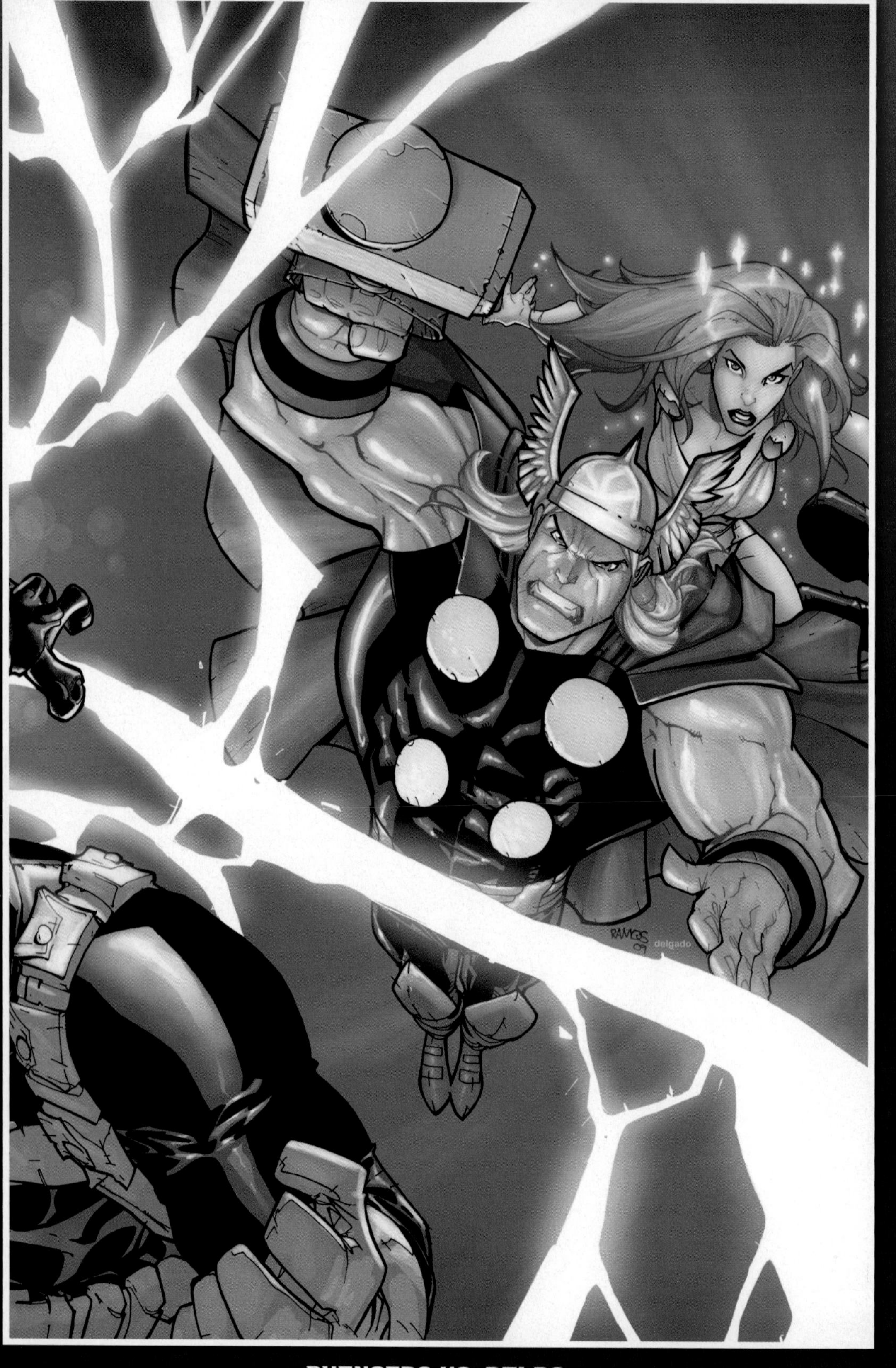
RAMOS
09
delgado

AVENGERS VS. ATLAS

#2

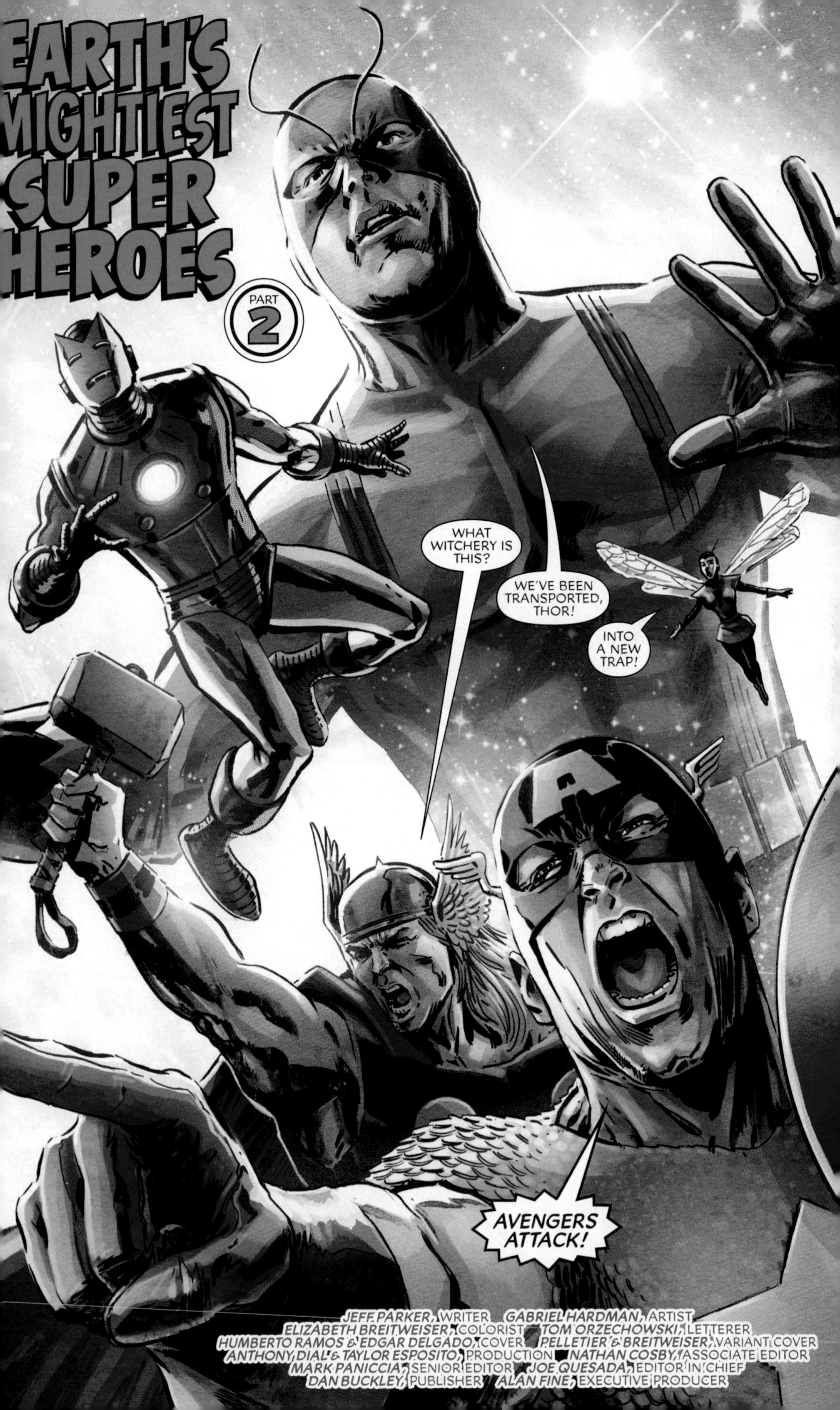

EARTH'S MIGHTIEST SUPER HEROES
PART 2
WHAT WITCHERY IS THIS?
WE'VE BEEN TRANSPORTED, THOR!
INTO A NEW TRAP!
AVENGERS ATTACK!
JEFF PARKER, WRITER GABRIEL HARDMAN, ARTIST
ELIZABETH BREITWEISER, COLORIST TOM ORZECHOWSKI, LETTERER
HUMBERTO RAMOS & EDGAR DELGADO, COVER PELLETIER & BREITWEISER, VARIANT COVER
ANTHONY DIAL & TAYLOR ESPOSITO, PRODUCTION NATHAN COSBY, ASSOCIATE EDITOR
MARK PANICCIA, SENIOR EDITOR JOE QUESADA, EDITOR IN CHIEF
DAN BUCKLEY, PUBLISHER ALAN FINE, EXECUTIVE PRODUCER

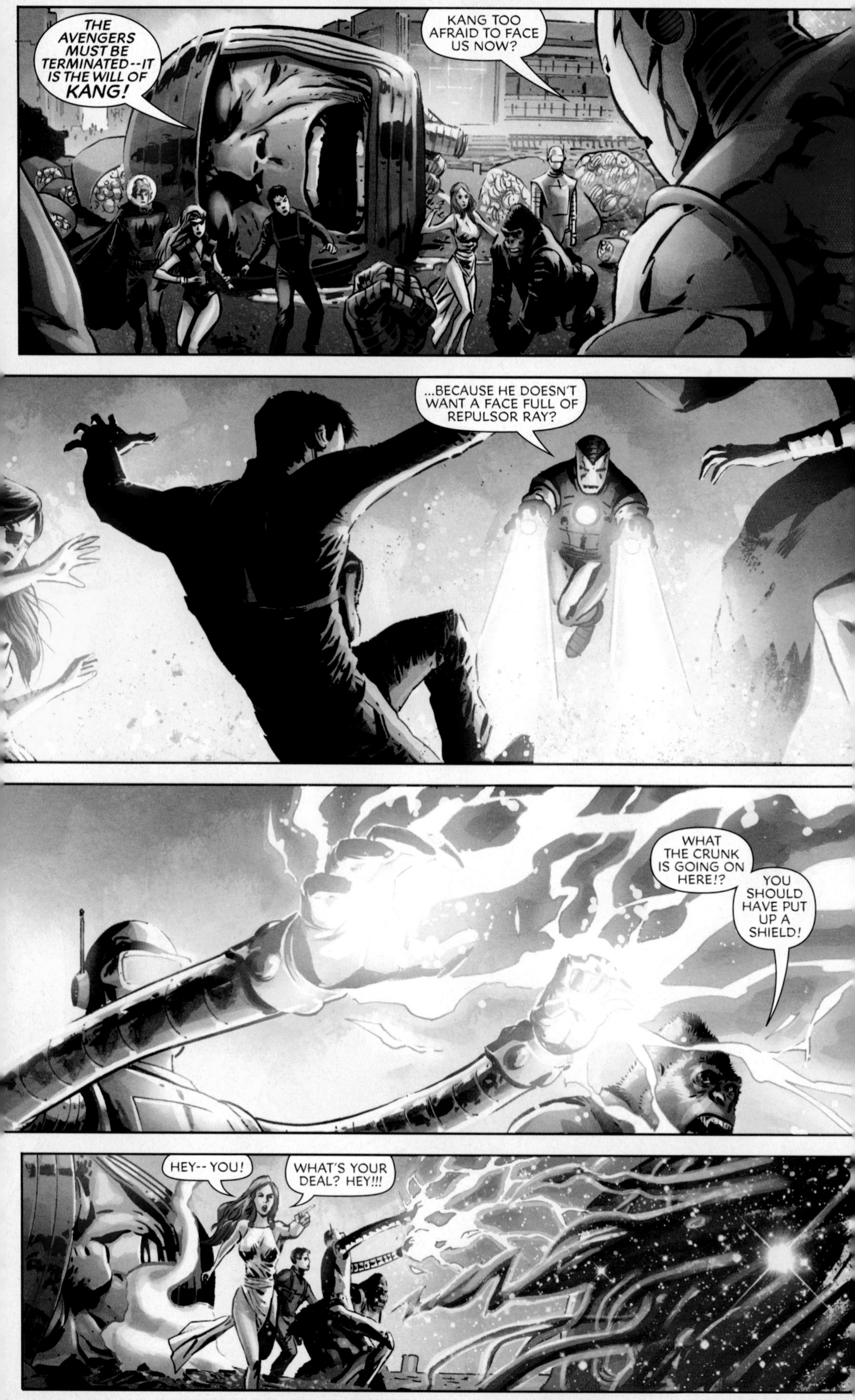
THE AVENGERS MUST BE TERMINATED--IT IS THE WILL OF KANG!
KANG TOO AFRAID TO FACE US NOW?
...BECAUSE HE DOESN'T WANT A FACE FULL OF REPULSOR RAY?
WHAT THE CRUNK IS GOING ON HERE!?
YOU SHOULD HAVE PUT UP A SHIELD!
HEY-- YOU!
WHAT'S YOUR DEAL? HEY!!!

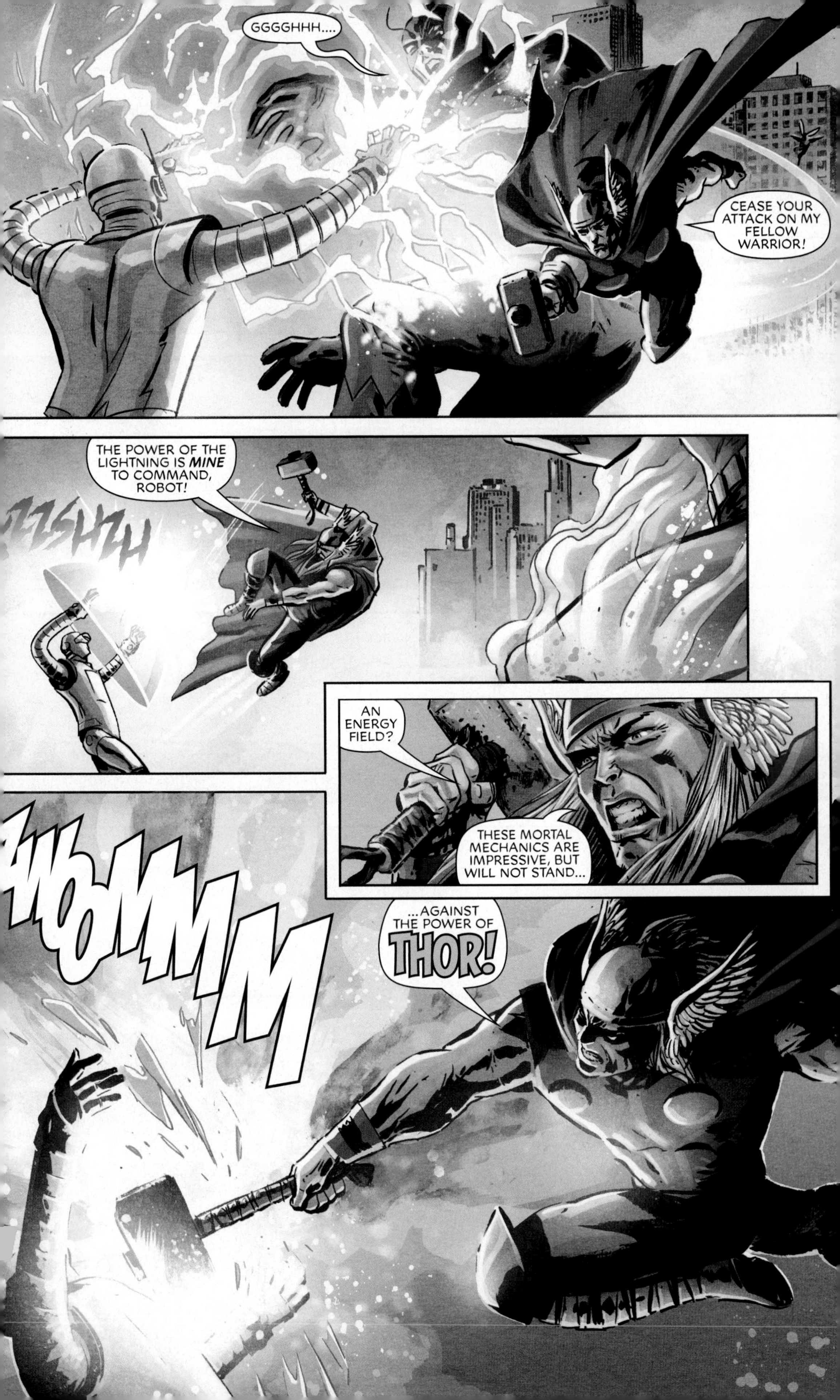
GGGGHHH....
CEASE YOUR ATTACK ON MY FELLOW WARRIOR!
THE POWER OF THE LIGHTNING IS *MINE* TO COMMAND, ROBOT!
ZZZSHZH
AN ENERGY FIELD?
THESE MORTAL MECHANICS ARE IMPRESSIVE, BUT WILL NOT STAND...
WHOMMM
...AGAINST THE POWER OF THOR!

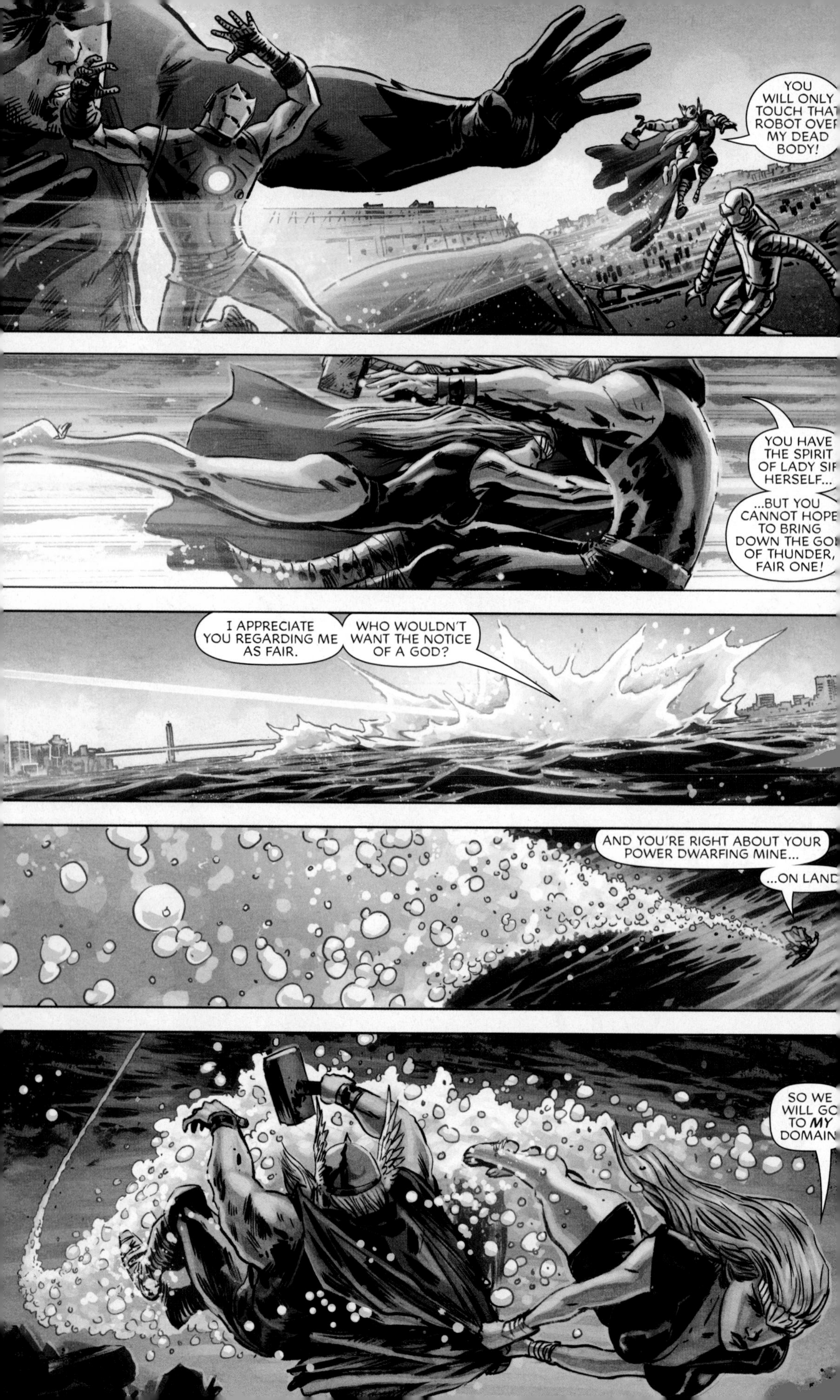

YOU WILL ONLY TOUCH THAT ROBOT OVER MY DEAD BODY!
YOU HAVE THE SPIRIT OF LADY SIF HERSELF...
...BUT YOU CANNOT HOPE TO BRING DOWN THE GOD OF THUNDER, FAIR ONE!
I APPRECIATE YOU REGARDING ME AS FAIR.
WHO WOULDN'T WANT THE NOTICE OF A GOD?
AND YOU'RE RIGHT ABOUT YOUR POWER DWARFING MINE...
...ON LAND
SO WE WILL GO TO MY DOMAIN

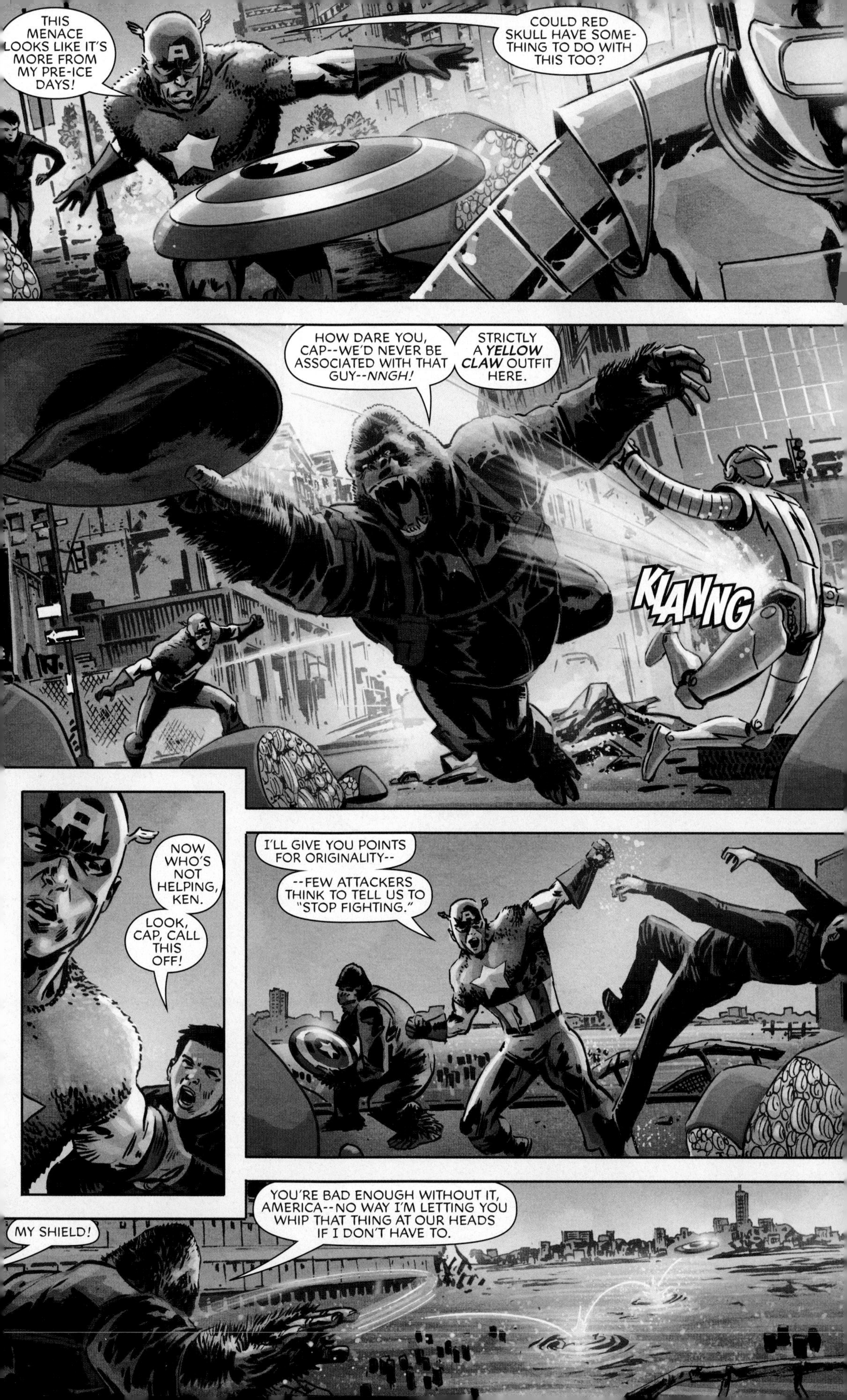
THIS MENACE LOOKS LIKE IT'S MORE FROM MY PRE-ICE DAYS!
COULD RED SKULL HAVE SOMETHING TO DO WITH THIS TOO?
HOW DARE YOU, CAP--WE'D NEVER BE ASSOCIATED WITH THAT GUY--*NNGH!*
STRICTLY A ***YELLOW CLAW*** OUTFIT HERE.
KLANNG
NOW WHO'S NOT HELPING, KEN.
LOOK, CAP, CALL THIS OFF!
I'LL GIVE YOU POINTS FOR ORIGINALITY--
--FEW ATTACKERS THINK TO TELL US TO "STOP FIGHTING."
MY SHIELD!
YOU'RE BAD ENOUGH WITHOUT IT, AMERICA--NO WAY I'M LETTING YOU WHIP THAT THING AT OUR HEADS IF I DON'T HAVE TO.

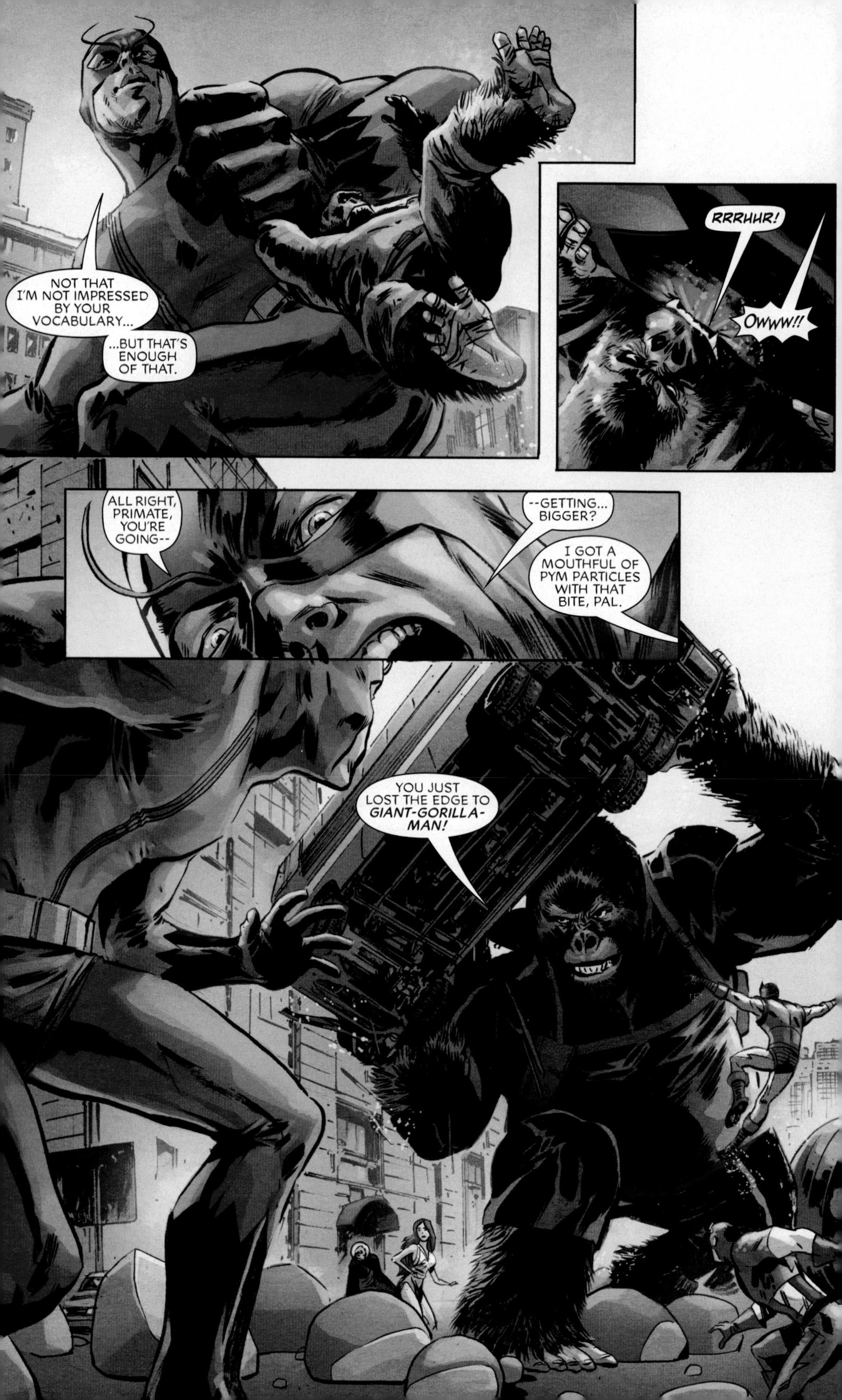
NOT THAT I'M NOT IMPRESSED BY YOUR VOCABULARY...
...BUT THAT'S ENOUGH OF THAT.
RRRHHR!
OWWW!!
ALL RIGHT, PRIMATE, YOU'RE GOING--
--GETTING... BIGGER?
I GOT A MOUTHFUL OF PYM PARTICLES WITH THAT BITE, PAL.
YOU JUST LOST THE EDGE TO *GIANT-GORILLA-MAN!*

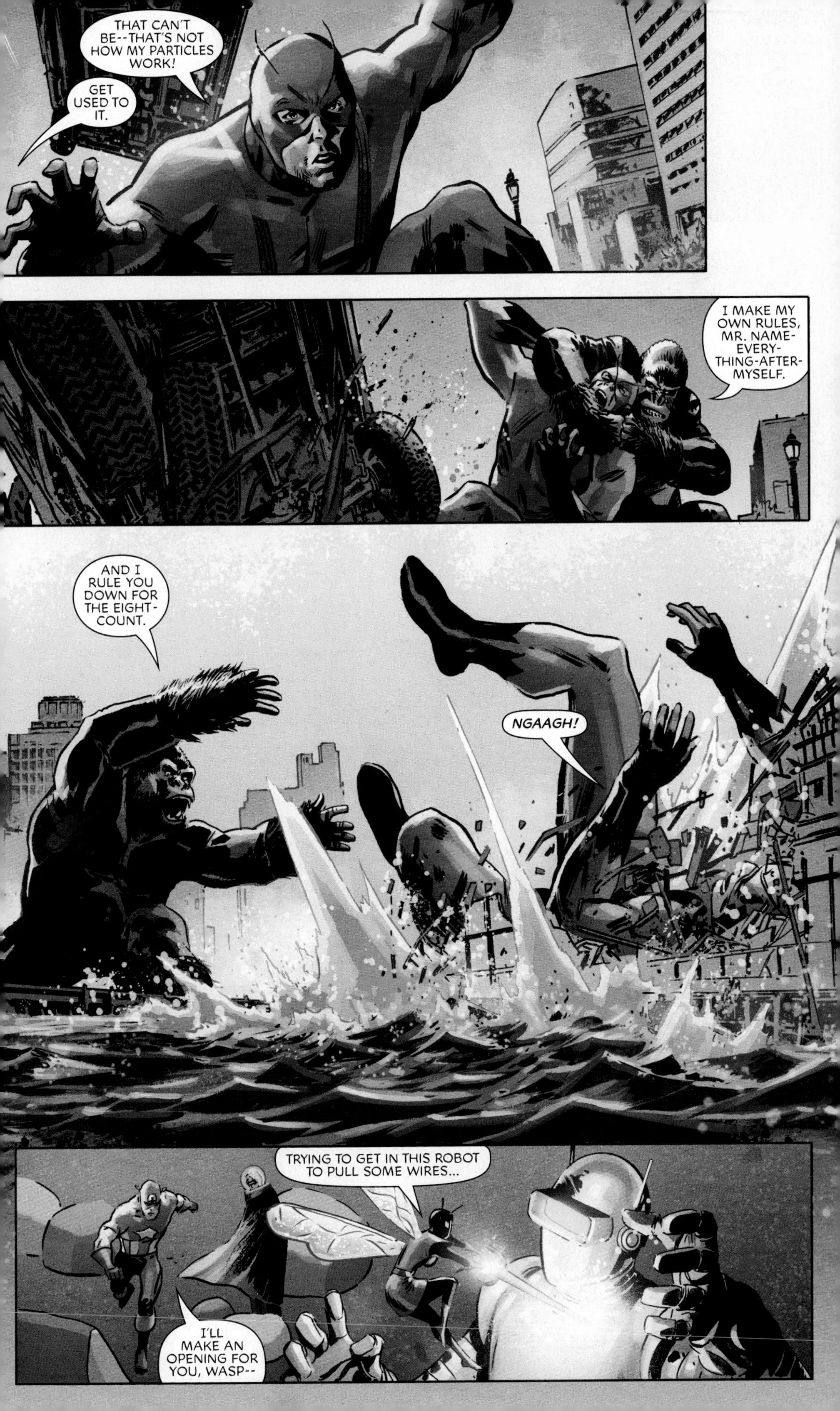
THAT CAN'T BE--THAT'S NOT HOW MY PARTICLES WORK!
GET USED TO IT.
I MAKE MY OWN RULES, MR. NAME-EVERY-THING-AFTER-MYSELF.
AND I RULE YOU DOWN FOR THE EIGHT-COUNT.
NGAAGH!
TRYING TO GET IN THIS ROBOT TO PULL SOME WIRES...
I'LL MAKE AN OPENING FOR YOU, WASP--

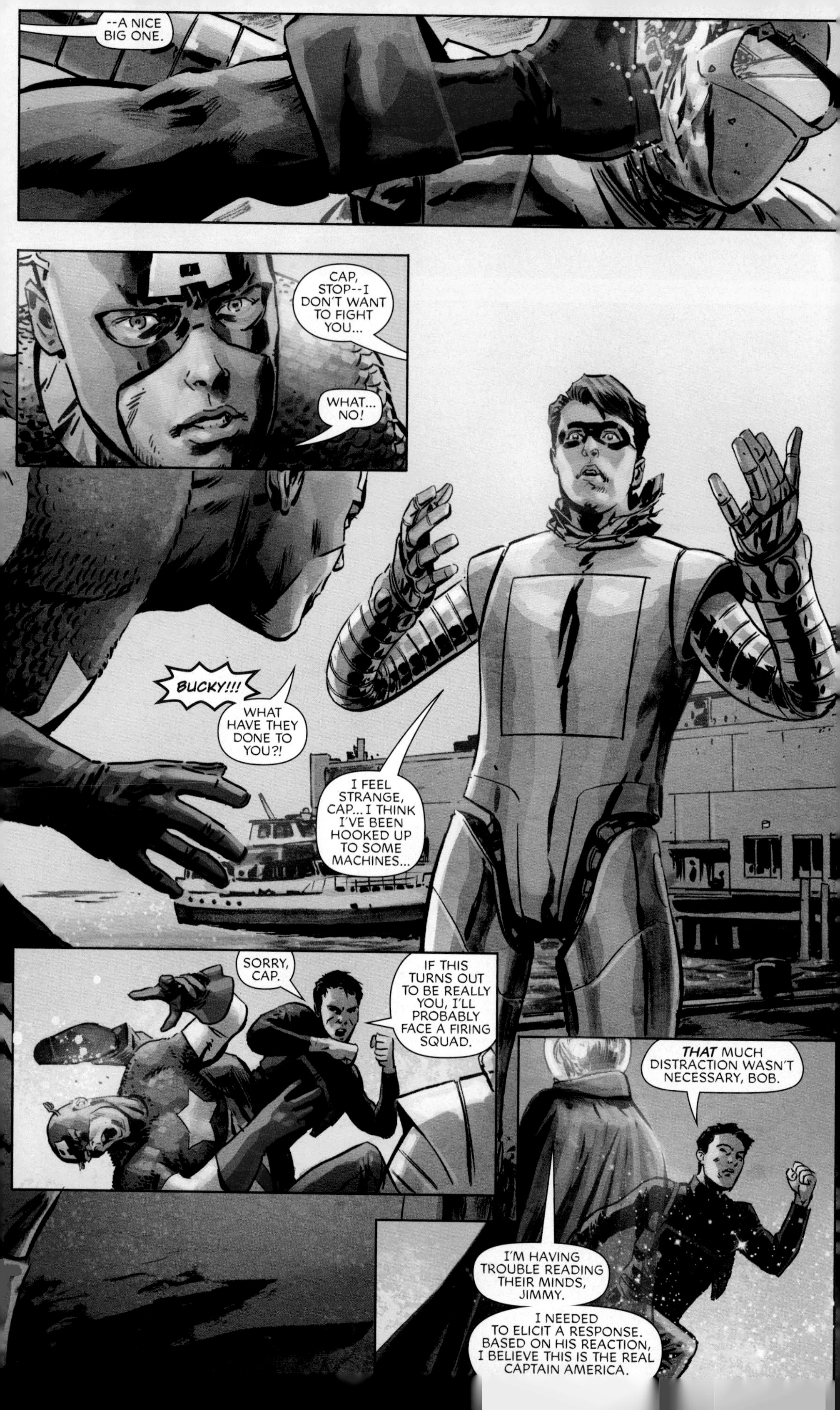
--A NICE BIG ONE.
CAP, STOP--I DON'T WANT TO FIGHT YOU...
WHAT... NO!
BUCKY!!!
WHAT HAVE THEY DONE TO YOU?!
I FEEL STRANGE, CAP... I THINK I'VE BEEN HOOKED UP TO SOME MACHINES...
SORRY, CAP.
IF THIS TURNS OUT TO BE REALLY YOU, I'LL PROBABLY FACE A FIRING SQUAD.
THAT MUCH DISTRACTION WASN'T NECESSARY, BOB.
I'M HAVING TROUBLE READING THEIR MINDS, JIMMY.
I NEEDED TO ELICIT A RESPONSE. BASED ON HIS REACTION, I BELIEVE THIS IS THE REAL CAPTAIN AMERICA.

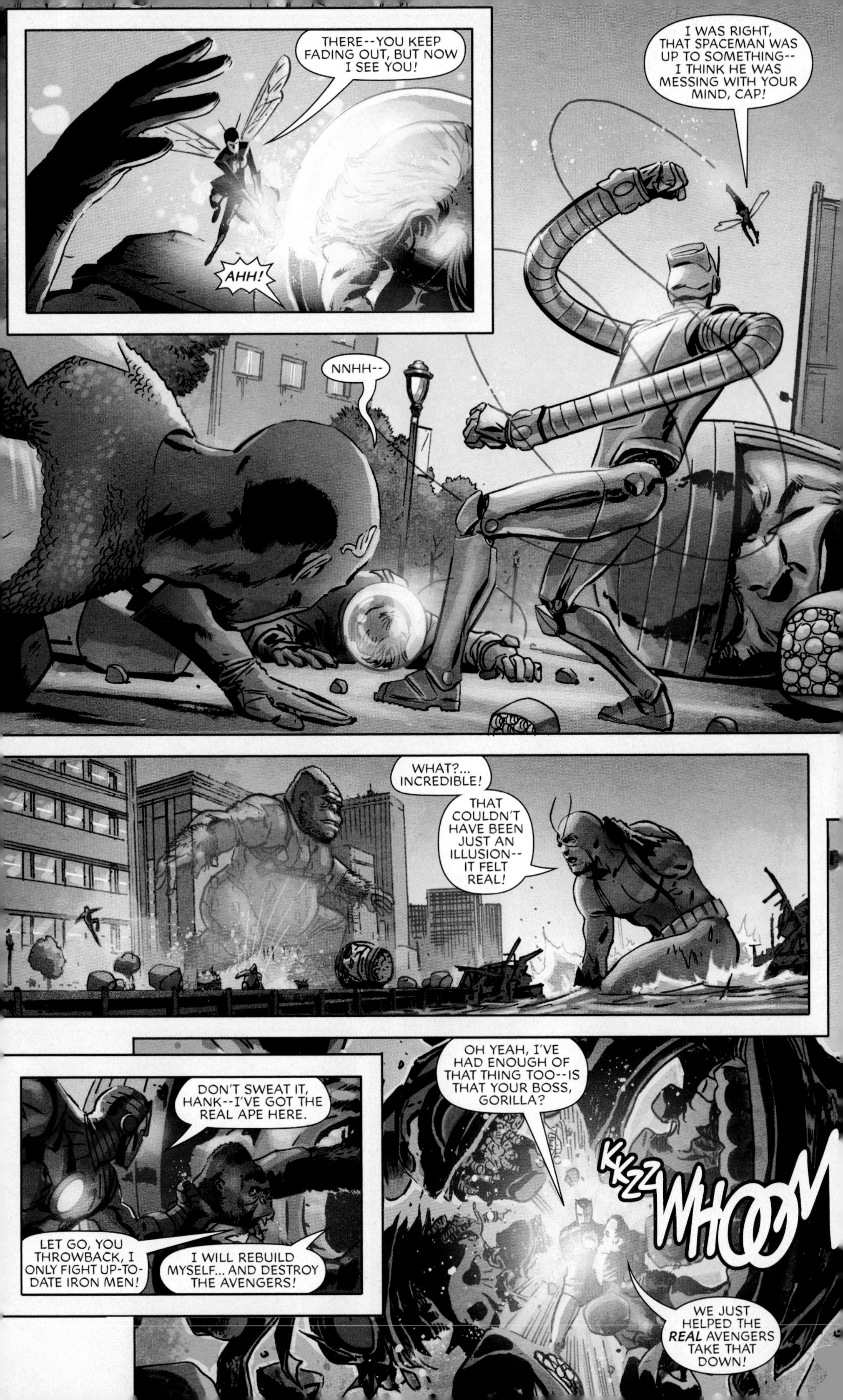
THERE--YOU KEEP FADING OUT, BUT NOW I SEE YOU!
AHH!
I WAS RIGHT, THAT SPACEMAN WAS UP TO SOMETHING-- I THINK HE WAS MESSING WITH YOUR MIND, CAP!
NNHH--
WHAT?... INCREDIBLE!
THAT COULDN'T HAVE BEEN JUST AN ILLUSION-- IT FELT REAL!
DON'T SWEAT IT, HANK--I'VE GOT THE REAL APE HERE.
LET GO, YOU THROWBACK, I ONLY FIGHT UP-TO-DATE IRON MEN!
I WILL REBUILD MYSELF... AND DESTROY THE AVENGERS!
OH YEAH, I'VE HAD ENOUGH OF THAT THING TOO--IS THAT YOUR BOSS, GORILLA?
KKZZ WHOOM
WE JUST HELPED THE REAL AVENGERS TAKE THAT DOWN!

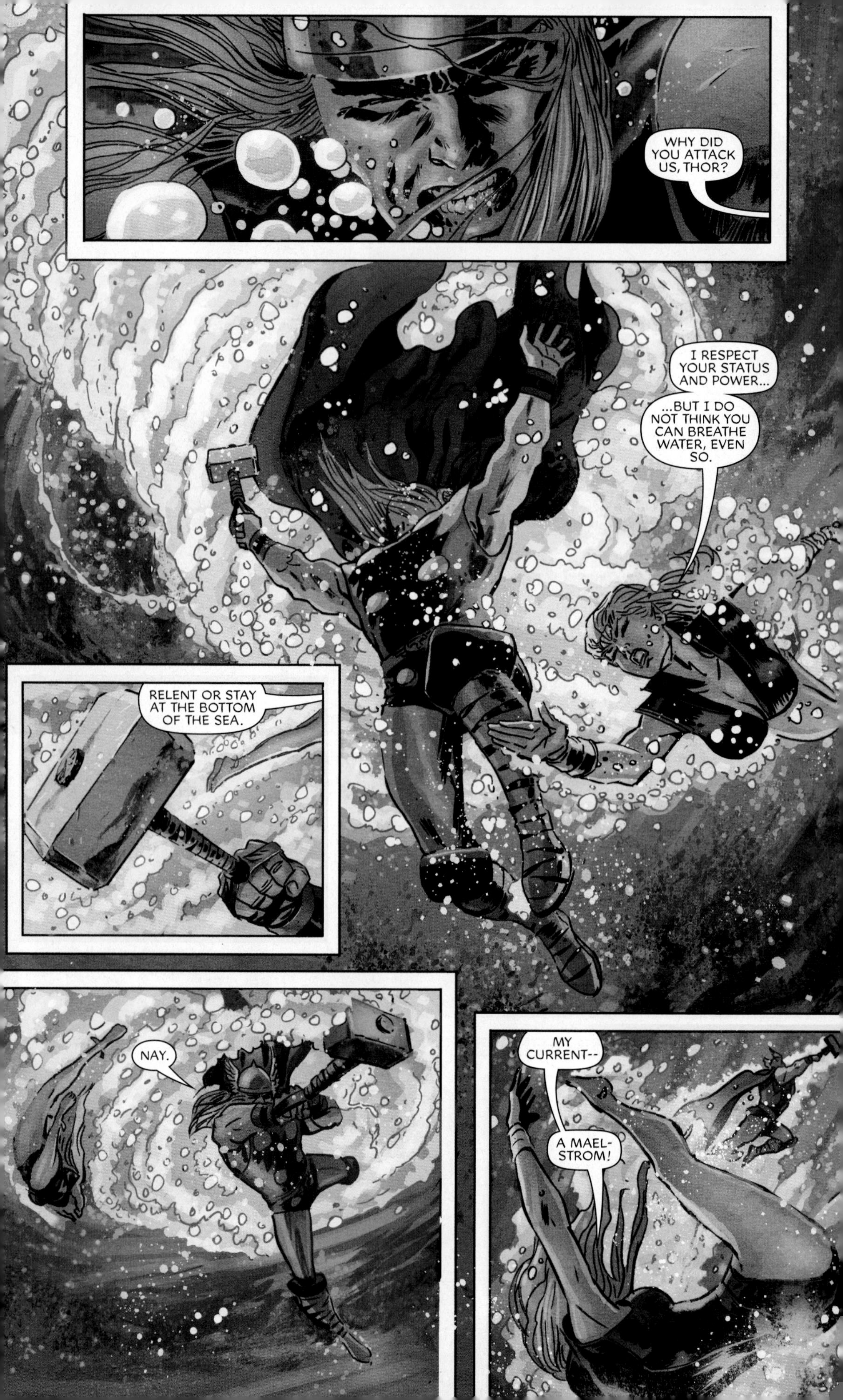
WHY DID YOU ATTACK US, THOR?
I RESPECT YOUR STATUS AND POWER...
...BUT I DO NOT THINK YOU CAN BREATHE WATER, EVEN SO.
RELENT OR STAY AT THE BOTTOM OF THE SEA.
NAY.
MY CURRENT--
A MAEL-STROM!

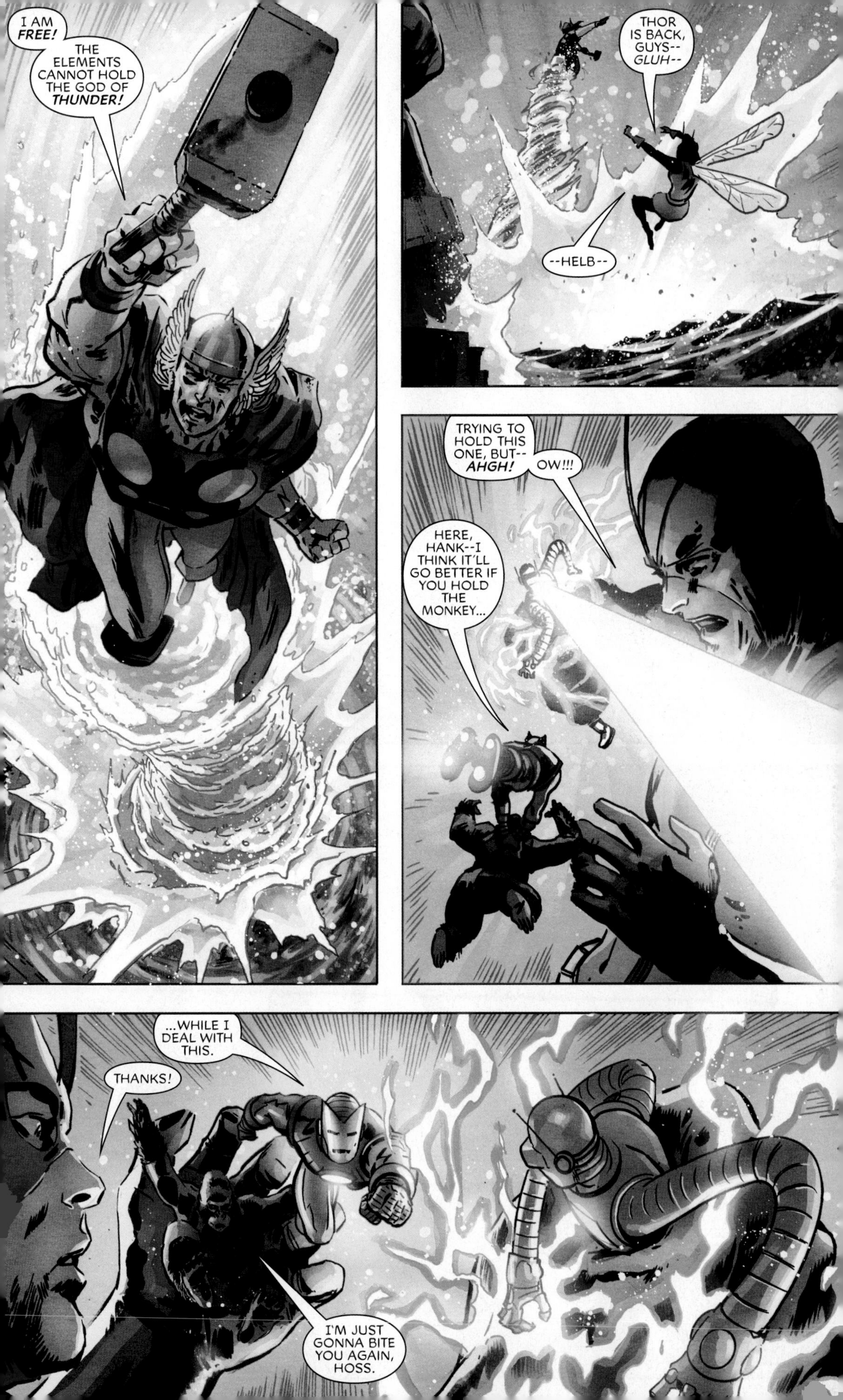
I AM FREE!
THE ELEMENTS CANNOT HOLD THE GOD OF THUNDER!
THOR IS BACK, GUYS-- GLUH--
--HELB--
TRYING TO HOLD THIS ONE, BUT-- AHGH!
OW!!!
HERE, HANK--I THINK IT'LL GO BETTER IF YOU HOLD THE MONKEY...
...WHILE I DEAL WITH THIS.
THANKS!
I'M JUST GONNA BITE YOU AGAIN, HOSS.

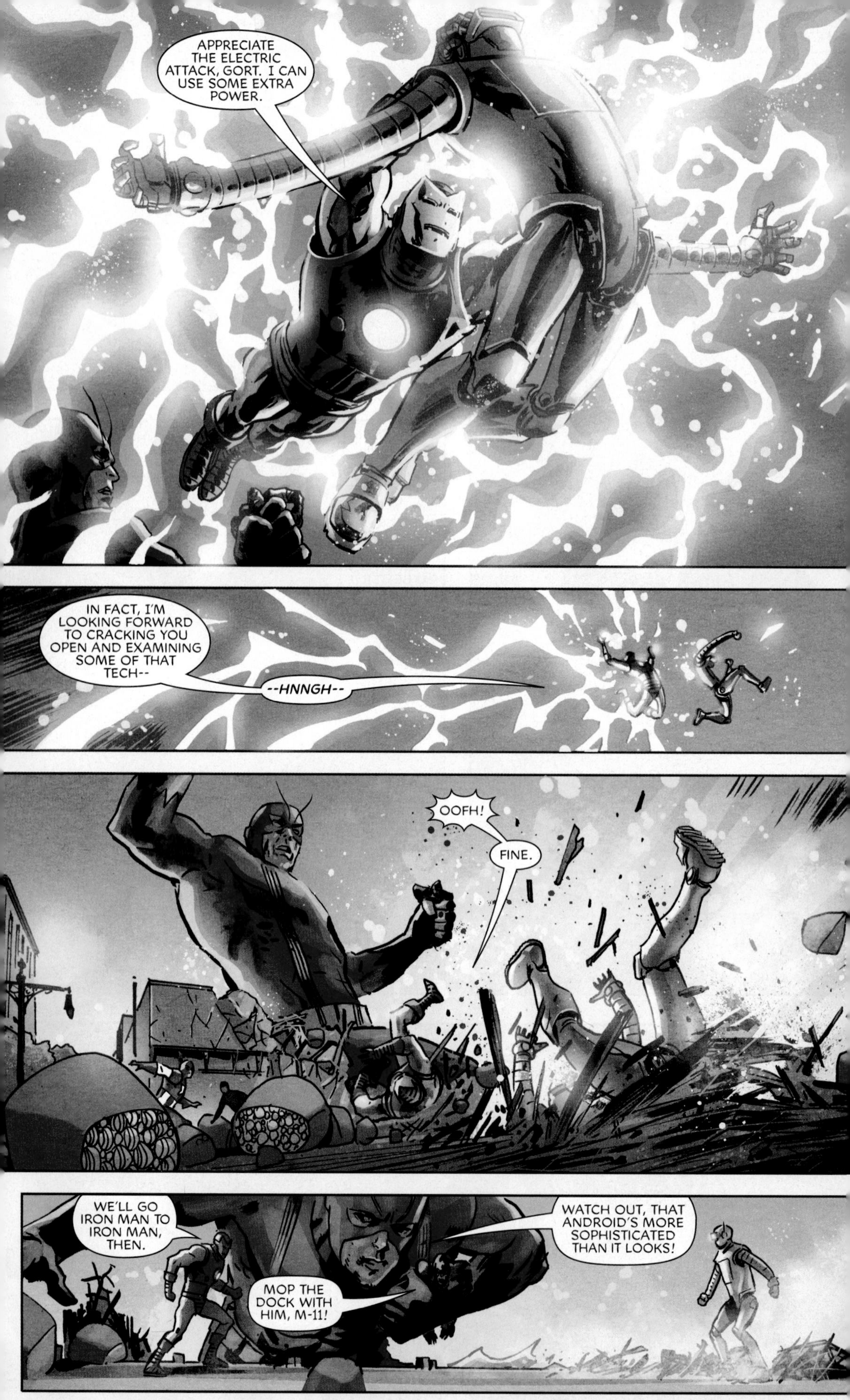
APPRECIATE THE ELECTRIC ATTACK, GORT. I CAN USE SOME EXTRA POWER.
IN FACT, I'M LOOKING FORWARD TO CRACKING YOU OPEN AND EXAMINING SOME OF THAT TECH--
--HNNGH--
OOFH!
FINE.
WE'LL GO IRON MAN TO IRON MAN, THEN.
WATCH OUT, THAT ANDROID'S MORE SOPHISTICATED THAN IT LOOKS!
MOP THE DOCK WITH HIM, M-11!

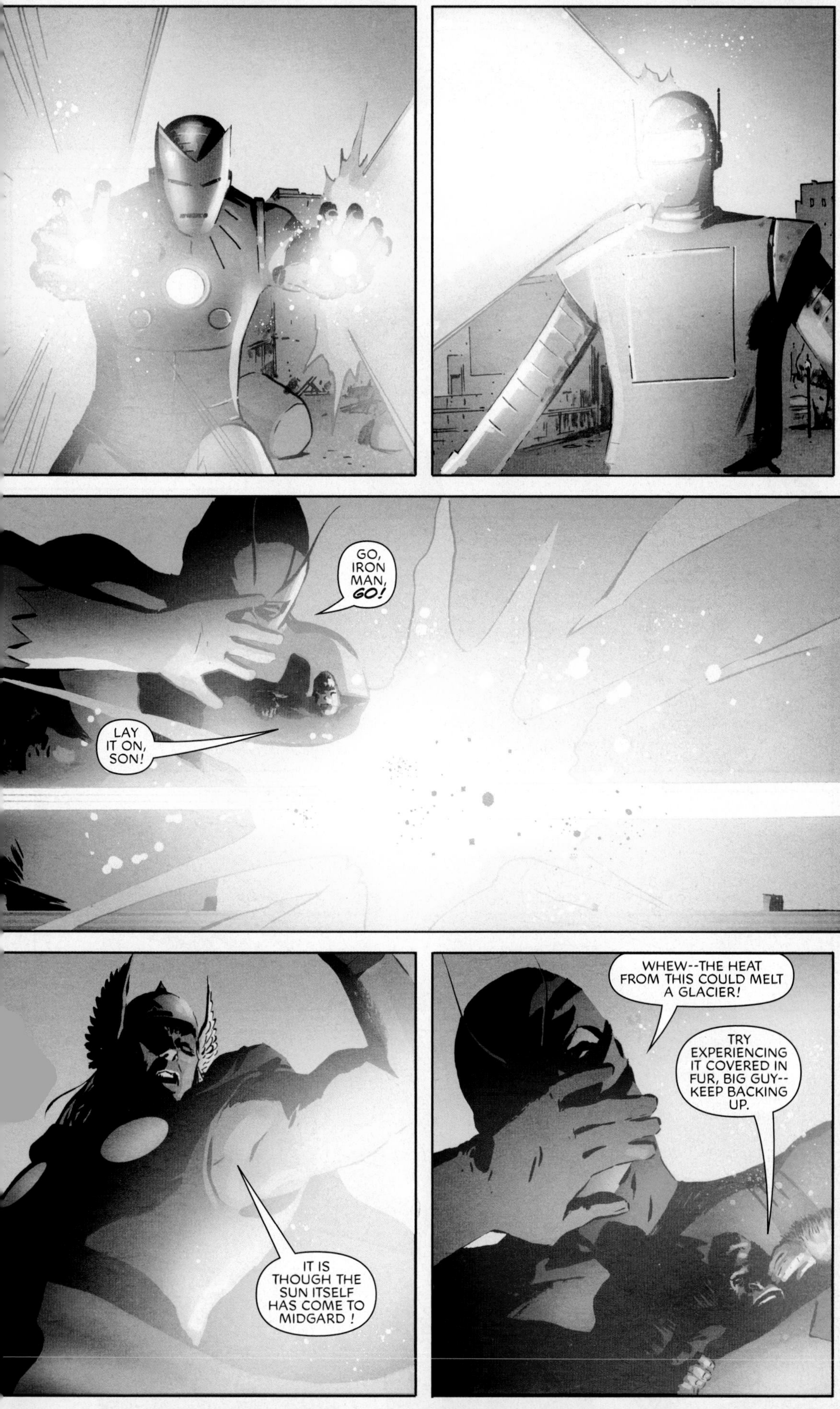
GO, IRON MAN, GO!
LAY IT ON, SON!
IT IS THOUGH THE SUN ITSELF HAS COME TO MIDGARD !
WHEW--THE HEAT FROM THIS COULD MELT A GLACIER!
TRY EXPERIENCING IT COVERED IN FUR, BIG GUY-- KEEP BACKING UP.

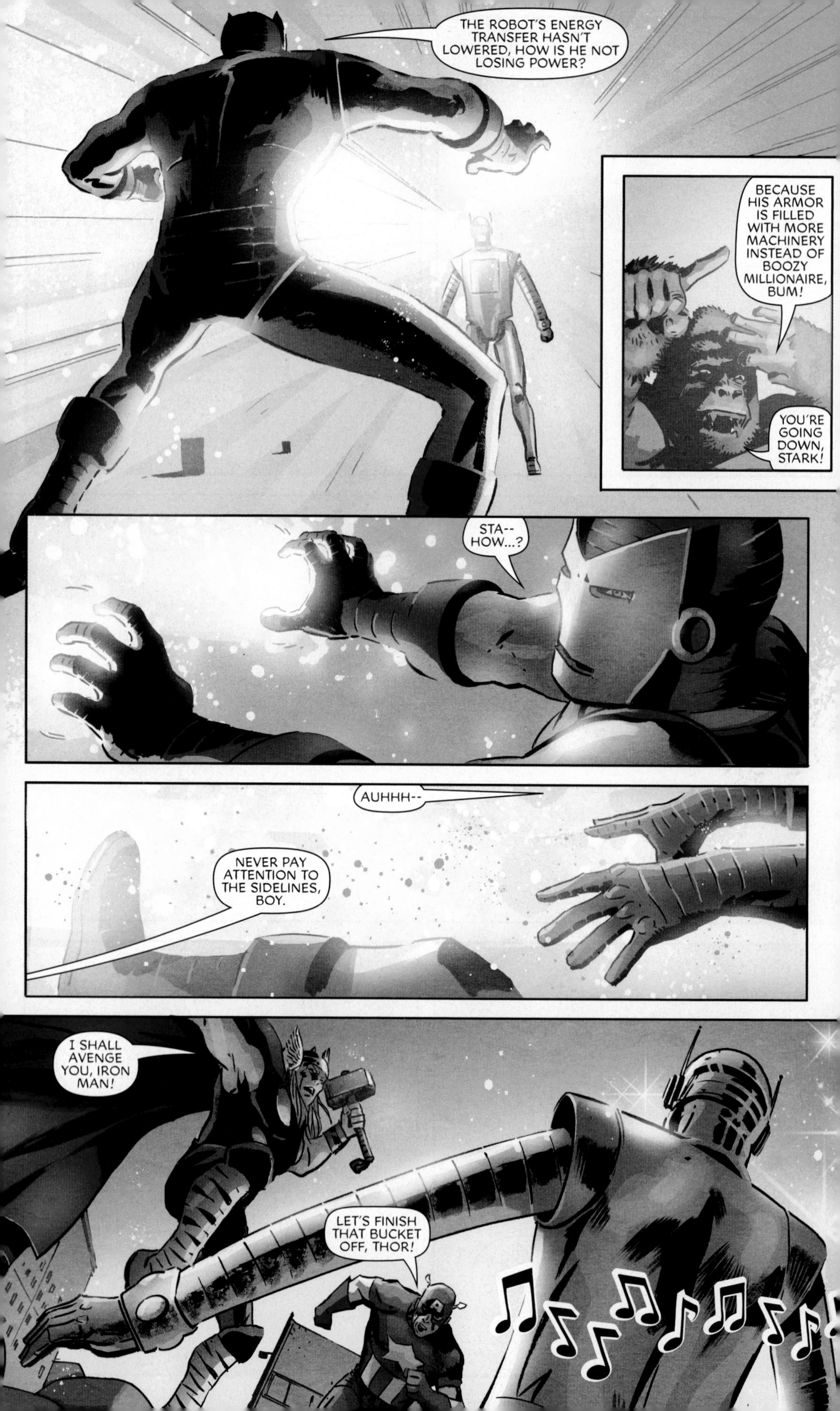
THE ROBOT'S ENERGY TRANSFER HASN'T LOWERED, HOW IS HE NOT LOSING POWER?
BECAUSE HIS ARMOR IS FILLED WITH MORE MACHINERY INSTEAD OF BOOZY MILLIONAIRE, BUM!
YOU'RE GOING DOWN, STARK!
STA-- HOW...?
AUHHH--
NEVER PAY ATTENTION TO THE SIDELINES, BOY.
I SHALL AVENGE YOU, IRON MAN!
LET'S FINISH THAT BUCKET OFF, THOR!

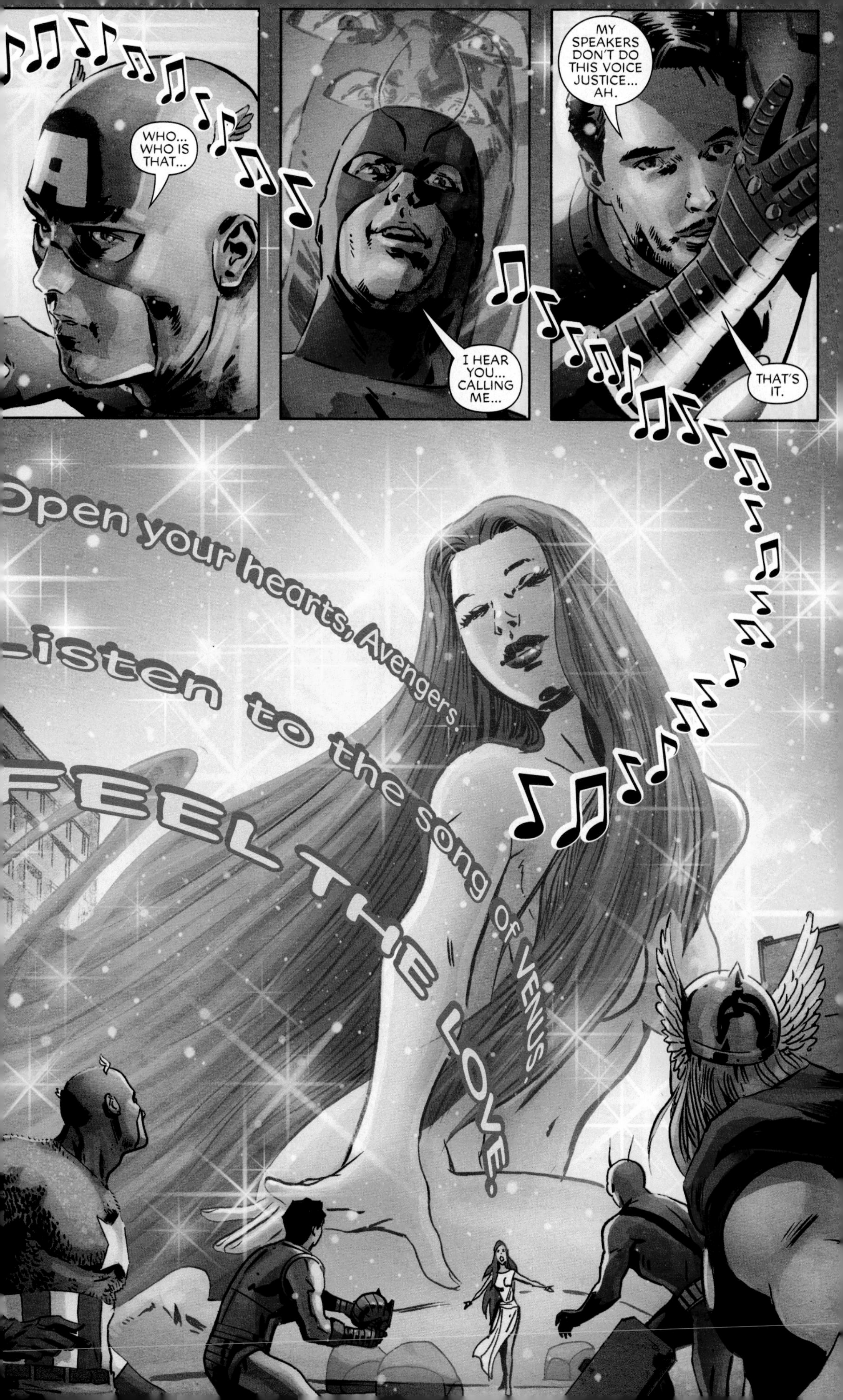
WHO... WHO IS THAT...
I HEAR YOU... CALLING ME...
MY SPEAKERS DON'T DO THIS VOICE JUSTICE... AH.
THAT'S IT.
Open your hearts, Avengers.
Listen to the song of Venus.
FEEL THE LOVE.

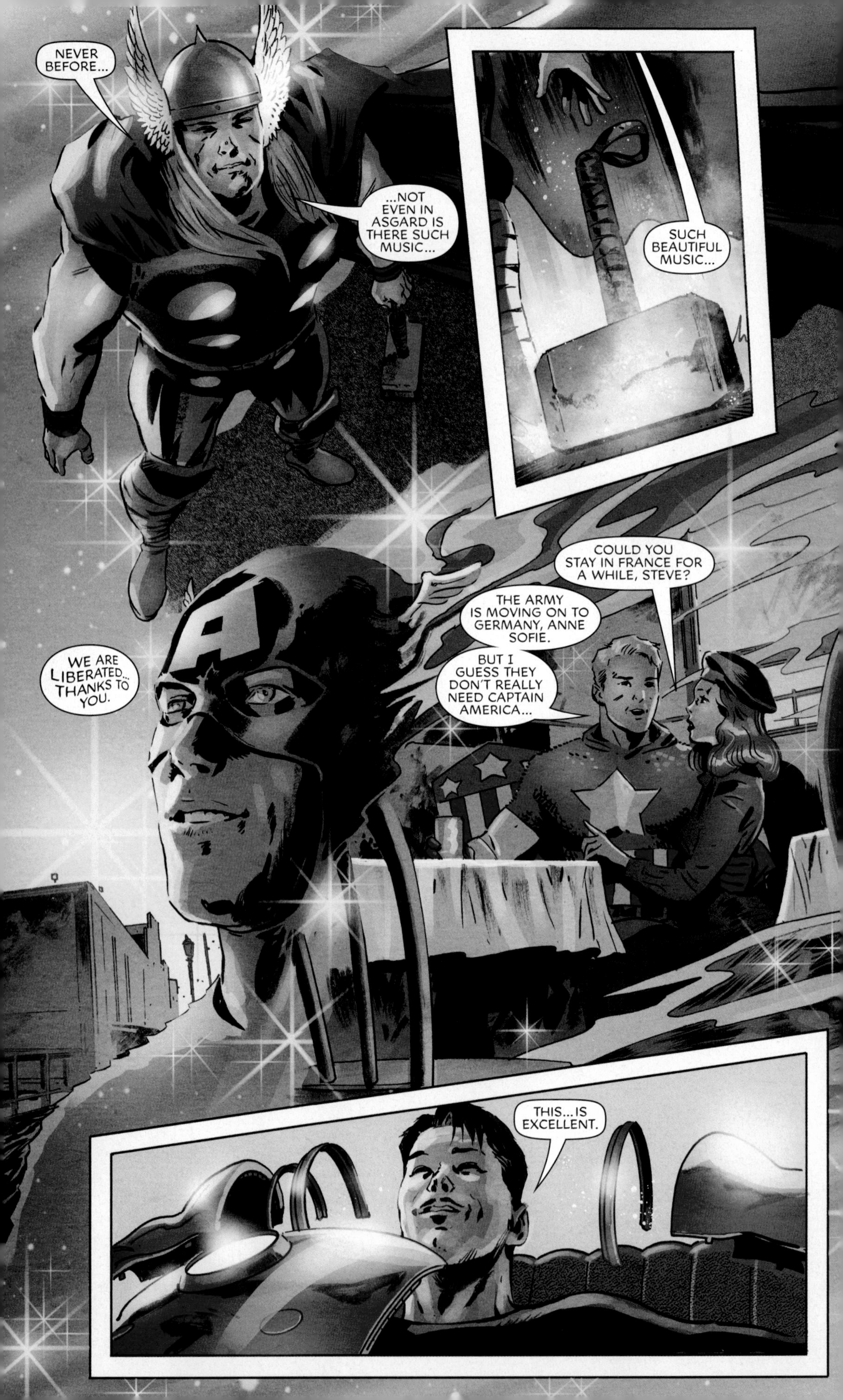
NEVER BEFORE...
...NOT EVEN IN ASGARD IS THERE SUCH MUSIC...
SUCH BEAUTIFUL MUSIC...
WE ARE LIBERATED... THANKS TO YOU.
COULD YOU STAY IN FRANCE FOR A WHILE, STEVE?
THE ARMY IS MOVING ON TO GERMANY, ANNE SOFIE.
BUT I GUESS THEY DON'T REALLY NEED CAPTAIN AMERICA...
THIS...IS EXCELLENT.

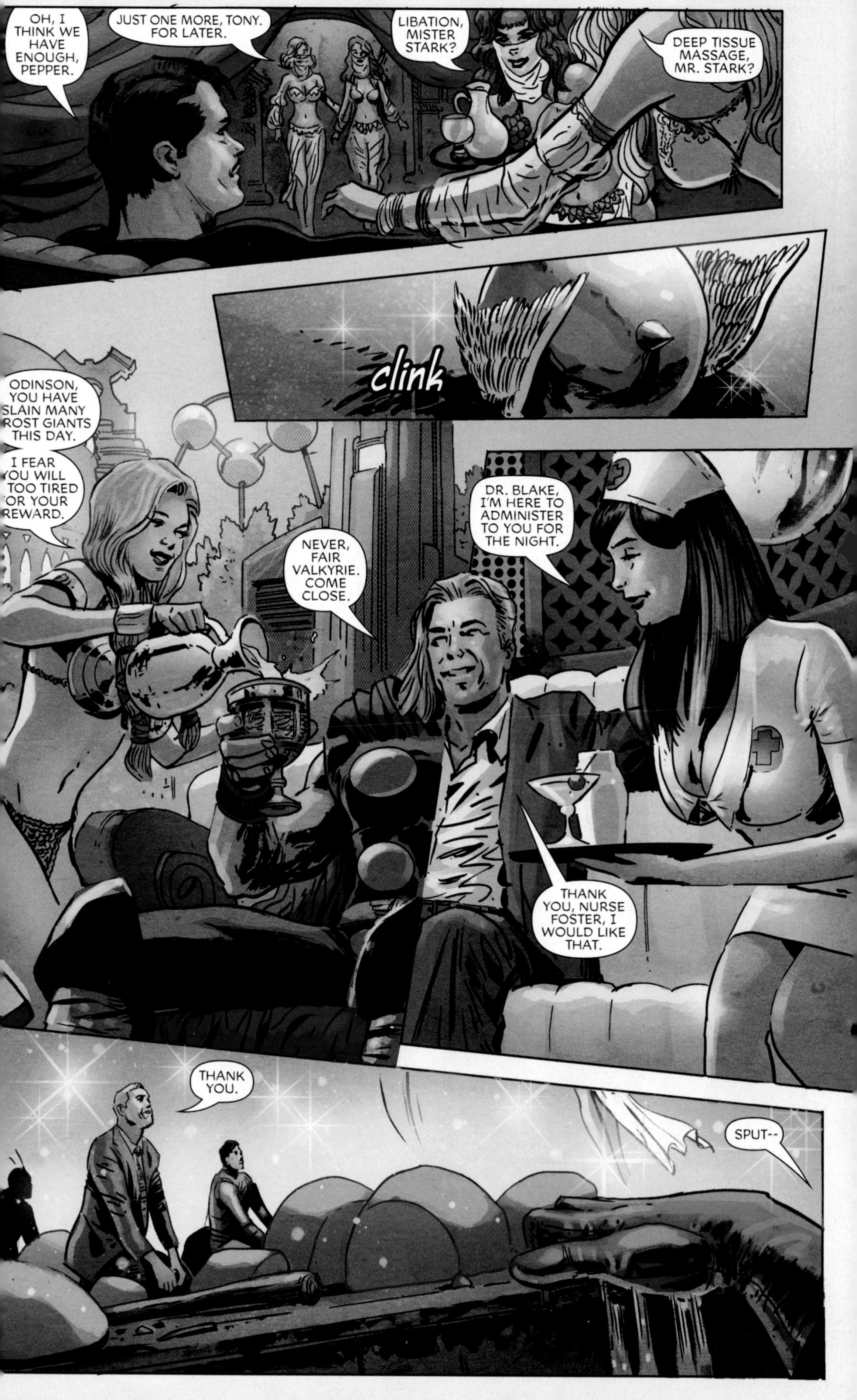
OH, I THINK WE HAVE ENOUGH, PEPPER.
JUST ONE MORE, TONY. FOR LATER.
LIBATION, MISTER STARK?
DEEP TISSUE MASSAGE, MR. STARK?
clink
ODINSON, YOU HAVE SLAIN MANY ROST GIANTS THIS DAY.
I FEAR YOU WILL TOO TIRED OR YOUR REWARD.
NEVER, FAIR VALKYRIE. COME CLOSE.
DR. BLAKE, I'M HERE TO ADMINISTER TO YOU FOR THE NIGHT.
THANK YOU, NURSE FOSTER, I WOULD LIKE THAT.
THANK YOU.
SPUT--

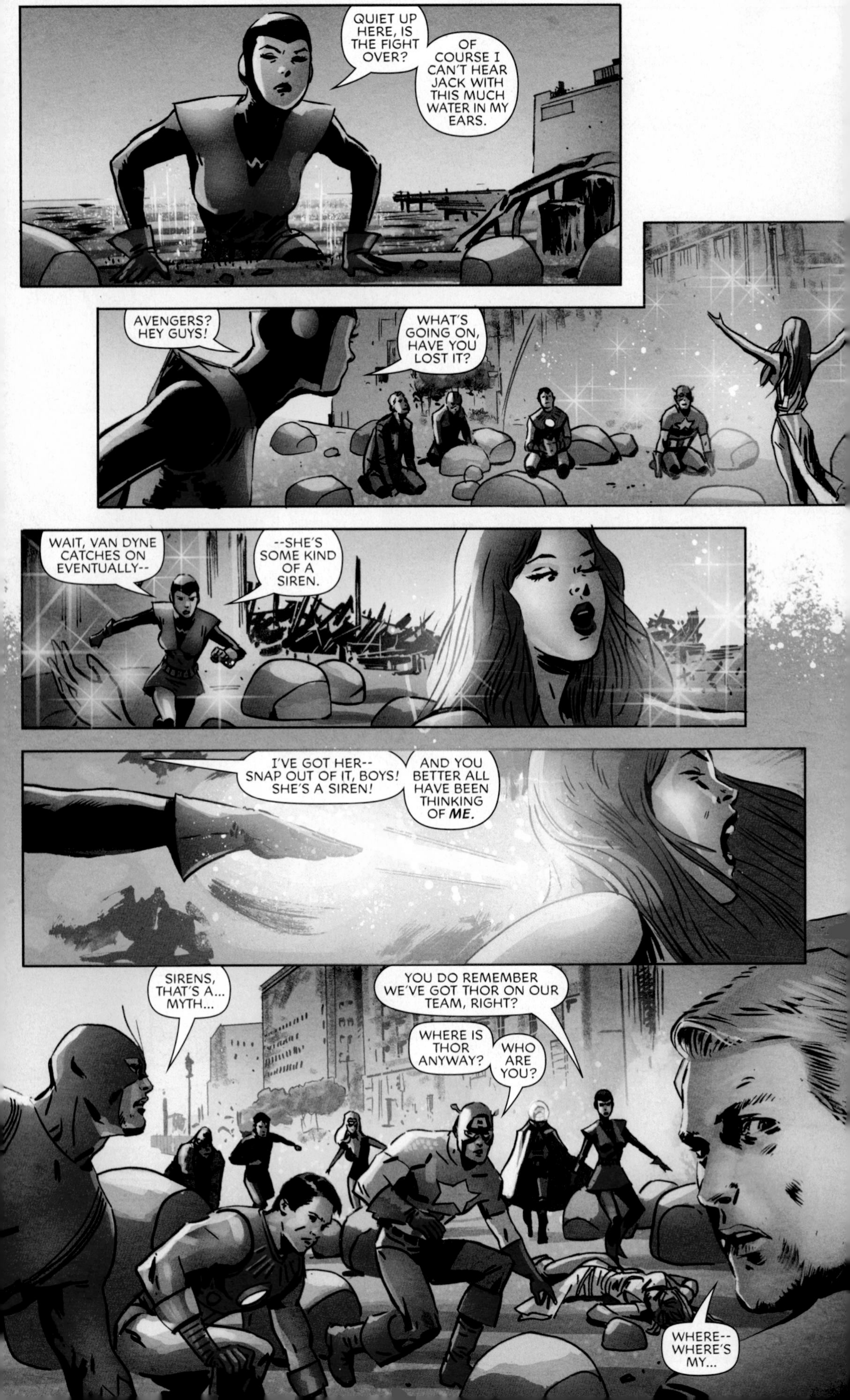
QUIET UP HERE, IS THE FIGHT OVER?
OF COURSE I CAN'T HEAR JACK WITH THIS MUCH WATER IN MY EARS.
AVENGERS? HEY GUYS!
WHAT'S GOING ON, HAVE YOU LOST IT?
WAIT, VAN DYNE CATCHES ON EVENTUALLY--
--SHE'S SOME KIND OF A SIREN.
I'VE GOT HER-- SNAP OUT OF IT, BOYS! SHE'S A SIREN!
AND YOU BETTER ALL HAVE BEEN THINKING OF ***ME.***
SIRENS, THAT'S A... MYTH...
YOU DO REMEMBER WE'VE GOT THOR ON OUR TEAM, RIGHT?
WHERE IS THOR ANYWAY?
WHO ARE YOU?
WHERE-- WHERE'S MY...

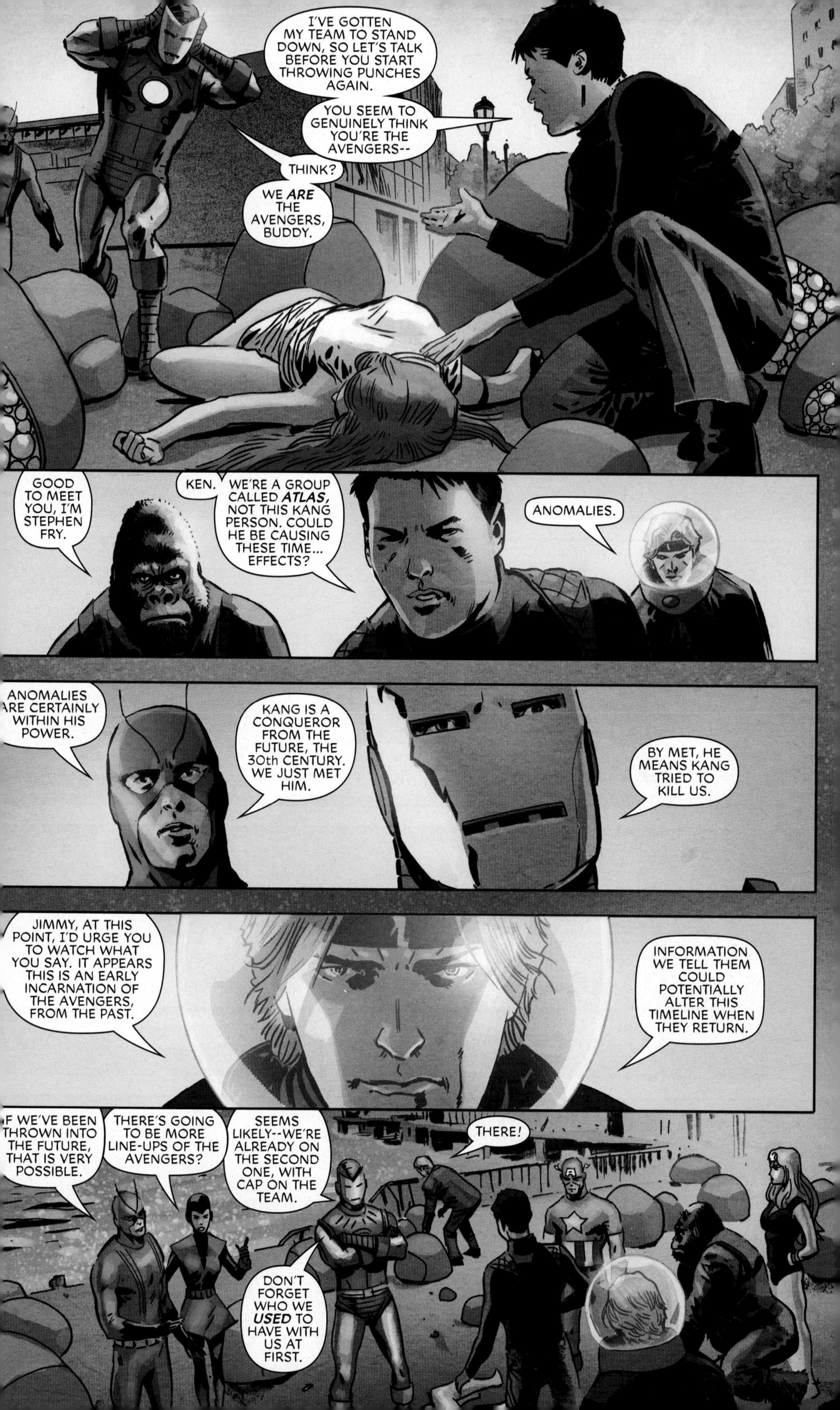
I'VE GOTTEN MY TEAM TO STAND DOWN, SO LET'S TALK BEFORE YOU START THROWING PUNCHES AGAIN.
YOU SEEM TO GENUINELY THINK YOU'RE THE AVENGERS--
THINK?
WE *ARE* THE AVENGERS, BUDDY.
GOOD TO MEET YOU, I'M STEPHEN FRY.
KEN.
WE'RE A GROUP CALLED *ATLAS,* NOT THIS KANG PERSON. COULD HE BE CAUSING THESE TIME... EFFECTS?
ANOMALIES.
ANOMALIES ARE CERTAINLY WITHIN HIS POWER.
KANG IS A CONQUEROR FROM THE FUTURE, THE 30th CENTURY. WE JUST MET HIM.
BY MET, HE MEANS KANG TRIED TO KILL US.
JIMMY, AT THIS POINT, I'D URGE YOU TO WATCH WHAT YOU SAY. IT APPEARS THIS IS AN EARLY INCARNATION OF THE AVENGERS, FROM THE PAST.
INFORMATION WE TELL THEM COULD POTENTIALLY ALTER THIS TIMELINE WHEN THEY RETURN.
F WE'VE BEEN THROWN INTO THE FUTURE, THAT IS VERY POSSIBLE.
THERE'S GOING TO BE MORE LINE-UPS OF THE AVENGERS?
SEEMS LIKELY--WE'RE ALREADY ON THE SECOND ONE, WITH CAP ON THE TEAM.
THERE!
DON'T FORGET WHO WE *USED* TO HAVE WITH US AT FIRST.

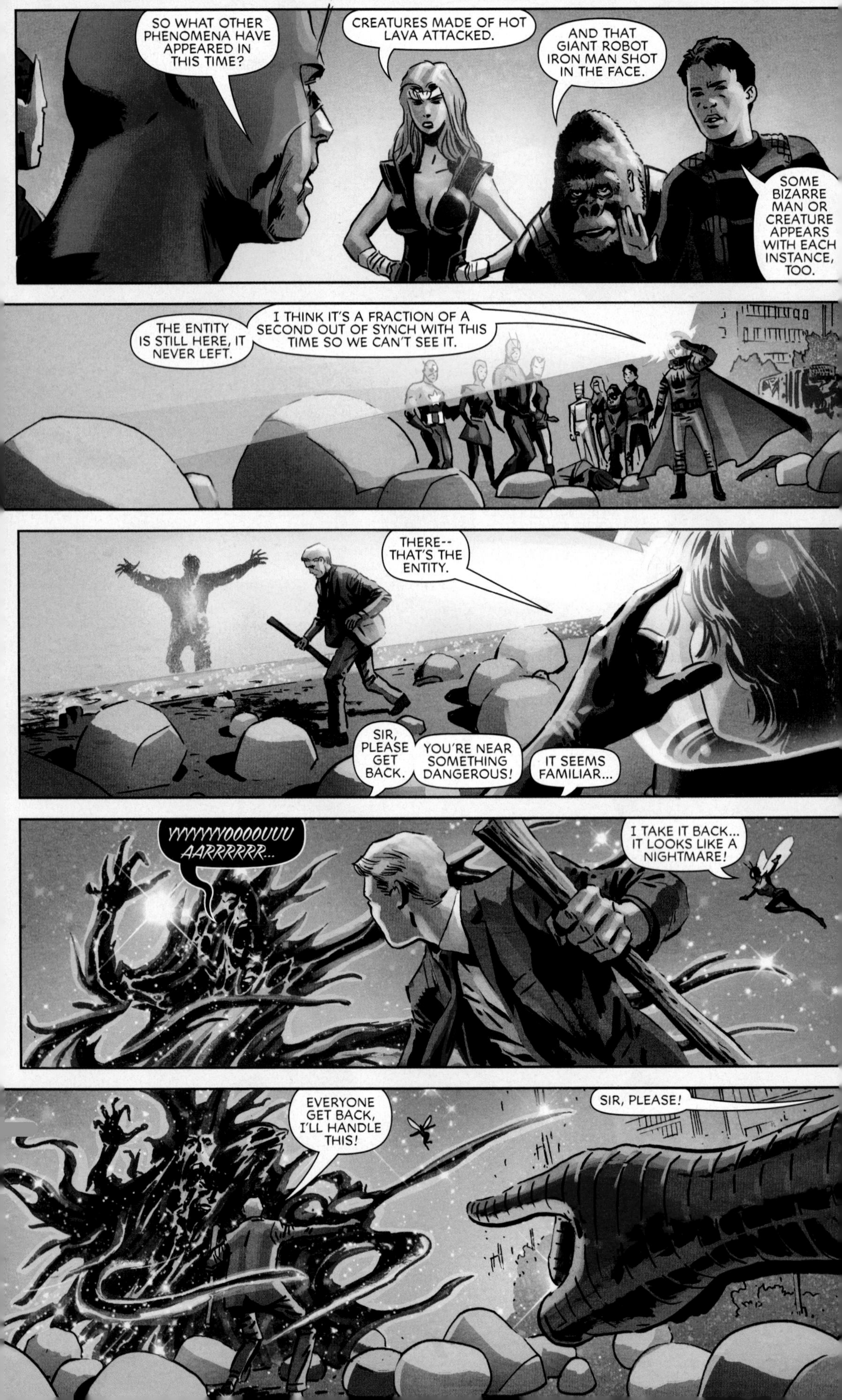
SO WHAT OTHER PHENOMENA HAVE APPEARED IN THIS TIME?
CREATURES MADE OF HOT LAVA ATTACKED.
AND THAT GIANT ROBOT IRON MAN SHOT IN THE FACE.
SOME BIZARRE MAN OR CREATURE APPEARS WITH EACH INSTANCE, TOO.
THE ENTITY IS STILL HERE, IT NEVER LEFT.
I THINK IT'S A FRACTION OF A SECOND OUT OF SYNCH WITH THIS TIME SO WE CAN'T SEE IT.
THERE-- THAT'S THE ENTITY.
SIR, PLEASE GET BACK.
YOU'RE NEAR SOMETHING DANGEROUS!
IT SEEMS FAMILIAR...
YYYYYYYOOOOUUU AARRRRRR...
I TAKE IT BACK... IT LOOKS LIKE A NIGHTMARE!
EVERYONE GET BACK, I'LL HANDLE THIS!
SIR, PLEASE!

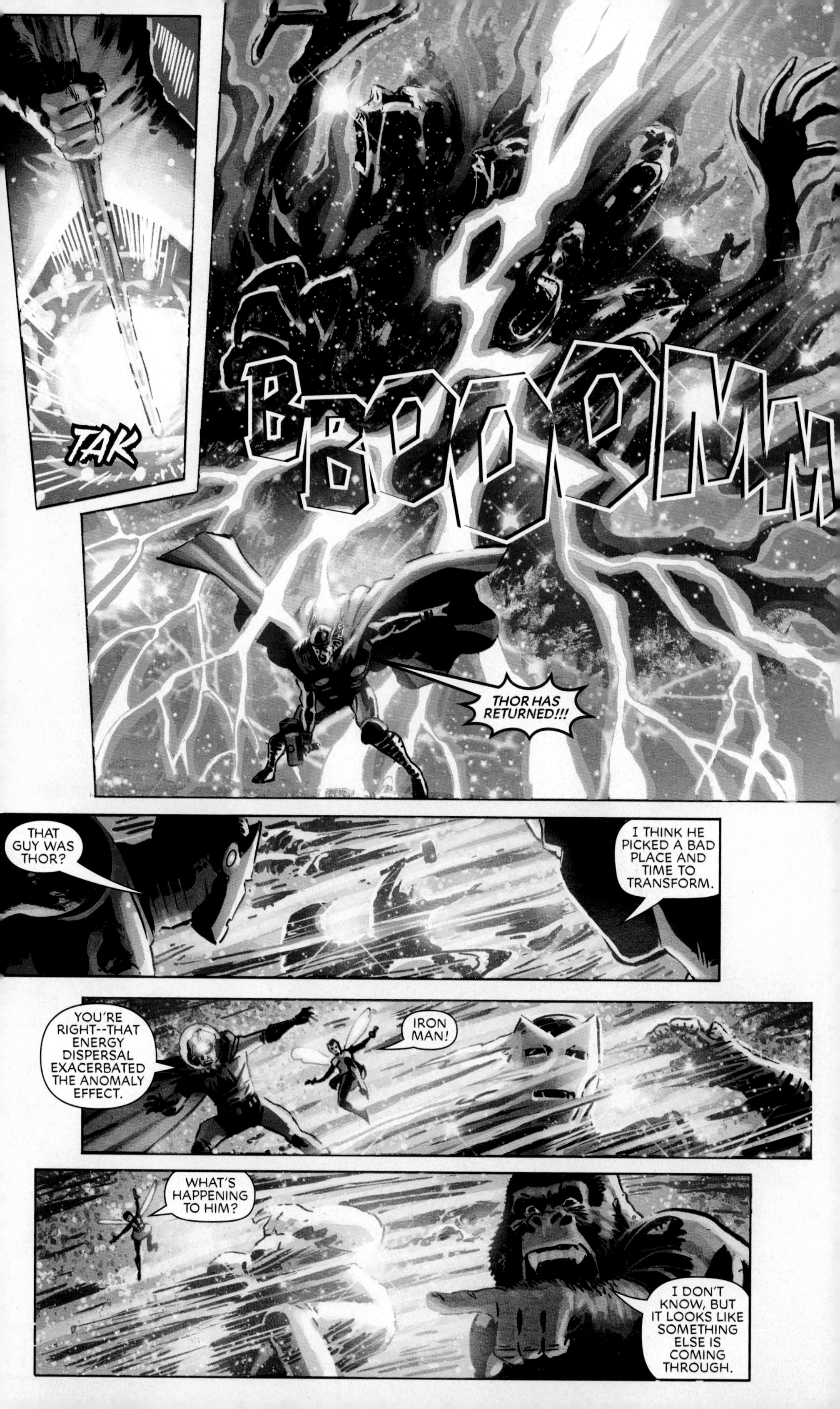

TAK
BROOOOMM
THOR HAS RETURNED!!!
THAT GUY WAS THOR?
I THINK HE PICKED A BAD PLACE AND TIME TO TRANSFORM.
YOU'RE RIGHT--THAT ENERGY DISPERSAL EXACERBATED THE ANOMALY EFFECT.
IRON MAN!
WHAT'S HAPPENING TO HIM?
I DON'T KNOW, BUT IT LOOKS LIKE SOMETHING ELSE IS COMING THROUGH.

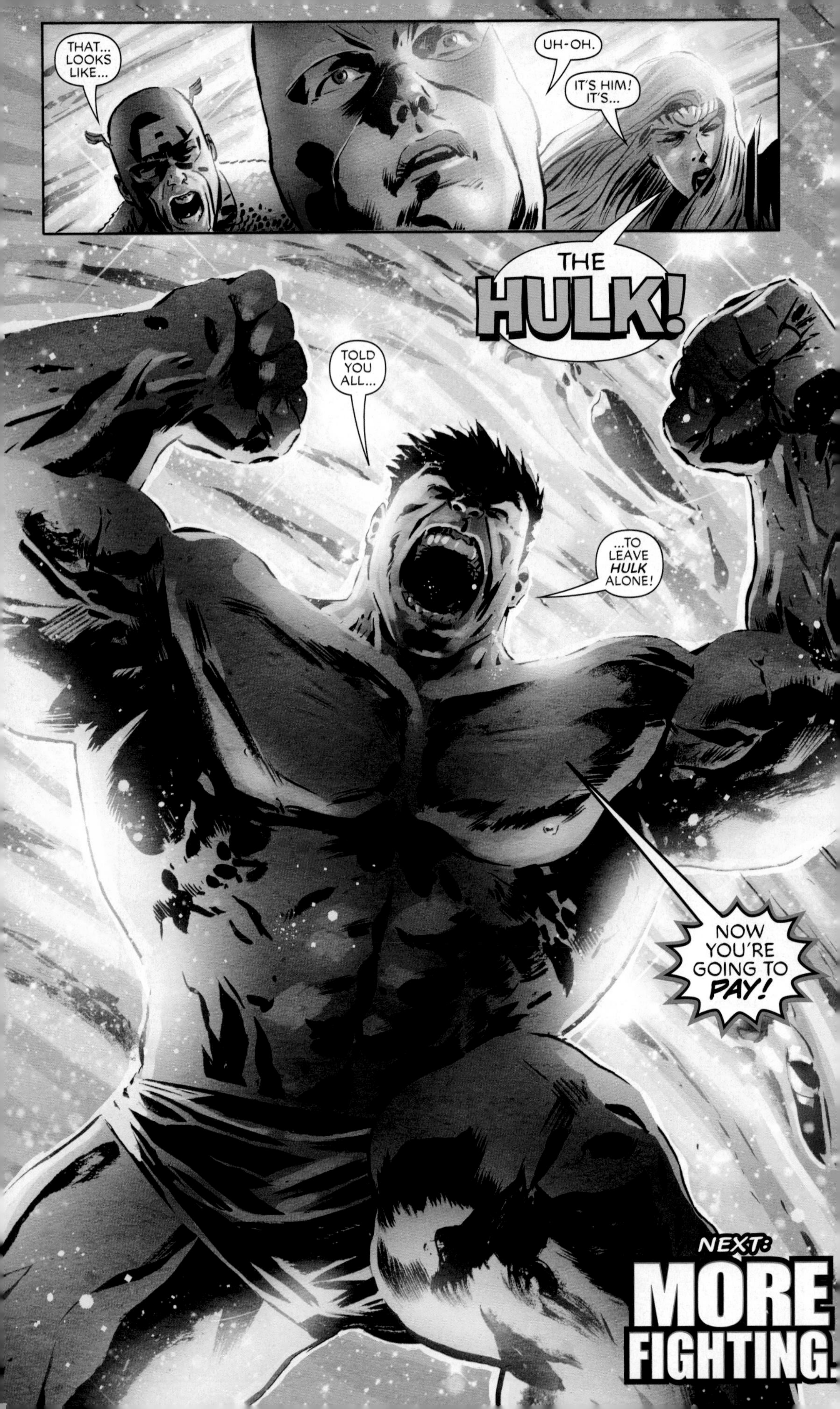
THAT... LOOKS LIKE...
UH-OH.
IT'S HIM! IT'S...
THE HULK!
TOLD YOU ALL...
...TO LEAVE HULK ALONE!
NOW YOU'RE GOING TO PAY!
NEXT: MORE FIGHTING.

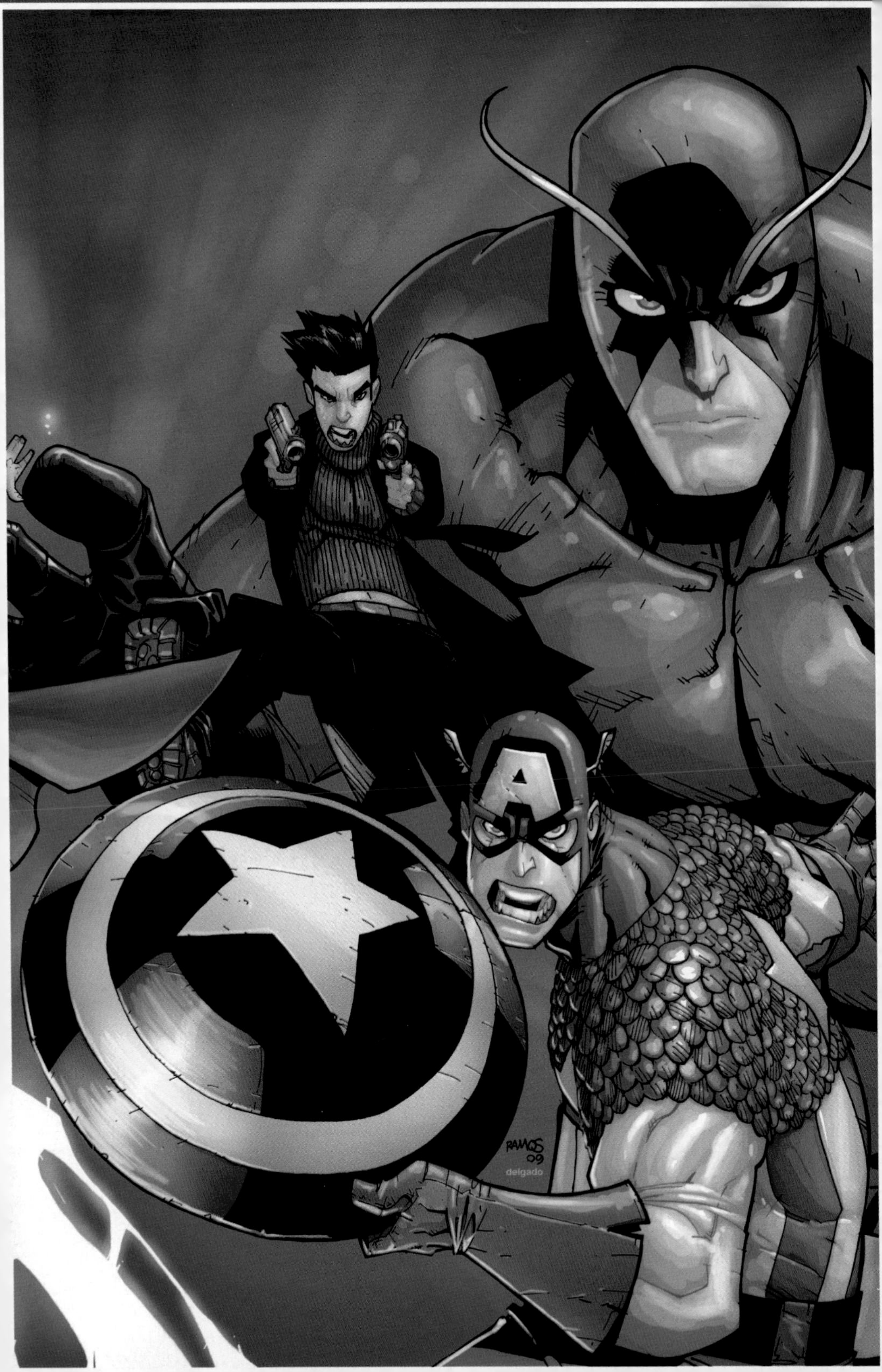
RAMOS
09
delgado

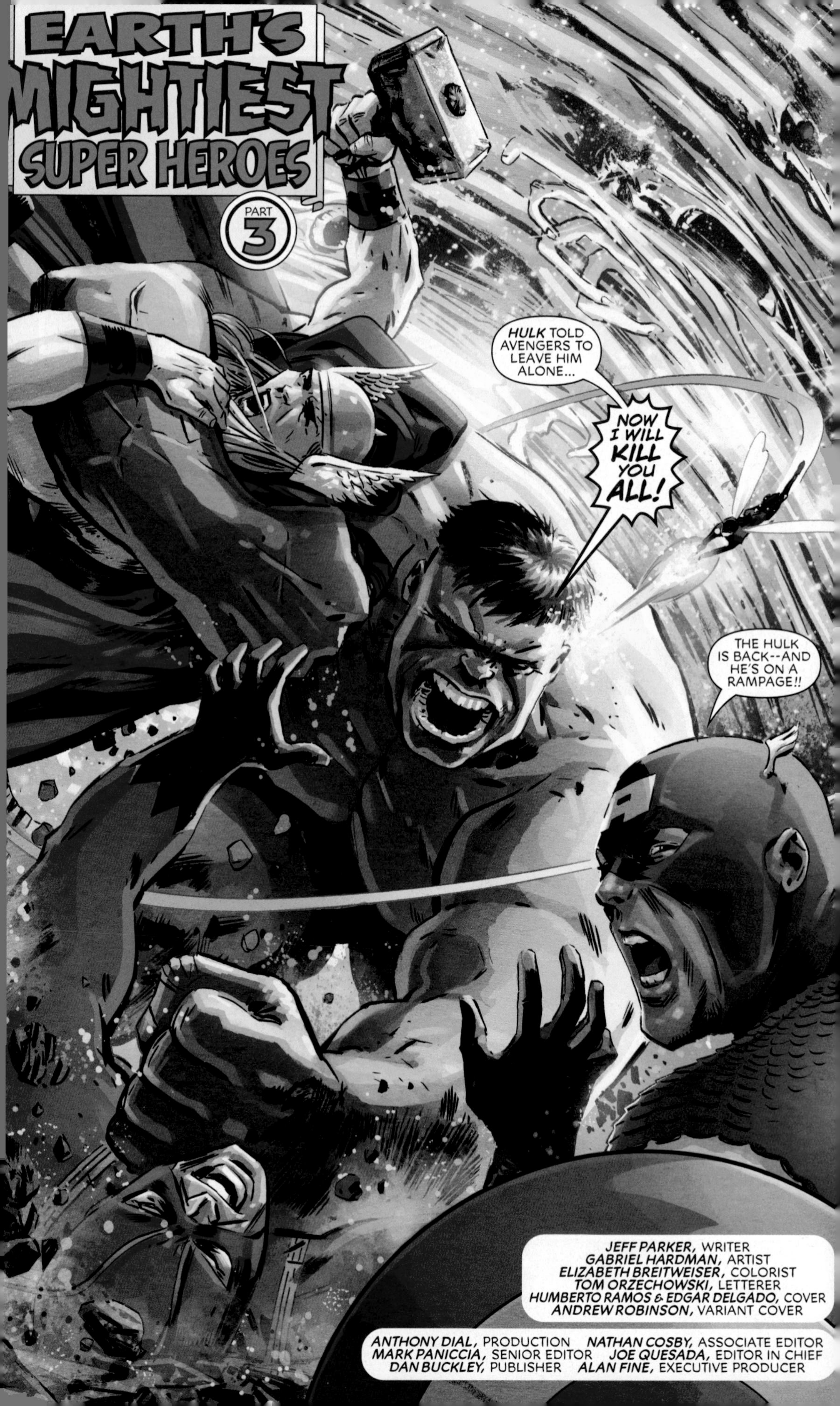

EARTH'S MIGHTIEST SUPER HEROES
PART 3
HULK TOLD AVENGERS TO LEAVE HIM ALONE...
NOW I WILL KILL YOU ALL!
THE HULK IS BACK--AND HE'S ON A RAMPAGE!!
JEFF PARKER, WRITER
GABRIEL HARDMAN, ARTIST
ELIZABETH BREITWEISER, COLORIST
TOM ORZECHOWSKI, LETTERER
HUMBERTO RAMOS & EDGAR DELGADO, COVER
ANDREW ROBINSON, VARIANT COVER
ANTHONY DIAL, PRODUCTION NATHAN COSBY, ASSOCIATE EDITOR
MARK PANICCIA, SENIOR EDITOR JOE QUESADA, EDITOR IN CHIEF
DAN BUCKLEY, PUBLISHER ALAN FINE, EXECUTIVE PRODUCER

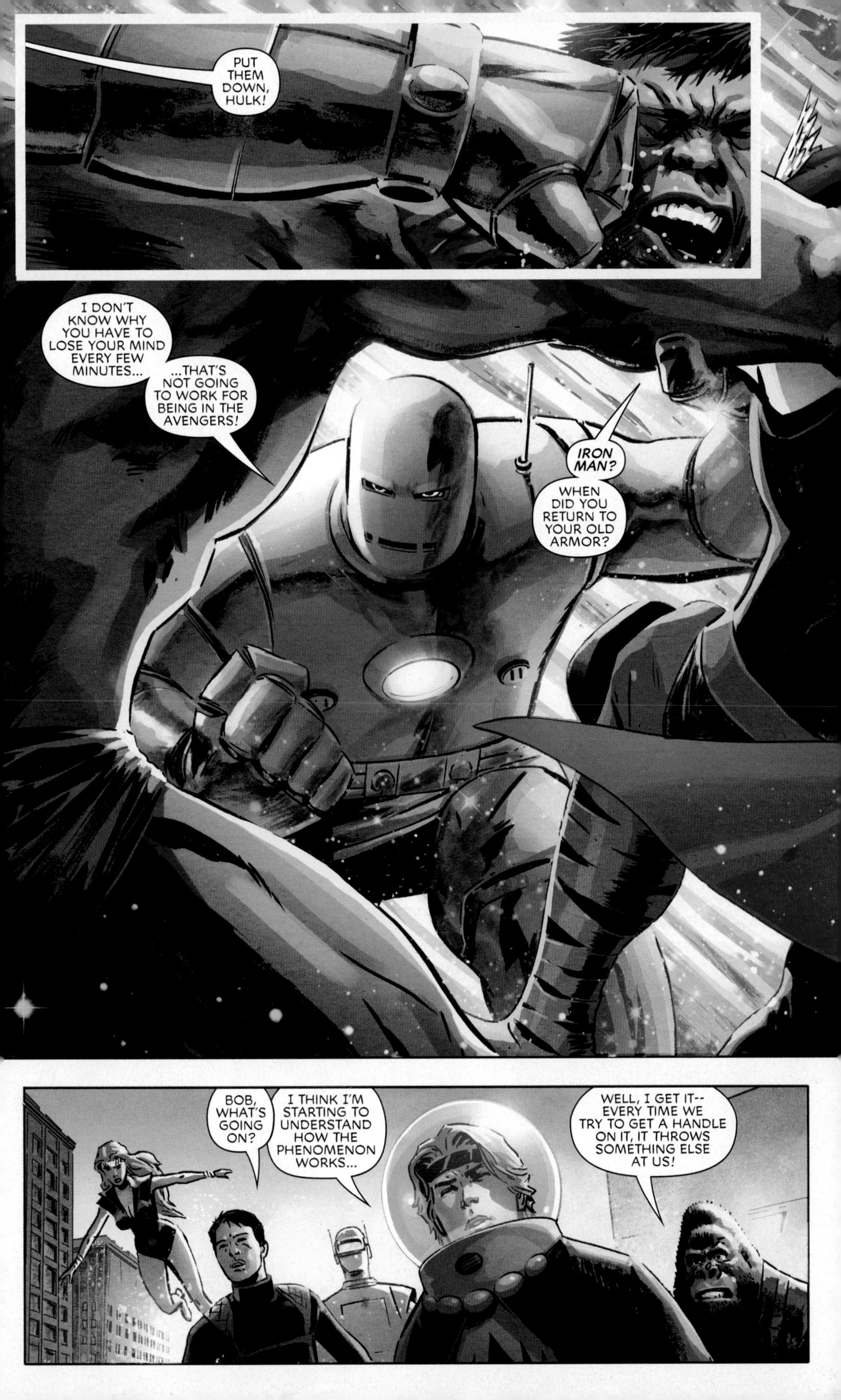
PUT THEM DOWN, HULK!
I DON'T KNOW WHY YOU HAVE TO LOSE YOUR MIND EVERY FEW MINUTES...
...THAT'S NOT GOING TO WORK FOR BEING IN THE AVENGERS!
IRON MAN?
WHEN DID YOU RETURN TO YOUR OLD ARMOR?
BOB, WHAT'S GOING ON?
I THINK I'M STARTING TO UNDERSTAND HOW THE PHENOMENON WORKS...
WELL, I GET IT-- EVERY TIME WE TRY TO GET A HANDLE ON IT, IT THROWS SOMETHING ELSE AT US!

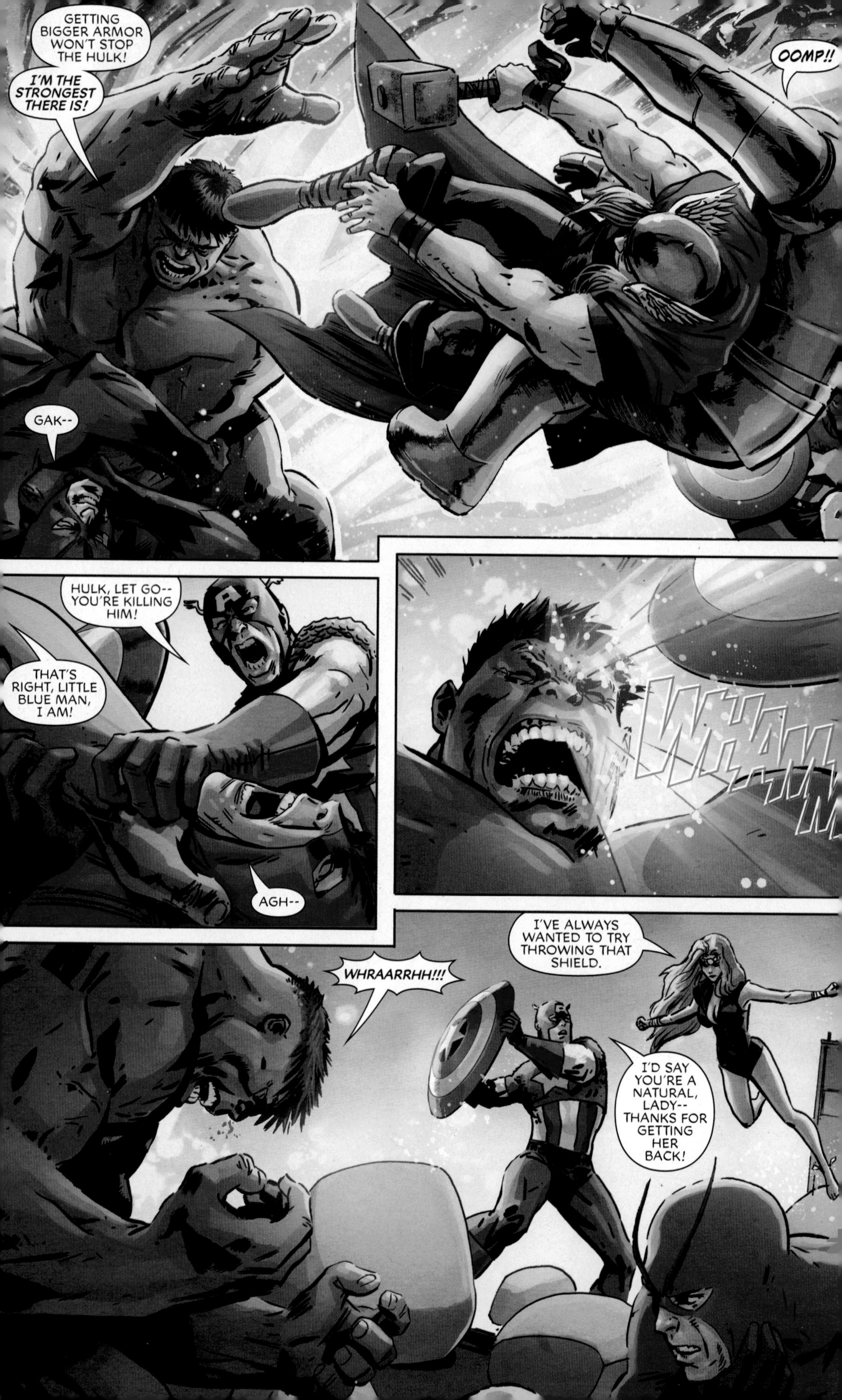
GETTING BIGGER ARMOR WON'T STOP THE HULK!
I'M THE STRONGEST THERE IS!
OOMP!!
GAK--
HULK, LET GO-- YOU'RE KILLING HIM!
THAT'S RIGHT, LITTLE BLUE MAN, I AM!
AGH--
WHAM
WHRAARRHH!!!
I'VE ALWAYS WANTED TO TRY THROWING THAT SHIELD.
I'D SAY YOU'RE A NATURAL, LADY-- THANKS FOR GETTING HER BACK!

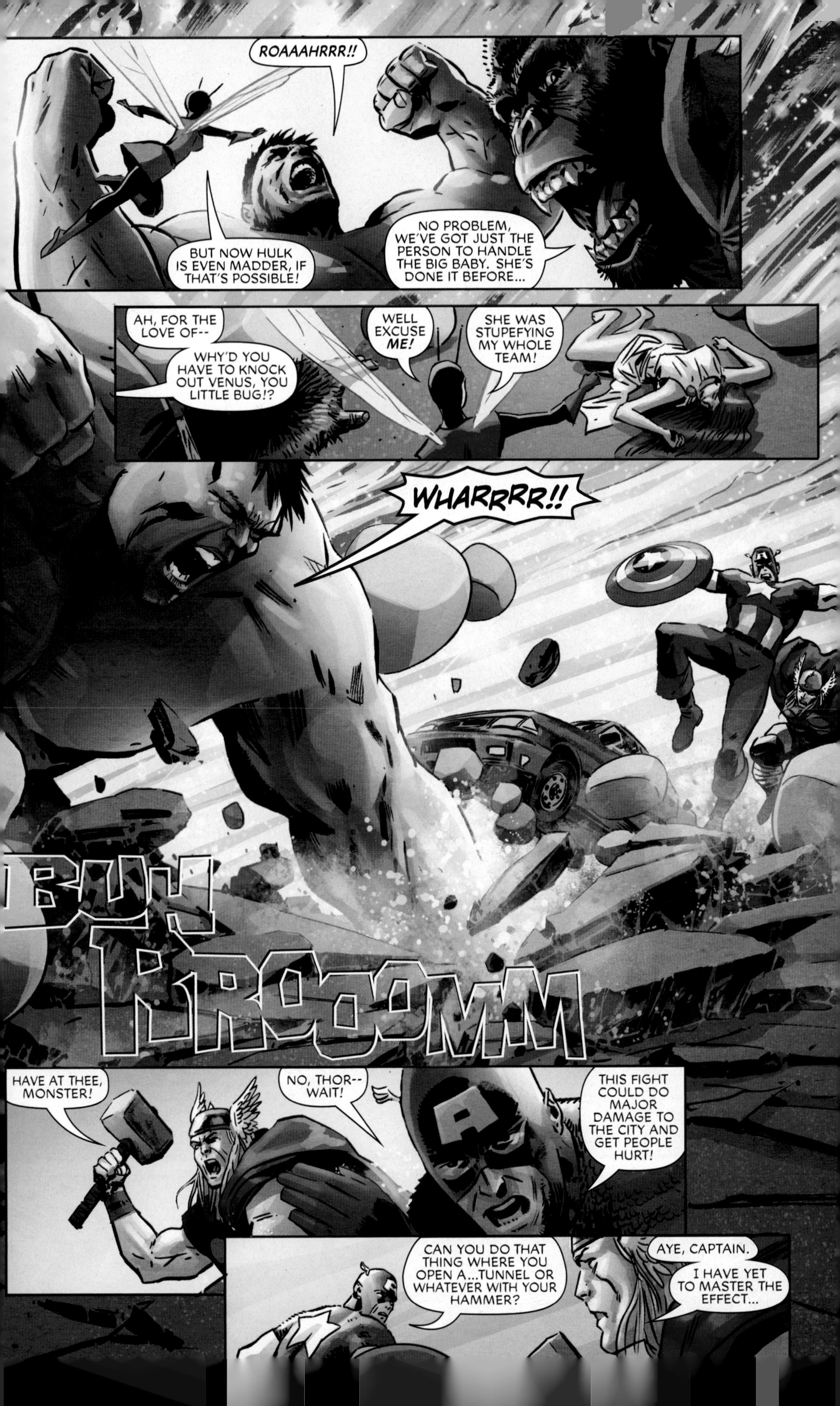
ROAAAHRRR!!
BUT NOW HULK IS EVEN MADDER, IF THAT'S POSSIBLE!
NO PROBLEM, WE'VE GOT JUST THE PERSON TO HANDLE THE BIG BABY. SHE'S DONE IT BEFORE...
AH, FOR THE LOVE OF--
WHY'D YOU HAVE TO KNOCK OUT VENUS, YOU LITTLE BUG!?
WELL EXCUSE ME!
SHE WAS STUPEFYING MY WHOLE TEAM!
WHARRRR!!
BUH KROOOMM
HAVE AT THEE, MONSTER!
NO, THOR-- WAIT!
THIS FIGHT COULD DO MAJOR DAMAGE TO THE CITY AND GET PEOPLE HURT!
CAN YOU DO THAT THING WHERE YOU OPEN A...TUNNEL OR WHATEVER WITH YOUR HAMMER?
AYE, CAPTAIN.
I HAVE YET TO MASTER THE EFFECT...

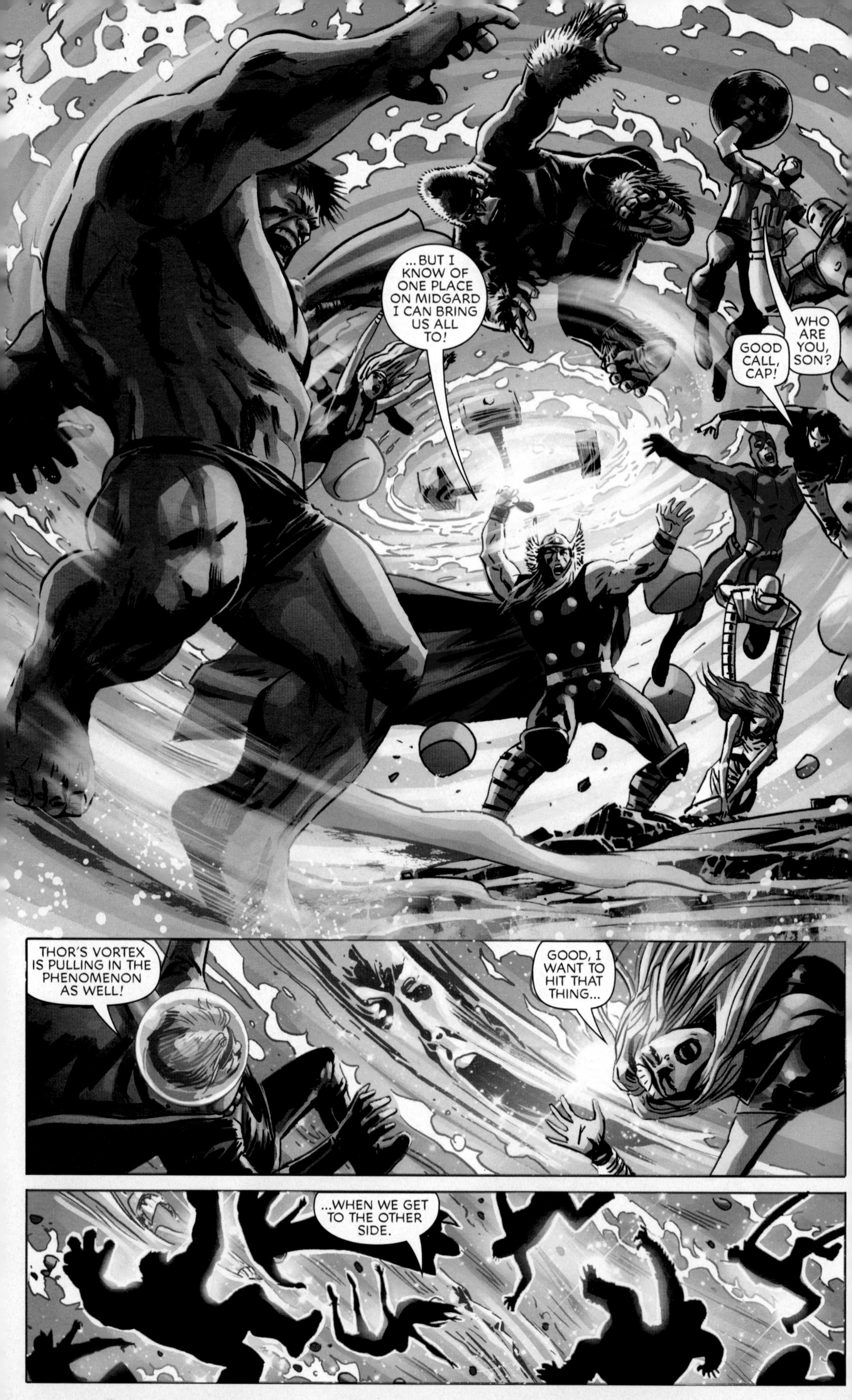
...BUT I KNOW OF ONE PLACE ON MIDGARD I CAN BRING US ALL TO!
WHO ARE YOU, SON?
GOOD CALL, CAP!
THOR'S VORTEX IS PULLING IN THE PHENOMENON AS WELL!
GOOD, I WANT TO HIT THAT THING...
...WHEN WE GET TO THE OTHER SIDE.

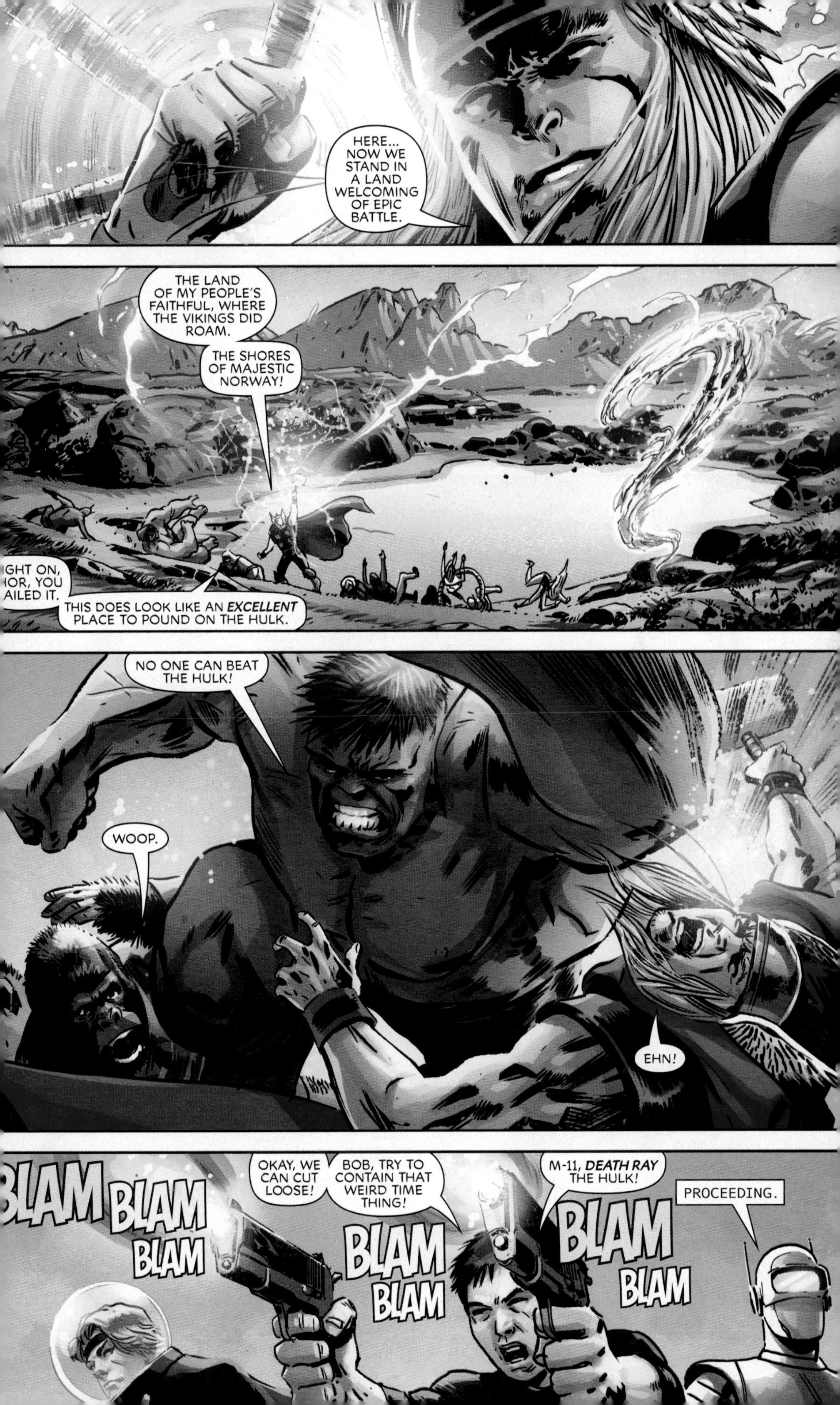

HERE... NOW WE STAND IN A LAND WELCOMING OF EPIC BATTLE.
THE LAND OF MY PEOPLE'S FAITHFUL, WHERE THE VIKINGS DID ROAM.
THE SHORES OF MAJESTIC NORWAY!
IGHT ON, HOR, YOU AILED IT.
THIS DOES LOOK LIKE AN EXCELLENT PLACE TO POUND ON THE HULK.
NO ONE CAN BEAT THE HULK!
WOOP.
EHN!
BLAM BLAM BLAM BLAM
OKAY, WE CAN CUT LOOSE!
BOB, TRY TO CONTAIN THAT WEIRD TIME THING!
BLAM BLAM
M-11, DEATH RAY THE HULK!
BLAM BLAM
PROCEEDING.

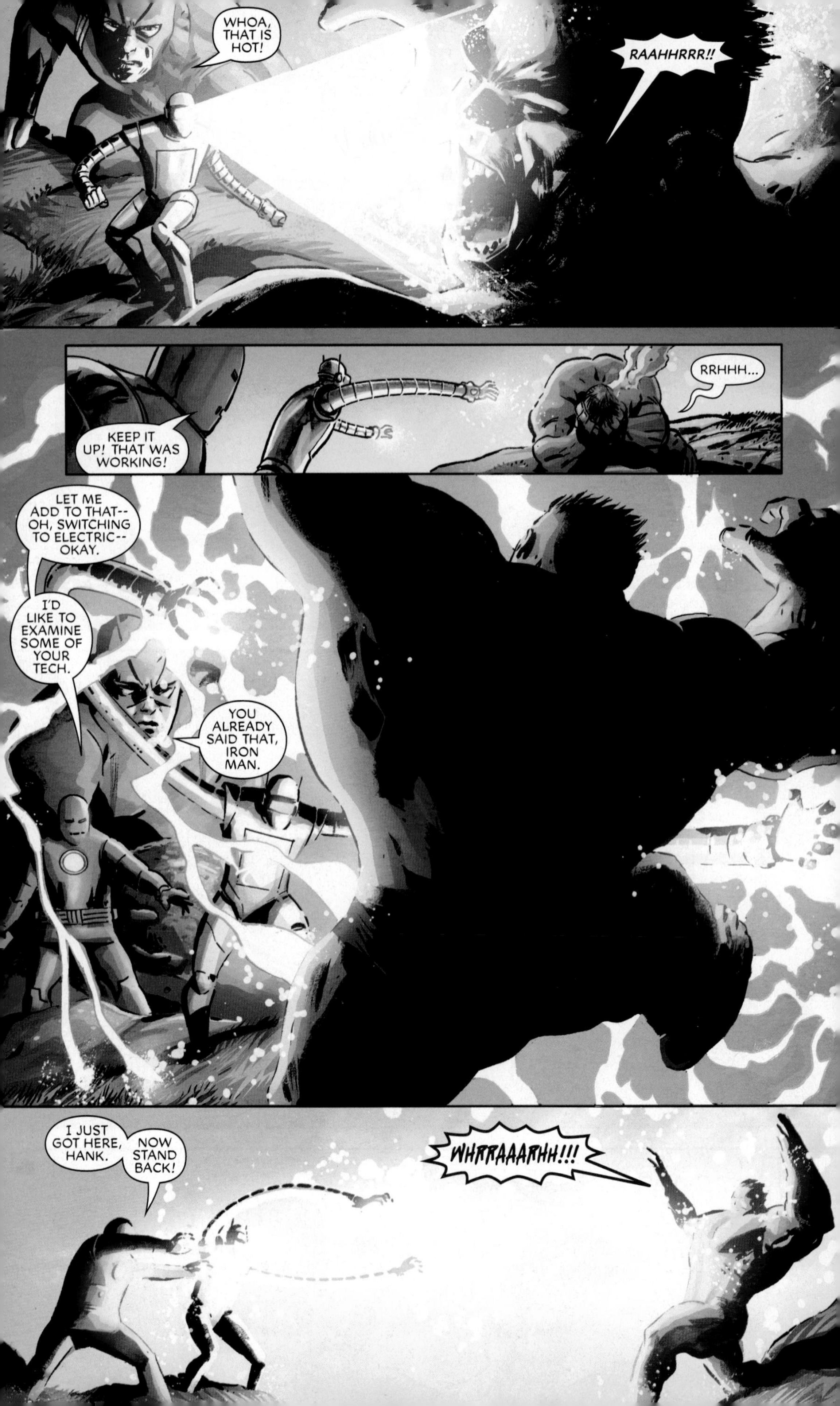

WHOA, THAT IS HOT!
RAAHHRRR!!
KEEP IT UP! THAT WAS WORKING!
RRHHH...
LET ME ADD TO THAT--OH, SWITCHING TO ELECTRIC--OKAY.
I'D LIKE TO EXAMINE SOME OF YOUR TECH.
YOU ALREADY SAID THAT, IRON MAN.
I JUST GOT HERE, HANK.
NOW STAND BACK!
WHRRAAARHH!!!

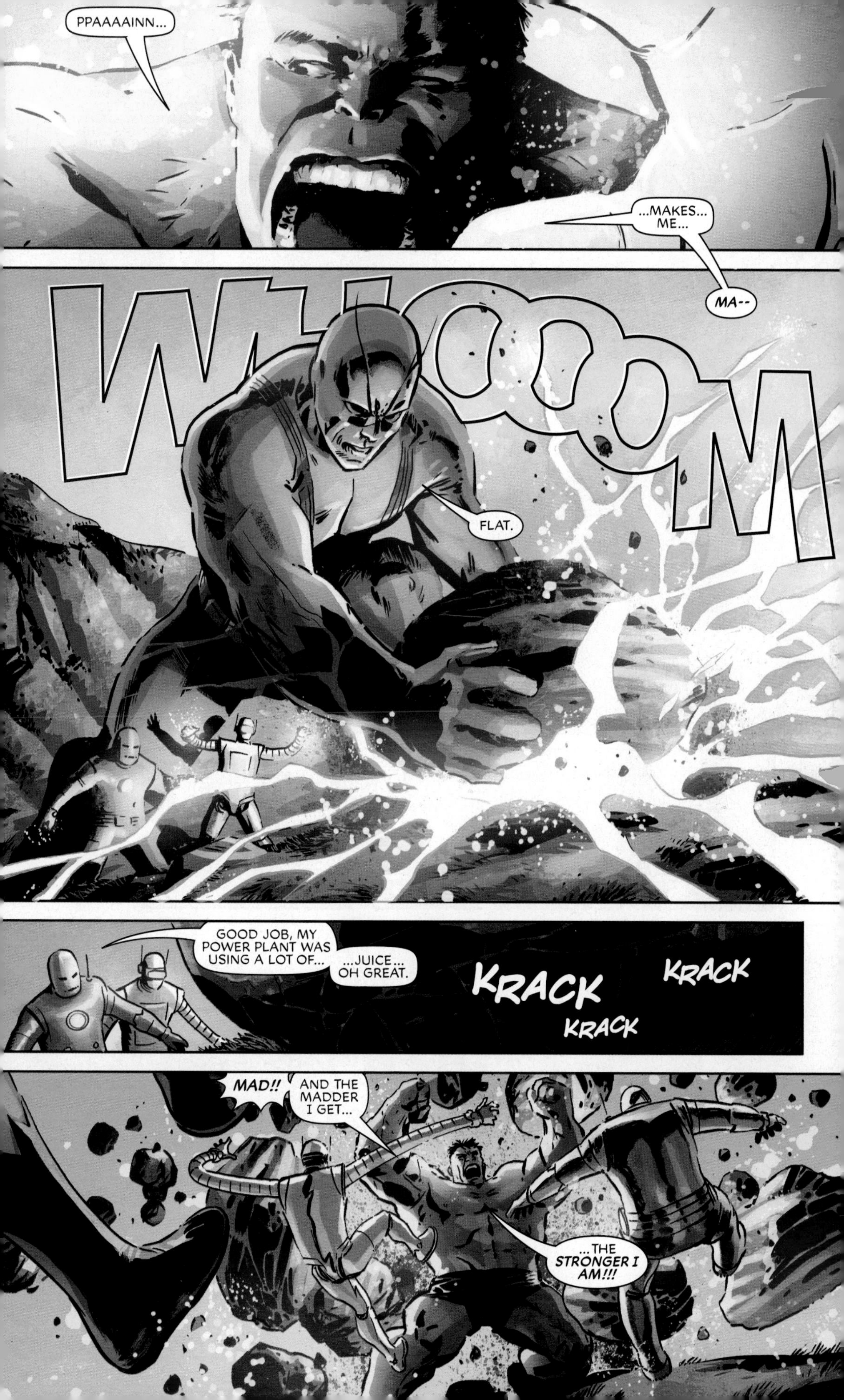
PPAAAAINN...
...MAKES... ME...
MA--
WHOOOOM
FLAT.
GOOD JOB, MY POWER PLANT WAS USING A LOT OF...
...JUICE... OH GREAT.
KRACK
KRACK
KRACK
MAD!!
AND THE MADDER I GET...
...THE STRONGER I AM!!!

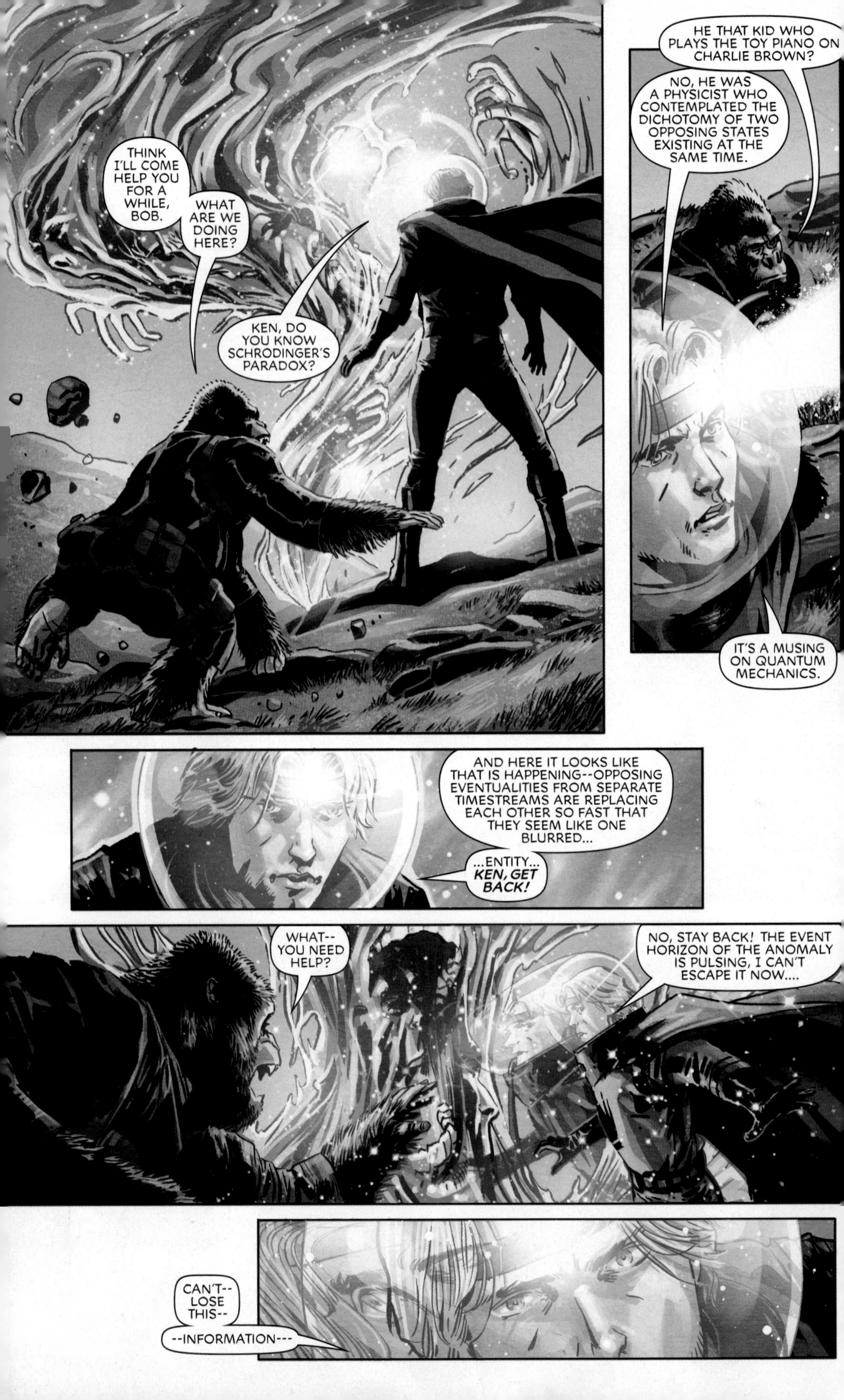
THINK I'LL COME HELP YOU FOR A WHILE, BOB.
WHAT ARE WE DOING HERE?
KEN, DO YOU KNOW SCHRODINGER'S PARADOX?
HE THAT KID WHO PLAYS THE TOY PIANO ON CHARLIE BROWN?
NO, HE WAS A PHYSICIST WHO CONTEMPLATED THE DICHOTOMY OF TWO OPPOSING STATES EXISTING AT THE SAME TIME.
IT'S A MUSING ON QUANTUM MECHANICS.
AND HERE IT LOOKS LIKE THAT IS HAPPENING--OPPOSING EVENTUALITIES FROM SEPARATE TIMESTREAMS ARE REPLACING EACH OTHER SO FAST THAT THEY SEEM LIKE ONE BLURRED...
...ENTITY... KEN, GET BACK!
WHAT-- YOU NEED HELP?
NO, STAY BACK! THE EVENT HORIZON OF THE ANOMALY IS PULSING, I CAN'T ESCAPE IT NOW....
CAN'T-- LOSE THIS--
--INFORMATION---

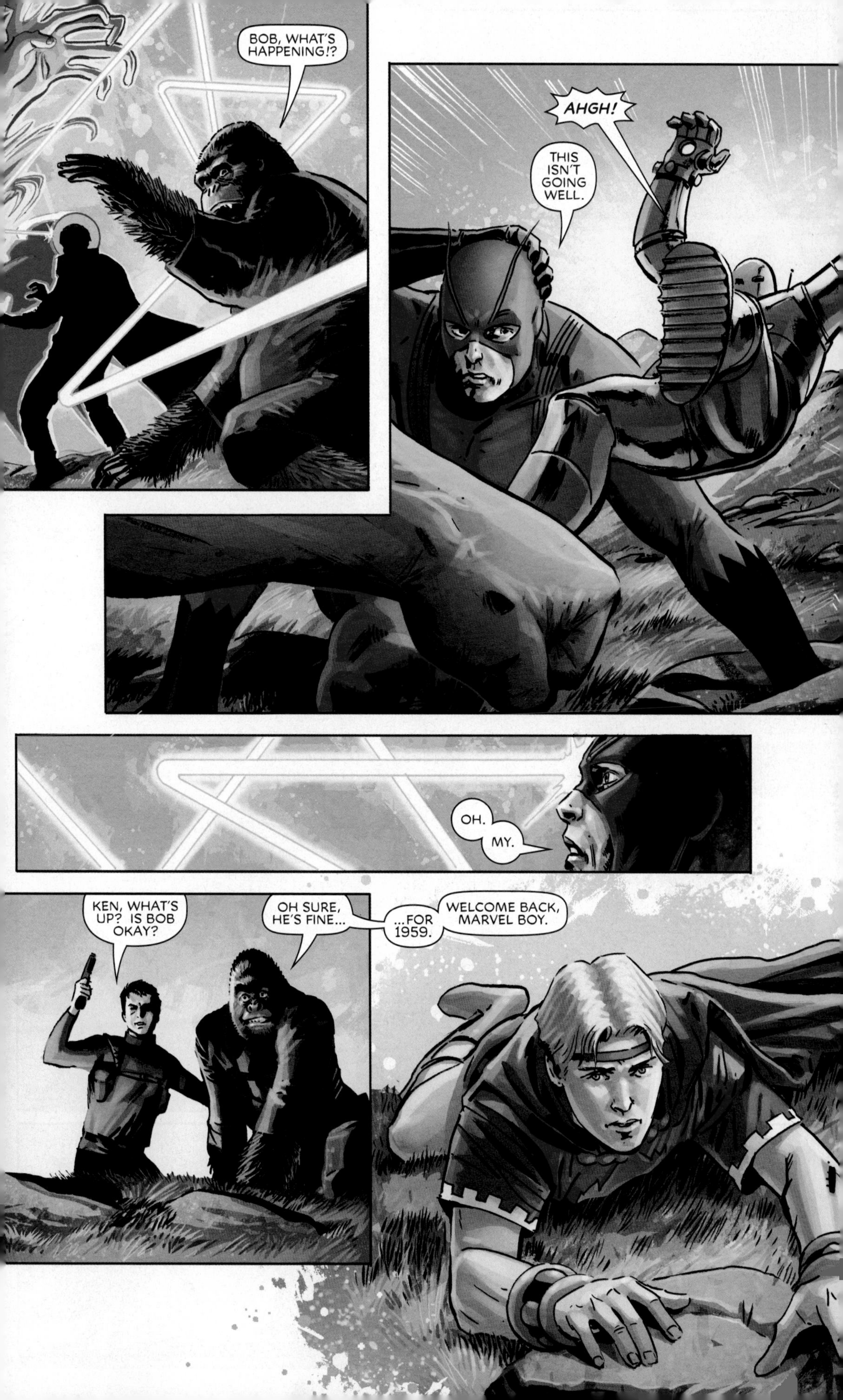

BOB, WHAT'S HAPPENING!?
AHGH!
THIS ISN'T GOING WELL.
OH.
MY.
KEN, WHAT'S UP? IS BOB OKAY?
OH SURE, HE'S FINE...
...FOR 1959.
WELCOME BACK, MARVEL BOY.

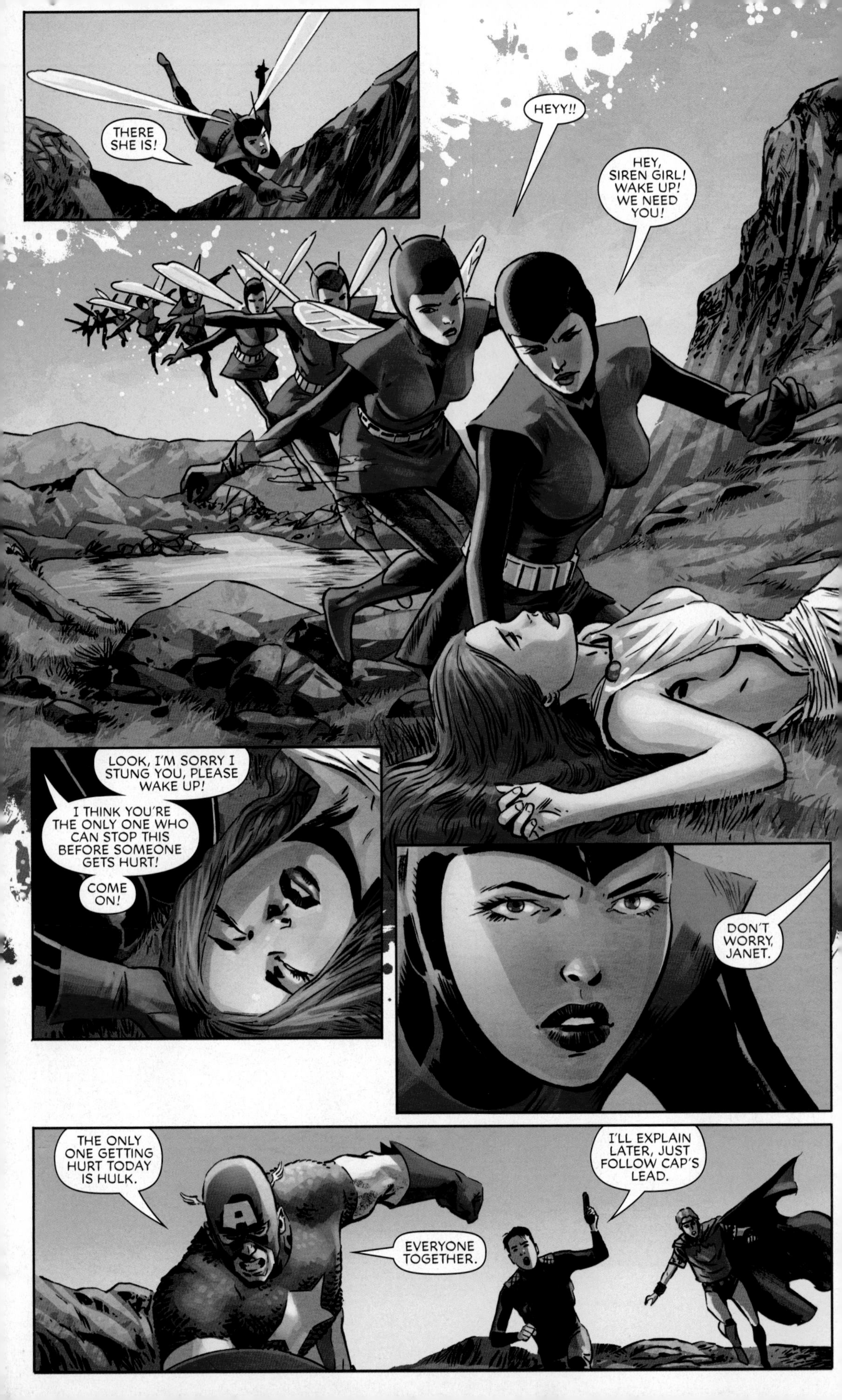
THERE SHE IS!
HEYY!!
HEY, SIREN GIRL! WAKE UP! WE NEED YOU!
LOOK, I'M SORRY I STUNG YOU, PLEASE WAKE UP!
I THINK YOU'RE THE ONLY ONE WHO CAN STOP THIS BEFORE SOMEONE GETS HURT!
COME ON!
DON'T WORRY, JANET.
THE ONLY ONE GETTING HURT TODAY IS HULK.
EVERYONE TOGETHER.
I'LL EXPLAIN LATER, JUST FOLLOW CAP'S LEAD.

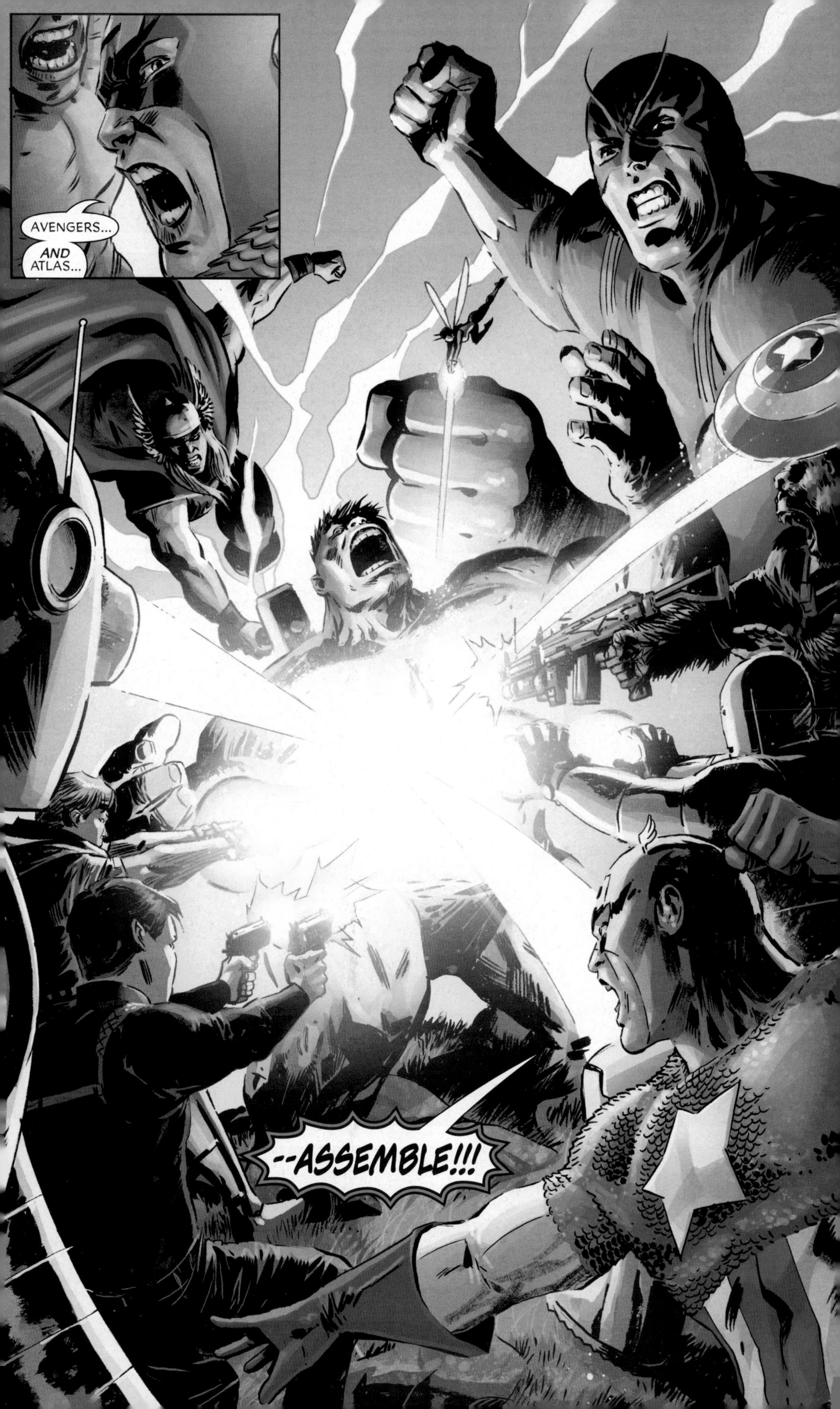
AVENGERS...
AND ATLAS...
--ASSEMBLE!!!

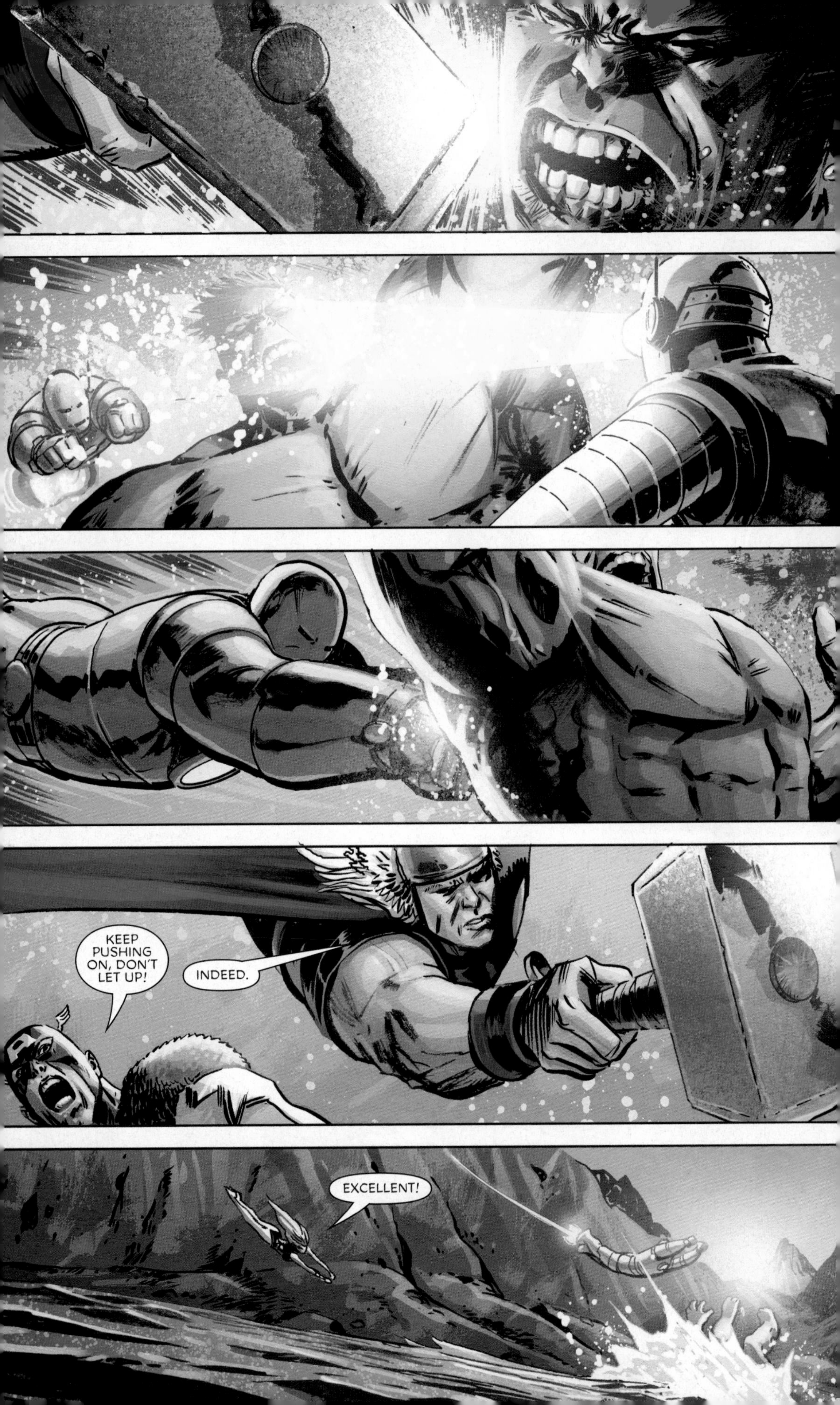
KEEP PUSHING ON, DON'T LET UP!
INDEED.
EXCELLENT!

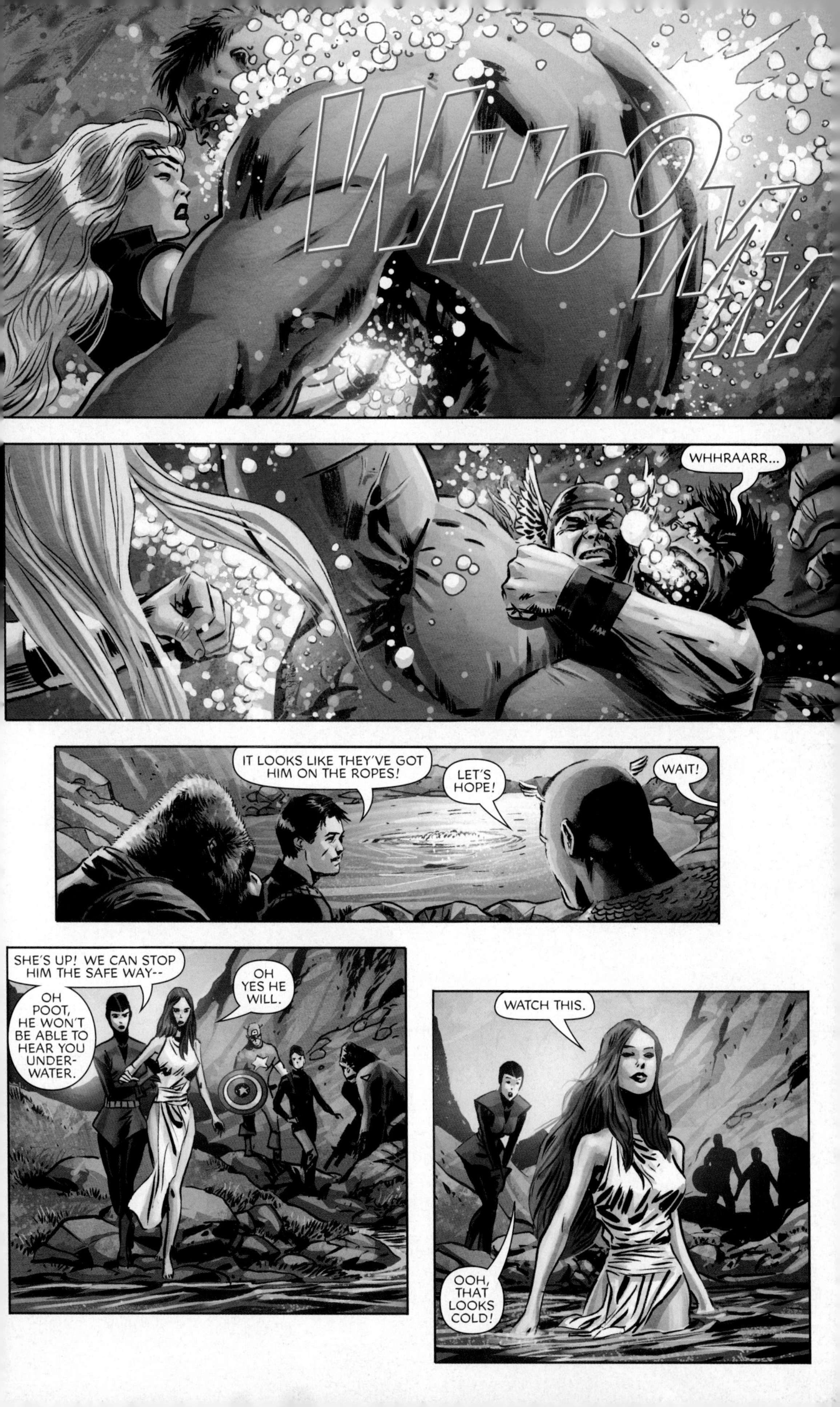
WHOOM
WHHRAARR...
IT LOOKS LIKE THEY'VE GOT HIM ON THE ROPES!
LET'S HOPE!
WAIT!
SHE'S UP! WE CAN STOP HIM THE SAFE WAY--
OH POOT, HE WON'T BE ABLE TO HEAR YOU UNDER-WATER.
OH YES HE WILL.
WATCH THIS.
OOH, THAT LOOKS COLD!

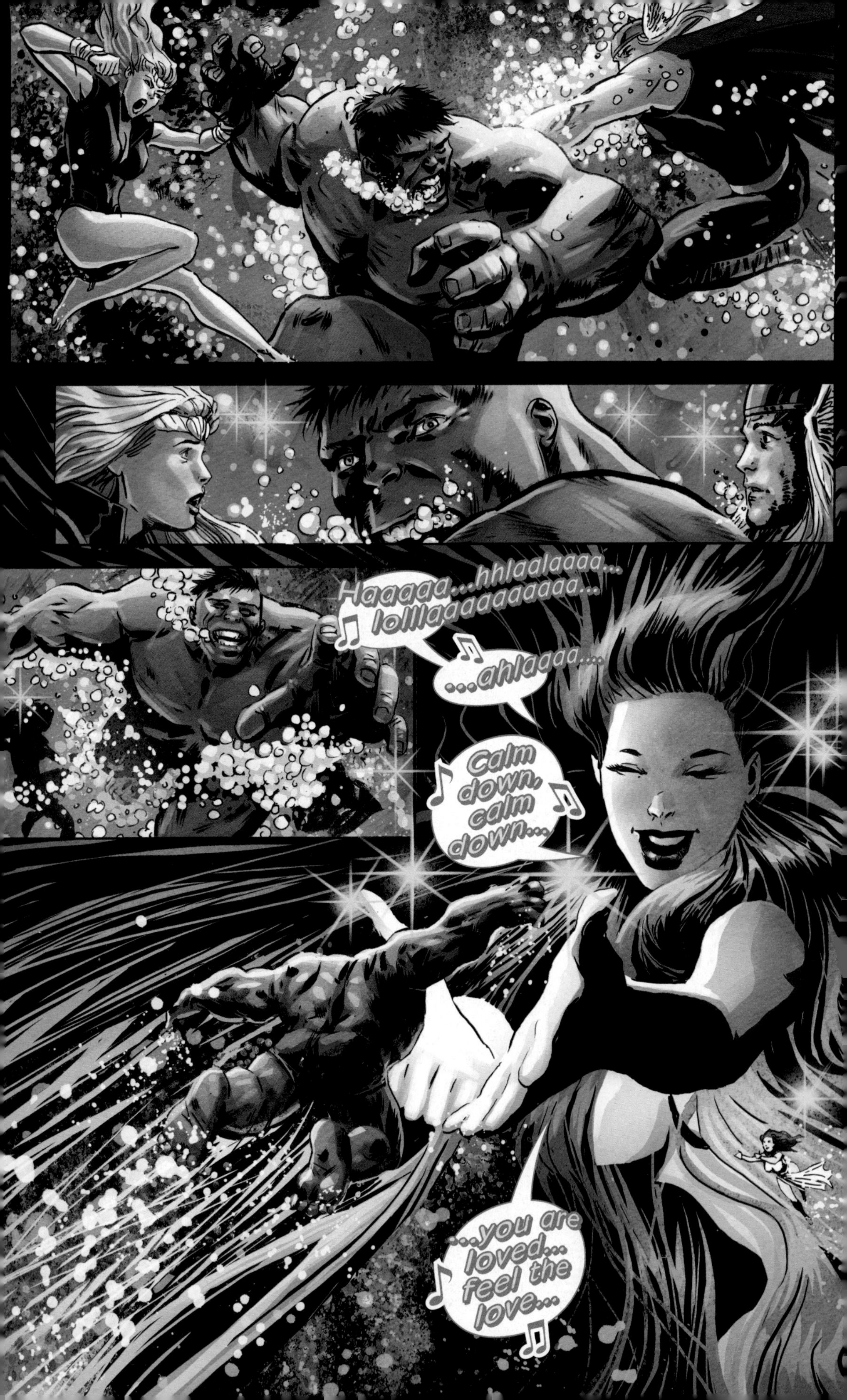
Haaaaa...hhlaalaaaa... lolllaaaaaaaaaa...
...ahlaaaa...
Calm down, calm down...
...you are loved... feel the love...

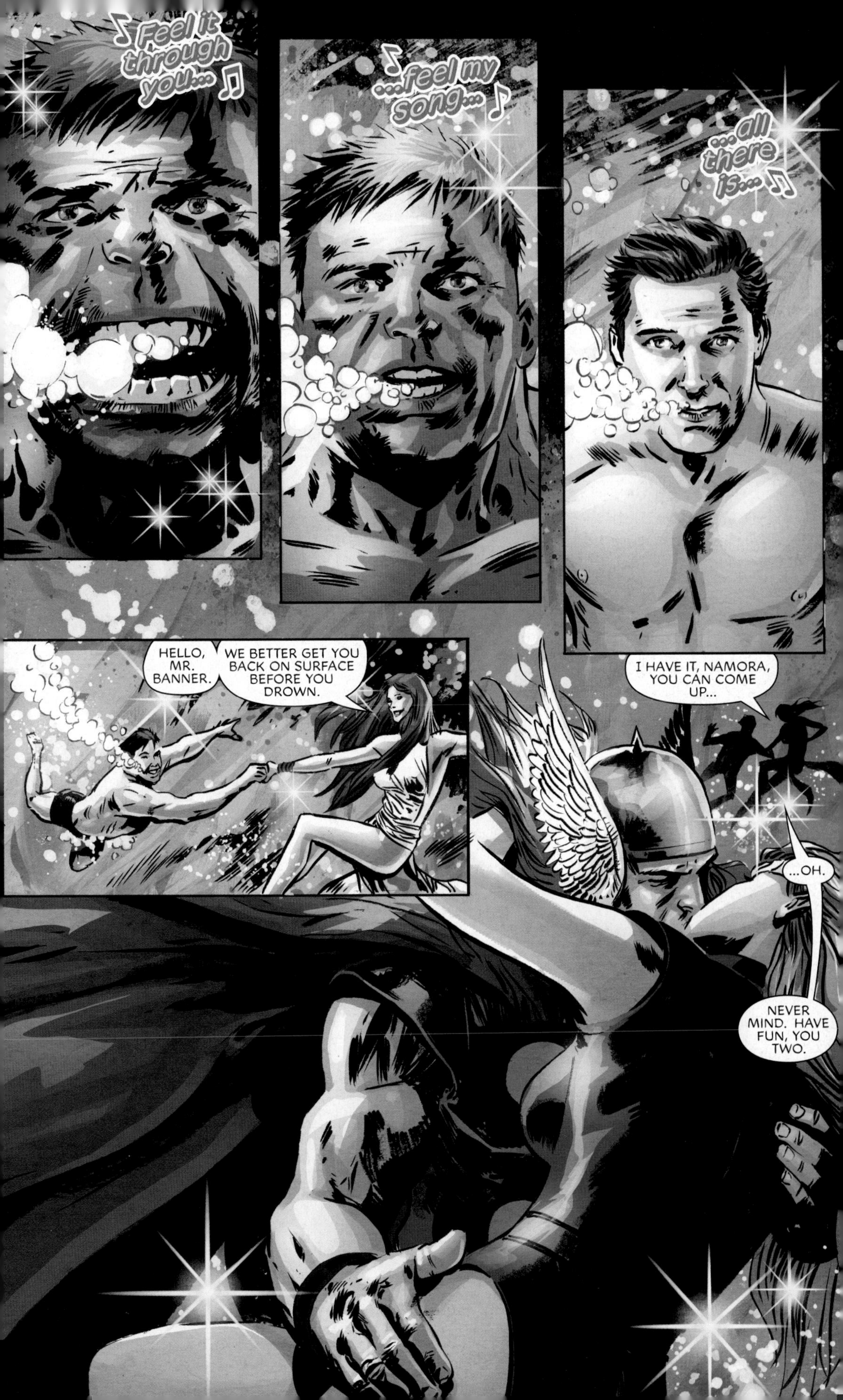
♪ Feel it through you... ♫
♪ ...feel my song... ♪
...all there is... ♫
HELLO, MR. BANNER.
WE BETTER GET YOU BACK ON SURFACE BEFORE YOU DROWN.
I HAVE IT, NAMORA, YOU CAN COME UP...
...OH.
NEVER MIND. HAVE FUN, YOU TWO.

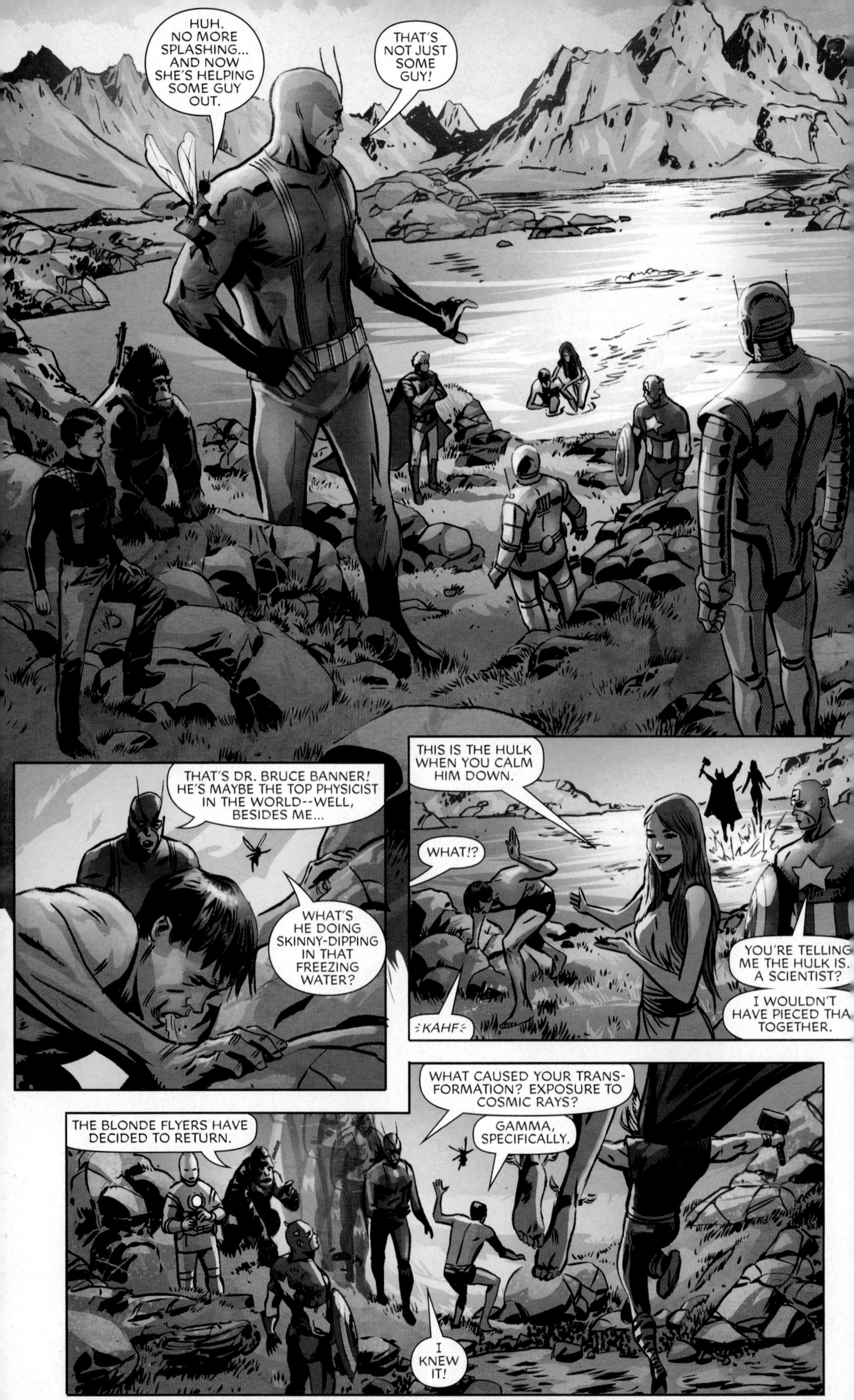
HUH. NO MORE SPLASHING... AND NOW SHE'S HELPING SOME GUY OUT.
THAT'S NOT JUST SOME GUY!
THAT'S DR. BRUCE BANNER! HE'S MAYBE THE TOP PHYSICIST IN THE WORLD--WELL, BESIDES ME...
WHAT'S HE DOING SKINNY-DIPPING IN THAT FREEZING WATER?
THIS IS THE HULK WHEN YOU CALM HIM DOWN.
WHAT!?
KAHF
YOU'RE TELLING ME THE HULK IS A SCIENTIST?
I WOULDN'T HAVE PIECED THA TOGETHER.
THE BLONDE FLYERS HAVE DECIDED TO RETURN.
WHAT CAUSED YOUR TRANSFORMATION? EXPOSURE TO COSMIC RAYS?
GAMMA, SPECIFICALLY.
I KNEW IT!

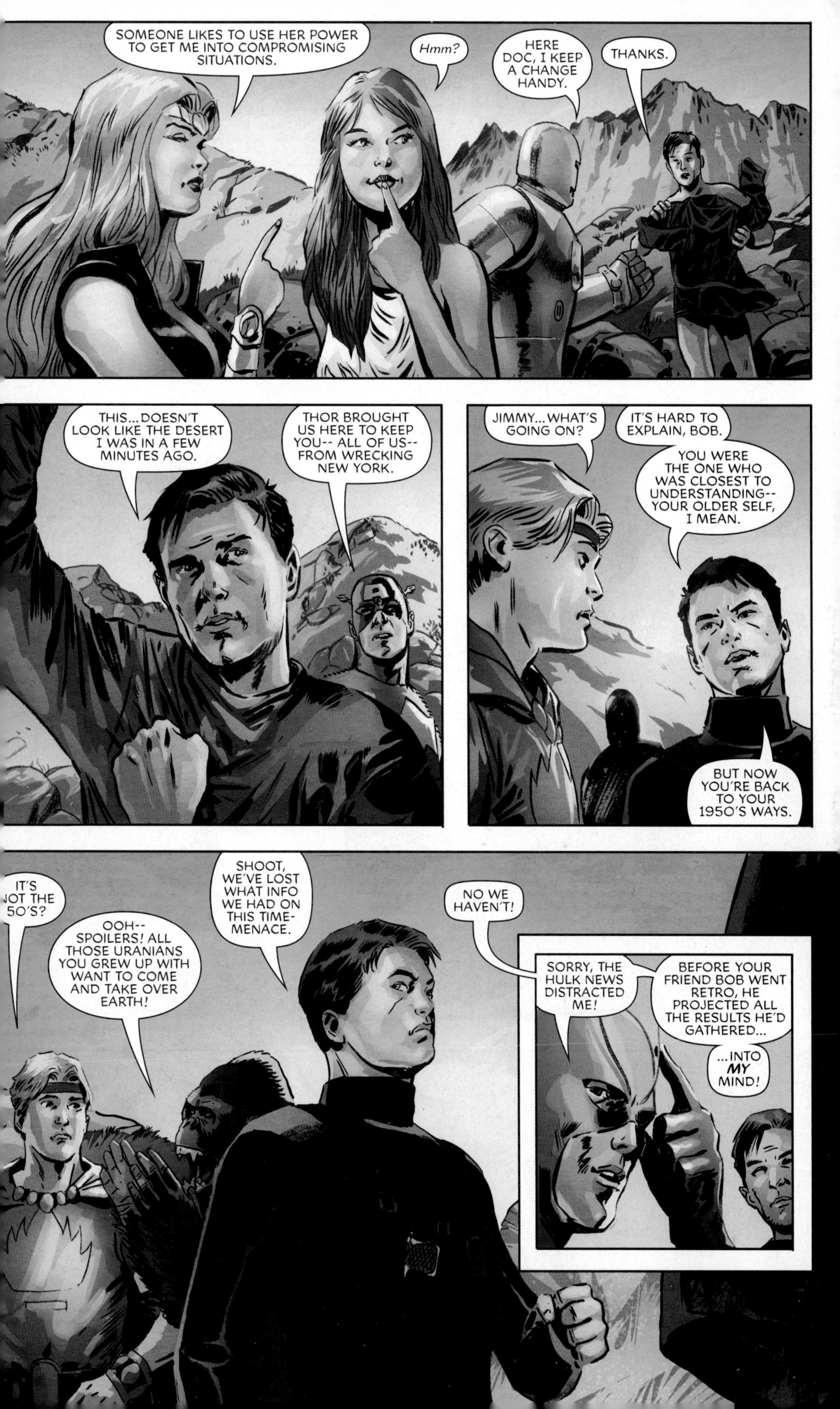
SOMEONE LIKES TO USE HER POWER TO GET ME INTO COMPROMISING SITUATIONS.
Hmm?
HERE DOC, I KEEP A CHANGE HANDY.
THANKS.
THIS...DOESN'T LOOK LIKE THE DESERT I WAS IN A FEW MINUTES AGO.
THOR BROUGHT US HERE TO KEEP YOU-- ALL OF US-- FROM WRECKING NEW YORK.
JIMMY...WHAT'S GOING ON?
IT'S HARD TO EXPLAIN, BOB.
YOU WERE THE ONE WHO WAS CLOSEST TO UNDERSTANDING-- YOUR OLDER SELF, I MEAN.
BUT NOW YOU'RE BACK TO YOUR 1950'S WAYS.
IT'S NOT THE 50'S?
OOH-- SPOILERS! ALL THOSE URANIANS YOU GREW UP WITH WANT TO COME AND TAKE OVER EARTH!
SHOOT, WE'VE LOST WHAT INFO WE HAD ON THIS TIME-MENACE.
NO WE HAVEN'T!
SORRY, THE HULK NEWS DISTRACTED ME!
BEFORE YOUR FRIEND BOB WENT RETRO, HE PROJECTED ALL THE RESULTS HE'D GATHERED...
...INTO *MY* MIND!

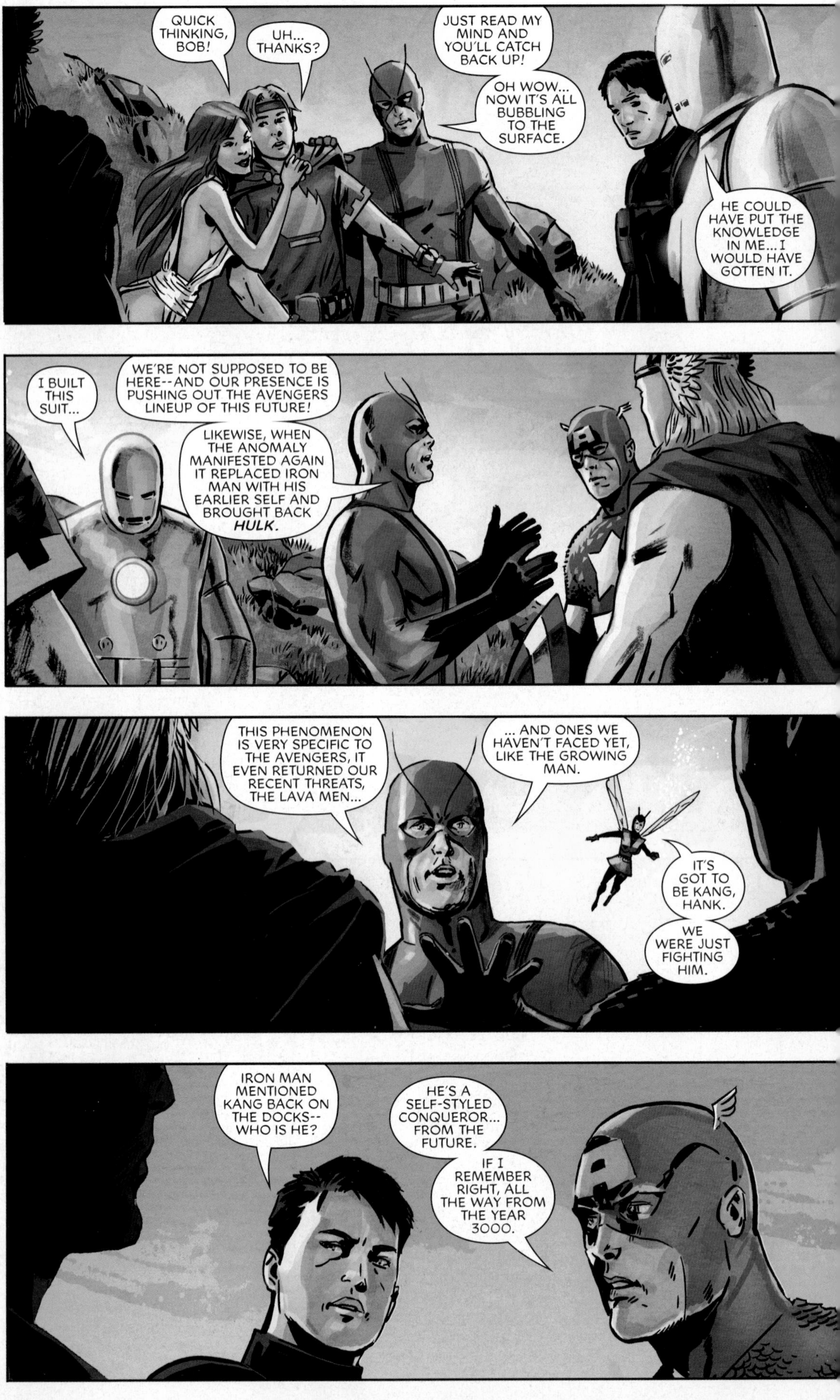

QUICK THINKING, BOB!
UH... THANKS?
JUST READ MY MIND AND YOU'LL CATCH BACK UP!
OH WOW... NOW IT'S ALL BUBBLING TO THE SURFACE.
HE COULD HAVE PUT THE KNOWLEDGE IN ME... I WOULD HAVE GOTTEN IT.
I BUILT THIS SUIT...
WE'RE NOT SUPPOSED TO BE HERE--AND OUR PRESENCE IS PUSHING OUT THE AVENGERS LINEUP OF THIS FUTURE!
LIKEWISE, WHEN THE ANOMALY MANIFESTED AGAIN IT REPLACED IRON MAN WITH HIS EARLIER SELF AND BROUGHT BACK *HULK*.
THIS PHENOMENON IS VERY SPECIFIC TO THE AVENGERS, IT EVEN RETURNED OUR RECENT THREATS, THE LAVA MEN...
... AND ONES WE HAVEN'T FACED YET, LIKE THE GROWING MAN.
IT'S GOT TO BE KANG, HANK.
WE WERE JUST FIGHTING HIM.
IRON MAN MENTIONED KANG BACK ON THE DOCKS-- WHO IS HE?
HE'S A SELF-STYLED CONQUEROR... FROM THE FUTURE.
IF I REMEMBER RIGHT, ALL THE WAY FROM THE YEAR 3000.

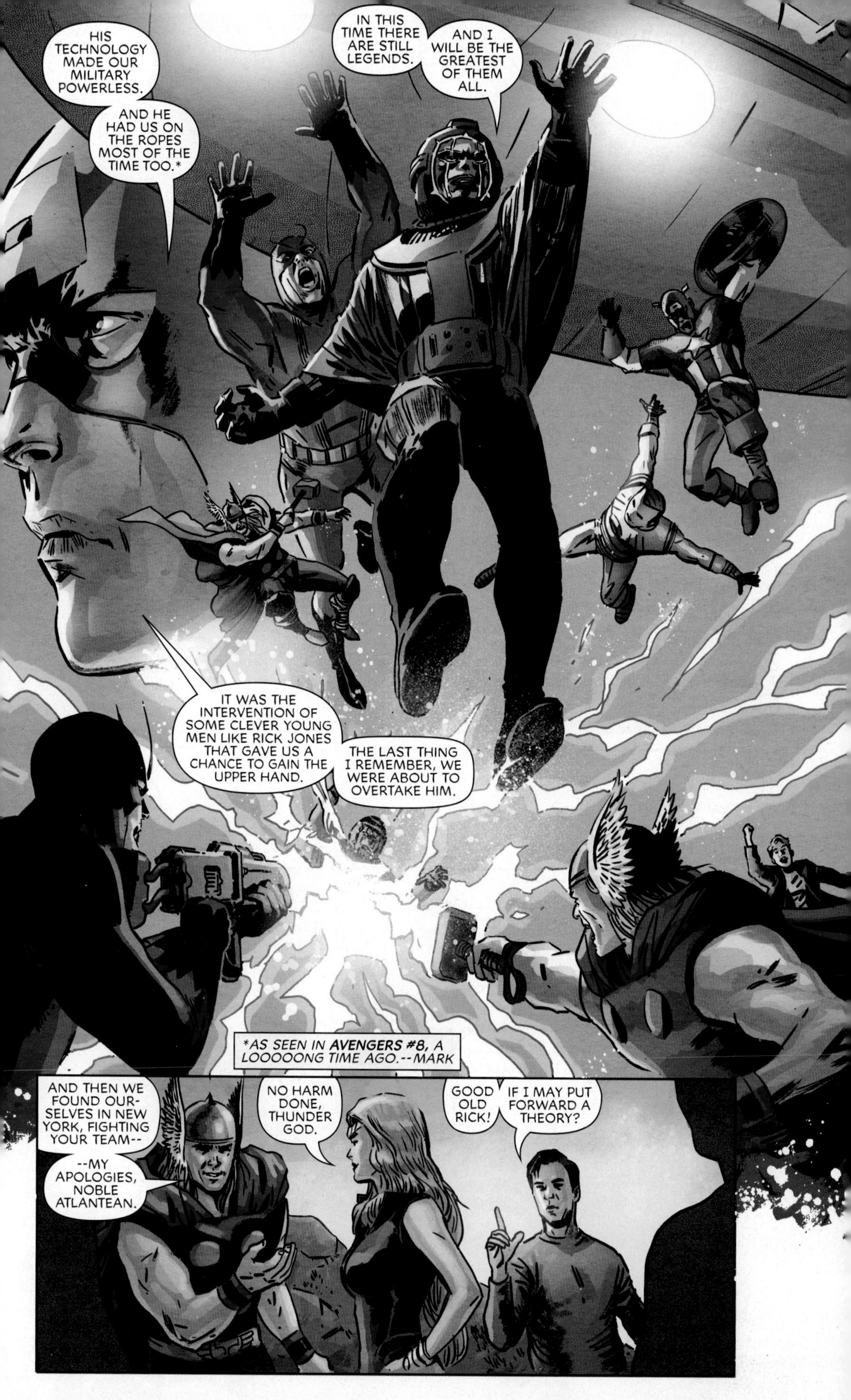
HIS TECHNOLOGY MADE OUR MILITARY POWERLESS.
AND HE HAD US ON THE ROPES MOST OF THE TIME TOO.*
IN THIS TIME THERE ARE STILL LEGENDS.
AND I WILL BE THE GREATEST OF THEM ALL.
IT WAS THE INTERVENTION OF SOME CLEVER YOUNG MEN LIKE RICK JONES THAT GAVE US A CHANCE TO GAIN THE UPPER HAND.
THE LAST THING I REMEMBER, WE WERE ABOUT TO OVERTAKE HIM.
*AS SEEN IN AVENGERS #8, A LOOOOONG TIME AGO.--MARK
AND THEN WE FOUND OUR-SELVES IN NEW YORK, FIGHTING YOUR TEAM--
--MY APOLOGIES, NOBLE ATLANTEAN.
NO HARM DONE, THUNDER GOD.
GOOD OLD RICK!
IF I MAY PUT FORWARD A THEORY?

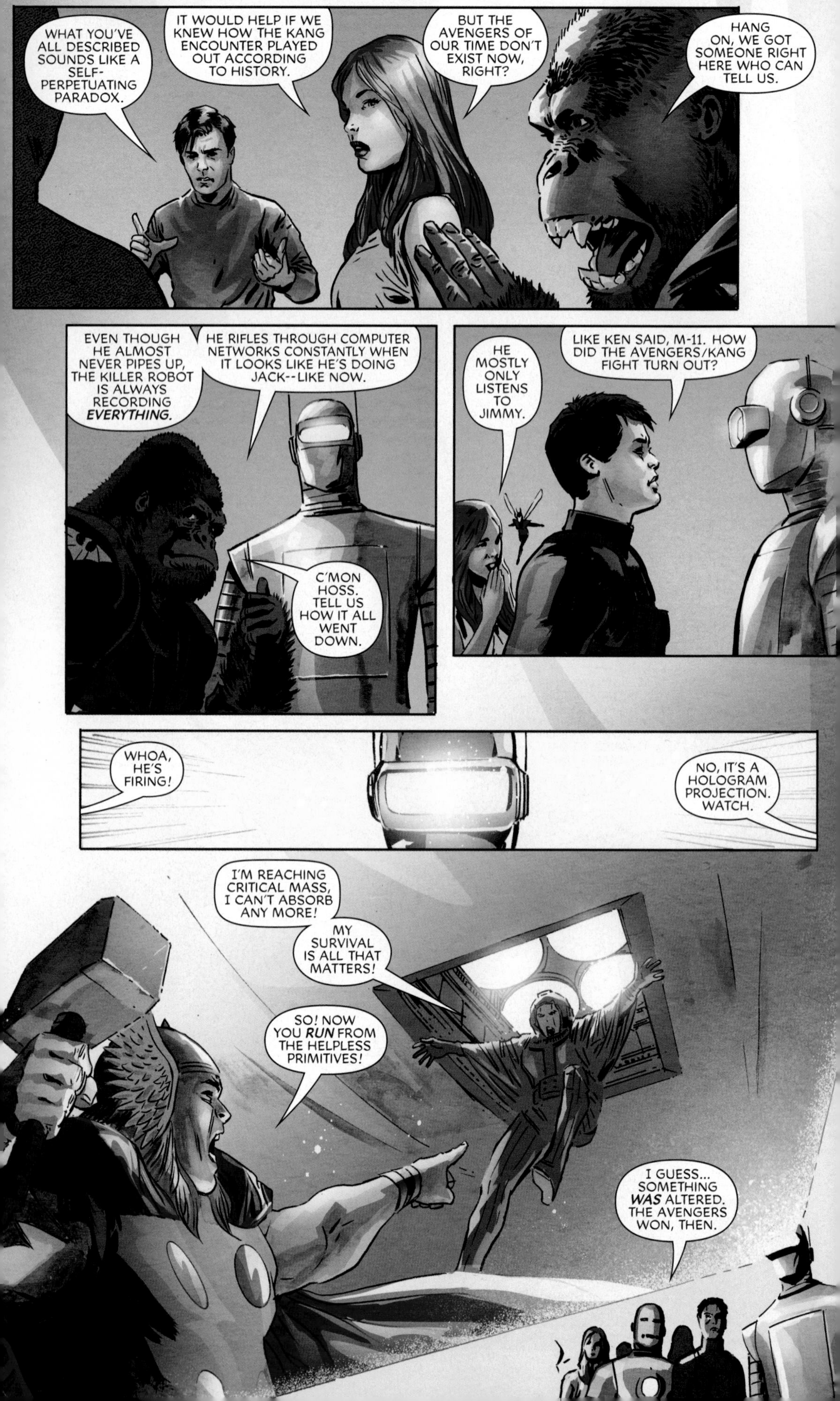
WHAT YOU'VE ALL DESCRIBED SOUNDS LIKE A SELF-PERPETUATING PARADOX.
IT WOULD HELP IF WE KNEW HOW THE KANG ENCOUNTER PLAYED OUT ACCORDING TO HISTORY.
BUT THE AVENGERS OF OUR TIME DON'T EXIST NOW, RIGHT?
HANG ON, WE GOT SOMEONE RIGHT HERE WHO CAN TELL US.
EVEN THOUGH HE ALMOST NEVER PIPES UP, THE KILLER ROBOT IS ALWAYS RECORDING EVERYTHING.
HE RIFLES THROUGH COMPUTER NETWORKS CONSTANTLY WHEN IT LOOKS LIKE HE'S DOING JACK--LIKE NOW.
C'MON HOSS. TELL US HOW IT ALL WENT DOWN.
HE MOSTLY ONLY LISTENS TO JIMMY.
LIKE KEN SAID, M-11. HOW DID THE AVENGERS/KANG FIGHT TURN OUT?
WHOA, HE'S FIRING!
NO, IT'S A HOLOGRAM PROJECTION. WATCH.
I'M REACHING CRITICAL MASS, I CAN'T ABSORB ANY MORE!
MY SURVIVAL IS ALL THAT MATTERS!
SO! NOW YOU RUN FROM THE HELPLESS PRIMITIVES!
I GUESS... SOMETHING WAS ALTERED. THE AVENGERS WON, THEN.

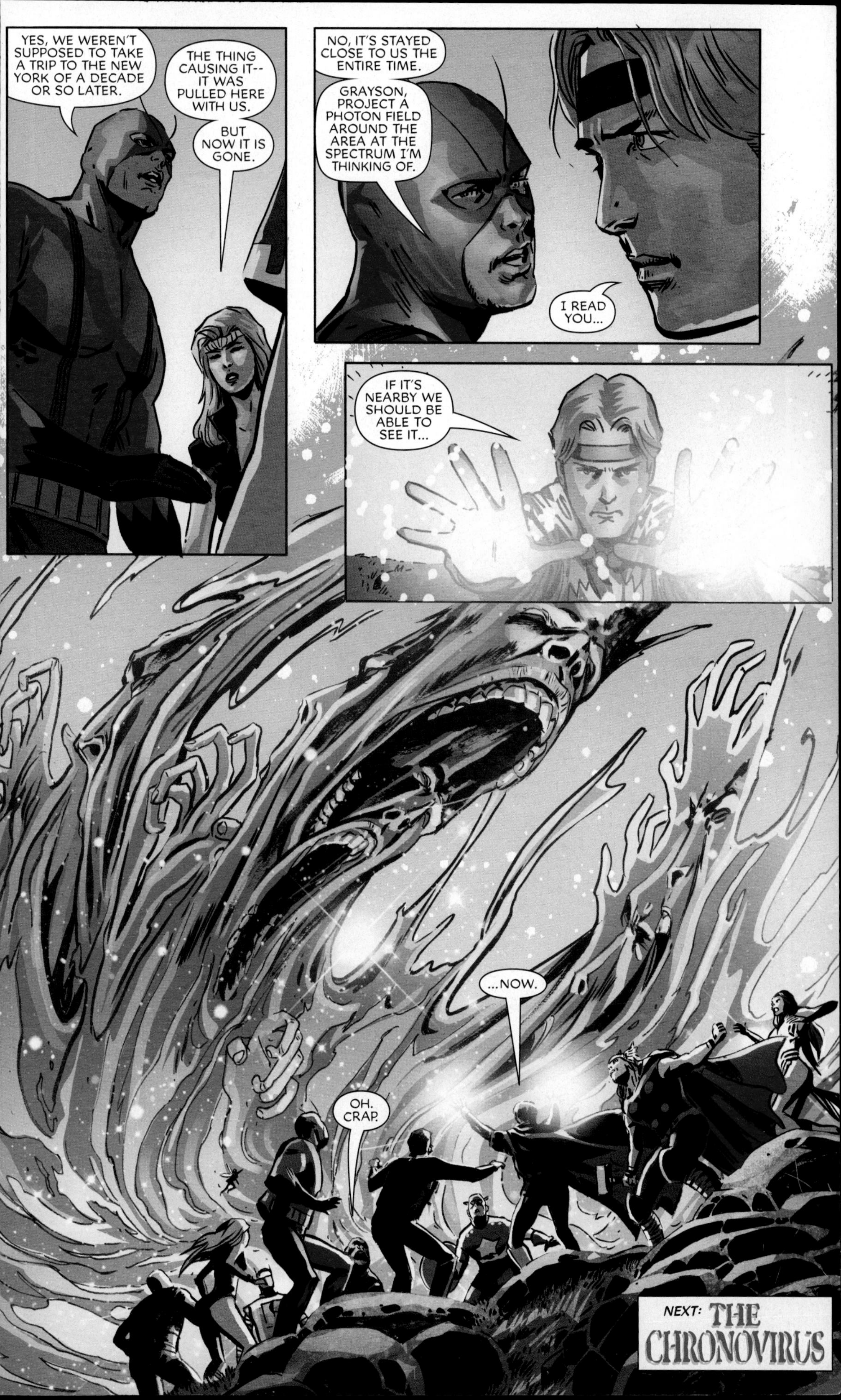

YES, WE WEREN'T SUPPOSED TO TAKE A TRIP TO THE NEW YORK OF A DECADE OR SO LATER.
THE THING CAUSING IT-- IT WAS PULLED HERE WITH US.
BUT NOW IT IS GONE.
NO, IT'S STAYED CLOSE TO US THE ENTIRE TIME.
GRAYSON, PROJECT A PHOTON FIELD AROUND THE AREA AT THE SPECTRUM I'M THINKING OF.
I READ YOU...
IF IT'S NEARBY WE SHOULD BE ABLE TO SEE IT...
...NOW.
OH. CRAP.
NEXT: THE CHRONOVIRUS

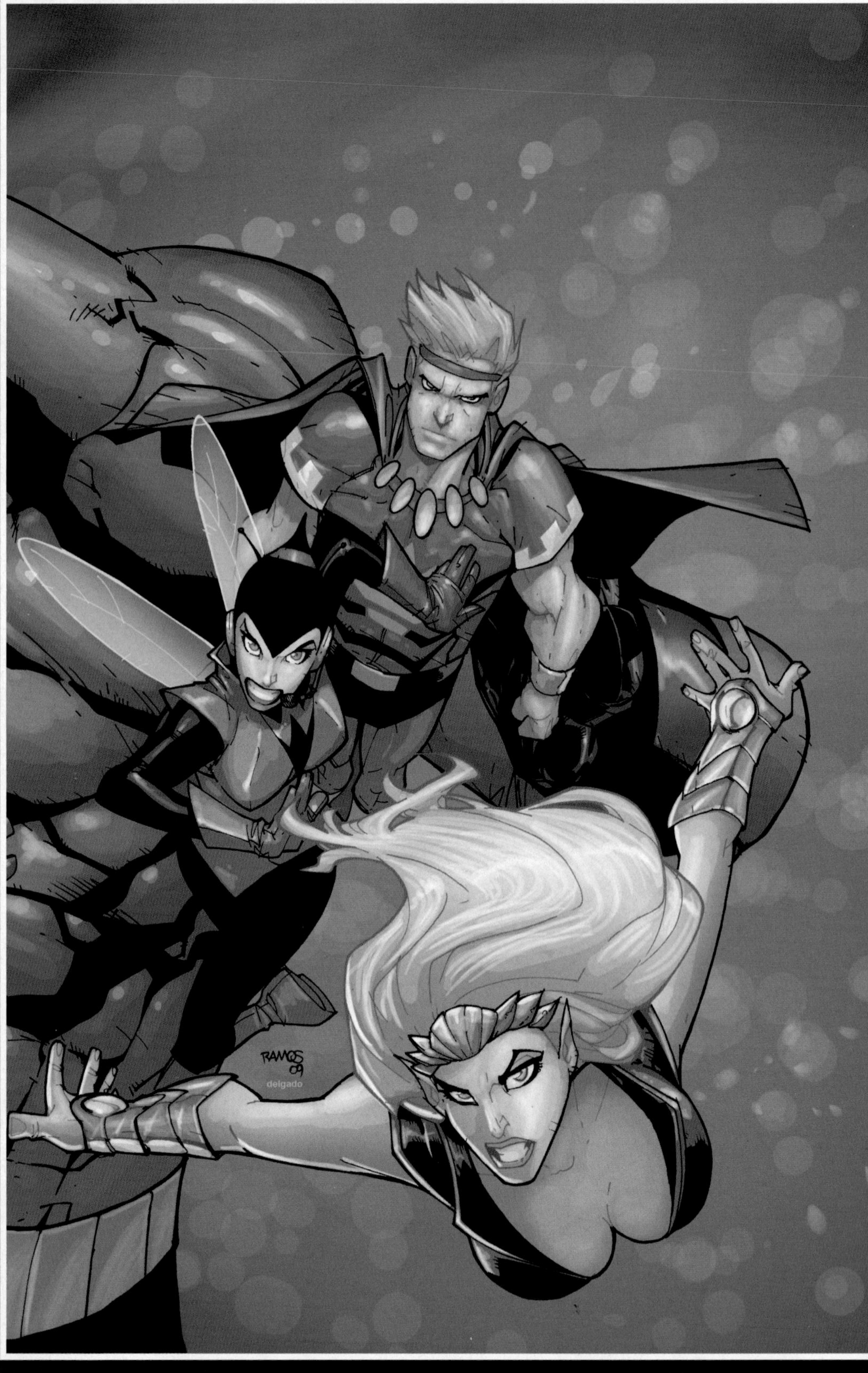
RAMOS
09
delgado

AVENGERS VS. ATLAS

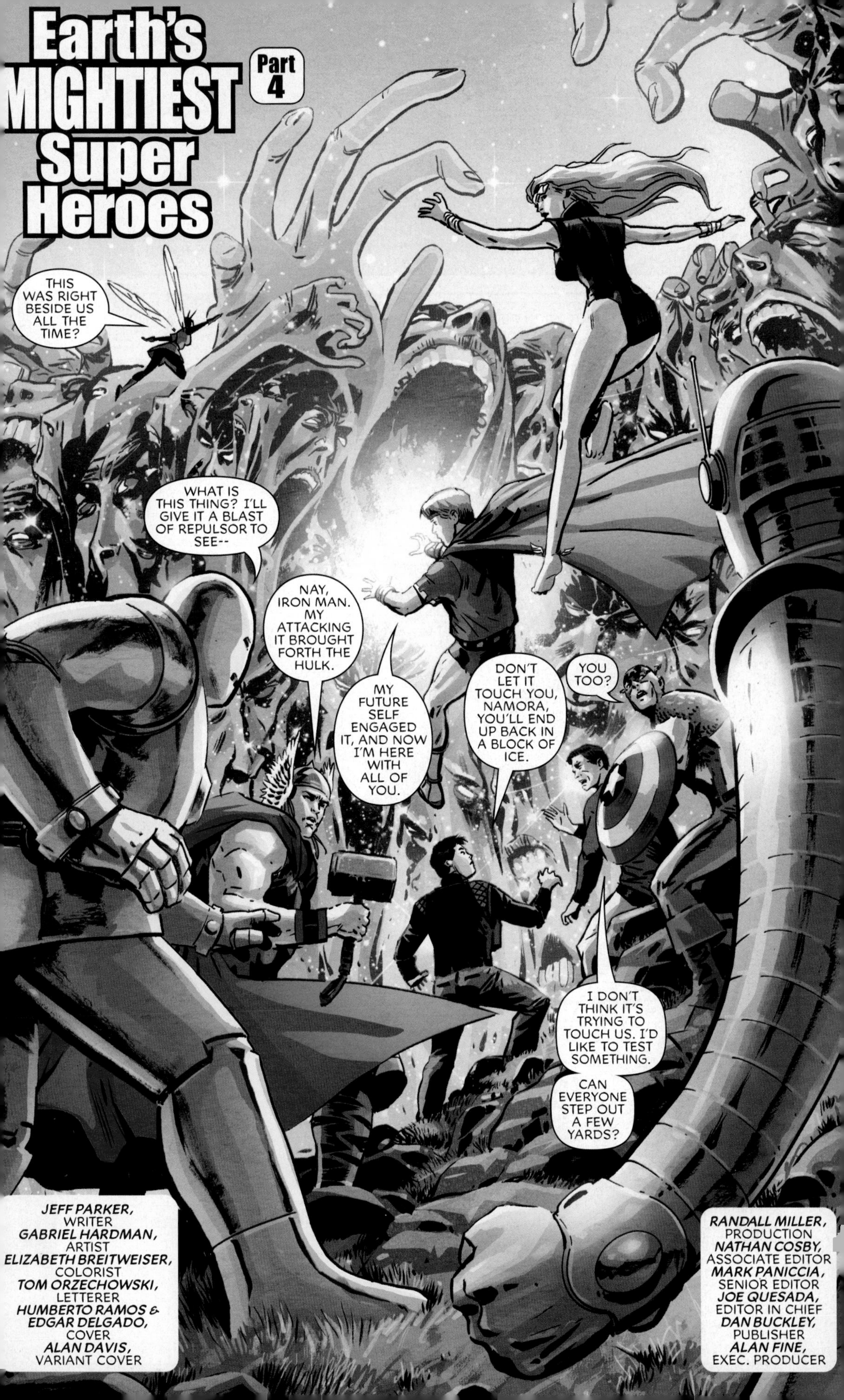
Earth's MIGHTIEST Super Heroes
Part 4
THIS WAS RIGHT BESIDE US ALL THE TIME?
WHAT IS THIS THING? I'LL GIVE IT A BLAST OF REPULSOR TO SEE--
NAY, IRON MAN. MY ATTACKING IT BROUGHT FORTH THE HULK.
MY FUTURE SELF ENGAGED IT, AND NOW I'M HERE WITH ALL OF YOU.
DON'T LET IT TOUCH YOU, NAMORA, YOU'LL END UP BACK IN A BLOCK OF ICE.
YOU TOO?
I DON'T THINK IT'S TRYING TO TOUCH US. I'D LIKE TO TEST SOMETHING.
CAN EVERYONE STEP OUT A FEW YARDS?
JEFF PARKER, WRITER
GABRIEL HARDMAN, ARTIST
ELIZABETH BREITWEISER, COLORIST
TOM ORZECHOWSKI, LETTERER
HUMBERTO RAMOS & EDGAR DELGADO, COVER
ALAN DAVIS, VARIANT COVER
RANDALL MILLER, PRODUCTION
NATHAN COSBY, ASSOCIATE EDITOR
MARK PANICCIA, SENIOR EDITOR
JOE QUESADA, EDITOR IN CHIEF
DAN BUCKLEY, PUBLISHER
ALAN FINE, EXEC. PRODUCER

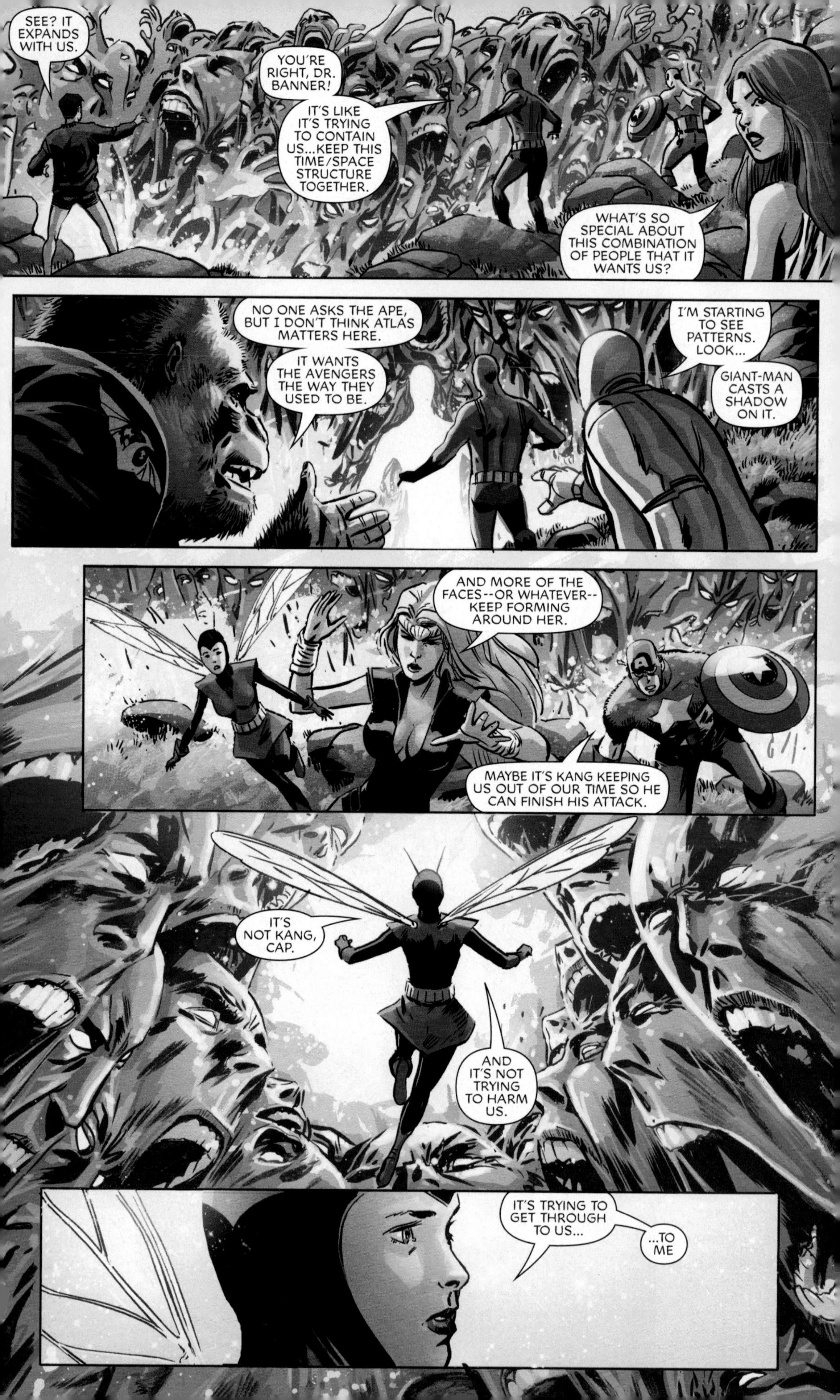
SEE? IT EXPANDS WITH US.
YOU'RE RIGHT, DR. BANNER!
IT'S LIKE IT'S TRYING TO CONTAIN US...KEEP THIS TIME/SPACE STRUCTURE TOGETHER.
WHAT'S SO SPECIAL ABOUT THIS COMBINATION OF PEOPLE THAT IT WANTS US?
NO ONE ASKS THE APE, BUT I DON'T THINK ATLAS MATTERS HERE.
IT WANTS THE AVENGERS THE WAY THEY USED TO BE.
I'M STARTING TO SEE PATTERNS. LOOK...
GIANT-MAN CASTS A SHADOW ON IT.
AND MORE OF THE FACES--OR WHATEVER--KEEP FORMING AROUND HER.
MAYBE IT'S KANG KEEPING US OUT OF OUR TIME SO HE CAN FINISH HIS ATTACK.
IT'S NOT KANG, CAP.
AND IT'S NOT TRYING TO HARM US.
IT'S TRYING TO GET THROUGH TO US...
...TO ME

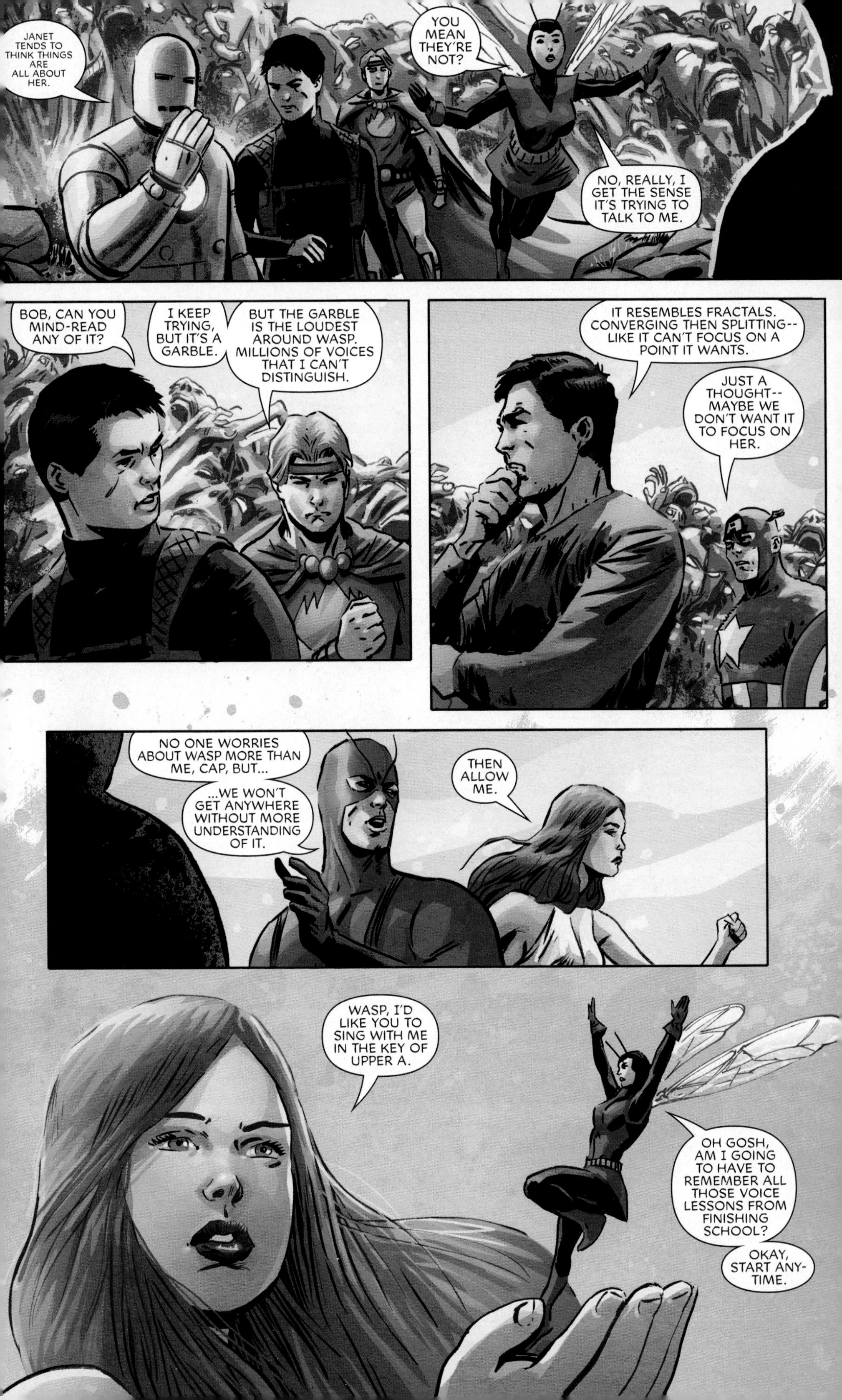
JANET TENDS TO THINK THINGS ARE ALL ABOUT HER.
YOU MEAN THEY'RE NOT?
NO, REALLY, I GET THE SENSE IT'S TRYING TO TALK TO ME.
BOB, CAN YOU MIND-READ ANY OF IT?
I KEEP TRYING, BUT IT'S A GARBLE.
BUT THE GARBLE IS THE LOUDEST AROUND WASP. MILLIONS OF VOICES THAT I CAN'T DISTINGUISH.
IT RESEMBLES FRACTALS. CONVERGING THEN SPLITTING-- LIKE IT CAN'T FOCUS ON A POINT IT WANTS.
JUST A THOUGHT-- MAYBE WE DON'T WANT IT TO FOCUS ON HER.
NO ONE WORRIES ABOUT WASP MORE THAN ME, CAP, BUT...
...WE WON'T GET ANYWHERE WITHOUT MORE UNDERSTANDING OF IT.
THEN ALLOW ME.
WASP, I'D LIKE YOU TO SING WITH ME IN THE KEY OF UPPER A.
OH GOSH, AM I GOING TO HAVE TO REMEMBER ALL THOSE VOICE LESSONS FROM FINISHING SCHOOL?
OKAY, START ANY-TIME.

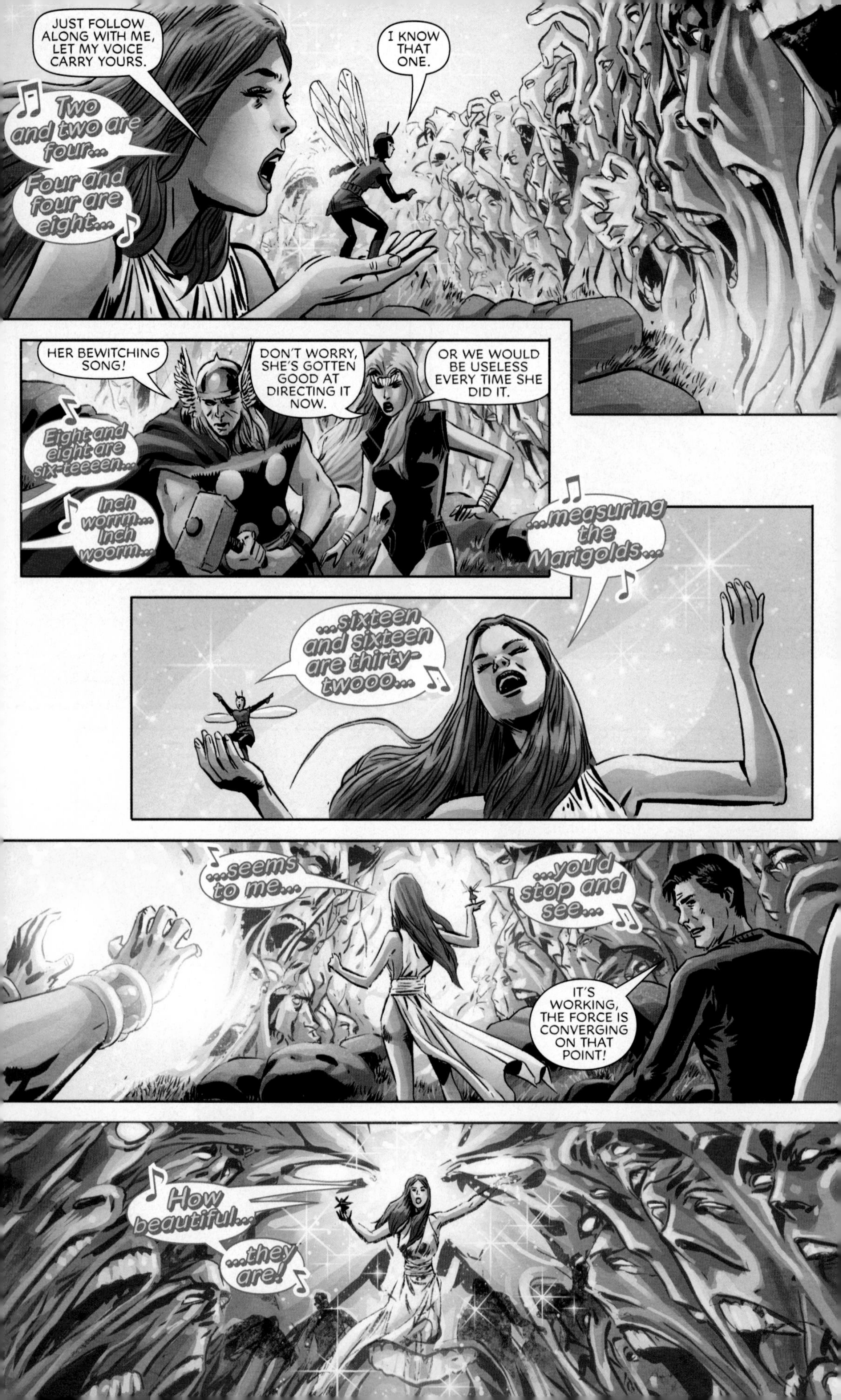

JUST FOLLOW ALONG WITH ME, LET MY VOICE CARRY YOURS.
Two and two are four... Four and four are eight...
I KNOW THAT ONE.
HER BEWITCHING SONG!
DON'T WORRY, SHE'S GOTTEN GOOD AT DIRECTING IT NOW.
OR WE WOULD BE USELESS EVERY TIME SHE DID IT.
Eight and eight are six-teeeen...
Inch worrm... Inch woorm...
...measuring the Marigolds...
...sixteen and sixteen are thirty-twooo...
...seems to me...
...you'd stop and see...
IT'S WORKING, THE FORCE IS CONVERGING ON THAT POINT!
How beautiful...
...they are!

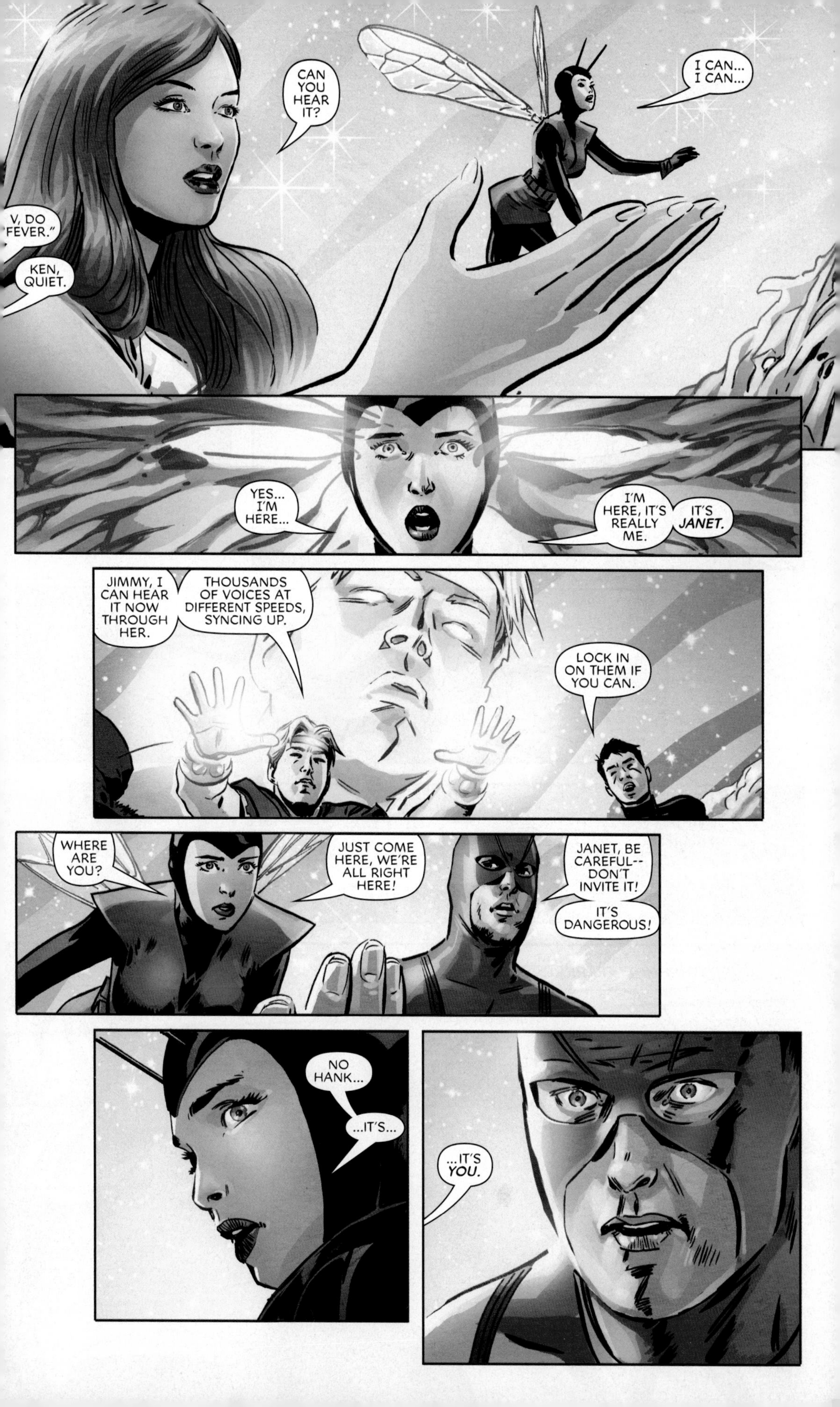
CAN YOU HEAR IT?
I CAN... I CAN...
V, DO FEVER."
KEN, QUIET.
YES... I'M HERE...
I'M HERE, IT'S REALLY ME.
IT'S JANET.
JIMMY, I CAN HEAR IT NOW THROUGH HER.
THOUSANDS OF VOICES AT DIFFERENT SPEEDS, SYNCING UP.
LOCK IN ON THEM IF YOU CAN.
WHERE ARE YOU?
JUST COME HERE, WE'RE ALL RIGHT HERE!
JANET, BE CAREFUL-- DON'T INVITE IT!
IT'S DANGEROUS!
NO HANK...
...IT'S...
...IT'S YOU.

SHE'S RIGHT--I CAN READ THEM--HIM--NOW.

THEN CONNECT ME THROUGH YOUR HEADBAND INSTRUMENT!

A PSYCHIC CONNECTION TO MY BRAIN SHOULD BRIDGE THE GAP.

I CAN'T DO THAT.

YES YOU CAN, BOB. THE URANIANS HAD AN INHIBITOR SET ON YOUR BAND, BUT THEY AREN'T AROUND TO LIMIT IT NOW.

THEY'RE NOT?

I'LL EXPLAIN THAT LATER.

I THINK YOU VISUALIZE A LOOP THAT CONNECTS OUR MINDS WHEN YOU DO IT.

I'LL GIVE IT A SHOOT.

SHOT.

IT'S WORKING!

GOOD JOB, MARVEL BOY.

NOW JUST BRING ME INTO IT...

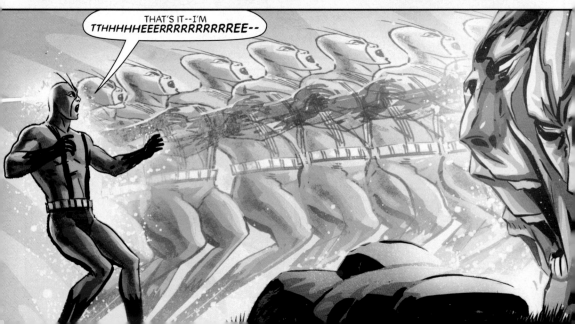

THAT'S IT--I'M TTHHHHHEEERRRRRRRRREE--

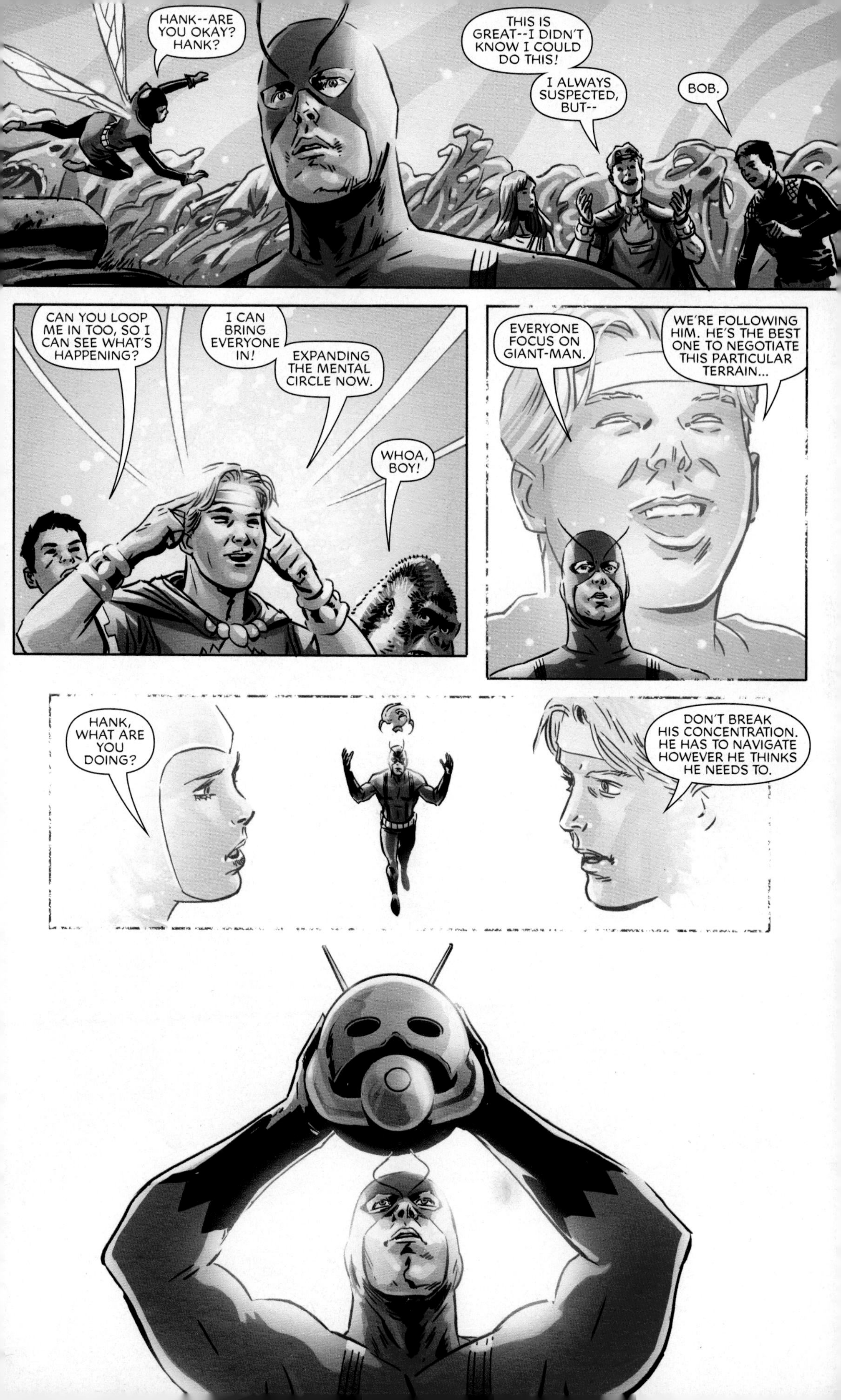
HANK--ARE YOU OKAY? HANK?
THIS IS GREAT--I DIDN'T KNOW I COULD DO THIS!
I ALWAYS SUSPECTED, BUT--
BOB.
CAN YOU LOOP ME IN TOO, SO I CAN SEE WHAT'S HAPPENING?
I CAN BRING EVERYONE IN!
EXPANDING THE MENTAL CIRCLE NOW.
WHOA, BOY!
EVERYONE FOCUS ON GIANT-MAN.
WE'RE FOLLOWING HIM. HE'S THE BEST ONE TO NEGOTIATE THIS PARTICULAR TERRAIN...
HANK, WHAT ARE YOU DOING?
DON'T BREAK HIS CONCENTRATION. HE HAS TO NAVIGATE HOWEVER HE THINKS HE NEEDS TO.

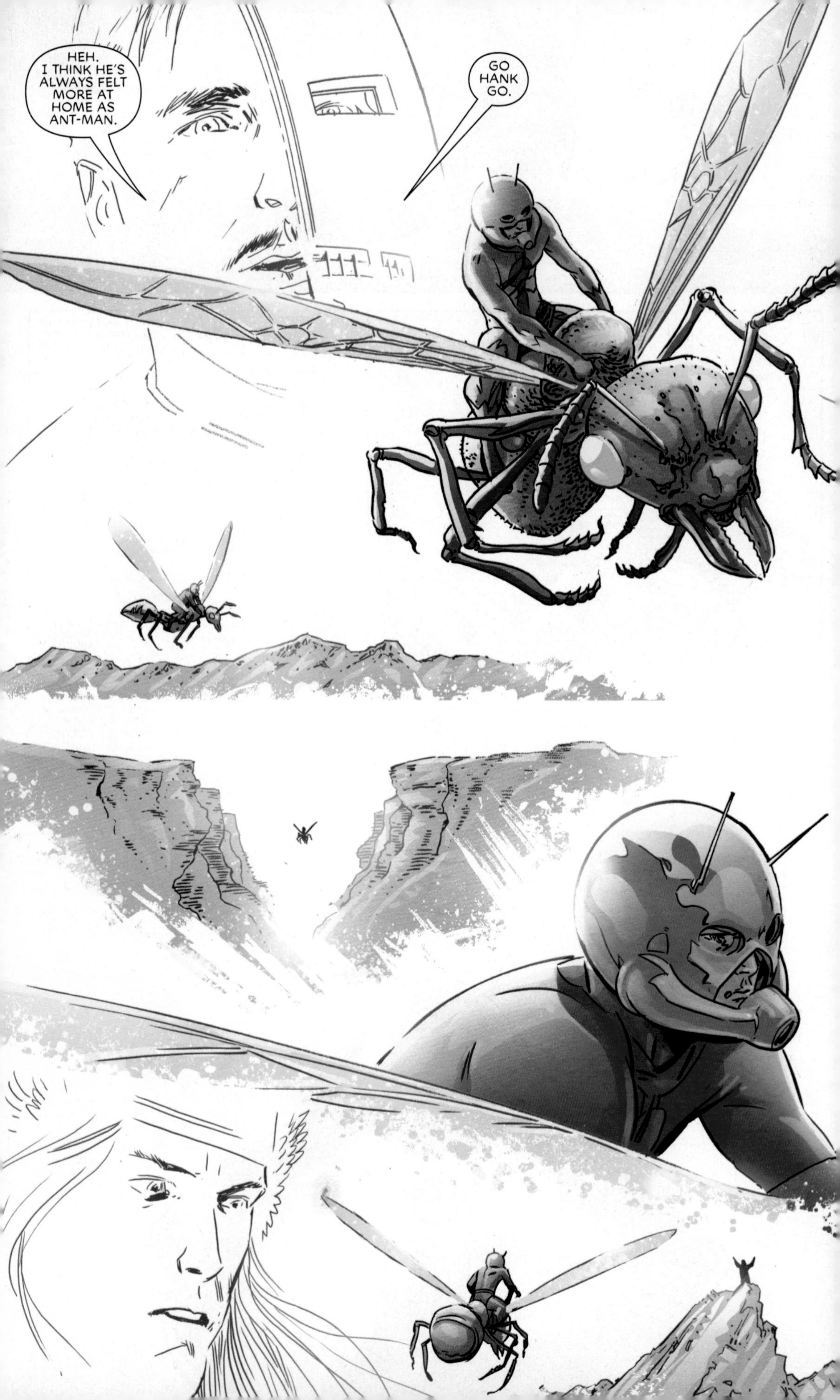
HEH. I THINK HE'S ALWAYS FELT MORE AT HOME AS ANT-MAN.
GO HANK GO.

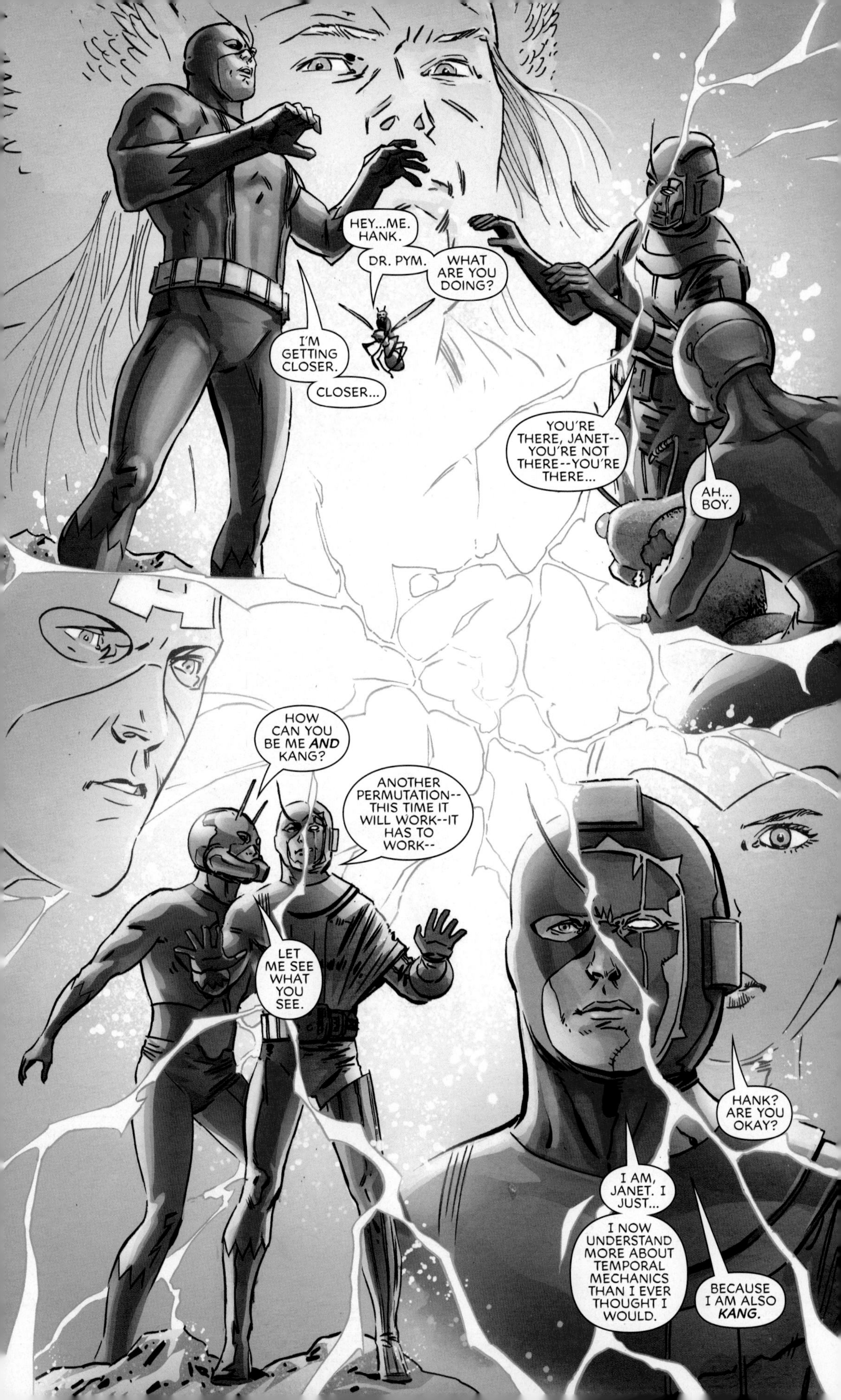
HEY...ME. HANK.
DR. PYM.
WHAT ARE YOU DOING?
I'M GETTING CLOSER.
CLOSER...
YOU'RE THERE, JANET-- YOU'RE NOT THERE--YOU'RE THERE...
AH... BOY.
HOW CAN YOU BE ME *AND* KANG?
ANOTHER PERMUTATION-- THIS TIME IT WILL WORK--IT HAS TO WORK--
LET ME SEE WHAT YOU SEE.
HANK? ARE YOU OKAY?
I AM, JANET. I JUST...
I NOW UNDERSTAND MORE ABOUT TEMPORAL MECHANICS THAN I EVER THOUGHT I WOULD.
BECAUSE I AM ALSO *KANG.*

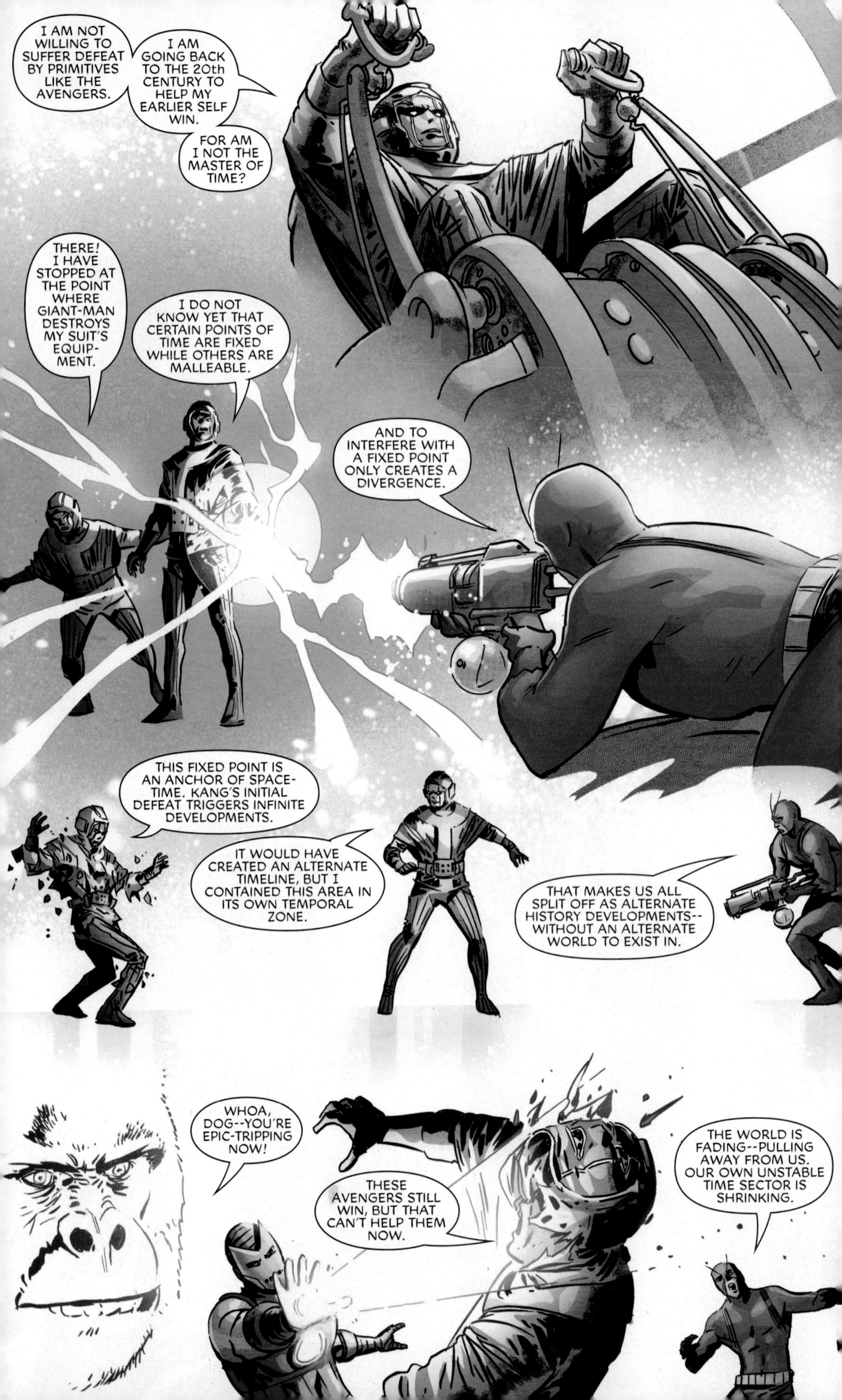
I AM NOT WILLING TO SUFFER DEFEAT BY PRIMITIVES LIKE THE AVENGERS.
I AM GOING BACK TO THE 20th CENTURY TO HELP MY EARLIER SELF WIN.
FOR AM I NOT THE MASTER OF TIME?
THERE! I HAVE STOPPED AT THE POINT WHERE GIANT-MAN DESTROYS MY SUIT'S EQUIP-MENT.
I DO NOT KNOW YET THAT CERTAIN POINTS OF TIME ARE FIXED WHILE OTHERS ARE MALLEABLE.
AND TO INTERFERE WITH A FIXED POINT ONLY CREATES A DIVERGENCE.
THIS FIXED POINT IS AN ANCHOR OF SPACE-TIME. KANG'S INITIAL DEFEAT TRIGGERS INFINITE DEVELOPMENTS.
IT WOULD HAVE CREATED AN ALTERNATE TIMELINE, BUT I CONTAINED THIS AREA IN ITS OWN TEMPORAL ZONE.
THAT MAKES US ALL SPLIT OFF AS ALTERNATE HISTORY DEVELOPMENTS--WITHOUT AN ALTERNATE WORLD TO EXIST IN.
WHOA, DOG--YOU'RE EPIC-TRIPPING NOW!
THESE AVENGERS STILL WIN, BUT THAT CAN'T HELP THEM NOW.
THE WORLD IS FADING--PULLING AWAY FROM US. OUR OWN UNSTABLE TIME SECTOR IS SHRINKING.

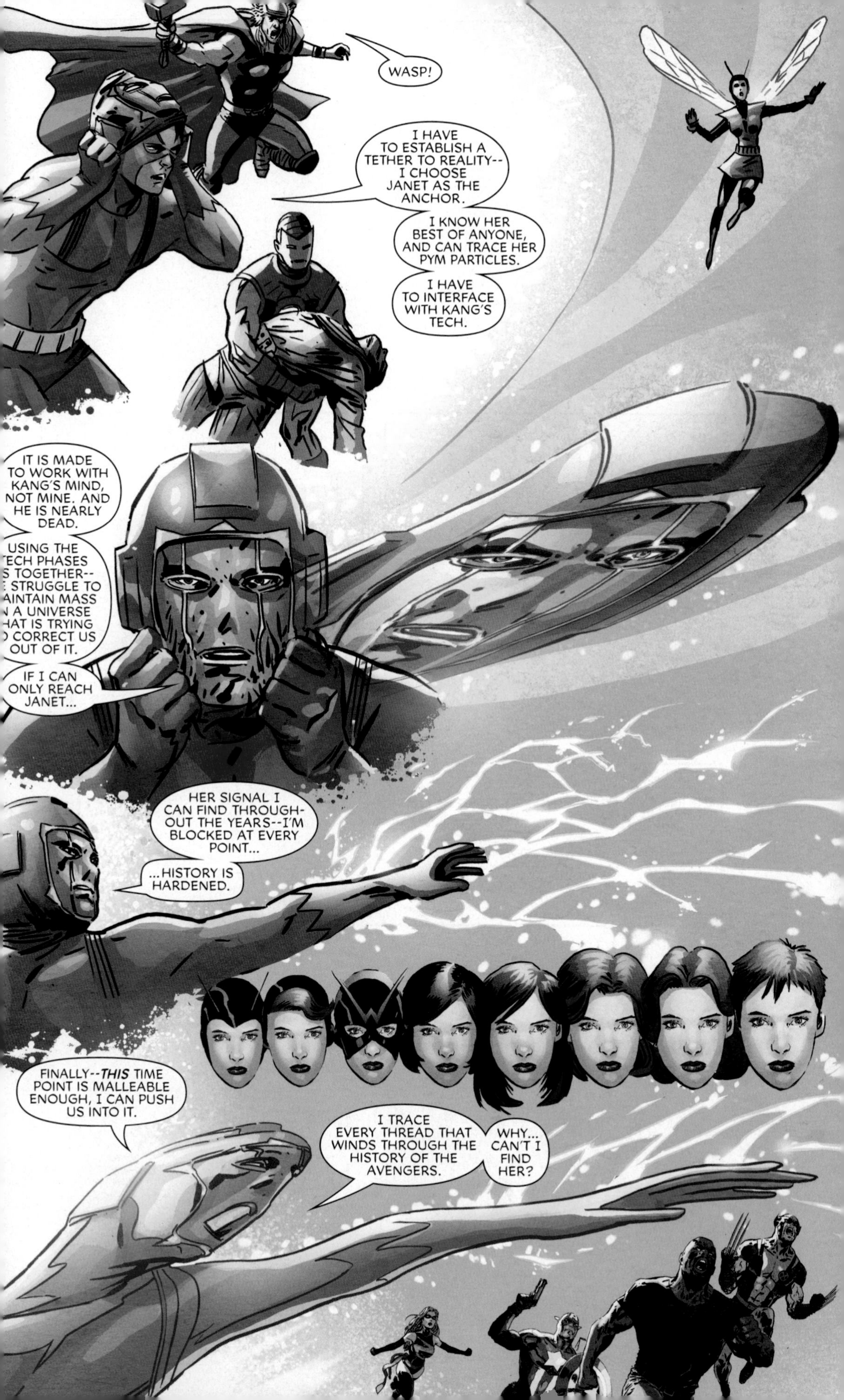

WASP!
I HAVE TO ESTABLISH A TETHER TO REALITY-- I CHOOSE JANET AS THE ANCHOR.
I KNOW HER BEST OF ANYONE, AND CAN TRACE HER PYM PARTICLES.
I HAVE TO INTERFACE WITH KANG'S TECH.
IT IS MADE TO WORK WITH KANG'S MIND, NOT MINE. AND HE IS NEARLY DEAD.
USING THE TECH PHASES S TOGETHER-- STRUGGLE TO AINTAIN MASS N A UNIVERSE HAT IS TRYING CORRECT US OUT OF IT.
IF I CAN ONLY REACH JANET...
HER SIGNAL I CAN FIND THROUGH-OUT THE YEARS--I'M BLOCKED AT EVERY POINT...
...HISTORY IS HARDENED.
FINALLY--*THIS* TIME POINT IS MALLEABLE ENOUGH, I CAN PUSH US INTO IT.
I TRACE EVERY THREAD THAT WINDS THROUGH THE HISTORY OF THE AVENGERS.
WHY... CAN'T I FIND HER?

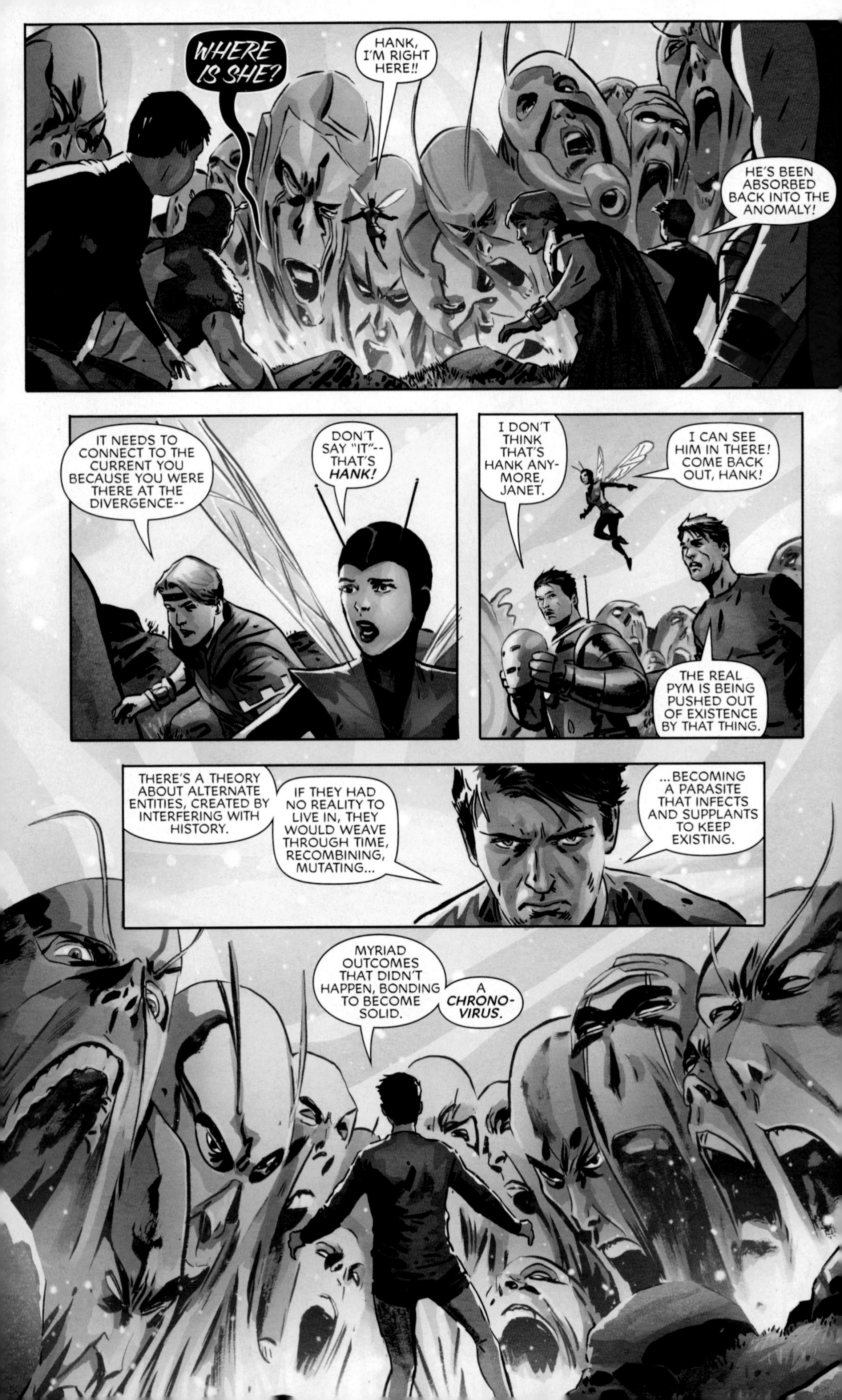

WHERE IS SHE?
HANK, I'M RIGHT HERE!!
HE'S BEEN ABSORBED BACK INTO THE ANOMALY!
IT NEEDS TO CONNECT TO THE CURRENT YOU BECAUSE YOU WERE THERE AT THE DIVERGENCE--
DON'T SAY "IT"-- THAT'S HANK!
I DON'T THINK THAT'S HANK ANY-MORE, JANET.
I CAN SEE HIM IN THERE! COME BACK OUT, HANK!
THE REAL PYM IS BEING PUSHED OUT OF EXISTENCE BY THAT THING.
THERE'S A THEORY ABOUT ALTERNATE ENTITIES, CREATED BY INTERFERING WITH HISTORY.
IF THEY HAD NO REALITY TO LIVE IN, THEY WOULD WEAVE THROUGH TIME, RECOMBINING, MUTATING...
...BECOMING A PARASITE THAT INFECTS AND SUPPLANTS TO KEEP EXISTING.
MYRIAD OUTCOMES THAT DIDN'T HAPPEN, BONDING TO BECOME SOLID.
A CHRONO-VIRUS.

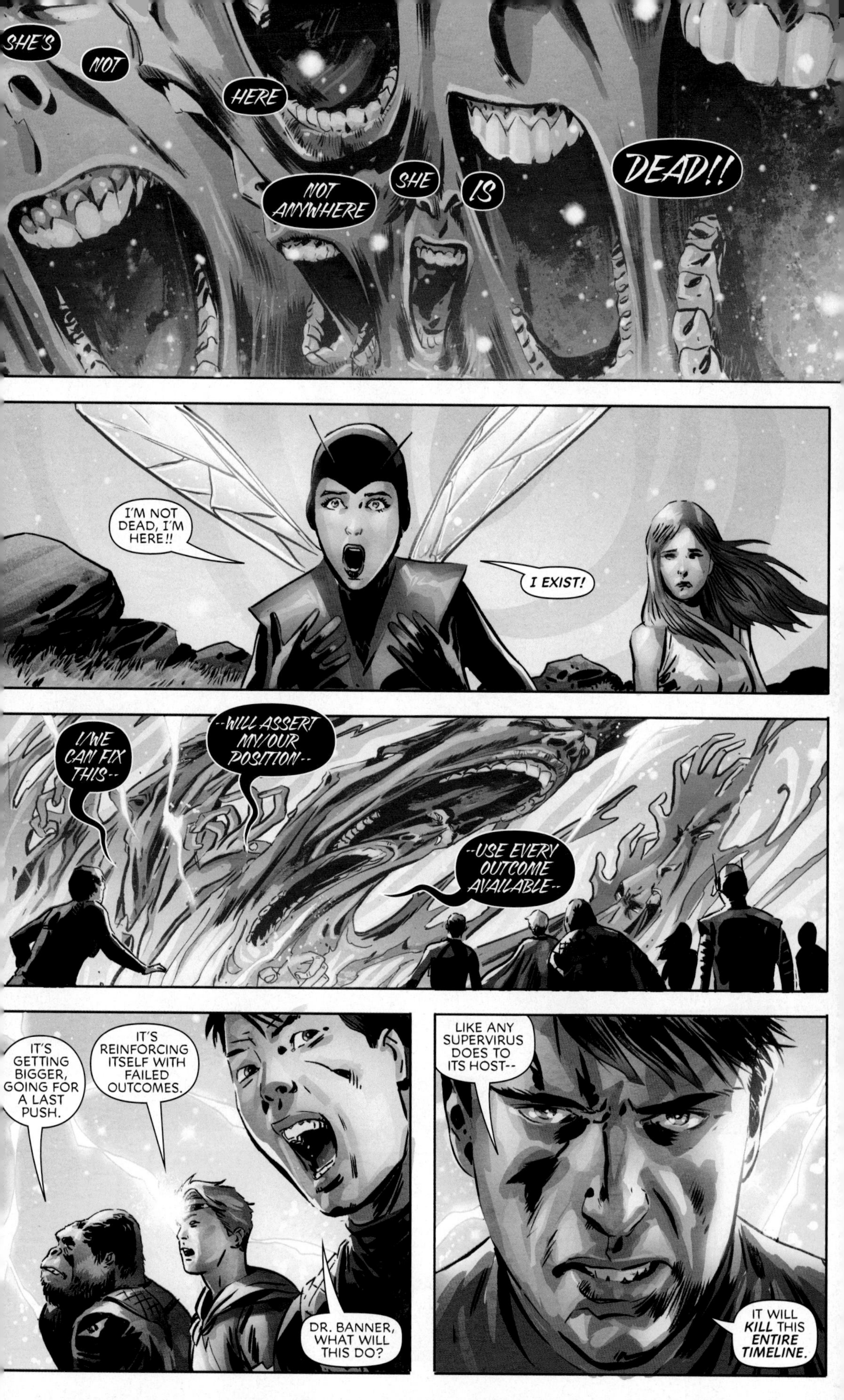

SHE'S
NOT
HERE
NOT ANYWHERE
SHE
IS
DEAD!!
I'M NOT DEAD, I'M HERE!!
I EXIST!
I/WE CAN FIX THIS--
--WILL ASSERT MY/OUR POSITION--
--USE EVERY OUTCOME AVAILABLE--
IT'S GETTING BIGGER, GOING FOR A LAST PUSH.
IT'S REINFORCING ITSELF WITH FAILED OUTCOMES.
DR. BANNER, WHAT WILL THIS DO?
LIKE ANY SUPERVIRUS DOES TO ITS HOST--
IT WILL KILL THIS ENTIRE TIMELINE.

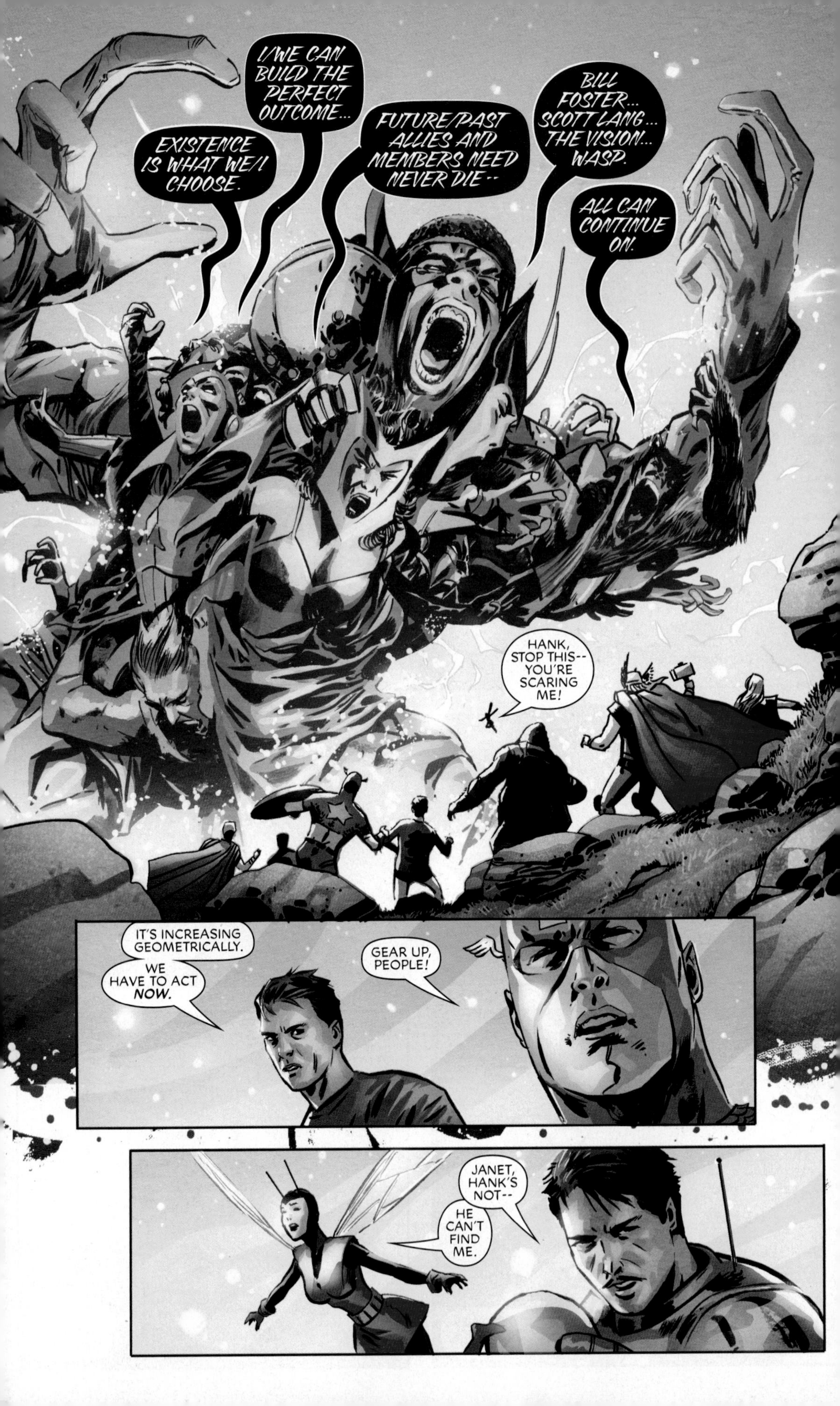
EXISTENCE IS WHAT WE/I CHOOSE.
I/WE CAN BUILD THE PERFECT OUTCOME...
FUTURE/PAST ALLIES AND MEMBERS NEED NEVER DIE--
BILL FOSTER... SCOTT LANG... THE VISION... WASP.
ALL CAN CONTINUE ON.
HANK, STOP THIS-- YOU'RE SCARING ME!
IT'S INCREASING GEOMETRICALLY.
WE HAVE TO ACT NOW.
GEAR UP, PEOPLE!
JANET, HANK'S NOT--
HE CAN'T FIND ME.

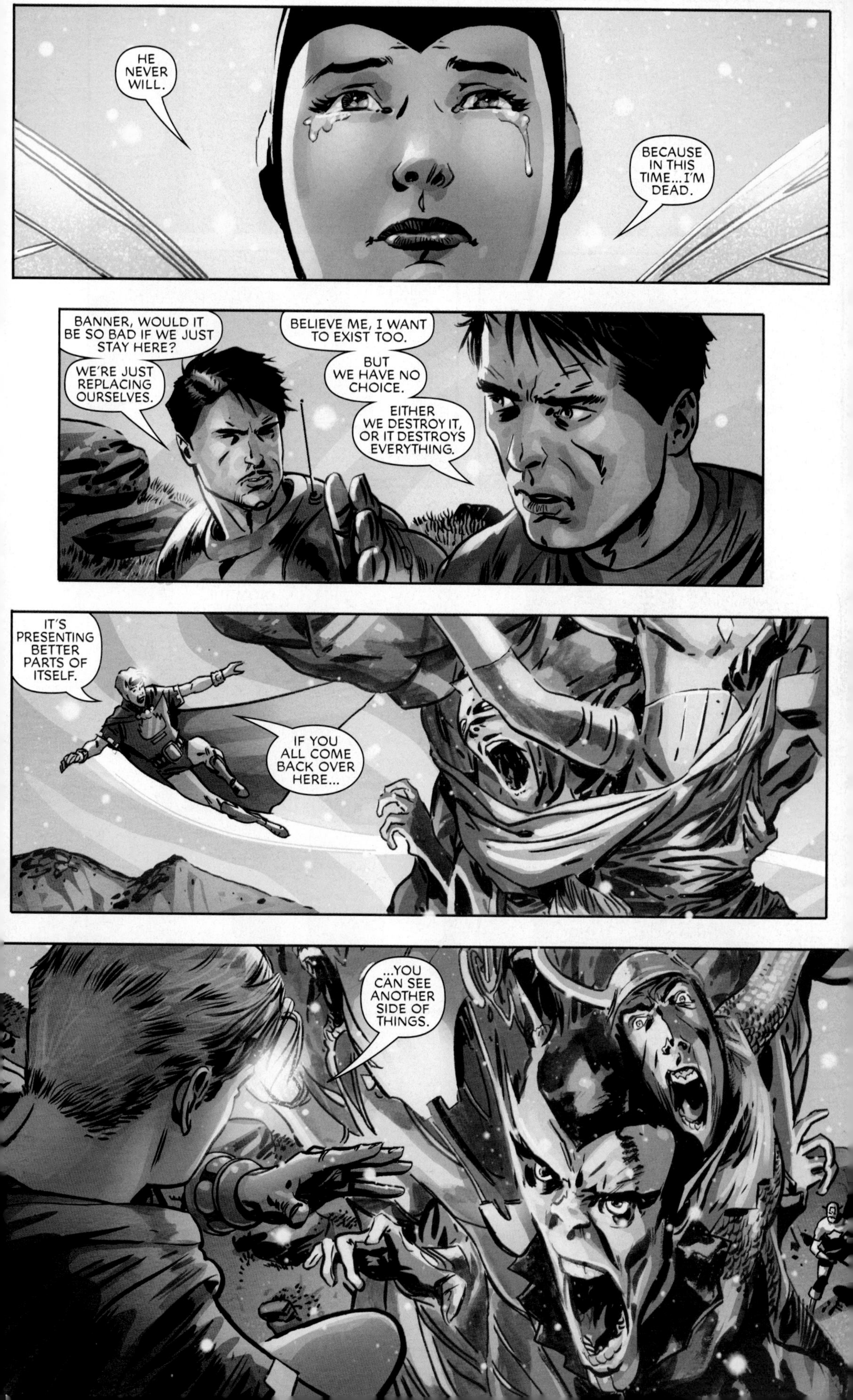
HE NEVER WILL.
BECAUSE IN THIS TIME... I'M DEAD.
BANNER, WOULD IT BE SO BAD IF WE JUST STAY HERE?
WE'RE JUST REPLACING OURSELVES.
BELIEVE ME, I WANT TO EXIST TOO.
BUT WE HAVE NO CHOICE.
EITHER WE DESTROY IT, OR IT DESTROYS EVERYTHING.
IT'S PRESENTING BETTER PARTS OF ITSELF.
IF YOU ALL COME BACK OVER HERE...
...YOU CAN SEE ANOTHER SIDE OF THINGS.

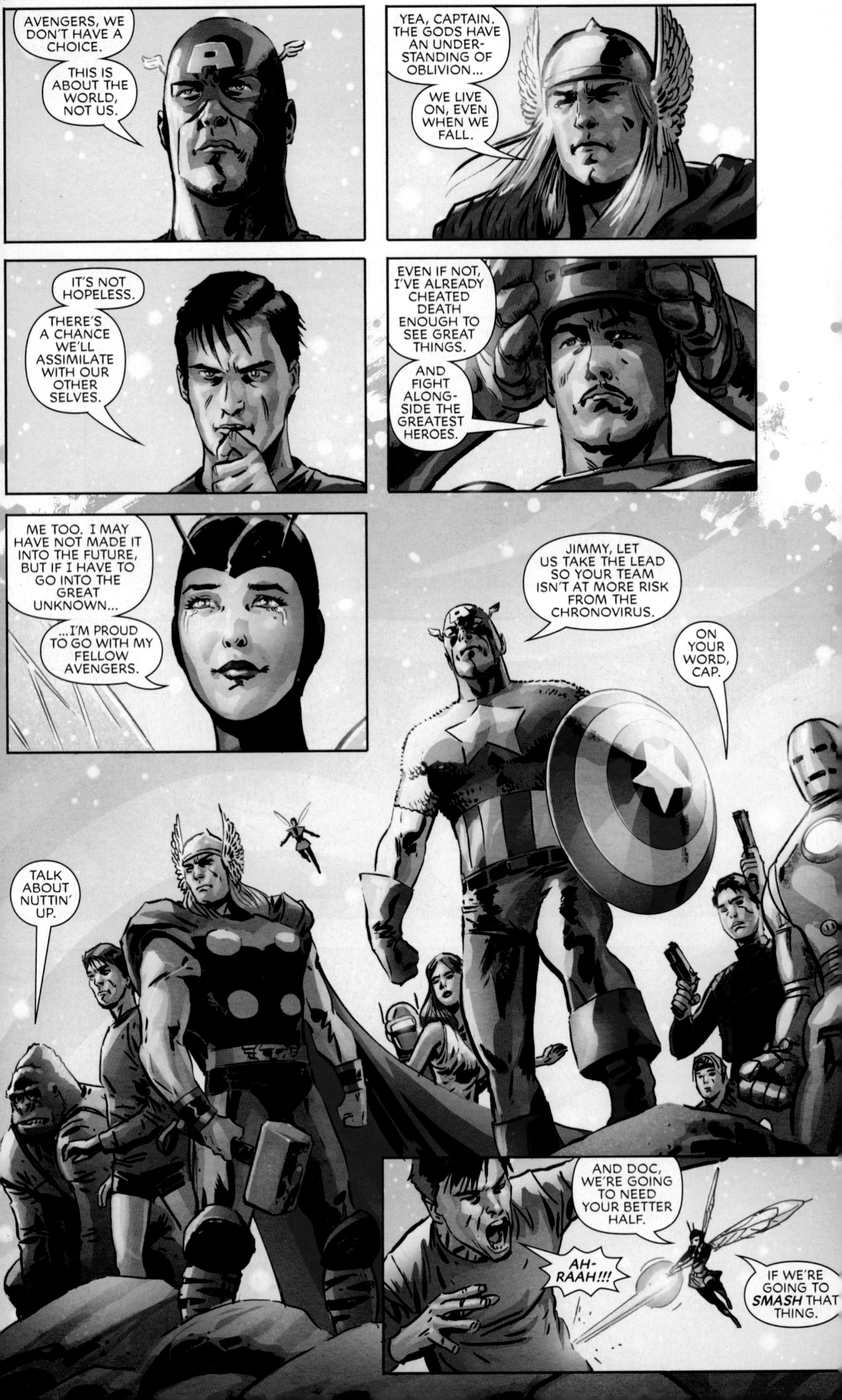
AVENGERS, WE DON'T HAVE A CHOICE.
THIS IS ABOUT THE WORLD, NOT US.
YEA, CAPTAIN. THE GODS HAVE AN UNDER-STANDING OF OBLIVION...
WE LIVE ON, EVEN WHEN WE FALL.
IT'S NOT HOPELESS.
THERE'S A CHANCE WE'LL ASSIMILATE WITH OUR OTHER SELVES.
EVEN IF NOT, I'VE ALREADY CHEATED DEATH ENOUGH TO SEE GREAT THINGS.
AND FIGHT ALONG-SIDE THE GREATEST HEROES.
ME TOO. I MAY HAVE NOT MADE IT INTO THE FUTURE, BUT IF I HAVE TO GO INTO THE GREAT UNKNOWN...
...I'M PROUD TO GO WITH MY FELLOW AVENGERS.
JIMMY, LET US TAKE THE LEAD SO YOUR TEAM ISN'T AT MORE RISK FROM THE CHRONOVIRUS.
ON YOUR WORD, CAP.
TALK ABOUT NUTTIN' UP.
AND DOC, WE'RE GOING TO NEED YOUR BETTER HALF.
AH-RAAH!!!
IF WE'RE GOING TO *SMASH* THAT THING.

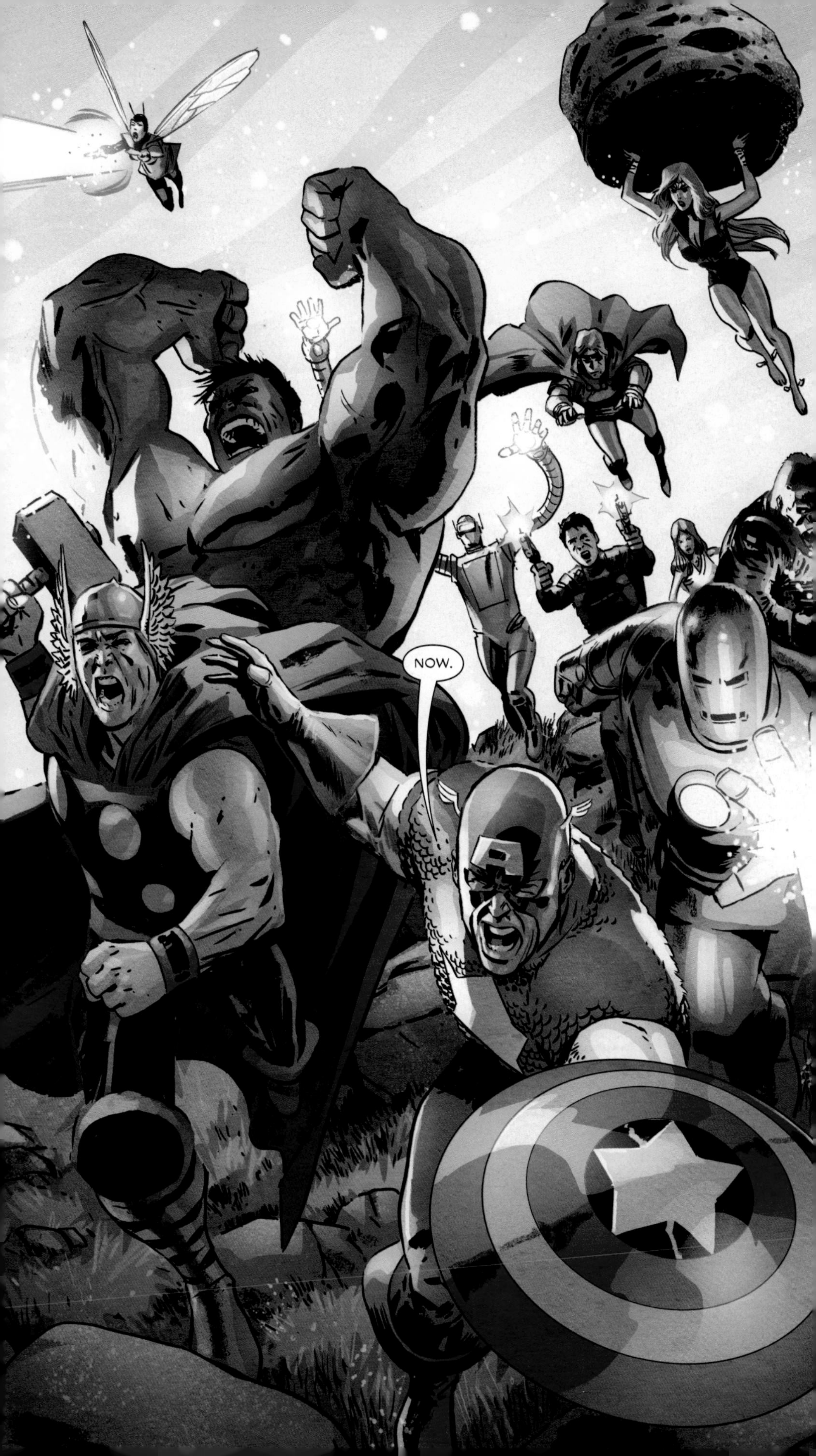
NOW.

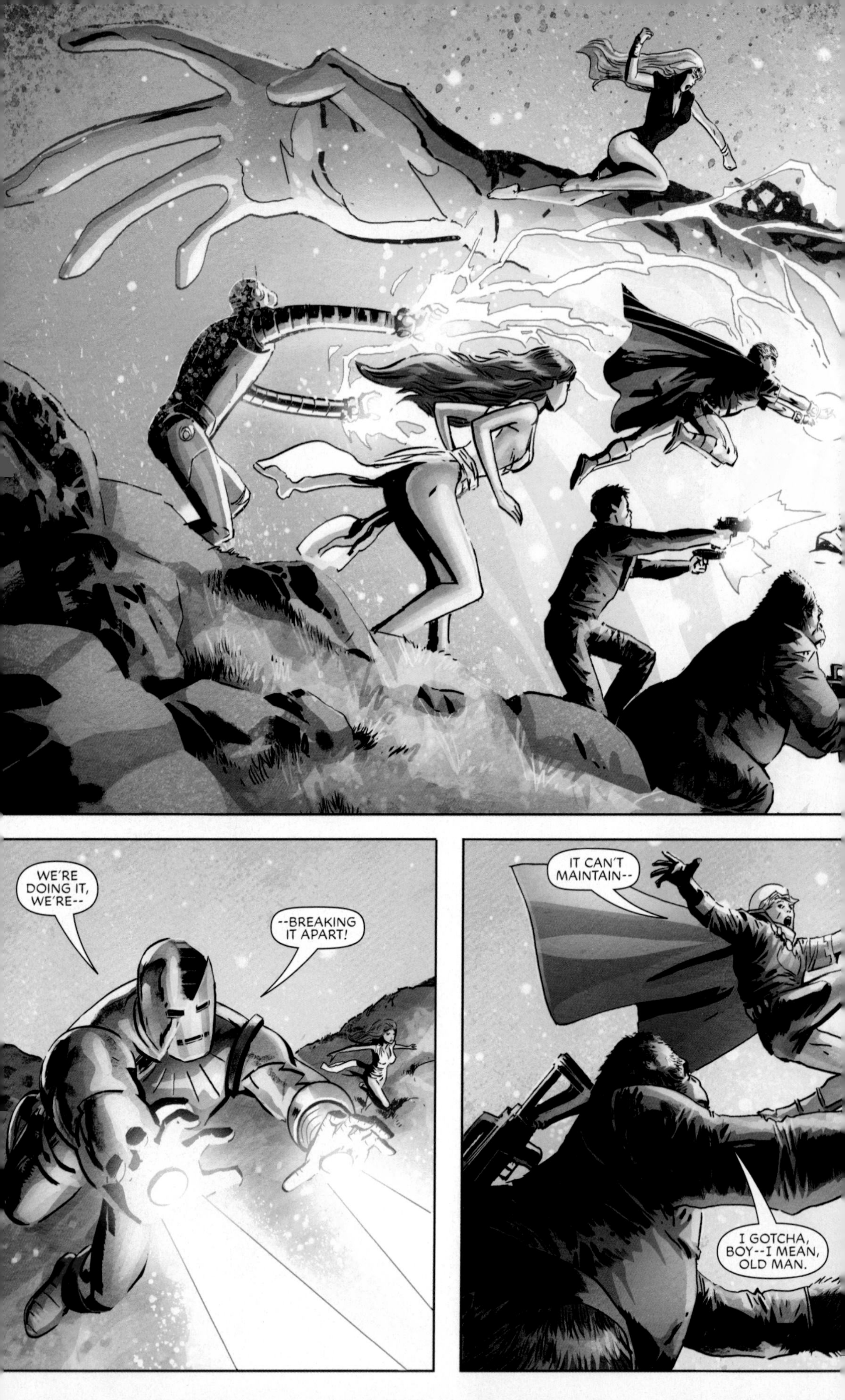
WE'RE DOING IT, WE'RE--
--BREAKING IT APART!
IT CAN'T MAINTAIN--
I GOTCHA, BOY--I MEAN, OLD MAN.

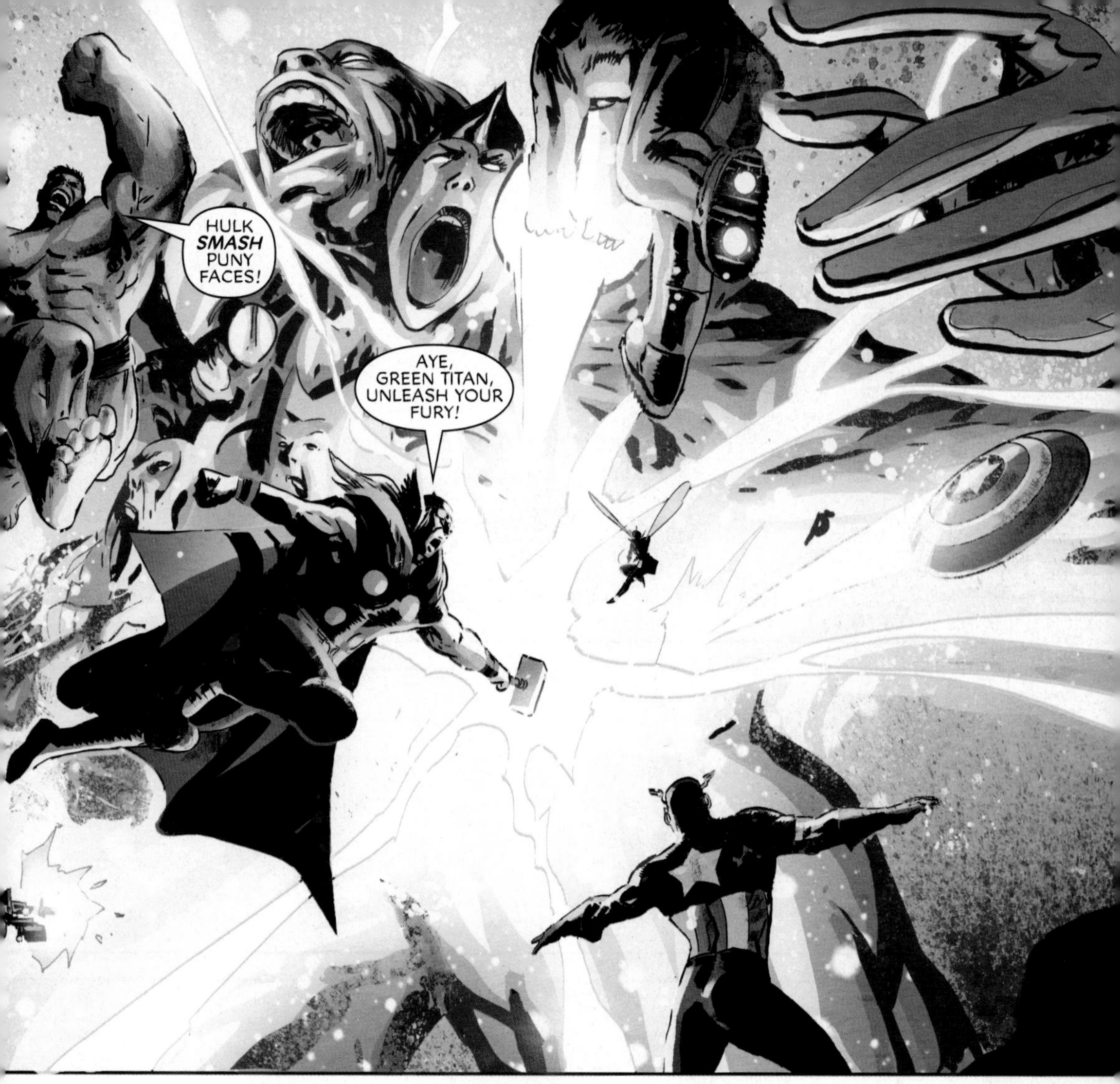
HULK *SMASH* PUNY FACES!
AYE, GREEN TITAN, UNLEASH YOUR FURY!

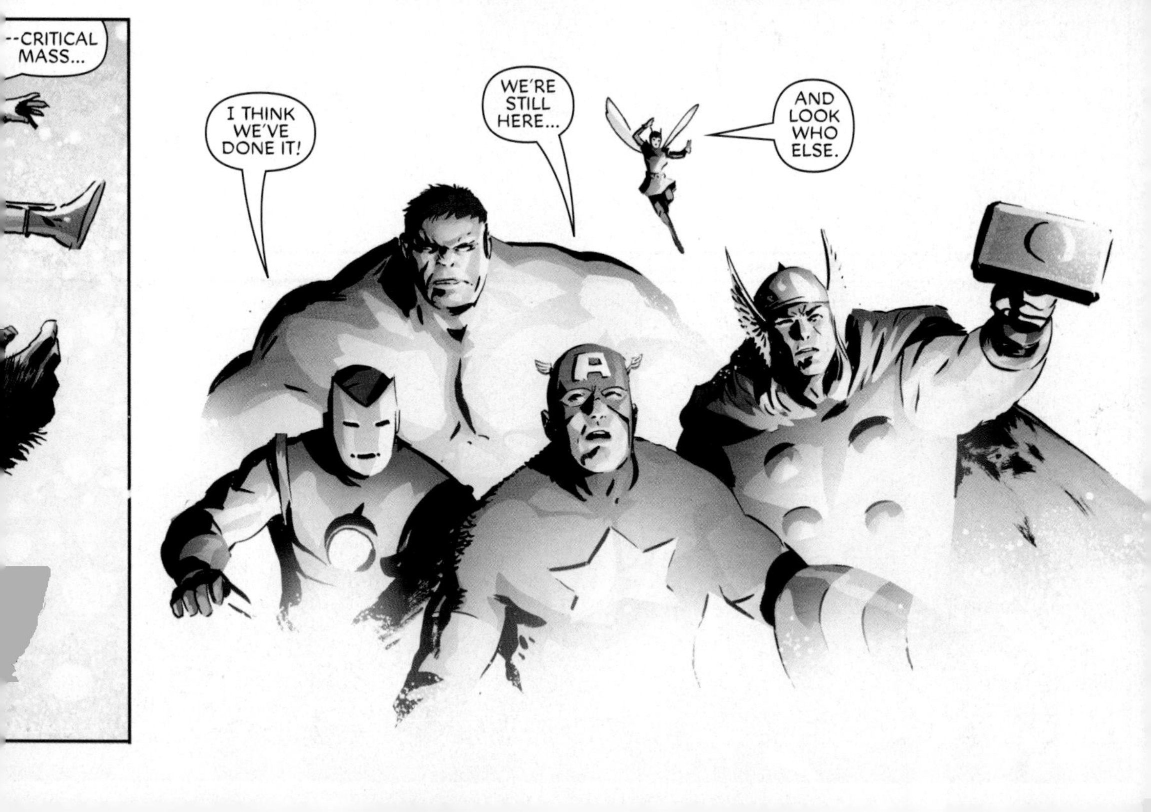
--CRITICAL MASS...
I THINK WE'VE DONE IT!
WE'RE STILL HERE...
AND LOOK WHO ELSE.

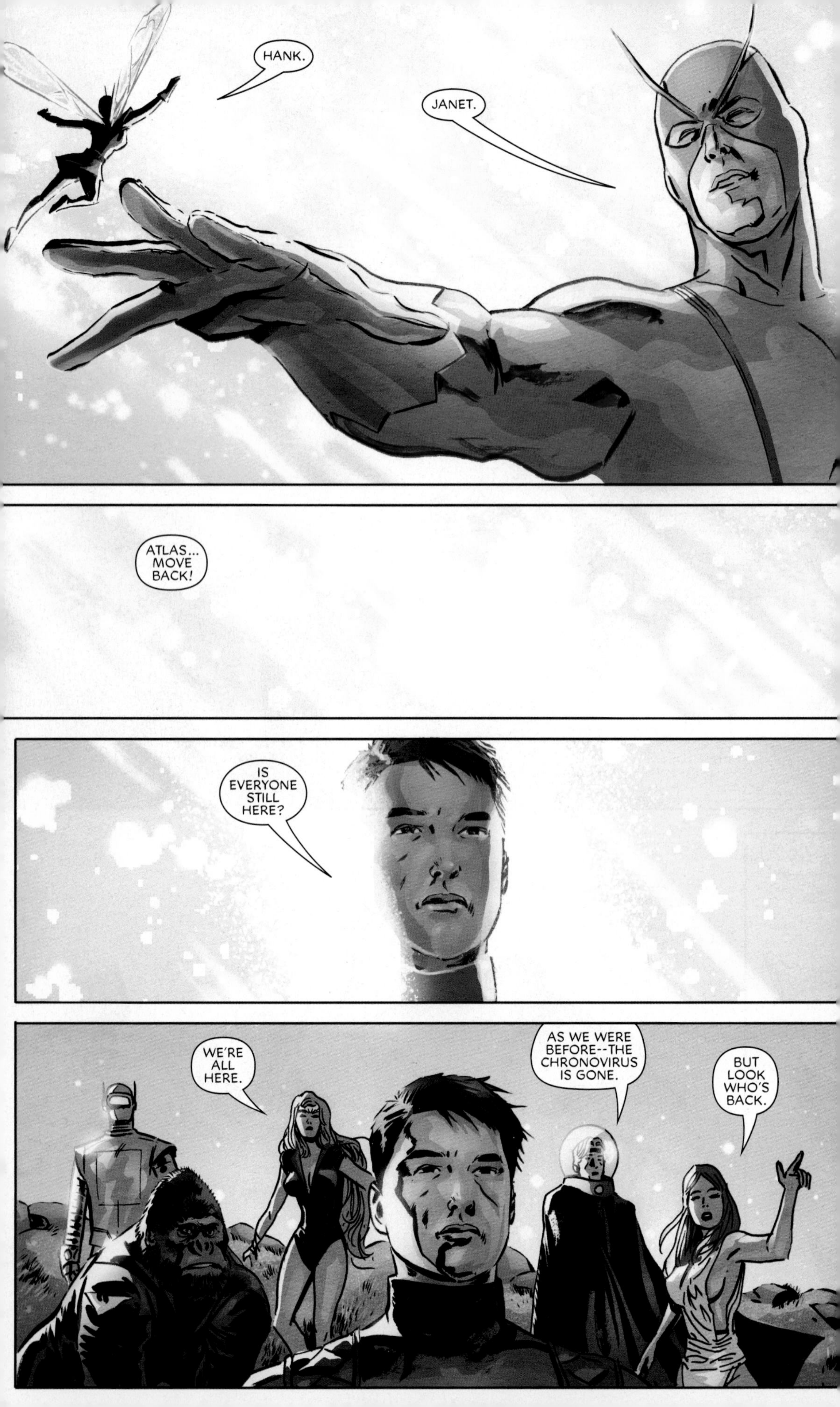
HANK.
JANET.
ATLAS... MOVE BACK!
IS EVERYONE STILL HERE?
WE'RE ALL HERE.
AS WE WERE BEFORE--THE CHRONOVIRUS IS GONE.
BUT LOOK WHO'S BACK.

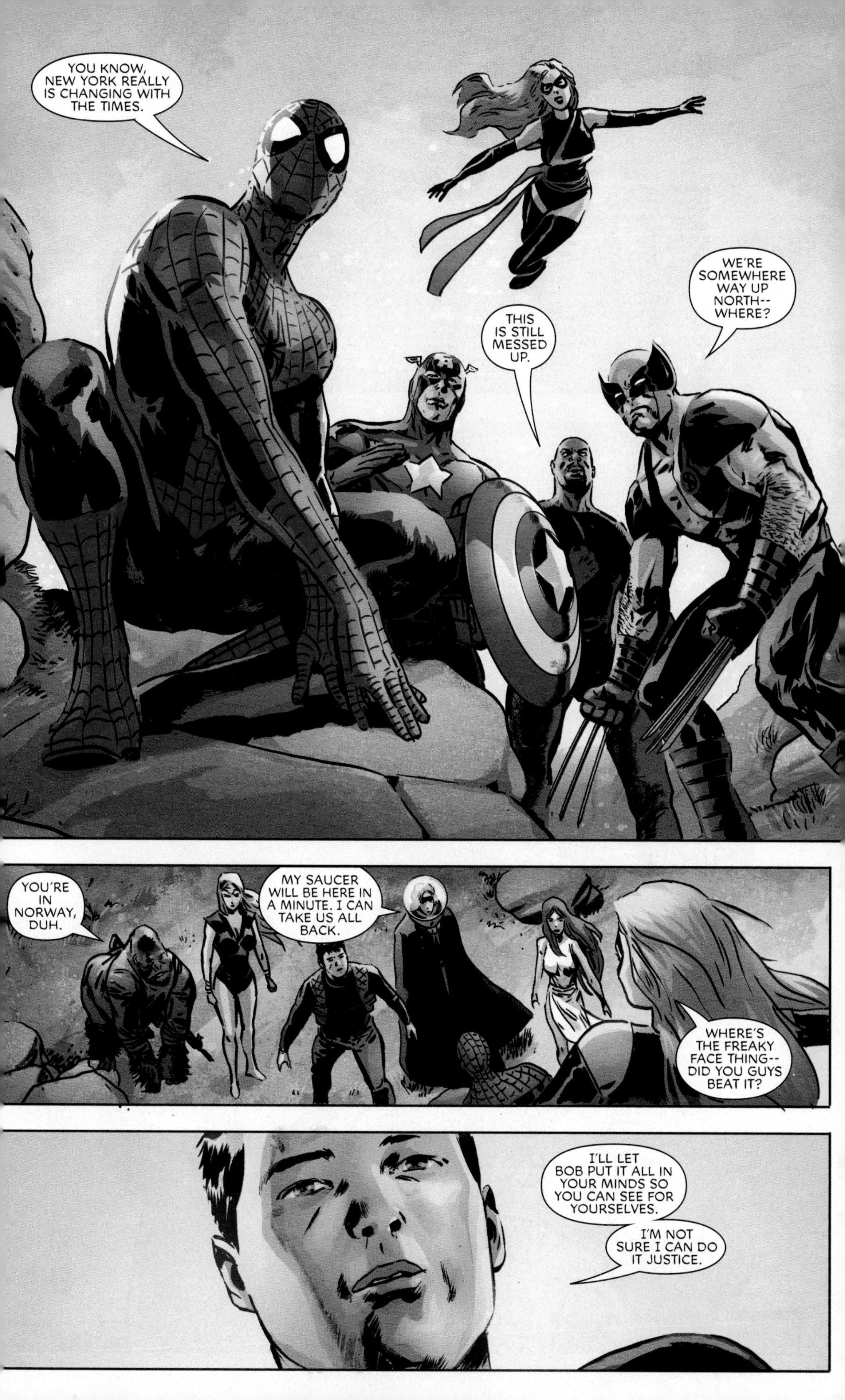
YOU KNOW, NEW YORK REALLY IS CHANGING WITH THE TIMES.
WE'RE SOMEWHERE WAY UP NORTH-- WHERE?
THIS IS STILL MESSED UP.
YOU'RE IN NORWAY, DUH.
MY SAUCER WILL BE HERE IN A MINUTE. I CAN TAKE US ALL BACK.
WHERE'S THE FREAKY FACE THING-- DID YOU GUYS BEAT IT?
I'LL LET BOB PUT IT ALL IN YOUR MINDS SO YOU CAN SEE FOR YOURSELVES.
I'M NOT SURE I CAN DO IT JUSTICE.

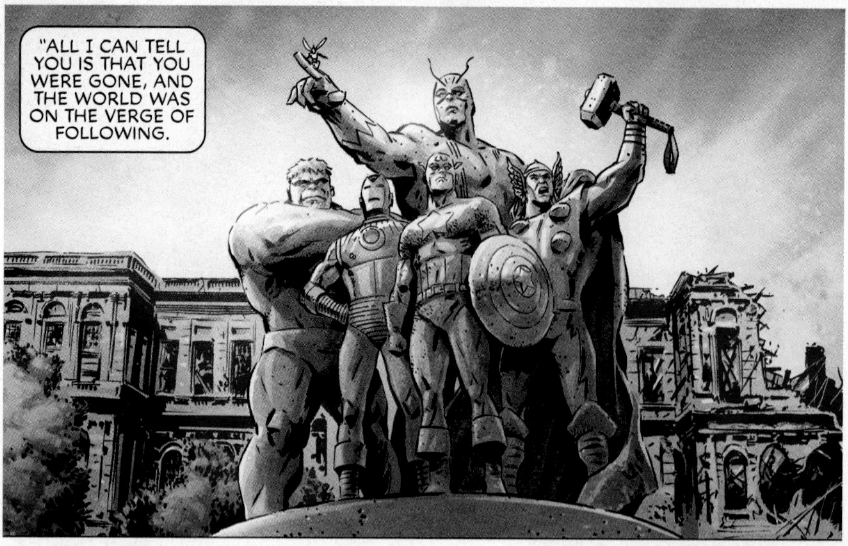
"ALL I CAN TELL YOU IS THAT YOU WERE GONE, AND THE WORLD WAS ON THE VERGE OF FOLLOWING.

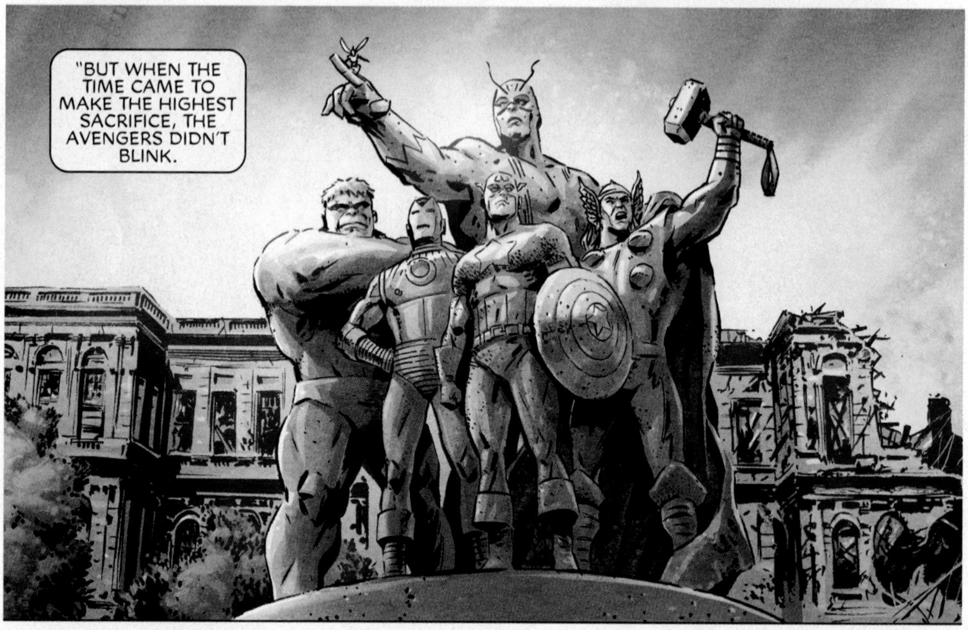
"BUT WHEN THE TIME CAME TO MAKE THE HIGHEST SACRIFICE, THE AVENGERS DIDN'T BLINK.

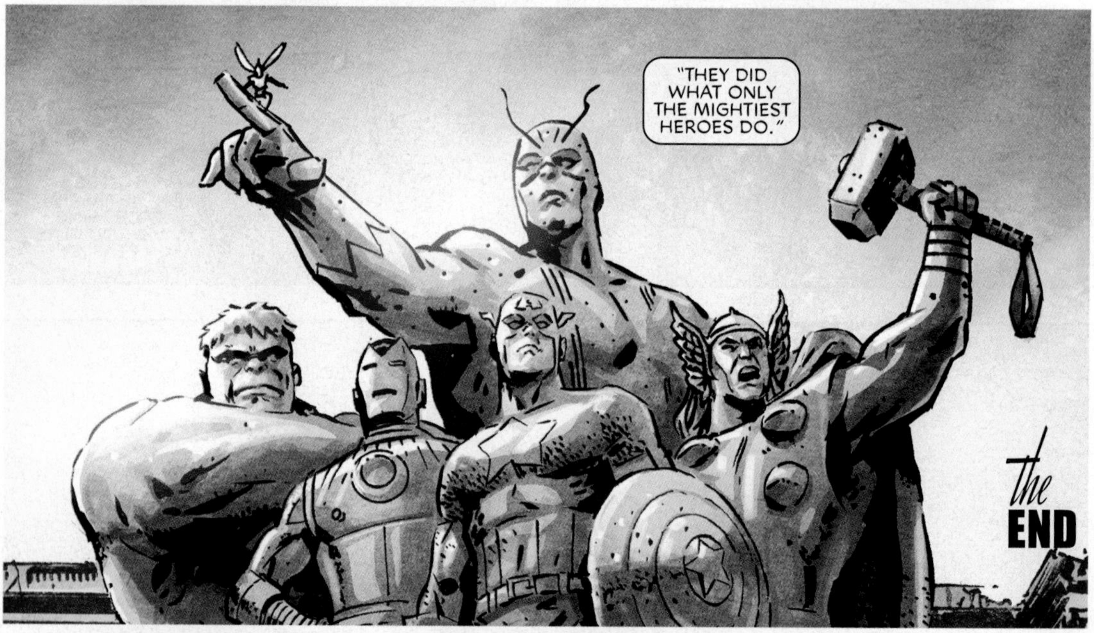
"THEY DID WHAT ONLY THE MIGHTIEST HEROES DO."
the END

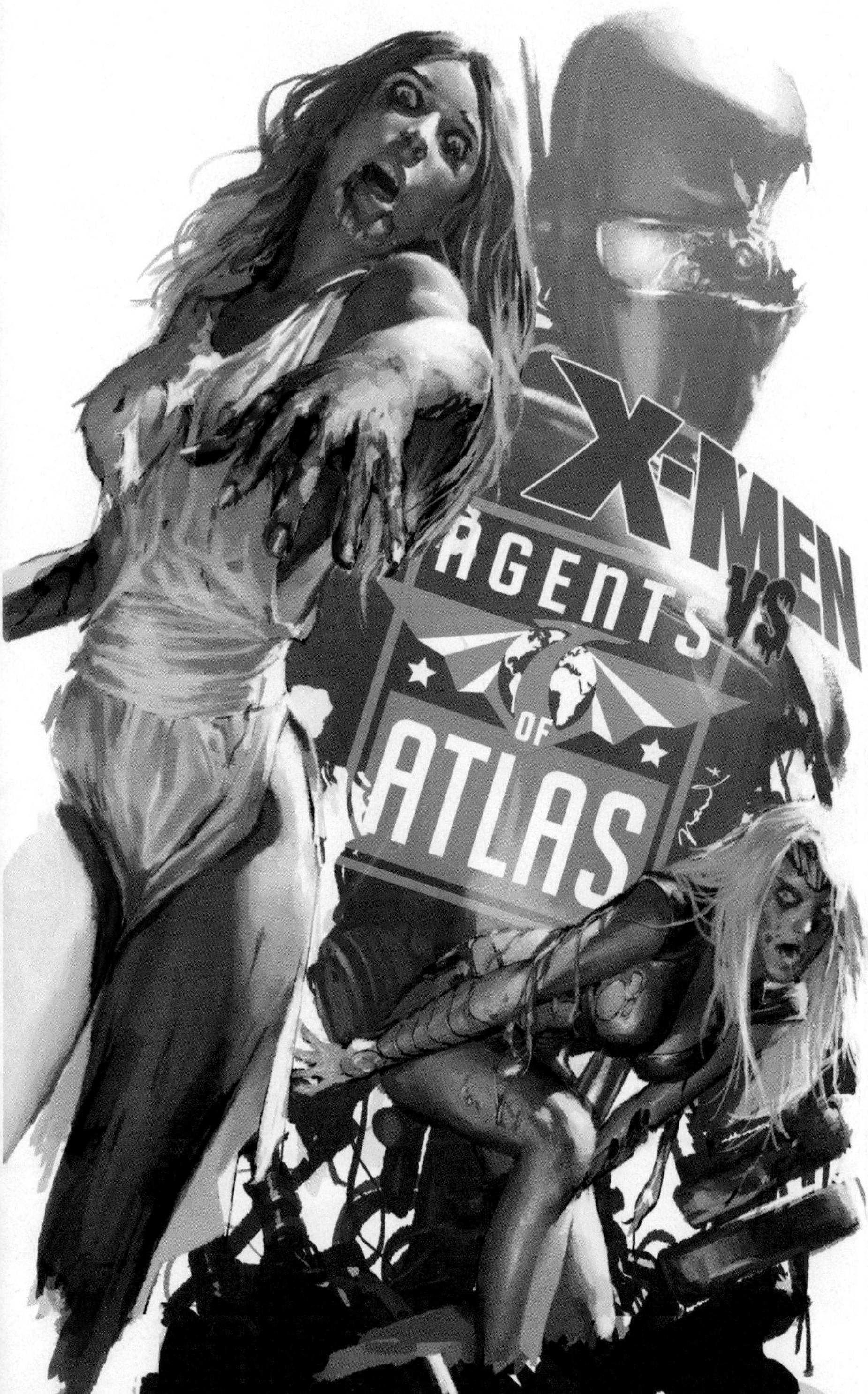
X-MEN
VS
AGENTS
OF
ATLAS

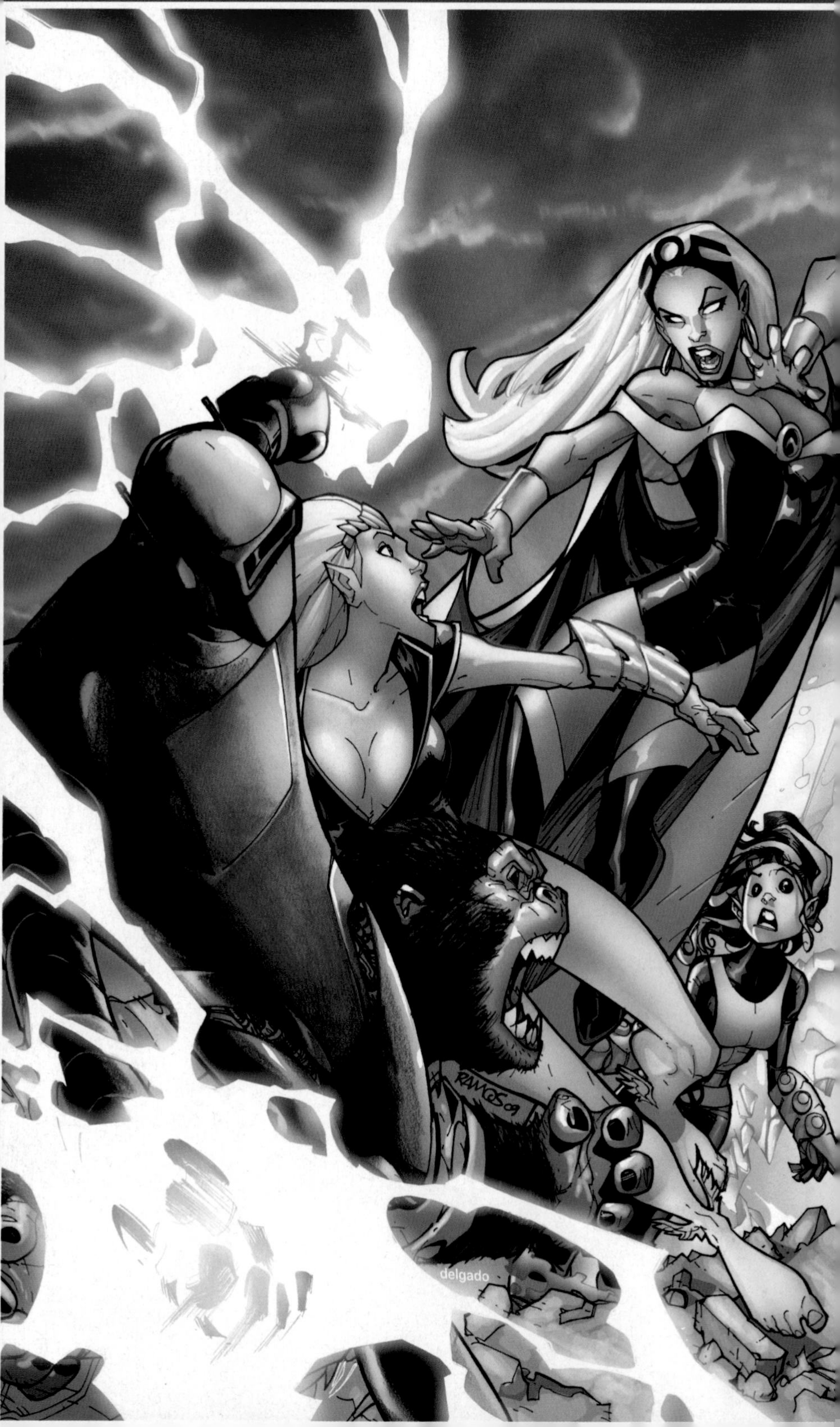
delgado

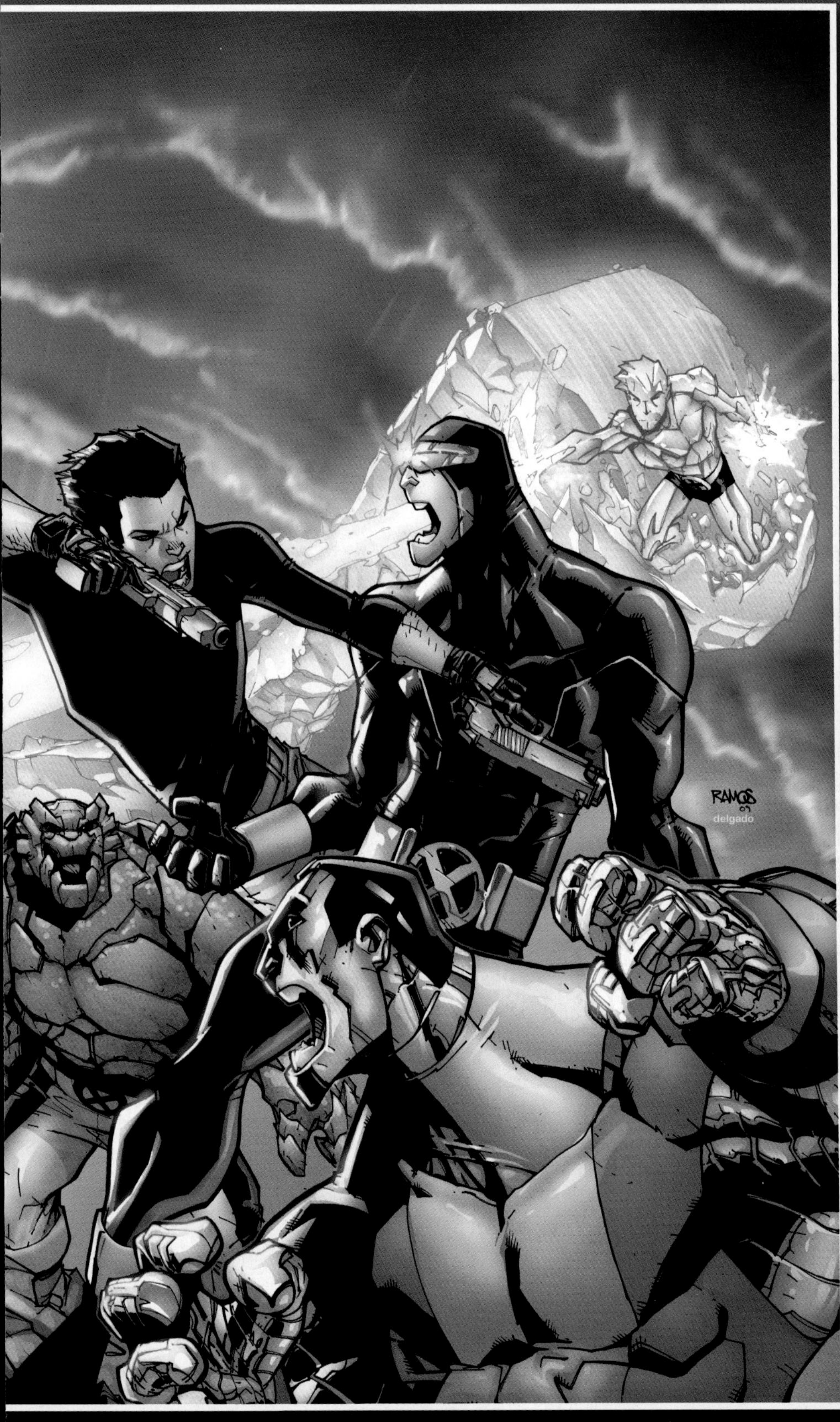
RAMOS 09
delgado

X-MEN VS. AGENTS OF ATLAS COMBINED VARIANT COVERS
BY HUMBERTO RAMOS

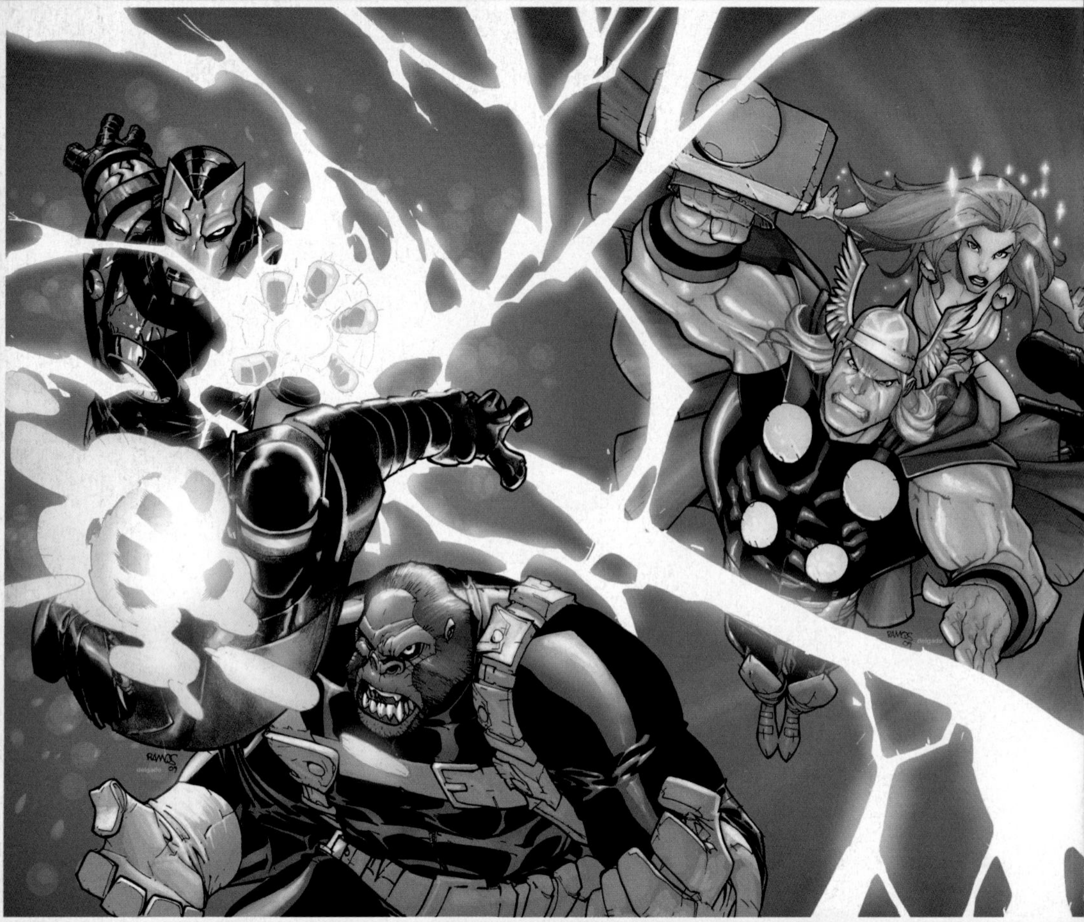

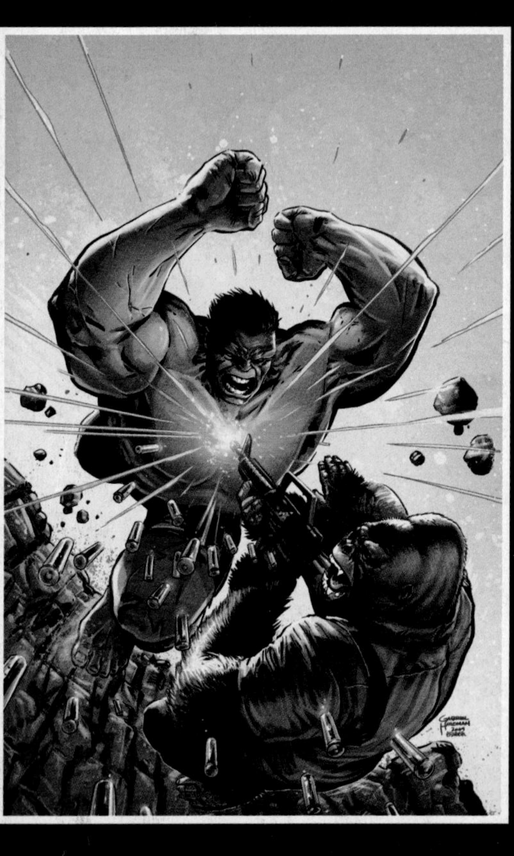

AVENGERS VS. ATLAS

#1

VARIANT BY GABRIEL HARDMAN

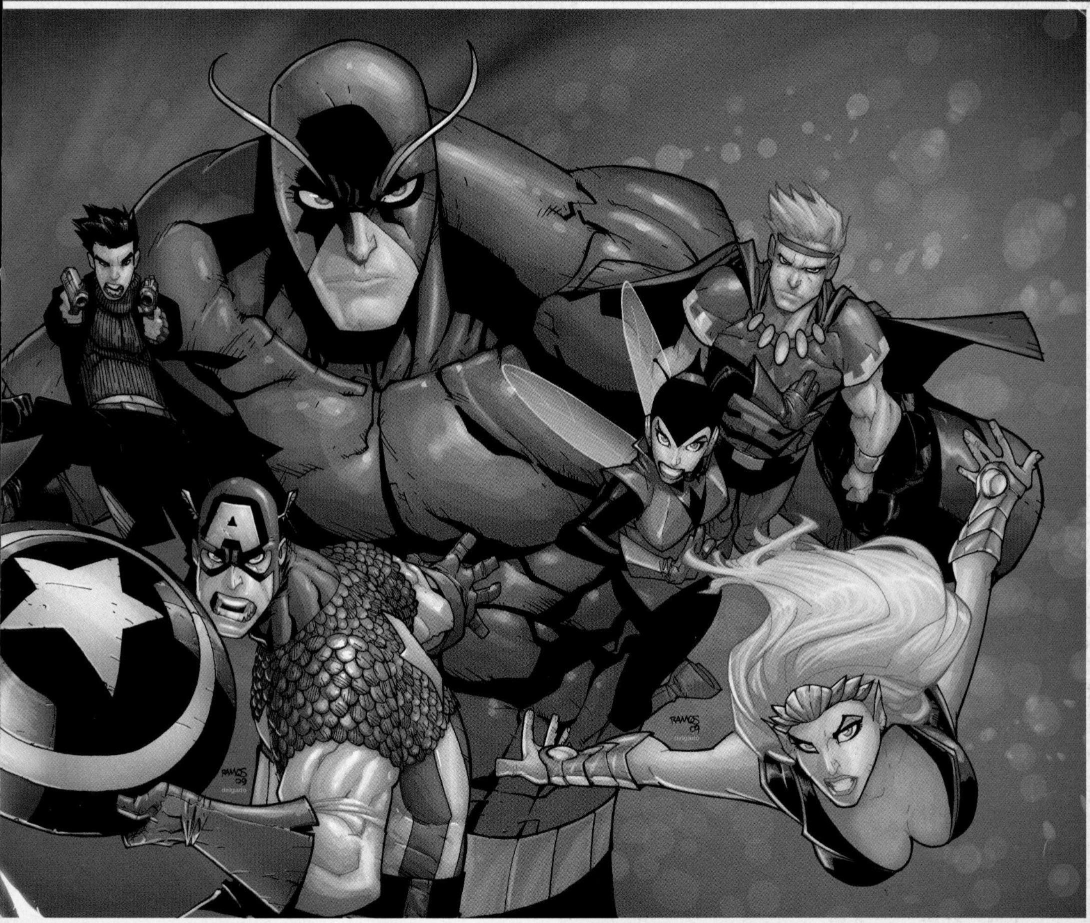

AVENGERS VS. ATLAS
COMBINED COVERS
BY HUMBERTO RAMOS

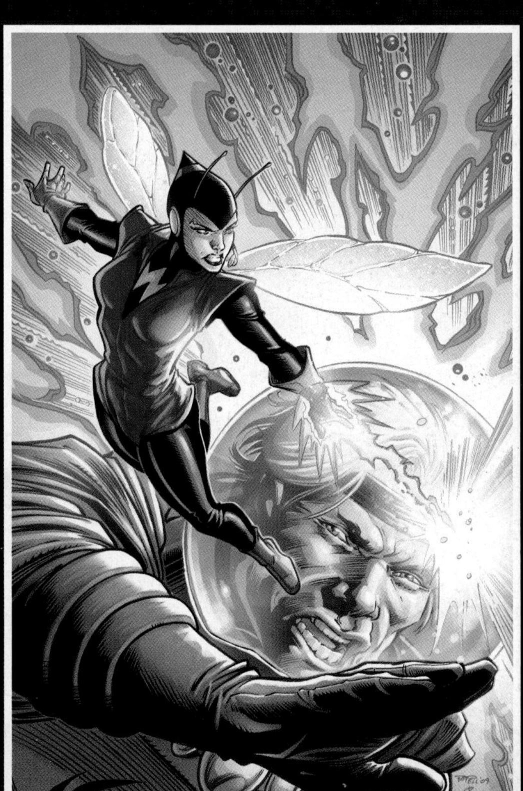

AVENGERS VS. ATLAS

#2

VARIANT BY PAUL PELLETIER

AVENGERS US. ATLAS

#3

VARIANT BY ANDREW ROBINSON

AVENGERS US. ATLAS

#4

VARIANT BY ALAN DAVIS